SUB

Inside the Notorious School District of Philadelphia

Clayvon C. Harris

Wyncote, PA

Grateful acknowledgment is made to: Eric Hanushek, Ph.D., Paul and Jean Hanna Senior Fellow at the Hoover Institution of Stanford University, for confirming the economic gains associated with growth in student achievement; The Education Trust for allowing the reprint of direct quotes from the *Funding Gap Reports*; Julian Vasquez Heilig, Dean and Professor, University of Kentucky School of Education, and Sr. Pat Suchalski, SBS and the Sisters of the Blessed Sacrament for permission to use quotes.

Library of Congress Control Number: 2020912144

Hardback ISBN: 978-0-9881797-3-8
Trade Paperback ISBN: 978-0-9881797-2-1
e-book ISBN: 978-0-9881797-4-5

Cover photo: Sid Holmes
Cover design: Elizabeth Shope/Joel Catindig
Book design: Elizabeth Shope

Angelwalk
grace·faith·truth

www.angelwalk.biz

Printed in the United States of America.

10 9 8 7 6 5 4 3

This book is dedicated to:

*All of the smart, funny, kind
and very extraordinary children I met along the way*

&

*my mother, Christina V. Wimberly,
who traveled every step of this journey with me.*

Thank you for your love and encouragement.

> Contents

PART 1: INSIDE THE SDP (2001-2002)

PART 2: UPDATE ON THE SCHOOLS

PART 3: BACK INSIDE THE SDP...*15 YEARS LATER*

This book literally sat on my shelf unfinished for over a decade. I first began writing it when I was substitute teaching in the School District of Philadelphia (SDP). I couldn't believe what I was seeing on a daily basis. So I started writing. In addition to sharing my experiences, I wanted to help make sense of it all: how policies were negatively affecting outcomes, how chaotic environments were fueled by a lack of accountability, and—most shockingly—how out-of-control students were undermining the learning process for both themselves and others.

The deeper I dove, the more complicated and convoluted the issues became. Many people with far greater experience were thoughtfully and intelligently weighing in on all sides of every issue: from high-stakes testing and *No Child Left Behind* to inclusion, school funding, charters, you name it. With so many education experts on the case, it seemed reasonable for me to step away from a problem that, frankly, had begun to weigh me down. Years passed and, I assumed, so had the relevance of my book. After all, nothing stays broken forever. Between the time I first started subbing and now, there have been four education superintendents, three mayors, one state-sponsored takeover, one statewide cheating scandal and a boatload of policy changes at the state and federal levels. Yet, each new education superintendent, along with the state-imposed and now defunct School Reform Commission, has been tasked with the very same thing—"fixing" the School District of Philadelphia.

"*They*" have hired and fired, introduced new initiatives and drafted new plans. They have set about eliminating 50,000 of the "lowest-performing seats" through school closings and consolidations. And, they have relied heavily on privatized charter schools[1], which more than doubled from 45 in 2003 to 103 by 2016.[2,3] Interestingly, back in 2007, the Rand Corporation—a nonprofit research organization that studied the progress of Philly's schools—concluded that "results for privately managed schools were no better than regular District-run schools, and in some cases they were worse."[4] In 2013, a national study determined that roughly 75% of charter schools across the U.S. were "no better" or "worse" than regular public schools.[5] And, in 2015, *another* study noted that students enrolled in online charters "significantly" trailed their counterparts in traditional schools.[6] (But during a pandemic, any online/virtual option is likely a safer choice than in-person classes.) Today, a growing number of U.S. states— California, Maine, Mississippi, Washington, New York and others—have banned or limited for-profit charter schools.[7] *Still* there are some who continue to push for more. Even if all charter schools were amazing, a system that offers only a limited number of "good" schools abandons the vast majority of students. It's not fair. More importantly, it doesn't reflect the ideals upon which America claims to be founded: liberty and justice for _all_, right? Not just the lucky.*

Unfortunately, nearly 15 years after my first subbing experience and tons of School District issues, articles and upbeat press releases later, I couldn't tell if Philly's public schools were any better. For me, the topic had become both more pressing and more personal because now I have three nieces and a godson who are all school age. The thought that any one of them, or any child for that matter, might not receive the education needed to successfully take advantage of life's opportunities both saddens and angers me. So much so that I reapplied to be a substitute teacher and headed back out into the School District to see for myself.

---

*For more information about the charter school issue, check out this video: _PISA 2015 Shows Education Privatization Doesn't Work_ by the American Federation of Teachers. PISA stands for Program for International Student Assessment, which is given to 15-year-olds all over the world, every three years to evaluate school systems...not students. The video compares Sweden, which invested heavily in privatized schools starting in the 1990s and subsequently dropped in world rankings (below the U.S.) and Poland, which has steadily climbed (above the U.S.) using a strategy of increased education spending, access to early childhood programs, annual testing only to improve instruction and student placement, and the reinvigoration of vocational programs. You can find the video at http://www.oecd.org/pisa/ or on YouTube. (In case you're wondering, Singapore was #1 across the board in 2015 and, in 2018, China was #1.)

Why should you care?

Because failing inner-city schools do little more than set children up for disappointment and disillusionment. Because underfunded and unsuccessful educational systems continue to graduate students with substandard skills that qualify them only to shore up America's permanent, self-replenishing underclass. Because though the systematic hunting and killing of black people by racist cops and other vigilante terrorists is beyond horrific—depriving millions and millions of black children of the education they need to reach their full potential is *just as insidious.*

The brutal murder of George Floyd and the resulting civil unrest demonstrated the inextricable link between America's black communities and the peace and prosperity of the rest of the nation. If you are still not convinced that we are all in this together, perhaps these hard financial facts I first discovered in *High School & the Future of Work*, a guide from The XQ Super School Project[8] will help explain why the health, welfare and future success of black (and brown) children should be a relevant concern for all Americans:

- In 2017, only 39% of _all_ U.S. students were prepared for college-level work in 3 or 4 subjects.[9] Tuition payers across the U.S. spend $1.3 billion dollars a year on remedial college courses for high school graduates who are unprepared for college classes.[10] That means black, white, brown, etc., college is more expensive for students from underperforming schools.
- Closing the racial achievement gap (between black and Hispanic students and native-born white students) would boost America's GDP (Gross Domestic Product) by over $500 billion a year.[11] This waste of human potential has been described as "imposing the equivalent of a permanent recession on the American economy."[12]
- Raising the level of academic achievement for _all_ U.S. students to at least the **basic** level of achievement (as defined by the National Assessment of Education Progress [NAEP] standardized test[†]) would, over time, raise the GDP of the United States by $30 *trillion dollars.* That's way more money than the amount needed to properly fund all public schools. PA's

[†] Not to be confused with state-administered standardized tests, the NAEP is administered by the National Center for Education Statistics and given only to fourth-, eighth- and twelfth-grade students. Scores are ranked Advanced, Proficient and Basic, which equals only partial mastery of fundamental skills.[13] Roughly 27% of our nation's children are scoring _below_ the Basic threshold on the NAEP.[14]

economy alone would increase by nearly $1.1 trillion, New York's by $2.4 trillion, California's by $6.7 trillion.[13,14]

- Raising the level of academic achievement of <u>all</u> students across the country to match the U.S. state with the highest student achievement (Minnesota) would increase the value of our GDP by $70 *trillion* over time.[14] Bringing all U.S. students up to the level that Finland's students achieve would add $81 trillion to America's GDP.[14]

Hopefully, this book about my journey as a substitute teacher in the School District of Philadelphia will help shine a light on the key challenges so many public school students and teachers are facing every day.

—C.C. Harris

> Author's Note #1

This book is based on my personal experience as a classroom teacher and my substantive research into the various conflicts and controversies that arise in the field of public education. The issues that are reported and discussed here are focused on the School District of Philadelphia, but they can be found in school districts across the United States. *Sub* is my effort to join in the public debate that continues to be conducted in government and media and among the stakeholders in public education.

The names and other identifying characteristics of all schools, students and staff mentioned in this book have been changed, fictionalized or omitted. All names that have been changed or fictionalized are shown between quotation marks at first mention, and all "P.S." numbers for schools are fictional. Some individuals and institutions are composites. Any similarities between changed or fictionalized names and characteristics of real individuals and institutions are strictly coincidental.

Actual names of individuals have been used only to identify public figures, interviewees and subject-matter experts who granted permission to use their names and biographical information, and when quoting from published media sources and public records.

PART 1

Inside the SDP
(2001-2002)

If we wish to serve God and love our neighbor well, we must manifest our joy in the service we render to Him and them. Let us open wide our hearts. It is joy which invites us. *Press forward and fear nothing."*

—Saint Katharine Drexel, Founder
Sisters of the Blessed Sacrament &
Over 60 Schools for African-American
and Native-American Students

> "Public School #1"

November 5, 2001 (Day 1 of 21)

High School: Nearly 2000 students; 97.9% African American, 0.1% Asian, 0.8% Latino, 1.0% White, 0.1% Other.[1]

After tossing and turning all night, I was exhausted and leaning toward starting my illustrious career as a substitute teacher tomorrow, but the phone rang at exactly 6:30 a.m. I answered, only to hear a loud, annoying automated voice: "*THIS IS THE SCHOOL DISTRICT OF PHILADELPHIA. We have an assignment for... Clayvon Harris. Please enter your PIN number using the telephone keypad...*"

I scrambled out of bed searching for both my glasses and the stupid PIN. Luckily, both were nearby. Punching in the numbers, I waited expectantly for my first assignment: English as a Second Language (ESL) at a nearby middle school. *What?* I didn't sign up for ESL. I wasn't even sure what it meant. Would I have one class all day and be expected to teach English, Math, etc. to a bunch of kids who couldn't understand me? Or would I be rotating through English class after English class with several different bunches of kids who couldn't understand me? My Spanish is rusty at best. And Korean? Oh hell no.

Feeling somewhat cowardly, I declined, fell back into bed and back asleep until the phone rang again at 7:45 a.m.: "*THIS IS THE SCHOOL DISTRICT OF PHILADELPHIA...*" (really annoying). This time, for some elementary school downtown starting at 8:05 a.m. Even if I were dressed, I couldn't have gotten there on time. I'd need thirty minutes to get downtown, plus another ten to fifteen minutes to drive around lost. (I've never been able to find my way around Philly.) I turned this one down, too. But I was awake and realizing that my fear of not being called for assignments was completely unfounded. The phone rang again as I stepped out of the shower at 7:55 a.m. This time, the subject was

English at (for lack of a better code name) Public School #1—the high school I would have been assigned to if my mother hadn't sent me to private school. P.S. #1 was within walking distance, but it was worlds away from the small, private Catholic, racially diverse, all-girls school I attended. In the years between then and now (2001) P.S. #1's reputation as one of the most dangerous schools in Philadelphia had only grown. I couldn't help but feel a little excited. Here was my chance to see what high school could have been like for me.

Arriving at 8:15 a.m., with my sub handbook and poetry books in tow, I stood for a moment staring up at the imposing edifice of P.S. #1. I was intrigued by the large panels of brick-red paint and wondered what else they might be covering besides random graffiti. Hundreds of students poured toward the entrance, some loud and laughing, others more reserved, anxious—all submitting to bag checks and a pass through a metal detector. Identifying myself as a "guest teacher," I was waved around the metal detector, which struck me as odd because the security officer had absolutely no proof that a) I was who I said I was or b) that I wasn't toting an Uzi.

Inside was spacious and kind of nice; gorgeous murals and mosaics balanced worn fixtures and flooring; definitely not the hellhole I was expecting. I signed in at the office and waited for directions. They gave me a list of classes to cover and told me someone would bring the student lists and assignments later. (Still no request for the I.D. I stood in line for an hour to get.)

Here we go.

My first class was "Strategies for Success," a bogus title if ever I've heard one, with a bunch of 9th graders. Finding no assignment from the instructor and month-old notes on the blackboard did not quell my suspicions. The kids explained their daily routine: ten minutes of journal writing, then chatting amongst themselves for the rest of the period. There was no class list, so I had no idea if they were all there. What I did know was that they talked incessantly and complained because I made them a) move to the front of the class, b) quiet down, c) stop cursing and d) stop mocking their classmates and me. All in all, this was my best class.

The students swore they were behaving better than they normally did because their usual teacher was "too fat and too lazy to do anything." I, on the other hand, being the patient woman that I am, came very close to sending a girl covered head-to-toe in traditional Muslim clothing to the principal within the first ten minutes of class. I didn't understand why she couldn't be quiet. She didn't understand why she should have to. I threatened to kick her out. She stopped mouthing off.

It took me another ten minutes to get the rest of the class settled. Not completely quiet, but quieter. Somehow, I felt the poetry lesson I had planned would not be well received. Or maybe I doubted my ability to keep them quiet and focused. Whatever. I decided to flow with the "Strategies for Success" theme, asking them to introduce themselves and tell me if they were planning to go to college. This was a joke. Most refused to stand up. Almost all of them skipped the "is" in "My name is…" along with their last names:

"My name 'Malik.' I'm going to University of Maryland. I'm a play ball for the Terps."

Geez. How many black boys are deluded into thinking this is a legitimate option? If that wasn't bad enough, at least three of the students, as I was informed, "didn't talk at all…*ever.*" (So what were they doing in this classroom?) To make up for them, I had an overabundance of L&Rs—Loud and Rowdy students who mock and loud-talk pretty much everyone, including me.

Most of the kids said they wanted to go to college to study law, business, accounting, basketball, etc. The young Muslim girl, however, told me her plans were to go to Afghanistan, stay with her cousin and help fight the Americans because "They started first." She sat back with a confrontational smirk on her face, waiting for my response.

I decided to take a pass. "I see your point," I said and moved on. Unfortunately, "Muslim Girl #2" also wanted to be a terrorist—or a muralist. She wasn't sure which. "Okay," I said and again moved on. Focusing on the non-terrorist options, I began my "you-can-do-anything-you-set-your-mind-to" speech, but "Muslim Girl #1" yelled out, *"That's a lie right there!"* I stopped short. There's encouragement and then there's full-on fantasy promotion. Might as well be real.

"You're right," I said. "That is a lie. But this is the truth. There will be things you can do and things you can't do. And you won't know which is which until you try."

She sat back, glaring as the others nodded. I moved on, asking if they thought any of them would have impressed a prospective employer or admissions counselor with the way they introduced themselves. They were a little insulted, but a couple of the L&Rs took my question as a challenge and agreed to re-do the exercise, standing in front of the class—this time using verbs.

"Hi, my name *is* 'Malik Jones'..." He continued, pretending to introduce himself to a scout for a Division 1 school. He did a nice job this time but I had to ask: "What if they don't recruit you?"

"Then I'll keep trying different schools until I get one of them to say 'yes,'" he responded. Determination is a good thing. Having a great transcript to go along with that determination is better. I should have said that but I didn't want to pick on him too much after he'd volunteered.

Muslim Girl #2, the terrorist/muralist, was also much better this time. She introduced herself to someone at an art program, then went on to share that she had been in an art program and had a mentor...when she was on probation.

"Then they tested my urine and I passed. So I got off probation. Then they kicked me out of the program."

I stood there, uncertain of which thing I should be more disturbed by: that she was only in ninth grade and had already been on probation; or that when she was in trouble she had support and encouragement for her dream, but when she straightened up, they booted her out of the program. Where's the safety net for these kids?

Turnabout is fair play, so they wanted to know about me. I hate public speaking of any kind. I broke into a little sweat just walking into the classroom. But I needed to get over it if I planned to teach. So I started talking.

I smiled and extended my hand to shake. "Hello, my name is Clayvon Harris and I wanted to write for television..."

"And you couldn't, right?!" they yelled out.

When I told them I could and had, I finally had their complete attention. Even the L&Rs were shushing each other, as I gave a modified version of "the spiel" I developed for LA meet-and-greets:

"I grew up in this neighborhood, got good grades in school, went to Swarthmore College, worked in corporate America, went back to school to get a Master's degree in Cinema-Television from the University of Southern California, and wound up writing for a couple of TV shows: *Star Trek–Voyager*, *Living Single* (they gasped), *Soul Food*: The Series, blah, blah."

Suddenly, hands shot up. They politely asked questions, mostly about Queen Latifah (never underestimate the power of a rapper-turned-actor) and the other folks who starred in *Living Single*. I answered, hoping to steer the conversation back toward how working hard in school pays off. Unfortunately, before I could really drive the point home, the bell rang and the students broke for the door.

Advisory or what we used to call homeroom.

I rushed through the hallways weaving in and out of students, trying to locate a tenth-grade classroom. No one was there when I arrived. While I waited for someone, anyone, to show up, the "Section Coordinator" called. I told her it was my first day subbing and it was a little overwhelming.

"Only a little? That's good." She laughed...for quite some time, before telling me that someone would stop by to "get me up to speed." She also mentioned something about checking on me later and hung up.

Soon after, a curt, middle-aged man in a bow tie showed up. He instructed me to take roll, gave me class lists and assignments for the remainder of the day, as well as a few hall passes, though he cautioned me to use them sparingly.

"I'm next door if you need help."

"Why don't we take roll first thing in the morning?"

"Because," "Mr. Short & Sweet" answered, "we have to give our students a sporting chance."

Advisory turned out to be a fifteen-minute piece of cake. So far, this teaching thing was alright.

This is not what I signed up for.

As the eleventh graders trickled in, it became immediately obvious that there would be many more Loud & Rowdies than in the ninth-grade class, and they would be even louder and rowdier. I couldn't have talked over them if I wanted. The students rolled past me, mostly late, some stopping to point out their names on the roll sheet. "Thas me." I was sort of stunned by the number of kids pouring in. I couldn't tell who had been checked off and who hadn't. I repeated over and over, "Please make sure I've checked you off." They weren't listening and couldn't have heard me if they were. After a while, I figured it was on them. They sprawled in their desks as if they were on the subway, grouped together in little informal chat clusters of five or six students. They didn't care about the roll sheet. They didn't care about the assignment. And they certainly didn't care about me.

I truly had a problem comprehending this situation. I went to private and Catholic schools—nursery through graduate school. I had never witnessed such blatant disrespect and disregard for an adult, particularly a teacher, in a school setting. I contemplated leaving, but then I thought, *some of these kids must want to learn something.* I approached them individually, asking if they were interested in the assignment of putting together a résumé. Most of them dismissed me without pause. The few that bothered to listen said they'd done the assignment already. And even if they hadn't, one girl informed me, "This is like a college class. You do your work or you don't. It's on you."

She stared at me blankly when I replied that it wasn't anything like a college class. "In college, you sit quietly taking notes while the professor lectures. If you don't believe me, go visit one."

Finally, one boy raised his hand and said he wanted to do some work. Maybe he felt sorry for me. Who cares? It was a start. I wound up working with a group of five. Most of them didn't have much to put down, so we pretended this was after college and they were trying to get their first serious job. The kid who got things rolling for me put down "going out," "talking to girls" and "getting money" as his hobbies. I made him erase "getting money" since it made him sound like a pimp when he was actually referring to his mother's generosity.

One of the kids surprised me. He was doing a *real, usable* résumé. He'd had quite a few jobs at restaurants, UPS, etc. When I encouraged him to put down hobbies, he said he didn't have time for "all of that." He worked. A lot. I guess that's how he could afford the diamond stud earrings he was sporting. He also told me he was going to auto mechanic school (not thinking about it, *going*) and asked if mechanics made good money.

"Oh yeah," I said. "I've forked over enough money to them to know." He smiled and finished the assignment, references and all.

One of the girls had been a clerk in a state senator's office though she had no interest in politics. Bright and articulate, she explained that she wanted to be a lawyer.

"But look around," she said, referring to her classmates who were having what amounted to recess. "Coming from this school, I need all the help I can get."

Another kid finished up the format and asked if he could keep it. "My pops is looking for a job. I want to show this to him."

Toward the end of class, a few others belatedly copied the format I had put on the board and handed in slapped-together drafts. As they filed out, I asked one of the girls if this class was always so deafeningly noisy.

"Pretty much," she said. "But you had two classes in here because both of our teachers are out."

"Wow..." I thought, "way to take advantage of a sub."

Hall sweep?

All they had to do was watch a video and answer a few stupid extra-credit questions. Out of thirty something kids, only fifteen or sixteen students even bothered to show up. Only nine of them seemed remotely interested in learning something. The rest were rude, disrespectful and couldn't have cared less about *Othello*.

I was grateful for the nine who huddled around the VCR trying to watch the movie. One had even set it up for me. When I asked if he planned to go to college, he said, "Yes." When I asked where, he looked at me with a fatigue he shouldn't even be familiar with at his age.

"It doesn't matter," he said, cutting his eyes toward his clowning classmates. "Anywhere...out of state."

I spent half the class trying to keep six or seven students quiet so the others could watch a movie. We traded comments back and forth until they didn't have good comebacks and shut up. I asked the last two L&Rs if they were interrupting the movie because they couldn't understand it. One kid, who told me his name was "Derrick," said he didn't see why he should waste time on Shakespeare. It didn't have anything to do with his life; he planned to get a job.

"How do you expect to get a job if you can't sit still and be quiet?"

"You don't have to be quiet at Pizza Hut," he explained.

Hard to argue with that logic, especially since he got up and walked out, along with four or five others. Finally, we were able to watch the movie in peace. I handed out extra credit, which most of them got to work on right away. Just for a few minutes, it seemed like a real class. Then, ten L&Rs including Derrick and his tall, skinny sidekick burst in with no notes, no excuses and snacks. They strutted around, joked, passed the chips, threw things (luckily not at me) and, basically, I lost control of the class.

As I headed toward the phone, they begged me not to call. I asked if they would behave. Some said, "Yes." Others jumped up on the desks and screamed. Needless to say, I dialed and seven students ran out. I don't know why they were rushing. It took forever to get an NTA (non-teaching assistant) on the phone and even longer for him to get there. I flipped on the overhead lights and waited by the door. (In case I had to run.) The students kind of chilled out at this point. Or, at least, took their seats—though there was still a lot of joking and yelling going on. Those who were watching the movie gave up because they couldn't hear it. They sat back in their seats disgusted.

Fifteen minutes later, when the NTA finally showed up, the students greeted him by name. "Yo Mr. So & So, wasssssup?" He looked around the room, then at me as if to say, "What's the problem?" It seemed pretty obvious to me, but I proceeded to explain that they had been throwing things, jumping on desks, eating unauthorized snacks. "Some of them ran out when I called you."

"They'll probably catch them in the next hall sweep," he said. (*Probably?*) Then, he walked over to a female student and whispered to her that her thong was showing. She pulled her shirt down over her jeans. Before leaving, he casually told the students to behave and told me to dial 100 for the school police next time. That's when it hit me: disrespect and disruption aren't a big deal. *Blood* would be a big deal.

The L&Rs huddled in the back of the room, laughing and talking, but keeping it to a dull roar. Seems no one wanted me to call the school police. The kid who had set up the VCR wound the tape back a little and asked if I could shut the lights back off. I flipped off the light and stood arms crossed, watching them and feeling each of the few remaining minutes of the period passing like hours. I was infuriated by their total disregard for me, someone who wanted to help. "Why bother?" I thought. As I struggled to come up with an answer, Derrick's six-foot-tall sidekick struck up a conversation.

"See now, why'd you call the office? You didn't have to do that," he said in a singsong voice.

"I think I did," I answered, not sure where this was headed.

"You're not going to report me, are you?" he went on. "'Cause I didn't do anything."

Was he kidding? "You've been disruptive. You walked out. Didn't tell me where you were going..."

"I don't tell my regular teacher where I'm going. I, for damn sure, ain't telling no sub." He laughed. *I* was not amused and couldn't have reported him if I wanted to because I didn't know his name. I walked away. He followed.

"Sike... I'm sorry. I'm playing." He paused, grinning at me expectantly. "For real though, I don't need you getting me in trouble. I'm going to college." I just looked at him. "I am," he said. "I got good grades. You can ask."

"Please stop talking to me," I said flatly and walked away. Again he followed, sitting at a nearby desk. We had the same conversation three different times. During one of our exchanges, he actually handed in the extra credit work. I didn't believe it was his paper. So, he showed me his I.D. His name was "Naeem W." Who harasses someone, then flashes his I.D.? I suspected that this kid had some issues. Or, maybe, he was trying to threaten me and I was just too shell-shocked to realize it at the time. Finally, the period ended and Naeem and the rest of the students filed out, thank God. I was starting to feel weak.

I'm out.

A thirty-minute lunch break would not have been enough for me to regain my composure. I had *had* it. This situation was untenable. The kids wouldn't listen, didn't respect me and were hell-bent on giving me a hard time. I felt like I was wasting my time and being humiliated as repayment for my trouble. I went in search of the Section Coordinator. I found her chitchatting with a student about a TV show. After five or so minutes, I interrupted, "Just wanted you to know, I'm leaving." Suddenly, she had time for me. But realizing I was steadfast in my resolve to get the hell outta there, she insisted I had to speak to the principal before leaving. I gave her Derrick's and Naeem's names and made my way to the main office, where the principal was standing in the hallway waiting for me (in case I decided to sneak out, I guess). She politely but firmly told me I'd be leaving them in the lurch.

"We've got a lot of teachers out."

Maybe she should have thought about that before doubling up one of my classes without warning me. I wasn't feeling a lot of sympathy for her, but not being able to make it through my first day of subbing didn't sit well with me. And what if this woman reported me? Would that jeopardize my future with the School District? Did I *want* a future with the School District? I felt coerced, more so by my own sense of duty than by the principal. When I agreed to stay, she thanked me and offered to cover the beginning of my class so I could grab something to eat. I only had ten minutes left and one of the guards had already warned me not to go into the cafeteria.

Since I was from the neighborhood, I knew where to get a quick bite. As I walked up the street away from the school, my anger turned to anguish. What planet do these kids live on? P.S. #1 is not the real world and they'll be in shock when they find this out. They don't have skills. They, "for damn sure," don't have knowledge. What do they have that somebody, anybody is not only waiting for but willing to pay them to have access to? Life can be hard when you're well educated. These kids are being taught just enough to maintain the ranks of the underclass; to be cashiers, clerks, car-wash attendants and dishwashers. And that's fine, if that's what you want. But if not, you're screwed. Suddenly, an image came to me—thousands upon thousands of black children drowned in an ocean of despair, lost to themselves and their communities. Tears stung my eyes. My heart ached. I felt overwhelmed and utterly powerless in the face of it all.

Trying to get a grip before going back in, I stumbled into a local fast-food spot and stood in line. I watched as the young guy behind the counter messed up a customer's order three times. "Two medium cokes, two large fries, a double-meat cheeseburger and a chicken sandwich, no mayo!" I wanted to scream at him. Instead, I shook my head. He probably went to P.S. #1.

Second chances are for suckers.

I was about five minutes late for the next class. The principal was standing in the hallway, chatting with Mr. Short & Sweet from next door. Squinting at me, he asked, "You okay?"

"No," I said. "Didn't you hear all that noise?"

"Didn't seem any louder over here than usual," he shrugged, shooting me a sympathetic look before returning to his class.

The principal offered to take roll for me. See who was missing. Most of the students still weren't there but she didn't wait any longer. She quickly and loudly rattled off names. If she didn't hear an immediate "here" or "yo," she marked them absent. I'm sure it helped that she knew a lot of them, but I had to admit, she definitely started off in a more authoritative manner than I had. She threatened to suspend anyone who gave me a hard time. They weren't shaking in their boots, but they seemed to hear her.

Of course, as soon as she left, one of the students strolled to the VCR to pop in a *Def Comedy Jam* tape. When I explained that we would be watching *Othello*, he started to argue with me. "*Othello*," I reiterated firmly, trying to mimic the principal's tough stance. He seemed to be trying to decide whether or not to take me seriously when the Section Coordinator popped in.

"Sit down and shut up," she yelled, then warned the rest not to give me any trouble. (I guess if you threaten to leave, you get some backup.)

After she left, most of the students settled down. There was still a lot of talking but at least it was about the movie. But really, how many times could they call Iago a "f****t?" They had mentioned something about "lowering expectations" in sub orientation, but how low is low enough? I wasn't even sure why I was there anymore. I wasn't teaching; I was barely interacting with the students and I was really okay with that. For most of the period, I stood at the back of the class watching. I felt so bad for these kids. Trapped in this substandard school, learning next to nothing, reinforcing each other's ignorance and bad behavior…and generally missing out on developing the skills they need to become productive citizens. It was a lot to take in.

At this point, most of them were behaving but, of course, there was one "particularly nasty young man" sitting in the corner, talking very loudly to a young lady. I asked him to be quiet.

He mouthed off: "What's the problem? We're just talkin'."

I explained at least three or four times that he was disturbing the rest of the students. Eventually, the girl was so embarrassed, she moved away from him. So he had nothing else to do but watch the flick. I started to relax, even glanced at the movie for a few minutes, just in time to see Othello slap Desdemona. While most of the kids reacted strongly, the "Particularly Nasty Young Man" was the only one to do so favorably.

"Yeah, girls need to be smacked more!" he said, cutting his eyes toward me. I glared back, teetering between frustration and wanting to give him the finger.

The students lost interest after Othello killed himself. Luckily, the movie was almost over. Most of them had already answered the extra credit questions, so they were talking, passing pictures around, whatever. As long as they weren't too loud, I didn't care because class was almost over. Suddenly, one of the guys was trading punches with a girl. I shouted for them to stop, but he complained that she hit him first. Granted, she was a big girl, but this guy was at least six feet three and very solid. I was pretty sure he wasn't hurt. I told them to stop or I'd report them. The girl giggled like an idiot as the guy claimed they were just joking. They separated and, thinking it was squashed, I turned to shut down the VCR. Next thing I knew, he had her pinned up against the door with the help of the Particularly Nasty Young Man. This time she wasn't laughing.

I rushed over, stepping between them. I told the guy to let her go. He claimed she was holding *him*. She wasn't. I looked him in the eye and firmly said, *"Let her go."* He held my gaze for a few seconds, then let go. Really out of whatever sense of right and wrong he already possessed because truly, there wasn't much I could have done beyond insisting. All three of them towered over me.

Begrudgingly, the Particularly Nasty Young Man snatched away, *"You just took the girl's side!"*

"You had her pinned against the door," I replied. "What did you expect?"

Just then, the PA speaker buzzed. The kids claimed it was the bell. I suspected it wasn't, but didn't care anymore. I wanted them gone just as much as they wanted to be gone. Probably more.

"Go," I said, and they poured out. The two guys pushed roughly past the girl, almost knocking her down. She looked to me but what could I do, other than let her wait there until they disappeared down the hall?

Free at last.

I gathered my things...slowly. Next to the fourteen absences on the attendance sheet, I noted the names of the boys who had jacked the girl up against the door. I remembered them from roll call. I felt absolutely drained. How many times had I been called a bitch under someone's breath? At one point, a kid had walked in to deliver hall passes asking, "Where the fuck's the teacher?" He was embarrassed when the students pointed to me though not nearly as embarrassed as I was for him.

I made my way down the hall to turn in the attendance sheets and extra credit. On the way, I stepped in a puddle of yellow liquid, hoped it was Mountain Dew and kept walking. I just wanted out. When I reached the Section Coordinator's office, she thanked me for staying, but had questions about the boys I reported earlier. Seems Derrick was absent and Naeem claimed I had him confused with another student. Even said he'd come by so I could look at his face.

"Get him over here," I responded.

While we waited for Naeem, I acknowledged that perhaps I had the other guy's name wrong but that's what he told me. I described him in detail—up to and including the big silver medallion he wore around his neck.

"*Huge* medallion, right?" another teacher chimed in. He knew exactly who I was talking about.

Then, in walked Naeem. "That's him," I said without hesitation. He seemed surprised, even hurt. Maybe this boy really had been trying to intimidate me. Well, the chance of reprisal was slim because I will never *ever* set foot in P.S. #1 again.

"Naeem, you're getting dumber and dumber each year. It was your idea to have her look you in the face," the Coordinator smirked.

His response to all of this? "But I said I was sorry."

"Three or four times," I acknowledged. "All followed by, 'For real though, I don't need you getting me in trouble.'"

The Coordinator interrupted, "Did he get on your nerves?"

None of this struck me as appropriate, but I answered, "Yes."

"That's all that matters," she said.

Naeem objected as a burly, male instructor escorted him to detention.

The teachers hanging out in the Coordinator's office found this whole episode quite amusing. They had a huge belly laugh, then assured me the students I reported would be "dealt with." Somehow, I didn't believe an hour's detention would be much of a deterrent for any of them.

As I stepped into the hallway, the Coordinator yelled after me, "Please come again!" I looked next door to see Naeem in detention, yukking it up with another student until he caught sight of me. His smile faded and his eyes narrowed.

"Come again?" I thought. "Not a snow ball's chance."

P.S. #1: PERCENTAGE OF 11th-GRADERS
SCORING BELOW BASIC:[*,2,3]

2000–2001

Math } 79%   Reading } 66%

In March of 2002, *The Philadelphia Inquirer* published the "Report Card on the Schools," which listed the 2000-2001 results (the year before I started subbing) of Pennsylvania's Standardized Student Assessment (PSSA) for 5th, 8th and 11th graders throughout the state. Scores fell into four categories: Advanced, Proficient, Basic and the lowest category—*Below Basic*. I noted the results of the schools where I subbed and confirmed them on the state of PA's Education website. They are listed at the end of each school's chapter to demonstrate the dire academic situation we were facing in Philadelphia.

---

*Percentages are rounded.

> This May Have Been a Huge Mistake

Four months earlier...

$\mathcal{A}$fter ten years of pursuing a career as a television writer, I had burned out on the feast or famine nature of Hollywood and ached to do something that would make an immediate impact. Teaching seemed like the perfect solution. Since public schools in Philadelphia were just as bad as those in Los Angeles, I decided to go home, where I discovered a school district on the verge of state takeover.

Rumor had it that a hundred-million-dollar deal had already been struck with Edison Schools, Inc., a private education management firm with a debatable track record. People were pissed off. The mayor was pissed. Parents were pissed. Civic groups came out of the woodwork. Some folks were angry because the deal seemed to be a fait accompli though the Commonwealth and the City were still "in discussions." Others were angry because they didn't have a shot at the lucrative contract. Many were convinced that a for-profit company would never put the education of the students before its bottom line. Still others were upset because there was so much opposition to a solution that had yet to be given a chance. The uproar seemed less about educating children and more about the spiraling costs of funding a system that is obviously broken.

Despite the raging debate, classes were about to start. And while requirements for a full-time faculty position were quite rigid (no PA state certification, no job), the School District was practically begging for substitute teachers because, according to one of the area experts who conducted my sub training, on any given day they have "5,000 or more absent teachers." There are only around 12,500 teachers employed by the District. How could 5,000 teachers be absent in one day? If she was trying to shock me, she succeeded. I went to Catholic school—nursery through twelfth grade. Nuns show up to work. And lay teachers who work in Catholic schools are expected to follow suit. Apparently, in public school, absenteeism is not only tolerated, it's anticipated. New subs are practically guaranteed daily work, as long as they're willing to teach outside of their comfort zone—academically, logistically and emotionally. That means a large chunk of educating the youth of this fair city is being left in the hands of—for lack of a better word—temps. Having worked as an administrative temp for eight months in Los Angeles while trying to break into sitcom writing, I can confidently say: temps don't know squat. What's more, they're not expected to know squat. If you can show up on time, accurately take a phone message and not get yourself or anyone else fired, you're considered *really* good. I hoped that wasn't the case with substitute teachers. Regardless, the School District needed help and I was eager to get started.

Follow the yellow-brick paper trail.

The application process itself took over two months. I filled out form after form, including a Criminal Record Check, a Child Abuse Clearance and an FBI fingerprint card that no one at the School District followed up on.

"But you should send it in anyway," I was told.

I nodded. After spending over $250 for a physical, urinalysis and a chest X-ray ordered by the doctor because the tuberculosis skin test was "at best, inconclusive," I had no plans to pay for anything else that wasn't absolutely required.

Once all the paperwork was done, I was given an appointment along with fifty or sixty other would-be subs to fill out more paperwork. When asked to choose the subject area I wanted to teach, I proudly declared high-school English. It made sense. I majored in English literature in college. I have a master's degree from USC's Graduate Screenwriting Program. It was all right there in my transcripts.

"What else?" The woman reviewing my application asked.

"What else, what?" I responded.

"What other subjects can you teach?" she clarified.

I wasn't prepared for that question. Reportedly, kids are graduating unable to read and write. So shouldn't the School District be chomping at the bit for English teachers?

"We got a lot of English already," she added.

Being flexible, I offered, "Social Studies." I was runner up for the Social Studies award in high school. (I won the English award, but hey...)

"Um-hm. What about math?" she asked, unenthused.

"Do I look like I can teach math?" I wanted to ask. I think that's something you can tell about a person right away. Like if they're "not from around here" or they buy all of their clothes at The Gap. (Not that there's anything wrong with that.) The only thing I remember from high school math is how to calculate a percentage off at a sale. Or maybe my mother taught me that.

"*No math*," I said firmly.

She pressed on, "What about art?"

Art sounded like fun. "Sure...sure... I can try art."

Finally, she explained that I could choose up to four subject areas. The more I chose, the more assignments for which I'd be called. She suggested elementary for my fourth choice. I'm sure I must have had a blank expression on my face because she added, "You know, like fourth grade." As I continued to stare at her, she wrote "elementary" on my card. Sensing my hesitation, she pointed out that I could always turn down any assignments that made me uncomfortable. She smiled encouragingly and nodded for me to shove off.

At some point along the way, I was encouraged to sign up for the Literacy Intern program: a full-time teaching position, a full-time salary of $32K per year (you heard me), benefits and a shared class assignment. I decided to pass. I wasn't ready to commit to going back to school to get certified. I decided to stick with subbing; make sure I actually liked teaching first. I was pretty sure I would. I love kids. I have fond memories of school. For a couple of summers, I was a teaching assistant in a summer program for kids and I had a ball. I couldn't wait to get started.

Dis-orientation.

Despite all of the paperwork, no doubt designed to give the School District a clear picture of its applicants, there was no formal interview process. Perhaps if there had been, someone might have noticed that the woman sitting across from me during orientation was struggling with some issues. She was absolutely incensed that I had signed up to teach both high school and (not my idea) elementary school.

"You have to choose one. Or, at least not sit over here with the rest of us who aren't so greedy." She also claimed to have subbed before. *How did that happen?*

Despite being harrassed by this woman, I was still enthusiastic about orientation. Unlike some, I was under no delusion that teaching would be an easy gig. In Los Angeles, subs are required to pass the California Basic Educational Skills Test (CBEST), which isn't difficult but does require some brushing up. After passing the CBEST and taking a full week's worth of training classes, subs are given the go-ahead to start teaching. I decided to leave LA just as they called me for orientation. In Philly, orientation turned out to be a leisurely paced, five-hour session (including breaks and lunch) conducted by longtime employees of the School District. To their credit, they were well-versed in their topic areas. They casually went over classroom strategies and activities, lesson plans, employee benefits and HERBS (Human Resources Employee Record Base for Substitutes) the automated assignment system. You know...the loud recording... *"THIS IS THE SCHOOL DISTRICT OF PHILADELPHIA..."*

Given the brevity of time, our presenters stressed three things: 1) Have something for the kids to do; sometimes teachers don't leave assignments. 2) Dial six on the classroom phone to get help. And 3) Keep an eye on the students. That last one seemed pretty obvious, but they explained that in the late nineties, two male students had raped a 13-year-old, female special ed. student at "Public School X," *while* a substitute teacher was on duty. The sub claimed she didn't realize anything was happening behind the portable chalkboard. (Again, people should be interviewed.)

To be fair, most of the people I met were exceptionally nice and seemed very competent: a retired teacher who couldn't maintain his standard of living on his pension; a flight attendant who initially wanted to supplement her schedule with subbing until 9/11 wiped out her job altogether; a finance guy who abandoned his high-paying position to become a special ed. teacher because he couldn't take the stress of corporate America; a Ph.D. student from Temple who needed to supplement his student-teaching stipend and, of course, "My New Buddy."

While I felt confident in the abilities of the others, this lady worried me. She was a bit too cavalier. For example: Though it may not be official District policy, teachers are not encouraged to intervene in fights between students. During a quickie group discussion on conflict resolution, I commented that I would find it hard to stand by and let two kids beat the hell out of each other. I guess my comment struck her as particularly naïve. In fact, she said just that.

"You are *sooo naïve.*" She went on to suggest I carry a cell phone, call the police and stay out of the way if a fight breaks out.

"*That* will keep you out of the obituaries." She nodded at me, wild-eyed and emphatic.

We exchanged a few more words. Exactly what I said, I don't recall but I'm pretty certain the words "fine example" and "bully" slipped out of my mouth. She leapt up, motioning as if to jump on me. Luckily for one of us...probably me...a five-foot, sixty-year-old woman was able to hold her back.

Eventually, we were distracted by a significant piece of information: our salaries. The woman in charge of this section told us PA-certified substitutes are paid $95 per day for the first twenty-one days of employment and $115 per day thereafter. Out of the fifty or sixty people in the room, there were maybe two certified teachers. A few others were working toward it. Continuing, the woman apologized for having to tell us this, but the rest of us would be paid $95 a day—once we completed our 22nd day of subbing. For the first twenty-one days, we'd be making $40 a day; probably less than we'd make for a full day of work at McDonald's. Some of us laughed; others grumbled. My New Buddy was enraged.

"Something is *wrong* when they're paying teachers forty bucks a day!" she declared before storming out.

She had a point, but instead of letting the nearly nonexistent wages upset me, I decided to view the first twenty-one days as an internship. After all, it's about the kids, right? Besides, starting on day twenty-two, we'd graduate from welfare wages to those of the working poor.

With that, the ladies wished us well, told us we'd be "in the system" by Monday and sent us off with a three-hundred page, jerry-rigged handbook filled with photocopies of activities, teaching theories and numbers for nearly every educational office in Philadelphia proper. I found myself clutching that handbook as if my life depended on it.

> "Public School X"

Middle School: Over 800 students; 91.3% African American, 7.2% Asian, 1.1% Latino, 0.2% White, 0.1% Other.[1]

B is for the bullet that wasn't meant for "Brian." Wary of starting my new job armed with little more than determination and my sub manual, I called on a family friend, who also happened to be the new principal of the infamous Public School "X." Given an opening, "Principal Williams" invited everyone to visit what he called "The New P.S. 'X'." I arrived at 8:30 a.m. sharp to find him embroiled in a crisis. One of his students, "Brian J.," had been killed over the weekend by a bullet that "... wasn't meant for him." I wound up accompanying Principal Williams from class to class as he broke the news of the fifth grader's death to teachers who, in turn, had to tell their students.

By the time we arrived at Brian's homeroom, his classmates already knew. Far from being hysterical, they seemed almost impassive. The staff, on the other hand, was a mess. "Miss Smith," one of the assistant principals, collapsed into the Principal's arms crying. He escorted her from the room while Brian's homeroom teacher turned away to privately grieve. Slowly, the kids began to lose their battle with stoicism. As they began to cry, they were quietly escorted from the room.

"Let them cry!" I wanted to shout, painfully aware of my status as a visitor and untested sub. The shaking shoulders and bowed heads were clear signs they needed to let it out. I couldn't understand why they were trying to be so brave. They weren't asking for help. They weren't reaching for hugs. They just sat there, wiping silent tears as some man droned on, explaining the stages of grief.

"Who is this idiot?" I thought. "He can't possibly be a real counselor. Does he realize these kids are in fifth grade?" In hindsight, I realized he was probably just as much in shock as everyone else and didn't know what to say. Finally, a School District psychologist arrived and took over. Thank God. She told the kids it was okay to cry; okay to be sad. I don't know that they believed her. They still fought the tears. And when they lost the battle, they were still being ushered away. I guess that was the opportunity to put an arm around their shoulders and give them the hugs and reassurance they needed.

Teachers dropped by from all corners of the school to show their solidarity and support. When Principal Williams returned, he planted himself quietly but firmly in the middle of the room, as if to say, "I know we lost one but the rest of you, you're under my watch now. And for the time being, you are safe." The kids settled down and began to open up and talk about Brian. How he liked to tell jokes. How he could throw a basketball with one hand from center court and sink the shot. As I listened, thinking all the usual platitudes about a wasted life, the psychologist tried to assure the students that this was just a freak accident... that it wasn't Brian's fault or his parents' fault. It just happened.

A shoot-out in broad daylight on a Sunday afternoon? It was definitely somebody's fault. The gunman, definitely; the parents, maybe. There's always something on the news about parents who neglect their kids...then I heard the teachers whispering, expressing sympathy for the parents, who apparently were very involved with the school and their only child. They were the kind of parents who would pop by school in the middle of the day to check on him. Make sure he was okay and, even more importantly, to make sure he was getting his work done. Brian had transferred in from a charter school the previous year and he wasn't up to speed academically; so he had been held back. His parents were determined that this wouldn't happen again. Sadly, they'll never have the opportunity to see what he could have accomplished.

Suddenly, the conversation turned. Many of the twenty-something kids in the class began to share similar stories of "freak accidents," similar to their classmate's:

"My brother got shot in the subway. And they pushed him onto the tracks..."

"My cousin got hit by a bullet..."

"My uncle..."

Too many of the stories ended with "…but it wasn't meant for him." For these children, this type of occurrence is less of an anomaly and more of a probability. The girls teared up, but the little boys broke down. Perhaps because in their minds, they could easily be next. They can't stay at school forever. And they can't remain locked in their homes for the rest of the time.

"I heard about Brian the same day it happened," said one little boy. "Then my mom asked me to go to the store. I ran all the way there and all the way back."

I guess it never occurred to him to say, "I'm scared. I don't want to go." I can only hope that his mother didn't know about Brian.

Inevitably, the kids all wanted to know when they would arrest "the guy." "Why was it taking so long?" All of them had heard "things." They wanted to know he would be punished. There needs to be a consequence to shooting someone, even if it wasn't meant for him…especially if it wasn't meant for him. The principal assured them the police were looking for the murderer.

"What if we find him?" one of the kids offered and others nodded, causing fear to flicker across the face of every adult in the room. Knowing who killed Brian could put the children and anyone they told in danger.

Though he explained that they needed to let the police do their job, the kids insisted, *"But if we found out and told the cops?"*

How do you explain to eleven-year-olds that doing the right thing isn't always the best thing?

I observed no teaching that day, though I did witness a staff that truly loves its kids and that ached over the loss of a young boy's life. Later, Principal Williams told me they were used to whatever happened in the community spilling over into the school.

"We often hear about kids in the neighborhood being shot, but Brian was one of ours. I can't get used to that."

Who knows what kind of effect this murder will have on these kids in the future. Or perhaps they're numb to these random acts of violence, which may be the greatest tragedy of all. I left P.S. X at midday, my eyes burning and my throat aching from choking back tears.

P.S. #X: PERCENTAGE OF 8th-GRADERS
SCORING BELOW BASIC:[*2,3]

2000–2001

Math } 81%   Reading } 79%

---

* Percentages are rounded.

> St. Athanasius Catholic School

November 2, 2001

*N*ext, I turned to Sister Joan Alminde, the principal of my old grade school, St. Athanasius (St. A's). Initially, I didn't want to observe at St. A's because it wouldn't be representative of the public school experience. But teaching is teaching, right? St. A's is a good school and Sr. Joan—a holy force to be reckoned with—was named Principal of the Year in 1999 for the Archdiocese of Philadelphia. St. A's is one of the few elementary schools accredited by the Middle States Association of Colleges and Schools. But if I'm honest, another reason I chose to observe at St. A's is because, although it's an inner-city school, I knew the chances of something "spilling over from the community" were pretty slim...and I desperately needed to see some teaching in action.

Sr. Joan immediately sat me down and, in her serene, soft-spoken manner, warned me that she'd heard the public schools were "severely understaffed and undersupplied." She gave me four loose-leaf notebooks, two packs of pencils and three pens. She even offered to give me her briefcase because "it's big and roomy and looks like a real teacher's bag." But I couldn't take it.

Explaining that my main challenge would be controlling the students, Sr. Joan commented, "You're small and you look young. They'll size you up and try you. Don't smile at them."

I smiled.

"I'm serious, Clayvon. You cannot smile. They perceive kindness as weakness."

"Much like adults," I joked, smiling again.

"Practice a stern look," she said calmly but seriously, and I did. "But never raise your voice or publicly confront a child who's misbehaving. Just quietly encourage him to work."

I mentioned that my friend "Nora," a Harvard-educated, ex-Wall Street lawyer who was subbing in New Jersey (yes, really) had suggested that I kick out the most disruptive kid in the class right away to set an example. Sr. Joan shook her head in dismay.

"Putting a child out sends a message: 'There's nothing I can do with you.' And that message resonates in the child's mind long beyond the time of the incident."

I quickly jotted down, "No putting kids out."

After our discussion, Sr. Joan escorted me through the immaculately clean and quiet halls. It struck me that St. A's hadn't changed much. Sure, it now has a state-of-the-art computer room and a studio arts center, but the environment is the same: clean, orderly, safe. That's how it was when I went here. Not that kids didn't act up. There were arguments and fights. But if you got caught, parents were called, suspensions were given and some students were invited to never return.

"Perhaps after you've experienced the public schools, you'll give us a try," Sr. Joan pointedly slipped in.

"It's not that I don't want to teach in Catholic school," I quickly explained. "I just think the public schools might need more help."

"Hmm...." she replied. "Still."

We stopped in three or four other rooms on our way to fifth grade. In each class, the students stood to greet Sr. Joan, who encouraged me to give an impromptu talk about my education and "Hollywood career," as she put it. At the end of the spiel, "Catholic School, Swarthmore, corporate America, USC, *Star Trek, Living Single,* blah, blah..." Sr. Joan drove home the idea that studying and working hard could lead to wondrous things. She wished them a productive day and whisked me off to the next class.

Finally, installed at the back of Miss Jordan's class, I observed this tough, no-nonsense young woman who didn't smile, not even at me; though she never failed to compliment a student on a well-answered question. She put her kids through their paces: thirty-some questions spread out over the desks. They had thirty seconds to write down an answer before she called for them to "change." Then, in an incredibly orderly fashion, they rose and moved to the next desk to answer the next question. There was no pushing, no giggling, no talking. I was even more impressed when they went over the answers. Since when do fifth graders know how to pronounce (much less, spell) "esophagus." And I had no idea what a "nephron" was. Fifth-grade science had long ago disappeared from my frame of reference.

Suddenly, the absurdity of this substituting thing hit me. How on earth am I supposed to waltz in off the street and start teaching any old grade, first through twelfth with no experience? What are those people at the School District thinking? As I stood at the back of the room munching a soft pretzel and panicking, a few of the kids hesitantly approached. It didn't take long for them to get to the burning question: "Do you know Queen Latifah?" I could feel my cool points rising as I told them we had chatted a few times when I worked on *Living Single*, but that we didn't hang or anything. They had tons more questions but Sr. Joan whisked me off to the next class. On the way, I hesitantly confided my concerns about being ill-equipped to teach. Sr. Joan offered to lend me some textbooks. "Which grades will you be teaching?"

"All of them."

"Hmm," she responded, "the instructor editions of the textbooks come with the answers." We exchanged a look, both knowing that wasn't nearly enough.

"Listen, Clayvon," she said, "what you have to offer these kids is your experience. You've done a lot. And you can bring those experiences into the classroom. You'll do fine." I nodded, hoping the queasiness in the pit of my stomach was translating into a stern look on my face.

Next, we stopped outside an eighth-grade room. "Five times this woman has been nominated for Who's Who in American Teachers by her students," Sr. Joan proudly shared, "after they've graduated and gone on to high school."

Pressing on, she introduced me to Miss Bonner, another stern-faced woman with a twinkle of good humor in her eyes. As I finished "the spiel," Miss Bonner commented, "And now you want to teach? God bless you. Have a seat."

The kids were smart, enthusiastic and very tidy—including the meticulous braids worn by some of the boys. I watched intently as she drew the students into a lively discussion about a book in which a teacher is kidnapped by his students. (An odd, brave choice.) At the end of my visit, Sr. Joan wanted to know how everything had gone. I told her I had learned a lot and that I was very impressed. She beamed proudly.

"Clayvon, be a substitute teacher who really teaches. The kids will notice. They'll say, 'Miss Harris really teaches.' And they'll respect that."

Of course, that was the plan, but hearing it reiterated by Sr. Joan helped crystallize my resolve. I thanked her for her advice and kindness. In those few hours, she had instilled in me a belief that, even with my lack of experience and training, I could make a difference.

>————————————————————————————————<

As a Catholic school, St. Athanasius does not participate in the PSSAs; therefore, no scores are included here.

>————————————————————————————————<

> "Public School #2"

Middle School: Approximately 900 students; 98.3% African American, 0% Asian, 0.8% Latino, 0.7% White, 0.3% Other.[1]

*A*fter one day of subbing at P.S. #1, I was shaken and upset; no longer certain that I was cut out for teaching. That's when the phone rang with an assignment at a nearby middle school. The computer didn't indicate which grade or subjects; however, it did say that the position was a vacancy: something most subs hoped for because it meant steady work and more pay. Honestly, I wanted to pass, but I decided it'd be better to get back on the horse before I completely chickened out. After accepting, I asked my mother if she'd heard anything about this particular school.

"Only that you can smell the urinals from the street," she said matter-of-factly. Noting my obvious distress, she added, "...but that was a long time ago."

Stepping into the lobby of the school that next morning, I was thrilled to smell nothing at all. In fact, though rather run down, it seemed fairly clean. There were no metal detectors or school police. P.S. #2 definitely seemed safer than P.S. #1...or less prepared. One or the other.

Signing in at the office, I discovered a secretary who couldn't tell me anything except that the vacancy wasn't really a vacancy. Another teacher commented that they were "trying to do something." For any other information, I'd have to wait for the Coordinator. She said "Coordinator" almost the same way one would say "Mighty Oz." So I waited, legs aching from standing all day yesterday. "Why hadn't I taken the day off?" I wondered. "Oh yeah...the horse." After a while, I asked a passing teacher where I could get a cup of tea. He was kind enough to walk me around to a room that turned out to be locked. No tea, but in the process, he let me know he'd be out for three days next week and I could have the "gig" if I wanted it. I asked how the school was.

"Tough…definitely tough," he said. "But it's getting better."

I wasn't sure if he was trying to convince himself or me. I thanked him and said I'd let him know by the end of the day. I plopped down on a bench next to another waiting sub who told me he'd been at it for over a year and hated it. He asked where I'd been assigned. When I told him my first day had been at P.S. #1, he chuckled, "And you made it out, huh?" I shrugged, thinking "barely."

The Coordinator finally showed up just before the bell rang. Dapper and nonchalant, he handed us attendance sheets and escorted us to our rooms. I let him know right away this was only my second day of subbing.

"Doesn't matter," he said. "Middle school is middle school." Unapologetically wussing out, I quickly informed him that I'd prefer the younger kids. "You can handle sixth, right?" he sarcastically replied.

"We'll see," I answered in complete honesty.

The classroom was orderly, clean, well decorated and the teacher had left assignments for each of her classes. But before I could read through the notes carefully, students started streaming in. They were loud, talkative and kind of small in comparison to the high school students.

"Good," I thought, "anything jumps off, I should be able to take 'em."

Despite the fact that I hadn't a clue about the normal routine, I managed to get through advisory just fine. The kids sort of steered me through, while testing me at the same time. There was a lot of jumping up and down, running back and forth and noise—lots of noise. They weren't listening at all. I couldn't believe I was going through this again. With sixth graders. Uhn-uh. It was time for me to put my foot down. I raised my voice, insisted that they make name signs for their desks; then, I took roll. The kids weren't totally quiet, but they were responding.

Things were moving along when the Coordinator dropped off a little black binder. (I didn't realize until later that I had no idea what I was supposed to do with it.) Before he disappeared, I asked him to give the kids a talk about expectations and behaving for the guest teacher. (Sr. Joan told me she does this on the rare occasions she has a sub.) He looked at me like I was crazy, then hurriedly threatened to cancel the school trip for any students I reported. I'm pretty sure there was a collective "oooo," followed by giggles. And the "Mighty Oz" was off. Amazing: The veterans don't seem to give the subs much help or guidance. They act as though teaching is the easiest, most self-explanatory job in the world. Yet teachers constantly complain (and everyone else on their behalf) that they have a tough and important job for which they're not adequately compensated. Which is it? 'Cause if a forty-dollar-a-day sub can waltz in on Day 2 and just figure everything out, maybe teachers are overpaid.

Since I had a free period, I decided to go over the assignments: journal writing, language arts exercises, an essay and a practice science quiz. Seemed reasonable until I realized the teacher hadn't bothered to leave the answers to the quiz. Just as I started to panic, one of the students popped back in: "We need the co-op book."

"The what?"

He didn't wait for me to clue in. He grabbed a white binder off the teacher's desk and rolled out. I decided not to worry about it. I knew where to find him. Besides, I had to deal with this quiz. I thought back to Miss Jordan's quiz on the digestive system. I still don't know what nephrons are. Luckily, this quiz was on the metric system. Something people use every day—in Canada. I hadn't studied metrics since...actually, I wasn't sure I had ever really studied it.

With no teacher's edition in sight, I had no choice. For the next thirty minutes, I figured out the answers by process of elimination. It was kind of tough. Some of the questions were poorly worded and confusing. Others seemed to have more than one answer or none at all. And to top it off, the quiz wasn't typed. It was handwritten, somewhat illegibly at that, and scrunched onto half of a piece of paper. At least the material was challenging. I was kind of impressed that the kids were up to this type of work and somewhat amazed that, at some point, I must have studied the metric system. Maybe at Raven Hill, a private Catholic Montessori school I attended for a couple of years. They were pretty progressive.

I was almost done but the answers to the last two questions seemed interchangeable. I searched the desk for notes. Flipped through old science quizzes. Walked the room studying the science posters on the walls. Nothing. Finally, in a corner at the back of the room, I found the children's science books and started reading. Better to be a little anal than to give them the wrong answers. If I were the regular teacher, I would have left the key.

My first couple of classes were pretty much…ridiculous. It was difficult to get anything done because the kids were so unfocused. They were whiny, fidgety and unprepared. (I don't know how many of Sr. Joan's pens and pencils I let them borrow, but I only got two back.) It was almost as if they were physically incapable of sitting still and being quiet. I had never seen anything like it. I don't know if they were hopped-up on candy and soda, or what? The free breakfast provided by the school was a sugary, fruit-filled pastry and juice or chocolate milk. I'm sure that didn't help. I shifted pretty quickly from, "Please lower your voices." to "Hey! You're too loud!" I constantly moved around the room—standing next to the most talkative students expecting them to quiet down. And they did, until I moved away.

And the phone seemed to ring at least twice each period with some kind of request from the office. "Is so and so here today? Can you give me such and such's home number?" (Shouldn't they have that info in the office already?) Or they wanted me to send this kid to the office or that kid to the nurse. How are teachers supposed to teach with these constant interruptions? Not to mention trying to maintain discipline. And who's watching the kids when they're out in the halls by themselves? Maybe I was overly paranoid but P.S. #1 had traumatized me with its school police, roaming packs of kids and hall sweeps.

Despite the interruptions and disorder, I was determined the day would not be a waste. I ploughed through the lessons, running over into lunchtime for both the kids and for me. And, once again, I hadn't brought food, didn't know where to find any and didn't have much time. At least today, though far from thrilled, I didn't want to run screaming from the building. I was starting to get the idea that subbing just ain't fun. The Coordinator had encouraged me to call on my "grade partner" for guidance, so I went next door looking for help. I found two teachers who were annoyed that I had interrupted their lunch—especially my grade partner. But I had questions, like what do I do with the little black binder? Is there a cafeteria? And where's the bathroom? Begrudgingly, she explained that after I marked the kids absent on the attendance sheet, I was supposed to mark them absent again in the "roster" (the little black binder) using an "o" to indicate absences. (Wouldn't an "a" make more sense?) Faculty and staff don't eat in the cafeteria. And there was nowhere in the area to get a quick bite.

The other woman had a little more compassion. She had subbed before, eventually working her way into a full-time position. She told me where the bathroom was. Before leaving, I mentioned that I'd seen a kid copying his social studies homework from another student. Seeing her blank, unconcerned look, I added, "If it matters." Before I disappeared around the corner, she muttered, "Yeah, thanks."

Returning from the ladies room, I found a soda machine. In the absence of food, caffeine would have to do. I returned to the classroom and updated the roster. By the time I finished, the noise in the hallway was deafening and I was keenly aware of two, distinctly hostile voices floating above the rest. Opening the door, I found two girls separated by a matter of feet, screaming insults back and forth. I peered down the hall to see the Grade Partner standing at her door, arms folded, as if to say, "Let's not let this get out of control." But wasn't it already? I recognized both of these girls from the morning classes. They were chatty, but fairly well behaved. I approached the closest one. Relieved, she told me she'd been talking with the other girl and accidentally spit on her. Neither the spitter nor the spittee had noticed until someone else made a big deal about it.

"Girl #1": "She ain't even say nothin' 'til that other girl said somethin'. I dunno why she's actin' all like that." I did. Who, besides 1960's Civil Rights demonstrators and Gandhi, reacts calmly to being spit upon?

"But it was an accident?" I asked.

"Yeah," she answered.

I asked her to come with me. She did so willingly, hoping that I'd be able to somehow "fix" this situation. We walked over to the other girl, who, by this point, was screaming at the top of her lungs.

"That's so nasty! She's just nasty!!! Spittin' on somebody!"

I tried to calm her down, explaining that it had been an accident, but she continued to rant: "She's still nasty!!! You don't do that!!!" Of course, you don't. But accidents happen. Kids were gathering, expecting a fight I suspect. Girl #1 had a look of dread on her face. I wasn't sure what to do and I was getting a headache. I cast an eye toward the Grade Partner who looked away. I quieted "Girl #2" long enough to tell her the other girl wanted to apologize. She paused for a second, took note of the growing audience, then continued screaming, "She's just nas-teee!!!"

I encouraged her to accept the apology, but she refused. "Fine," I finally said, turning to the other girl, "forget it." I steered her back down the hallway in the opposite direction and sent her on to class. The disappointed looky-loos quickly dispersed and "The Scream Machine"—stunned by the disappearing attention—stopped screaming. Who knows what happened in the next class, or after school? For the time being, the situation was squashed.

The next group of students poured into the room, loud and rowdy like the rest. My patience had begun to wear thin. A boy came in and announced he wasn't doing any work and proceeded to kick back with his feet up on the desk. Before I realized it, I had said, "You. Out!" He was taken aback. So was I. As I escorted him to the door, he said I was doing him a favor. I told him he was doing me one, too. I beckoned to a non-teaching assistant who was chatting at a desk near the end of the hall. "Can you come get him?" I yelled. "Be happy to," she responded. As she took him away, I remembered seeing a sign in the office that very explicitly stated, "Students are not to be sent out of the classrooms." Oh well, I thought. They can fire me.

This was the best class I had all day. More of what I had in mind when I signed up to teach. The kids were cooperative and focused. Did they get a little rowdy? Yes. Did I have to threaten to put another student out? Yes. But then, we moved on and did the work. I felt like they were learning something. Not only did we get through the quiz in a timely fashion, we went over the answers twice to make sure everyone understood. Then we went over homework.

Lovely children that they were, they also explained the co-op book to me. (The white binder the kid had snagged off the teacher's desk earlier.) Apparently, each homeroom has a co-op (for "cooperative learning," I think) book that travels with them from class to class. The teachers make notations next to the name of any student who has been misbehaving, for example, "ET" for excessive talking. The kids didn't agree on how many notations they could receive before getting into trouble, nor on exactly what the trouble would be. They thought parents might be called. You'd think somebody—the Mighty Oz, the grade partner—would have mentioned this to me.

I decided to comply with school policy and not put any more kids out of class. And I suffered the consequences. Just as good as the last class had been, that's how bad the next one was. The homeroom kids had returned and they were even worse than they had been in the morning: talking, playing around, getting out of their seats. I wondered if they had gotten hold of more sugar or if this was a leftover high from lunch candy. Trying to get these kids to focus on the science quiz was next to impossible. Few of them completed it. Some filled in any old answer. Others didn't even do that. They just whined and complained, "I don't understand." The more I explained what they were supposed to do, the less they claimed to understand. Whereas the last class grasped the material well, these kids seemed to have never heard of the metric system and they were in the same grade.

I gave up on all of them completing the quiz. I decided to just go over the answers. Unfortunately, the majority of them wouldn't shut up. They talked over the kids who were trying to participate. They talked over me. They got up out of their seats. It was like a game to them. Raising my voice, making notes in the co-op book, nothing mattered. When I was in sixth grade, they could have sent a monkey to watch us and we would have behaved. These kids were very much aware that there wasn't a whole lot I could do, but I kept trying...

I put more names on the blackboard. (There were some there from the morning.) I told them if I circled a name, that student would be reported to the Coordinator and he or she wouldn't be allowed to go on the trip. You'd think they would chill out, but no. Not until I put a name on the board and circled it right away. They gasped (as if I had broken the rules) and quieted...a bit. The kid whose name I circled told me he was still going on the trip, "Watch."

Fed up, I announced if they weren't ready for the test tomorrow, it was on them. And I started whipping through the answers. To my surprise, some of the kids were right with me, excited that I was pressing forward. And guess what? They had the correct answers. Turns out, the knuckleheads were holding them back. At that point, I decided that to the best of my ability, I would make sure the kids who were really trying got the attention they deserved—at least from me. We moved on to essay writing. I handed out the paper, wrote the topic on the board and told them to start writing. Quite a few got right to work. And to my surprise, one at a time, the kids whose names were on the board started calling me over to their desks.

"If I'm good for the rest of the day, can I get my name off the board?" they whispered, not wanting the others to know they were trying to cut a deal. It was both amusing and appalling, but I was negotiating with ten-year-olds.

"Maybe," I responded, playing hardball. "But I want to see a total turn around in behavior. And I want a full page for the essay." They groaned, bowing their heads and muttering under their breath; but they actually began to put pen to paper.

Of course, there were still a few kids who just didn't give a damn. I had to separate two of them from the rest of the students. The boy was playful and fidgety, unable or unwilling to concentrate on work, angry when reprimanded. After he stripped the shirt off of another student (Who does that?) I sent him to the back table. I should have separated him earlier but he had also been helpful, coming back for the co-op book when I didn't send it along with the class. As the day wore on, however, he became more and more disruptive.

The girl was just hostile—provoking others to fight, refusing to do her work and stopping others from doing theirs. Separating these two disruptors helped calm the other students. Ironically, they had both gone straight to the back table when they first arrived in the morning. I'm the one who insisted they join the rest of the class. Lesson learned: if a kid is separated, there's probably a reason for it. In a logical world, they probably wouldn't be in this class.

Even after they were separated, they still didn't do any work. The girl sat chatting incessantly, as much to herself as to the boy because he was quite preoccupied with drumming on the table with his pencils. I spotted Oz in the hallway, snatched open the door and called him over, hoping that he would at least calm the boy down. Leaning in, Oz pointed, as if warning. He didn't say anything; just pointed. And the boy kept drumming. Noting the names on the board, Oz threw out another half-hearted reminder about missing out on the school trip and left. The girl kept talking. The boy kept drumming.

I hate to say it, but standing there watching those two kids, I could see how people came to view Ritalin and similar drugs as an answer. It may be the wrong answer, but it is an answer. People probably just want something, anything that will help some of these children. I felt so bad for them, but they still needed to do their work. I casually reminded them that I would be reporting them at the end of the day and if I were them, I wouldn't want to be reported and not have my work done. They saw the logic and got to work.

They were smart kids. They could do the work. It just wasn't on their agenda. You can tell when kids (and adults) know there will be no consequences for their actions. That was the case with the boy. The girl was just angry. I wanted to call their mothers but under what authority? And what would I say?

"Hi, I taught your kid for one day and I think he/she has a deep-seated psychological problem. Can you do something about that?"

At the end of the day, three different students protested the fact that I planned to rat them out. Since I wasn't buying the excuses, the girls gave up, but the boy was on fire with righteous indignation. He pointed out that he had asked for a deal and held up his end of the bargain. True, with thirty minutes left in the day, after I had warned him and circled his name, he promised to be good and do his work. But I never agreed to his deal. Those thirty minutes didn't make up for the whole day. He admitted that he'd been talking and arguing but the others were teasing him. Calling him "Clifford."

"That's a dog's name," he said.

I know what it's like to be teased about your name. My name is Clayvon while all the other little girls I went to school with were named Monica, Dena and Robin. Still…

"Clifortin," I said gently, "you just have to ignore them. You have to stay in your seat. You have to face the front of the class and you have to do your work." He started crying, bemoaning the unfairness of it all.

"Did you try to help me out at all here, today?" I asked.

After a few seconds, he finally stammered, "No, but nobody ever sees them messing with me. Everybody always sees me but never them. And I'm sick of it!"

Nothing hurts more than when you feel you're being treated unfairly. I wanted to pick up this little boy and give him a big hug. Instead, I said, "Well, Clifortin, I guess I'm not the only one who's catching you then, huh?" As he stormed out, I noted the twelve names on the blackboard. I erased all of them except the five that were circled. Those students I listed on a note to Oz. Even if he didn't do anything (and I had the distinct impression he would not) at least I held up my end of the bargain.

Right then, the teacher who offered me the "gig" stopped by. He confirmed my impressions, telling me that P.S. #2 has a huge discipline problem. Detention had been banned and they didn't have any other means of "punishing" the students for bad behavior.

"So how 'bout those three days, next week?" he smiled ruefully. "You want 'em?"

If sixth graders were bouncing off the walls with no accountability, what were the eighth graders doing? I decided to pass and he understood.

On my way out, I spotted Oz chatting with a few teachers. I told him I had left the roster, co-op book and list of students who really misbehaved in the office.

"Yeah thanks," he said and went back to chatting.

"Oh yeah," I thought. "He'll be all over those kids."

Heading out, I noticed that my throat was sore from yelling to be heard and my ears were buzzing from the noise. How can they stand it? Not just the teachers, the students, too. I've had jobs where I've worked twelve to fourteen hours a day. None of them had ever left me this drained. Is this what teaching is? Yelling at kids all day to be quiet? To get in their seats. To do their work. Maybe that's what subbing is. I felt like I hadn't made the slightest impact. Maybe you can't as a sub. I don't know. What I did know is that I was taking the next couple of days off.

P.S. #2: PERCENTAGE OF 8th-GRADERS
SCORING BELOW BASIC:[2,3]

2000–2001

Math } 80%   Reading } 60%

---

*Percentages are rounded.

> "Public School #3"

November 9, 2001 (Day 3 of 21)

Middle School: Approximately 700 students; 98.5% African American, 1% Latino, 0.1% White, 0.1% Other.[1]

*T*oday, I subbed for an art teacher at another middle school. I thought this would be an easy assignment. What kid doesn't like art? But as I walked toward this huge, run-down building, I had a queasy feeling in the pit of my stomach. Except for the mosaics peeking from beneath somebody's signature tag, the building reminded me of a minimum-security facility. There were no metal detectors but there was a security checkpoint inside. After identifying myself as a substitute teacher, the officer on duty waved me up the stairs without so much as a glance at my I.D.

Unlike the folks at P.S. #2, they were ready and waiting for me at P.S. #3. Two administrators signed me in, gave me a copy of the modified, half-day (woo-hoo!) schedule and escorted me to the art room where my first class, a subdued bunch of eighth graders, was just arriving. Both the administrators and the homeroom teacher warned the students to behave—and they did. They got right to work on their projects, using liquid ink to create stylized versions of their names. Those who were already finished took turns playing Tetris on the one computer in the room.

Since all of the students were occupied, I felt kind of useless. I tried striking up conversations with some of them, but they weren't very chatty, at least not with me. I did learn that as eighth graders, a lot of them were applying to high schools outside of their neighborhood because they didn't want to go to their designated area school.

"Anywhere but there," they said.

As far as discipline, I only had to ask a few students to quiet down, one guy to stop cursing and another to draw his own name instead of paying someone fifty cents to do it for him. I tried to explain why he should do his own work, but he either couldn't or wouldn't get it.

"If she can draw better and I have the money, why shouldn't I pay her to do it for me?"

Is eighth grade too early or too late to instill integrity in a child?

After the first class, I was informed that it would be more expeditious for me to go to the students than for them to come to the art room. Of course, no one bothered to inform them. Luckily, I ran into the fifth graders in the hallway. Their teacher, a concerned and helpful man from the West Indies, escorted us back to his classroom. He told me his students liked to draw and gave me a bunch of paper and pencils. Then he promised his students if they misbehaved, they'd be sitting in detention while the rest of the school was dismissed early. He even came by later to make sure we were okay. We were fine.

The class was divided, boys on the right, girls on the left, which struck me as a little old-fashioned and sexist but it gave me an idea. I asked them to write their names and an idea for something to draw at the bottom of the page. Then I gave the girls' papers to the boys and vice versa. What an uproar! The boys didn't want to draw flowers or families or anything the girls had picked. The girls had never heard of Dragon Ball Z so how were they supposed to draw it? One of the boys pulled out a picture. Immediately, the girls declared it "too hard." But one little girl picked up her paper, walked over to the boy with the picture and started drawing. The rest fell in line with a little encouragement. I was struck by the differences between the fifth graders at St. A's and these kids. They were not as well-behaved, more immature and probably not as academically advanced. Still, they had fifth-grade enthusiasm, so the class was fun.

When they finally traded back, almost all of them wanted the opportunity to comment on the drawing they had received.

"Look at this. It sucks. Does it look like a cat? Park? Basketball player?"

I wanted to laugh. Instead, we had a discussion about courtesy. Despite the harsh criticism, I thought it had been a good exercise. And it was obvious that some of the girls and boys had impressed each other. One kid made my day. He stood gingerly holding his drawing out in front of him.

"I got this lovely drawing of flowers from 'LaKeisha,'" he said.

He tenderly described each flower as if it were a detail from a Monet. For her part, LaKeisha had probably taken a whopping twenty seconds to toss off this masterpiece. Still, she was quite moved by his response to her art.

As the students sweetly waved good-bye, I realized I had jumped to conclusions about this school. I was actually having a pretty good day. Then I met the seventh graders. Their homeroom teacher was under the impression her free period had been cancelled because there was no art sub, so she was pretty happy to see me. She barked at her students to behave, then disappeared. They had already begun a drawing assignment. All I had to do was baby-sit. And as I look back now, I wonder why I didn't do just that: Keep the door shut. Let them talk as loud as they wanted, throw things, whatever—as long as they didn't kill each other or me. But no. Still high on my experience with the fifth graders, I wanted to connect. To make our time together valuable. What a fool.

As I introduced myself, there was one kid who sat with his back to me, carrying on a conversation at the top of his lungs. He rocked back and forth in his chair, grabbing things off a nearby shelf. "Hello...excuse me...?" He just kept talking. I wasn't sure if he was intentionally being rude, or if he was just oblivious to the fact that I was talking to him. I should have ignored him. Instead, I walked over and grabbed the back of his chair trying to get his attention. I think he thought I was going to snatch it and let him fall. I wouldn't have done that, but I did smile and introduced myself while some of the nearby students laughed...a little. I asked if the things he had taken off the shelf belonged to him. When he said, "No." I asked him to put them back. He did, squinting at me. I complimented his drawing (though it reminded me of something one of the fifth graders would draw) and encouraged him to keep working. Little did I know, the war had begun. He started with outbursts of laughter and loud-talking, meant to taunt me, I think. After a while, I tried to ignore his increasingly outrageous behavior. I had the feeling he needed only the slightest provocation to jump completely out of the box.

I flipped through all of the don'ts in my head: "Don't pay him special attention. Don't engage in a verbal tug of war. Don't raise your voice." At least I managed that last one. The more he acted up, the rowdier the other kids became: loud-talking, switching seats, throwing crayons. I tried to stay on top of them. I knew the noise had to be disturbing the other classes on the floor. I wanted to close the door but the room was stiflingly hot, which seems to be the norm. I flashed back to my experience at P.S. #1. Anger and resentment came flooding back. I studied this boy's messy, braided hair and baggy pants and found myself judging him: "This is what's wrong with public schools. Kids like him." Just last week, I was vehemently defending the rights of young men to wear their hair any way they want. You know...civil liberties and all. Suddenly, faced with a clear discipline problem, I was ready to extol the virtues of mandatory dress and grooming codes: neat clothes, ties, hair no longer than an inch. No Timberland boots, no jeans, no toothpick hanging out of his mouth...I mean, their mouths. I thought about how I would handle this young man if I were his regular teacher. As he glared at me across the room, his eyes narrowing, those thoughts were quickly replaced by how he might handle me. I tried shrugging off this line of thinking. I refused to be intimidated by someone in seventh grade, even if he was bigger than me.

Eventually, a young lady volunteered the names of the kids who were giving me a hard time. She suggested I put them on the board. "Oh yeah," I thought. "Because that works so well." What the hell, I had no other recourse. I wrote the names on the blackboard. When I asked about my friend, she hesitated. I acted as though I was annoyed and told her to sit down. I didn't want to create any problems for her. I saw the young man give her a nod. I reminded him that his teacher would return and she would certainly know his name. He turned his back to me.

I stood there wondering if perhaps I deserved this antagonism. After all, I did grab his chair. I was teasing him, but maybe he saw my actions as a challenge. Then I thought, "Wait a minute, I'm the teacher. He's the student and he's what, twelve? This behavior is not acceptable." I decided to try quietly talking with him. Before I could open my mouth, he put his hand within inches of my face, telling me to "Chill." I would never have spoken to a teacher that way. My normally low blood pressure pounded in my ears. Once again, I reminded myself that he was only a child. As I turned to walk away, he cut his eyes toward me and commented loudly to another boy, "I'll sock her." That was it. I wasn't getting paid forty bucks a day for this crap. I picked up the class phone and dialed. He watched with slight concern as I called the office and asked them to come get this boy because he had threatened to "sock me."

As I hung up, the regular teacher bolted through the door screaming at the top of her lungs. "I can hear you down the hall!" They quieted down. A little. She asked if they had acted up. "Of course," I responded. She was ready to give them all detention, but I didn't want the few decently behaved kids to suffer along with the rest. I pointed out the ones that gave me the most trouble.

She screamed at them. "I'm not surprised! What did I tell you?! You know better!" I pointed to the boy, asking his name. He scowled as she gave him up. Just then, a school officer showed up. He told me that I'd have to fill out a pink slip. He said it like he expected me to change my mind. I had no idea what a pink slip meant in the context of a school, but I figured it couldn't be good. "I'd be happy to," I told him. When the regular teacher realized I was actually filling it out, she turned to me and silently mouthed, "Thank you." Right then, I knew it wasn't just me. This kid was always a problem. He glared at me fiercely, as the officer took him away. I met his eyes without flinching, depriving him of whatever response he'd expected. As they disappeared through the chaotic change of classes, I slung my bag over my shoulder and headed down the hall.

The news spread quickly. One of the administrators and a couple of teachers were waiting for me as I passed through the library. They wanted to know if I was okay. I wasn't and I'm sure it showed all over my face.

"How can you stand it? How do you teach under these circumstances?" I asked.

"It's tough," one woman said.

"That's how it is," said another. "You should try to sub at 'this' school or 'that' school. I hear they're better."

I felt like an overly emotional wimp; totally unnerved, but still annoyed that the others were so resigned to a situation that is clearly unacceptable. They seemed like doormats, which made me feel like one, too. They helped me figure out where I was headed next—a sixth-grade class. They assured me this teacher was good; well liked and well respected. That her class would be "under control" and she'd probably stay in the room with me.

"Whatever," I thought. "Maybe she can show me how to manage a class."

They were right. This woman did have control over her class. She was about my height, 5'4, but heavier and a little older. She was mild mannered but still able to project her voice very loudly. And she didn't smile. Quite a few of her students were really engaged, raising their hands to read, giving answers. There was one boy who was desperately trying to get my attention: making faces, dancing in his seat. After the last class, I no longer had the same burning desire to connect. I just wanted to observe. But no matter where I moved in the room, I could feel him watching me. Finally, I looked up and he broke into a huge grin. I smiled (a little) and shot a look in the direction of his teacher, indicating that he needed to pay attention. Surprisingly, he settled right down.

Others weren't so easily dealt with. The teacher had to put one boy out. (An NTA was waiting for him in the hall. Apparently, he'd been put out of his last class too.) She stayed on the rest of the troublemakers from the beginning of class until the final bell: "'Marcus,' turn around. 'Kia,' be quiet. 'Haseem,' get on the right page."

Half of the class was wasted reprimanding students. There was a ton of material to cover on taking standardized tests: interpreting and responding to different types of questions, searching for clues within the text, etc. The kids were playing around just enough to slow the lesson down to a crawl. In the end, we barely made it through one practice exercise even with both of us working one-on-one with the students. And they couldn't take the workbooks home. They couldn't even write in them. These kids had no idea how important this lesson was in a pre-state-takeover environment, or even to their future academic success.

Finally, the end of the half-day arrived with a combination dismissal and fire drill. The alarm sounded, causing most students to file out in a fairly orderly manner. Others just hung out in the hallways, taking turns jumping down a flight of stairs. I couldn't understand why the passing teachers didn't say anything to them, but I decided to take the hint and mind my own business.

Outside, there wasn't a single parent in sight. I thought perhaps they were waiting at a different entrance, until I heard:

"Now, my mom knew we had a short day. *Where the fuck is she?*"

As the students dispersed, I complimented the teacher on the way she handled her class.

"Last week, I almost walked out," she responded. "It gets harder and harder to stay every day. The kids are out of control. They curse out teachers over and over before being suspended. Last year, a student threatened to 'drop' me. She raised her fist and started toward me. Instinctively, I put my hands up and the book I was holding flew out of my hand and hit the kid. That was the only thing that made her back off, but since the book left a mark, her parents called the police. The officer told me he'd try not to let it go anywhere. And it didn't...but if her parents had had any clout, I would've been out of a job."

I wanted to encourage her but I didn't know what to say. I just shook my head. She responded with a headshake of her own, thanked me for helping out and wished me luck in my teaching career.

When I first arrived, I was impressed by the fact that the administrators seemed to be so on top of things. In retrospect, I realize that staying on top of things was the only way to keep that place from imploding. It felt dangerous, like very bad things could happen. I decided not to waste any time getting out of there. As I walked along the back of the building, I heard footsteps running toward me. I turned, all types of possibilities flashing through my mind. Not the least of which was the young man I had "pink-slipped." Just then, two boys tumbled to the ground in front of me and collapsed into laughter. They looked up at me sheepishly. Not recognizing either of them, I shot them a look somewhere between disapproval and relief. Suddenly, a voice boomed over a mega-phone: "Get up! And move along! Now! Let's go!" We all looked to the man patrolling the second-story perimeter. Again, he directed them to get going. They did. And so did I.

Driving away, I wondered why people put themselves through this type of misery day after day. The kids have no respect for you. It's almost impossible to teach. It's dangerous. And you know what? I don't have to do it anymore. I quit.

P.S. #3: PERCENTAGE OF 8th-GRADERS
SCORING BELOW BASIC:[*2,3]

2000–2001

Math } 87%   Reading } 78%

---

*Percentages are rounded.

January 7, 2002

I thought a lot about this whole teaching thing over the holidays. After the first three assignments, I felt like I had been blindsided. I was over the shock of it. *Somewhat.* But I was disappointed in myself. What kind of coward quits after three days? Despite considerable effort, I was completely unable to come up with an acceptable answer. I should be able to make it through twenty-one days of subbing. The problem was I really, *really* didn't want to.

When I began subbing, I also started writing down my thoughts and experiences just to help alleviate some of my frustration and anger. Twenty-one pages later, I passed it to my friend Sid thinking he would say, "Yeah, girl. Run." Instead he said, "Clay, I think it's a book. I think you have to keep subbing and keep writing."

That was the last thing I wanted to hear. This was not the kind of book I would choose to write. I'm a sci-fi/fantasy/rom-com kinda chick. This education stuff is too serious, too real...

I decided to give it another shot.

> "Public School #4"

January 8, 2002 (Day 4 of 21)

Elementary School: Approximately 500 students: 91.4% African American; 5.1% Asian; 0.4% Latino; 1.5% White; 1.5% Other.[1]

*G*iving it another go, I eased back into the subbing scene covering for another art teacher. A pleasant but unorganized woman directed me to wait in the teachers' lounge while she looked for something to "keep the kids busy." The school was filthy. The teachers' lounge was junky. The soda machine kept my fifty cents and provided no caffeine in return. I casually mentioned this to the woman at the front desk, hoping that she would hook me up with the office's private stash of tea, coffee, Mountain Dew—I didn't really care at eight in the morning. Instead, she told me to "put my name on the machine."

"And what?" I wanted to ask. "Will the soda fairy leave me a can of Lipton tomorrow, when I'm not here?" Today, I worked for $39.50.

My first class was a group of sixth graders. I noticed the kids were all sitting in their coats even though it was nearly a hundred degrees in the room. I asked if they were hot. "No, it's cold." It was not cold. *I* am always cold...like verging-on-having-some-kind-of-medical-condition cold, but I felt like I was standing in a lit oven. Maybe they were worried about someone walking off with their stuff. Maybe they're just accustomed to that blazing hot room. Who knows? The thing that was painfully clear is that these kids were not happy to see me. Apparently, they "*neeever*" have art. That just made me all the more determined that they would have it today. I chose creating their own personal CD covers because all kids (including me) fantasize about becoming rappers or rock stars. Of course, they had already done this exercise, as well as the other three or four emergency art lessons I was given. Seems Art Gal *neeever* came to work.

Scrounging, I came up with drawing their dream homes and writing what they wanted inside the house on the back of the paper. (I'm always trying to work in writing.) Despite the fact that they complained about *neeever* having art, none of them were anxious to get to work. I had to personally encourage each one of them. They responded with stalling, whining and complaining. They even questioned my credentials. "Are you a real art teacher? Can you draw?" I told them the truth: "No and no." But I tried. I quickly drew a house with a fence, windows, a door and chimney. I expected them to laugh because I really can't draw. What I heard was, "That's alright." and "That's decent." I'm not sure if it was because I lowered the bar or because they felt that I was being a good sport, but it encouraged some of them to give it a try.

One student scribbled all over his paper and told me that his house had been hit by a tornado. I told him he had to list the contents of the house and their worth on the back for the insurance claim. Another girl told me she wasn't going to have a house. She would be homeless. I told her she needed to draw a little shopping cart with her blanket and newspapers for the cold weather. Yet another girl told me her house definitely wouldn't have any rent. I introduced her to the word "mortgage."

Turns out the key to getting the kids excited about this assignment was to tell them that they could have anything in their homes that they wanted: game rooms, pools, five bedrooms, sixty bathrooms, a Jacuzzi...they all wanted a Jacuzzi. So after being asked privately how to spell it for the twelfth time, I asked for a volunteer to spell it for the class. I expected the kids to raise their hands. Instead, two boys jumped up from their seats and raced each other to the board. As they each scrambled to get it up on the board, the other students spelled it out loud together. "J-A-C-U..." That was kind of a nice moment until I realized that many of them couldn't spell "house." If I could teach them how to spell Jacuzzi in 5 minutes, why hadn't any of their teachers in first through sixth grade taught them how to spell a basic word like house?

Next, I had an eighth-grade class that I was dreading. Bigger kids mean bigger problems. I had picked an elementary school hoping for smaller kids with smaller problems. Turned out the eighth graders were pretty cool. (Their homeroom teacher remained in the class grading papers. Bless her heart.) They were concerned that the few art projects they had done were never graded.

"It doesn't count for anything," they complained.

So I promised to speak to the principal about extra credit or something. They took me at my word and most of them got to work on the CD booklet. Some of them had no intention of doing anything and didn't. Since their homeroom teacher was right there and didn't see fit to press the issue, I didn't either. One enthusiastic group of boys moved to a back table and called themselves a record label. They were all members of a rap group and claimed to already have a bunch of completed raps. All they had to do was draw something on the cover, list the songs, some lyrics, who produced which tracks, along with their shout-outs and thank-yous to God and everybody. Not one of them finished the assignment because they couldn't agree on who had the right to list which songs in their booklets.

Another boy was asleep: head down, eyes closed, spittle dribbling. That was a little much. I woke him and invited him to participate. We chatted for a few minutes. He told me that he was from Guatemala and that he was tired. I encouraged him to stay awake and give the assignment a try. I figured he'd go right back to sleep when I walked away. Oddly, he was the only one who turned in a completed project. He also thanked me, though I had no idea why. I thanked him for making the effort and gave him a big fat A when I graded the assignments during lunch. Then, I delivered the grades to the principal, a middle-aged, nicely dressed African-American woman I couldn't quite get a read on. Initially, when I approached her, I got the impression I was intruding. She seemed somewhat pleased that I graded the projects because the kids didn't have any art grades at *all*. Then, she turned her back to me and went back to flipping through papers.

Fifth grade went pretty much like fifth grade at P.S. #3. They strongly objected to someone else getting to draw a picture they chose, but, after a lot of chitchat and clowning, they did it.

Second grade was great. Mostly because I just love little kids. As soon as I walked in, a little Pakistani girl came up, hugged me and introduced me to her best friend. I was charmed but I should have known: "Beware the first child to greet you." As delightful as she was, she was a handful. She wouldn't stay in her seat. She was always in the middle of any ruckus that arose; if not causing it, encouraging it. I had my hands full just trying to keep her and the rest of the kids in their correct seats. They were so talkative, easily distracted and accident-prone, that it was a little difficult to get the project done. We had a blast.

I turned my back for one second and a different little girl dumped a bottle of glue down her dress. (We weren't using glue.) I cleaned her up and gave her another piece of paper since she had lost the picture she was working on. In return, she drew me a lovely flower under which she wrote, "I love you." And I really wanted to keep it but one of the boys hadn't received a picture back. So I gave him mine.

"I understand why you had to do that," she told me.

Of course, as attentive as I was, the homeroom teacher walked in at the exact moment a little fight broke out and other students were running around the room. I was so embarrassed. She helped me get them back in their seats, then took points away they had earned toward a trip to the museum. And I had to suffer rather a withering glare. She also took gym away from the whole class, dispatching the kids to different rooms. Three of them wound up in my next class. I was surprised she was willing to leave them in my care again, but another thing I've come to realize: *Nothing* stands between a teacher and his or her free periods.

The next class was supposed to be second grade but the kids were too big and too bad. And it seemed like there were about a hundred of them. Okay, probably more like thirty-three, since that's the average class size in Philly public schools. Immediately, I had to put out a boy for being loud, disruptive, not working, etc. I hoped putting out one would calm the others. It didn't. They screamed, wouldn't stay seated, tore each other's papers and traded punches. I was really surprised because the teacher had assured me they would be good. They weren't. I even had to break up a fight between a boy and a girl. Not little love taps. He was really trying to pound her. He hadn't done the assignment and she said he was "a bad boy." He went berserk, launching himself across the room at her.

I jumped between them. I had a foot and a half on the boy and he still managed to get around me. How do you subdue an overwrought child without hurting him? I put my arm around his shoulder and firmly guided him from the room so he wouldn't jump on her. I called the office and asked them to send someone to get him. That didn't happen. What's worse is that two other boys punched the girl for "getting their friend in trouble." Tough little cookie that she was, she whacked them right back.

When the homeroom teacher finally showed up, apologizing for being late, she couldn't believe her class had behaved so poorly. I couldn't believe that boy was still raging—crying, breathing heavy, balling and un-balling his fists. I felt so bad for him. I tried to explain to him that the way to deal with someone calling him a bad boy was not to prove them right by attacking them. He was unwilling or unable to speak, but finally, he nodded that he understood. Right now, this child is difficult to handle. What happens when he gets older?

My last class was third grade and it was nothing but sunshine. They were already making Valentine's cards when I arrived. There were way fewer kids in this class than the last, less than twenty. In addition to the teacher, there was a classroom aide—a woman who was there in the class with the kids every day. The kids liked and respected her and she stayed on them. Even when the homeroom teacher left, she remained.

I wondered why some teachers had aides and others didn't. Why some classes were so large and others weren't. Why this aide stayed in the class with me, though others didn't bother. Having her there made a huge difference. I was much less worried about something tragic happening. All I had to do was encourage, compliment and help. In short, this experience was more like what I'd hoped teaching would be. One little girl left early, but stopped to hug both the aide and me before she left. It's amazing how something as small as an unexpected hug from a child can wipe away all the unpleasantries of a day.

Overall, P.S. #4 was sort of okay, now that I understand the scale. None of the kids cursed or threatened me. I didn't feel as though I might be jumped at any given moment. I guess the more accustomed to the environment I become, the less shocked I'll be. Though, perhaps, that's the risk.

At the end of the day, I had another chat with the principal.

"I think she's pretty much gone," she said about the regular art teacher.

Not once did she inquire about my credentials or status. She didn't even look directly at me. I would think that if I had an art teacher who never showed up, I'd be actively looking for another one, or at least a permanent sub. Maybe she had other things to worry about. Maybe it's not that simple to replace an AWOL teacher, but it should be. You don't show up, you don't have a job.

P.S. #4: PERCENTAGE OF 5th-GRADERS
SCORING BELOW BASIC:[*2,3]

2000–2001

Math } 46%   Reading } 58%

---

* Percentages are rounded.

> "Public School #5"

January 10, 2002 (Day 5 of 21)

Middle School: Approximately 927 students: 97.2% African American; 0% Asian; 2.3% Latino; 0.3% White; 0.2% Other.[1]

Since I hadn't left P.S. #4 in tears, shock or generally fearing for my life, I accepted an assignment for an art teacher at another middle school. It happened to be right next door to one of the most treacherous high schools in Philadelphia, one you survived vs. graduated. Feeling lucky that my assignment was next door at P.S. #5, I bounded into the huge, dilapidated building with long, unmonitored hallways which, I soon discovered, made it easy for students and other "visitors" to roam freely. Many of the kids wouldn't do the assignments and told me so. Quite a few cut. Others ran around the class or walked out at will. (I was told not to try to stop them because, "You can't do everything.") The kids fought and cursed at each other and me. I was called a "bitch" at least three different times. I was on edge all day long. Had it not been for the teacher down the hall, I would have left. In hindsight, I wish I had.

The assignments were on the desk with the seating plans. The students were supposed to use stencils to create a still life. I had paper but no pencils and all the closets were locked. (Luckily, I still had my stash from Sr. Joan.) The room was huge. It could have easily accommodated fifty or sixty students, excluding the blocked off back alcove with a running generator (a safety hazard if ever there was one). The woman who walked me to the room warned me to prop the door open if I had to go to the bathroom or something, otherwise it would swing shut and I'd be locked out. (Apparently, a key was out of the question.) As usual, she told me to "dial six" if I needed help, then introduced me to a teacher down the hall who told me straight off to "send any knuckleheads who act up" to his room. This was a first. Someone offering help *before* I needed it. He was my new hero.

My first class was a group of sixth graders, all boys. Nearly half the class was missing. Those who were present were kind enough to let me know where the others were: "absent," "out sick," "on in-house suspension," "transferred to a school for bad kids," etc. At least three kids had been "transferred," but the boy on "in-house suspension" was suddenly off and making his way toward the back of the class. He informed me that he couldn't sit near the door because "some dudes" were looking for him. He seemed older than the other boys, or maybe he was just living harder.

The boys didn't give me too much trouble. They chatted and joked a lot, but as long as I stayed on them, they did the assignment. I usually stand near the ones who are acting out the most. Most will settle down. The ones who don't—look out. The only tense moment I had with these kids was when they suddenly started crowding around the glass pane in the door. As I herded them back to their seats, I noticed two very tall young men lurking in the hallway. When they saw me looking, they casually headed in the opposite direction. One of the students told me they belonged in my class and pushed the door open. "That's okay," I replied, shutting it again. I was much more comfortable being the tallest person in the room. Besides, how was I going to *make* them come in? A few minutes later, they were standing outside the classroom windows, pointing into the room. They glared as I waved them away, but got moving as I started for the class phone. When I turned back, the kid with the in-house suspension was gone and never came back. I guess the boys skulking outside the building were the "dudes" he had been trying to avoid.

Next, I had seventh graders. Whereas the sixth graders attempted to do the art project, the seventh graders preferred to talk. A few chose to chase each other around the room. I spent a lot of time trying to get two boys to sit down. Luckily, a special ed. teacher wandered by and peeked in. (Someone probably gave him a heads up: "Sub in the building. Expect a mess.") I asked him to take the two boys who were giving me the most difficulty. Of course, they protested as he carted them off.

"*I ain't do nothin'!*" Really wish I knew what constituted "something."

Overall, these kids desperately craved attention and reassurance. Though most barely did any work, they constantly wanted to show it to me. I "oohed" and "ahhed" as best I could over minimal effort. There was only one child in the whole class who was seriously trying. So, of course, he was mocked and ridiculed. (When did underachievement become so popular? Kids and adults wear it so proudly, like a uniform. And it's not just "a black thing." The slacker mentality crosses racial and cultural boundaries.) Luckily, all this kid needed to keep his head up was a few encouraging words.

Finally, lunchtime rolled around, giving me a chance to sit down. I always stand when students are in the room because I'm not confident in my ability to control the class from a sitting position; probably because I don't have that ability. Likewise, the students must be seated. Once they're out of their seats, anything can happen. This I learned at P.S. #1.

After lunch, the same group of seventh graders returned. I thought they were messing with me, or had at least made a mistake but there it was on the schedule. What kind of school schedules students for art twice in one day, much less before and after lunch? Tomorrow they have art appreciation. Maybe that's why kids can't read. All that art. Well, we certainly weren't having art again. It wasn't very productive the first time around. Besides, everyone is always encouraging me to share my "experiences" with the kids.

"It doesn't matter if you get the lesson done, Clayvon. It's your job to be a bridge for those children to the outside world," one of my mentors proclaimed.

So there I was, ready to be a bridge. "Let's talk," I suggested. A little cheer went up and they proceeded to talk to each other. The notion that I wanted to have a discussion *with* them never occurred to them. I decided to skip my story and focus on current events: Kids from a nearby school had taken a parent's prescription Xanax to school, shared it and wound up in the hospital. I thought they'd find this interesting. I was wrong. They pronounced them stupid and moved on.

One girl said she wanted to talk about the drug dealers in her neighborhood. Another kid yelled out that he wanted to *be* a drug dealer. Yet another yelled back: "How you gonna sell coke, when you do coke?" And up went the first roar of laughter.

"Please keep it down." "*HEY*, you're too loud." Lights on and off. Nothing brought the volume down. One girl tried to help by doing some clapping game: "Clap two times if you hear me..." she sang out. And they clapped two times, until everyone was following suit. Then the game was over and they went back to talking and yelling. I cannot wrap my head around this whole ignore-the-teacher thing. *When did that become acceptable?*

Even the kid who was trying before was now chatty and hyped up. When I asked him to quiet down, he said, "It's me. Remember? I did the good work." I said I remembered and I was surprised by his behavior. He calmed down and sat quietly doodling for the rest of the period. Later, after class, I found a paper he left behind scribbled all over with "Miss Harris" in pink and silver ink. (Later, when I mentioned it to my friend Nora, she told me I should have kept the paper in case I needed to show it to the police. I laughed. She was serious.)

The seventh graders wasted the entire period. Finally, I bet them that they couldn't be quiet for five minutes—*five*. They had no intention of taking up my challenge. The same girl who had tried to help me quiet the class earlier tried to talk them into doing it. They shouted her down and waved her off. Disappointment clouded her face. I felt it too, but refused to give up. I badgered and provoked until some of them agreed to give it a try just to shut me up. (The others quieted because they were watching.) Almost all who tried, failed. These kids are nervous wrecks. One girl had to start over four times. When she stopped talking, she had to tap and write notes, dance in her seat, anything to keep moving. It took a while but finally, she was still and quiet...something she probably only experienced while sleeping. I thought back to a conversation with Sr. Joan. She said when kids transfer to St. A's from public schools, it's very difficult for them.

"They're so unaccustomed to being quiet, being still, staying in their seats, that St. A's must feel like a prison to them."

"No..." I thought. "*This* school is a starter prison if ever there was one."

I was dreading the eighth graders; but they arrived escorted by a homeroom teacher who seemed more like a drill sergeant: *"Shut up and sit down! I'm sick of you! I told you, you're on thin ice! Very thin!"* Then he turned to me, "If there are any problems, you just tell me who." And back to the students, *"I'll kill 'em! You... back there! You know you're wrong already, right? Stop acting stupid and sit down!"* He ranted for five minutes straight. Removed a couple of students he thought might be problems. Told me not to worry about the kids that hadn't showed up, or would walk out—"just mark them absent." But on second thought, he decided to take roll himself. Said he'd "*deal*" with the cutters later.

On one hand, I was impressed with the way "Sarge" took charge. On the other, I couldn't believe how he screamed and hollered at these kids. But after he left, they kept the noise down and did the assignment. I could walk around and be the nice guy because he had done the hard work. And despite the way he spoke to them, they all seemed to like him.

"That's just Sarge," one said.

"Yeah, he crazy," said another. "But he's alright."

These kids actually wanted to talk with me. In particular, they wanted me to know that a lot of the regular teachers yelled and cursed at them.

"One teacher called me a crack baby and my mom a crack ho."

"Yup. I heard it," said his friend.

"It's true," said another kid.

Despite the fact that several other students backed up this story, I wasn't buying it. It just sounded ridiculous to me.

Seventh graders are from hell.

My last class was another group of seventh graders. They came in jumping on the desks, screaming at the tops of their lungs, refusing to do any work. They were loud, unruly, unreasonable and violent. Within ten minutes, three or so of the girls had jumped a tall, skinny boy and beat him. The girls weren't huge. They were about five feet or a little taller, but meaty. Still, I didn't think it was serious at first. I certainly didn't think he was really afraid of them. I thought it was more like boys don't hit girls, but they don't let girls punch them either. So he stayed on the other side of the table in the back alcove, where they had trapped him. I was able to shut this down and get them all seated. But as soon as I turned my attention to keeping the students in the class from getting involved in the fight in the hallway, I heard, "*They fightin'!*" and it was coming from inside the room. I looked over to see those same girls punching that boy as hard as they possibly could. He rolled under a table that was pushed against a wall where the girls couldn't reach him with their hands anymore. So they kicked at him with all their might.

Right then, a tall thin man in a bright red turtleneck dropped more kids off at the door, as though I didn't have my hands full. I asked if he was their instructor. He just looked at me. I asked again.

"What do you need?" he responded.

"I could use some help here," I said pointing to the trapped boy and the girls, who paused to see what he was going to do.

He leaned casually on a table, "What's the problem?"

"Over there...*the boy trapped under the table.*" I answered wondering if he had lost his mind.

As he moved slowly and tentatively toward the fight, something told me to go in search of the "Hero Down the Hall." I ran to his room and blurted out that the students were fighting. He grabbed a ruler and sprinted down the hall. As we returned to the classroom, the other students started backing away from the fight scene. One of the girls was standing over the boy, who was now lying on the floor having an asthma attack.

"Say you fell," she urged him.

"He did not *fall,*" I said. "You *beat* him."

The "Thin Man" was hovering nearby, muttering something. What, I have no idea. Then he disappeared, leaving us to deal with his students. Gripping the ruler, the Hero made them take their seats and simmer down. He helped the boy back to his seat. Before he left, I commented that these kids were in the Thin Man's advisory.

"Yeah, that's the problem," said the Hero.

When the Hero and his ruler left, I felt abandoned—locked in this room with scary girls who needed to be expelled, but who were instead eyeing me with animosity. A couple of the larger boys walked out. I phoned the office and informed them that I needed some help with this class. They said they'd send someone up. Ten, fifteen minutes passed; no one came.

All day long, I had been asking kids to sit, to be quiet, to get out of the class if they didn't belong, to come in if they were supposed to be there, to put away the food, the drinks, the video games; to stop fighting and arguing, and to get off the class phone or away from the teacher's desk, where I kept my handbag. Kids cursed at me because I asked them to leave the class... "*Fuck you!*" Because I answered the class phone... "*Fuck you, bitch!*" Or just because I wouldn't let them do whatever they wanted to do... "*Bitch!*" My nerves were frazzled. I was literally afraid and trying to watch my own back. I kept a close eye on the girls who fought to draw blood; who scoffed at veteran teachers and who were now angry with me for reporting them.

In the midst of this nonsense, there was a nerdy kid who kept running around the class, hitting the other boys. Then he'd run to me for protection. He had been the first kid up on top of a desk when the class started. And he was harassing the few kids who were trying to do the assignment—snatching their papers, taking their pens, etc. He had those boys moving all over the class trying to find a spot where he would leave them alone. Usually, they moved toward me, as though that would deter him. I didn't stay in one spot for long. Making sure my back was to the wall, I kept circling so I could keep an eye on all of the students. I don't remember how many times the other boys complained. Or, how many times I actually saw that kid starting trouble. I tried to separate him; however, in a class where one boy has been beaten, ripping up some papers was clearly secondary. Next thing I knew, three of the boys had this kid upside down. I went over and made them put him down. When I asked if he was okay, the other boys were aghast.

"Is *he* okay?"

"He touched James's butt!"

The little pest made the most of the moment, getting up slowly, assuring me he was okay. I told the others to sit down and leave him alone. Then I caught him smirking out of the corner of my eye, so I also firmly told him to sit down and stay in his seat. Just then something else drew my attention. Kids walking in; kids walking out. I don't know. But as soon as it was settled, I scanned the room and noticed that same boy up in some girl's face...bothering *her.* I couldn't believe he was out of his seat—*again.* I walked over to him.

"She...she hit me..." immediately came the lie.

"*Boy, sit the hell down!*" I blurted out before thinking. I couldn't believe it. Shock and shame flooded through me. Not that I'm a stranger to profanity; I've been known to have a potty mouth. But cursing at a child?

"Ooo, teachers aren't supposed to curse," interjected a girl standing nearby.

"Tell somebody," I snapped, "maybe they'll send me home."

I walked away from them, needing to regroup. This was not the time for me to freak out. So I moved to check on the two or three students who were half-working. Then came those words again: *"They fightin'!"* The same girl who had said teachers aren't supposed to curse had a different boy down on the floor and she and another girl were stomping him. *With their feet.* I started toward them... well really, I was headed for the door...but they thought I was coming toward them. So, they backed away from the boy. He tried to play it off, but he was hurt. I stood between him and the girls while he got himself together. It took him a minute to get up. His lip was bleeding. I told him to come with me and we headed down the hall.

As we left, I heard, "She gettin' 'Mr. Hero.' Uh. Oh." Then from one of the girls, I heard, *"Lock her the fuck out!"* And the door slammed shut behind us.

As we rushed down the hallway, I hoped they wouldn't take the opportunity to steal my wallet.

"They're fighting again," I said to Mr. Hero. "And bring your keys. I'm locked out."

He grabbed his keys and his yardstick, glanced briefly at the boy, and headed down the hall. On our way, we ran into another teacher. He quickly told her what was happening. She said she knew this class; they were already in trouble. Wondering if she was the help I had requested, I pointed to the boy's swollen and bleeding lip.

"It'll clot naturally in three minutes," she casually commented.

Mr. Hero unlocked the door and we entered. The students were all seated, calmly chatting as though nothing had happened. Oddly, the two girls were sitting at the front of the class facing the others, as if on stage.

The female teacher asked the boy to point out who had jumped him. He dropped his eyes in the face of his classmates, "I fell," he said quietly.

"What? It was those two, right here," I chimed in pointing to the girls.

"She lyin'! I ain't do nothin'! She lyin' on me!" one of them screamed at the top of her lungs, then burst into laughter like it was the funniest joke.

I stared in disbelief. I felt like I was in a nightmare. Turning to the other two teachers, I put my foot down. "They can't stay. These two. Take them."

The girls were surprised (not sure why) and angry, but either they were going or I was going; and I meant it.

They stomped, argued and glared at me as the Hero marched them out. The female teacher remained a few minutes longer. She announced that the whole class was on a "ten-day lockdown." I had no idea what a "lockdown" was, but it sounded like prison jargon. Whatever it was, it was the first real punishment I had heard about since subbing. However, the students informed her that they were not "going on lockdown" because they had "stuff to do." The students argued back and forth with her, laughed and waved her off. She left, seemingly embarrassed, and I was alone with them again.

The rest of the students stared at me, angry because I had told on them. I didn't care. Okay, I did care, but I wasn't about to show it. One of them pulled out a deck of cards and started a game. The rest chatted; had some snacks. The other teachers have them all the time and couldn't get them to behave. I decided as long as they didn't beat on each other or me, perhaps I should let them be.

And, of course, the little boy I had cursed at was still bouncing around the room. Once the action had settled down, he started following me around like he wanted to say something. I was still circling the room because, you know, it's harder to hit a moving target. When I stopped to check on the group of boys who were working on the assignment, that little pest let forth a string of obscenities a mile long. They all waited for my reaction.

"*Boy...!*" I said, and he and the others fell out laughing. What more could I say? I had no moral ground to stand on. I smiled feebly trying to play it off but I was just in *hell*. And finally—mercifully—the bell rang.

The students poured out, leaving the room a mess. One of the boys stayed a few minutes to help me straighten up, despite the fact that neither of us threw food wrappers and paper on the floor, or turned over the desks and the trash can. As he scurried off to his last class, I grabbed my coat and headed out.

I stopped by the Hero's room to say, "thank you." Seeing how defeated I was, he told me the seventh graders from the second and third floors were "out of control." For the first time, I noticed how well behaved his class was. He said it was his job to "settle them down and get them ready for high school."

When I asked how he managed that, he confided that sometimes he had to "beat them because that's all they understand. I have to get them ready for eighth. And I have to get the eighth graders ready for high school. But look at them," he continued. "I can go across the street and get a soda. They'll be just like this when I get back."

I didn't know what to say, so I thanked him again and left. Outside, I walked slowly to my car and got in. Just then, *hundreds* of students from the high school next door poured into the streets blocking traffic. There were at least five patrol cars parked around the perimeter. Nightsticks out, police officers herded the students away from the school. The kids seemed to simultaneously take the situation in stride, while bracing for the one minor incident or misunderstanding that could turn this controlled chaos into something ugly and violent. As I waited for a path to clear, I reflected. "Is this what Mr. Hero is getting them ready for? God help us all."

Later, after a nap...

Earlier this year, I met a teacher from a high school in Camden who told me I could probably get a spot for the rest of the year at his school. They had just fired a sub for "allowing" the students to gamble and smoke marijuana in his class. I asked if the sub was smoking with them. "No," he said. "But I'd almost feel better if he had been."

I think that sub was in shock. I know I am. As bad as that experience at P.S. #5 was, what's worse is that I contributed to the hostile and negative environment of that school by cursing at a student. Fear is no excuse. Antagonistic behavior is no excuse. It'll be a long while before I can forgive myself. I think I'm going to take off a couple of days.

P.S. #5: PERCENTAGE OF 8th-GRADERS
SCORING BELOW BASIC:[*,2,3]

2000–2001

Math } 79%   Reading } 67%

---

[*] Percentages are rounded.

January 11, 2002

My mother mentioned that she'd been listening to a local talk radio show and the topic was teaching in Philadelphia's public schools. A veteran teacher of twenty-three years called in to say she felt teachers should be allowed to hit students. The other callers, mostly parents, nearly lost their minds. They termed it "abuse" and said teachers "had no right." And pointed out that "out-of-control teachers would abuse this privilege."

Other teachers called in and pointed out that hitting students might cause teachers to get hurt. After my experience at P.S. #5, I had no doubt that this was true. Even the seventh graders were big and aggressive. With each passing day, I became more aware that I could insist to the wrong student that he or she stop talking and that would be enough for them to hurt me.

I thought back to the Hero saying that he beat the students because that's all they understood. His method is appalling, but what happens when the next teacher isn't big enough or strong enough to intimidate the students or take them down? I guess the teacher gets taken down.

> "Public School #6"

Elementary School: Approximately 400 students: 97.4% African American; 0.2% Asian; 0.9% Latino; 1.2% White; 0.2% Other.[1]

*J*t occurred to me that teachers are not allowed to have personal problems. They're not allowed to be tired or depressed or sick. Regardless of how you may or may not feel, the kids come first: their problems, their best interest. Last night I couldn't sleep. Again. Just the thought that I might be going back into a situation like the one at P.S. #5 filled me with dread. Such a melodramatic and old-fashioned word, but that's exactly what it was...*dread*. What must the regular teachers feel like? Granted, students will push the limits with a sub, but the behavior is so far to the left of acceptable that I find it hard to believe they're much better with their regular teachers.

This morning, I was late. Yes, I was exhausted from lack of sleep, but truthfully I just didn't want to go. They're not usually ready for me when I'm early, sometimes not even when I'm on time, I justified. So what difference did it make? But as I sat in stop-and-go traffic, my good-Catholic-girl upbringing kicked in and I called to let them know that I was on my way. Ironically, today I was met by a warm, organized woman who thanked me for showing up. She hung up my coat, put my lunch in the fridge and steered me toward a cup of coffee. She admitted they have a problem getting subs.

"We have a lot of problem students," she confided. "But I still love this school and the students a great deal."

After announcing over the PA system that they had a guest teacher for (what else?) art who would be coming to the classrooms, she asked that homeroom teachers have something for me to do with the kids. She even gave me a tour of the school, which only went up to the fifth grade (*hallelujah!*). I was so caught off guard by this kind reception that I agreed to add an extra two days to my two-day assignment before I had even gotten a feel for the school. (Clearly, the caffeine hadn't kicked in.) She also mentioned that if any of the children acted up, they'd be removed from the class and taken to the Accommodation Room. *The what?* I had never heard of such, but I was pretty certain that it was just what it sounded like: a place to send the troublemakers—*nice.*

My day began with first graders. I was excited about working with them, but the homeroom teacher immediately popped *An American Tail: Fievel Goes West* into the VCR for them to watch. I was a little insulted. I could handle twelve first graders. "Do they like to draw?" I asked.

"They might get antsy," she responded, "but if that's what you want..."

Her words rang like a warning bell. Chickening out, I asked what she thought was best.

"The movie," she responded, flipping it on. She called the kids to the mat, asked them to be good and departed.

I plopped into the tiny chair behind the kids, and chugged my coffee. For the most part, they quietly watched the movie. During all of this, there was a nicely dressed, middle-aged African-American woman quietly talking with one of the first-graders off to the side. I had no idea if she was a parent, another teacher, or what. No one bothered to clue me in until the phone rang. A woman on the other end asked to speak to the principal. I was surprised. I rarely run across principals during my school visits, and usually nowhere near the classrooms. After she hung up, another woman showed up to take her place with the little girl. "Is everything okay?" I asked. The woman informed me that the girl wanted to go home. Every day they had to talk her into staying. At seven, she had just enrolled for the first time, late in the school year and late in life. They were particularly concerned that she wouldn't stay in the classroom with a stranger. So I introduced myself and told her she could sit next to me while we watched the cartoon. Surprisingly, she readily agreed and I pulled up another chair for her. Of course, two other girls migrated back to where we were, saying they wanted to sit on chairs too. I was happy to oblige.

Finishing off the sugar-filled muck that was passing for coffee, I watched the children with curiosity. I wondered what they were thinking and what they were learning from *Fievel*. Is this really teaching? Sitting them in front of a TV? Sr. Anthony let us watch *Sesame Street* when I was in kindergarten at

Gesù Bambino. I turned out okay. But I couldn't help myself, "What's that with the string?"

Them: *"A puppet!"*

Me: "And who's that?"

Them: *"Fievel!"*

Unfortunately, my little Q&A set off a storm of chatter so none of them could hear the movie and some of them hadn't seen it before. I restrained myself, looking around the classroom instead. I noticed how neat, clean and nicely decorated it was. There was also a ton of books. Then, I looked at the children. Some of them weren't well cared for at all. They wore ragged, dirty clothes and their hair was uncombed. One girl's hair was actually matted. I wanted to wash and comb it. If I were her homeroom teacher, it would probably already be done. Sometimes, parents are just crappy.

When the homeroom teacher returned, the kids were still watching the movie. As I rose to leave, the girls who sat nearby hugged me good-bye, while the boys waved and giggled. Well cared for or not, these children could not have been any more lovely.

Next, I had second graders, about 30 of them. A man and a woman greeted me, explained the assignment and directed me to a chair on the mat, where the kids gathered around. They had given out a piece of paper sectioned off in squares that told the story of Martin Luther King, Jr. in pictures and words. I read the story and asked questions. The students answered accurately and enthusiastically. Just as they were starting to get a little rowdy, I sent everyone to their desks to color the pictures, cut out the squares and staple them together to make a little booklet.

The kids were great. They got right to work. I did have a little problem getting them to comprehend the whole stay-in-your-seat-and-raise-your-hand-when-you-have-a-question deal. And they had lots of questions. Consequently, whenever I felt a little hand tapping me, I'd shake my head and say in a sing-song voice, "I can't see you if you're not in your seat. I can't hear you if you're not in your seat." After a while, they were doing it, too. Problem solved.

The male teacher came back to check on me. He watched for a while, then left again. I was fine. What I didn't know, the kids were happy to tell me. There was only one small glitch in this process. Some kids were using scissors that belonged to the classroom; others had their own. But they were all sharing. When one kid finished, I'd grab the scissors and give them to the next one. This would have been fine if I had remembered which scissors belonged to whom. But I didn't and suddenly two different boys were claiming the same pair. Silly me, I listened to the rest of the students who all agreed they belonged to "Kid A." By the time I made it back around, "Kid B" had the scissors in his possession. When I asked why, Kid A casually responded, "Oh, I forgot. Those aren't mine."

He forgot and what? The whole class forgot right along with him? Or had they all just lied? I asked him to apologize to the other boy. He did and so did I—twice. Kid B graciously accepted our apologies. In fact, later when he saw me in the hallway, he gave me a big hug. Kids can be so sweet and forgiving, except—you know—when they're not.

Near the end of class, the female teacher returned first. I started dialing it back waiting for her to take over, but she seemed content to let me continue while she gave out snacks. When the male teacher returned a few minutes later, I figured that was my cue but every time I started for the door, one of the kids called me to staple a booklet. Finally all done, the kids sung out, "Bye Miss Harris!"

The male teacher walked me out and told me I was "doing well." This was a first. I thanked him and chatted a bit. He had retired from the post office and gone back to school to get his master's in education. He told me that he and his partner team-taught the class, focusing on literacy. They were part of the whole Balanced Literacy Program I kept hearing about.

"The key," he said, "is splitting up the class. The kids are doing a lot better." He thanked me for coming and said good-bye.

At my next class, the regular teacher was having a discussion with the students about effort. She wasn't yelling—she was just laying it out. "Make some." She turned them over to me, but she and her aide hung out for a while to make sure I was okay. The students were cooperative, enthusiastic and yes, chatty; but all in all, not too bad. One of the boys didn't have a partner so we paired up. I drew a house on a hill and a tree by a lake for him. He drew a car on a tree-lined road for me. This time, I got to keep it. Just watching the way the kids presented the pictures that had been drawn for them, amazed me. In terms of maturity and ability, this fifth grade class was light years ahead of the class at P.S. #3. Maybe in a K-5 school, the fifth graders are the oldest and that requires more of them. Or, maybe this is just a better school.

Next, I had another group of second graders. The Coordinator had given me some worksheets, double-digit multiplication, just in case I needed something to do with the kids. I was tired of art and wanted to tackle something meatier. Multiplication seemed a little advanced for second graders but I wasn't sure. I asked the homeroom teacher if they had done this type of work before.

"No," she said. "But if you show it to them a couple of times, they'll get it."

I suggested that we do something else, but she insisted.

"No, that's how kids learn...just show them a couple of times. They'll be excited. Take care."

They didn't get it. *At all.* I tried scaling back to single-digit multiplication: "Eight times six is...?

"Twenty? Fourteen? Fifteen?" Then suddenly, one boy started getting all of the answers right.

"He's a math genius!" I thought. Then I found the multiplication tables in his desk. Smart boy. Not a math genius though.

I decided to start over with the two times tables. That worked a lot better. I wanted to move on to the three times table but I had four rowdies to contend with. One I was able to separate. One I kept at the board with me as my assistant. The other two fought, wouldn't stay seated and wouldn't listen. I called the office to ask if someone could come get them. The person on the other end wanted to know the names of the kids before she would send someone. I told them the girl's name but I didn't know the boy's name. They insisted I find out. Of course, the boy wouldn't tell me, but the others did. I love that about little kids. They have integrity. Being bad? They will dime you out. Most people lose that commitment to right and wrong later in life.

When the homeroom teacher returned, I told her I had sent two of her students to the Accommodation Room. She said they were troublemakers and that I had done the right thing. I told her when I called the office, they acted like they didn't want me to do it.

"They didn't," she said. "They make it as difficult as possible. You have to stop the class, fill out paperwork. (I didn't fill out any paperwork.) They don't really have any kind of discipline at this school. Notice one of the glass panes in my door is missing? Two of the kids in my class were fighting. I put one of them in the hall while I wrote up the slip. The kid was so angry he broke the glass. And I got in trouble for putting him in the hallway."

She smiled an excessively chipper smile and wished me luck. Whatever was going on, this woman was not letting it get her down.

At lunchtime, I swung by the office. The principal and a few other women (including the Coordinator) were standing around. I could smell the disapproval in the air. They thought I was just willy-nilly putting kids out. But I was trying to create a positive experience for the kids who were trying. I didn't even think the Accommodation Room was a big deal, especially since one little boy asked to go there when I pulled out the multiplication sheets. How rough could it be if kids were requesting it?

I asked the principal about the school policy for disciplining kids who are misbehaving. She couldn't wait to break it down.

"First, you speak to them. Then, you separate them. Then, if they're really still being disruptive, the Accommodation Room is a last resort—and only for one period. Then, the students return to the classroom."

"And I did exactly that, but it didn't stop them from fighting, talking, strolling around the room and ignoring the work we were doing."

"Oh," she said, "then, you did the right thing."

I nodded and headed to lunch where I struck up a conversation with an apprentice teacher who reflected the same disbelief that I was experiencing. She told me that whenever she had gone into the Accommodation Room, the kids were talking and passing notes.

"They don't have detention or expulsion because the principal 'doesn't believe in giving up on kids,'" she told me. "A kid brought a weapon to school and he was given an in-house suspension. So he spent all day in the Accommodation Room. *Come on.*"

My last class sucked. The apprentice teacher had warned me that this particular bunch of third graders was a handful. So I came in hard: no smiles, no chitchat. I let them finish word bingo. They booed the winner. I was going to read to them but they insisted that not a single teacher had let them use the bathroom all day. I knew they were probably lying, but I took them anyway. Mistake. One girl picked fights, argued, refused to stand in line. Finally, I told her she couldn't go to the bathroom and to return to the class. I might as well have said, "Please stay here in the hallway and sass me as much as possible." I actually had to chase her down the hallway. Eventually, I asked a passing teacher to walk her to the office. Screw the paperwork and the policy. I had other kids to deal with.

Once I got the students back to the room, I asked them to settle down, take their seats and stop talking so we could clean up and go home. The girls just completely ignored me. Then, they noticed that most of the boys had their coats and were headed to the hallway. Some of them quieted down. Others, four to be exact, led by the smallest girl in the class—"Little Miss Destiny"—jumped up and started for the closet, saying they were getting their coats because they "had stuff to do." I could not believe these little three-feet-tall people were acting like they were going to rush me. I planted myself in front of the closet and firmly told them to "Sit. Down." They returned to their seats but then either snuck into the other side of the closet or got someone else to sneak their coats out. They were so outrageous. The other kids were lined up in the hallway waiting but I refused to let any of these girls leave until they cooled out. And they did. But once I let them line up, they took off running down the hall. The other children generously supplied their names.

January 16, 2002 (Day 7 of 21)
Second day at P.S. #6

My classes started a little later today, so I wandered around the building killing time. I peeked in on the kindergarteners just to see how they were behaving. One little girl noticed and waved. The small ones are so open and loving. Many of the older ones are just angry. What happens in between?

I also noticed things that I had missed yesterday, like the fact that the whole school is very clean. It's funny how I notice right away if a place is dirty, but not so much if it's clean. The floors were polished and litter free. There were beautiful plants growing in the teachers' lounge and a soda machine that worked. And the kids spoke to me. Some, I recognized. Others, I'm pretty sure I hadn't met. They spoke just because.

The staff was also very friendly. Teachers spoke to each other and to me. They were sincerely interested in how my first day went. When I told them about the unruly third-graders, they encouraged me to speak to the homeroom teacher. Since her classroom was right across the hall, I figured, why not?

The kids were quite surprised when I strolled in. I don't think they expected to see me again. I informed the teacher that, overall, they had been pretty rowdy. Then I pointed out the ones who had run off without me at dismissal. My accusations were met with downcast eyes and pouting lips. They looked so remorseful, I almost felt bad—almost. The teacher told me to expect some letters of apology. "Yeah right," I thought, as I asked that she please have some real work for them to do. No more word bingo. (It was way too easy for a lot of them.) She assured me that she would take care of it. I thanked her and went on my way, wondering how they'd behave when I saw them later.

Teachers' lounge—lunchtime

A child was literally dragged out of my last class this morning. When I arrived, the homeroom teacher had already distributed paper and markers. All they had to do was color. Just *color!!* And keep the volume down. The homeroom teacher pointed out students who "might be trouble." She started to point to a not-so-little girl I'll call "Deja," but then changed her mind. "She's pretty cool today."

I introduced myself and asked the students to keep the noise down. After a few minutes, they started to get a little noisy. I asked them to be quiet again and they lowered their voices, all except for Deja. She yelled to her friends at other tables and encouraged them to change seats. I asked her quietly and nicely to please keep it down and work on her drawing. "Okay," she said and continued in the same manner. The louder and rowdier Deja became, the louder and rowdier the others became. I must have asked her ten times to keep it down. I told her I didn't like sending kids to the Accommodation Room but I would. She told me she went every day and would rather be there.

As I started toward the phone, she relented. "Okay, okay."

But I kept walking and picked up the phone to dial. "Are you going to behave, or am I dialing?"

She called my bluff. "I don't care what you do."

I dialed, as the other students reacted, "Oooo."

Deja's response? "I don't care who she calls. I'm not going."

Instead of sending someone for Deja, the woman who answered asked me to put her on the phone. Deja took the receiver, listened for a few seconds, then hung up. "I don't want to hear all that," she announced.

When I called back, the woman explained that she had asked Deja to come to the office. I passed the message along to Deja, who said, "I ain't goin' nowhere."

"She says she's not going anywhere," I told the woman on the other end, who promised to send someone for her.

As minutes ticked by, Deja talked more and more trash...mostly about me: "I don't like that lady. I'm sick of her. She mean. Don't y'all think she mean? I don't care if she called. I ain't goin' nowhere. Watch."

I really couldn't believe that a fourth grader was trash-talkin' me. How long would it be before the rest of the kids decided if Deja didn't have to listen, neither did they?

I walked over and stood next to her, thinking she might calm down. "You better get out of my face," she said. "I'm warning you. I have a bad temper." I couldn't believe this kid. I told her I had a bad temper, too, and asked what happened when she got mad. That seemed to make her pause for a moment—just a moment. Then she went back to the threats. I decided to walk away because I felt my blood starting to boil. I didn't want to get into a physical confrontation. She was about a foot shorter than me but pretty stocky. I could picture us rolling around the floor fighting. And, for me, that would be the straw after the last.

Luckily, a passing teacher offered some assistance. (Perhaps because I was hanging out of the classroom door, frantically looking up and down the hallway.) I asked if she'd mind taking a kid to the office. She was happy to oblige. Thank goodness because at this point, the other students were getting out of their seats, arguing with each other and passing hits back and forth. While I got the rest of the students under control, the other teacher went for Deja who hid in the coatroom. She took Deja's hand and tried to lead her out. In response, Deja threw herself onto the classroom floor and grabbed a nearby desk to anchor herself. Not to be outdone, the teacher proceeded to drag Deja, the desk and the boy in it toward the door. (So much for not touching the students.) I couldn't believe this girl would allow herself to be dragged across the floor. I was torn between being struck dumb and helping. I decided I could handle both at once. As I pried Deja's hand from the desk, the other teacher slid her across the floor and out the door. Shutting and locking the door, I asked the other students if she was always like this.

"Yeeess..."

I tried to encourage the students to get back to work, but fifteen minutes later, Deja was still in the hallway, surrounded by five grown women trying to coax her down the stairs. She chose, instead, to bang her head on a glass panel in the door. Eventually, a guard escorted her away...no doubt to the Accommodation Room. Most of the kids were relieved; even the ones who were supposed to be her friends. Apparently, Deja got dragged out every other day. Suddenly, art class was back on. Kids were drawing pictures for me like I was the hero who had slain the dragon. The sad thing was that in forty-five minutes, the dragon would be back.

The homeroom instructor returned at the end of the period shaking her head.

"I heard," she smiled before I could open my mouth. "All the kids in the class are afraid of Deja. If any of them stand up to her or tell on her, she and her buddies beat them up...she can curse me out, whatever...she still won't be expelled."

From the look of sheer frustration on this young woman's face, I got the impression she wouldn't be making teaching a lifelong career.

As for me, I couldn't believe how this day had gone south. It struck me that what's wrong with this school is also what's right with it: The principal. She doesn't believe in giving up on kids. She won't expel them or really punish them. She thinks love and patience are enough. *They're not.* That's why almost all of the teachers I've met at this school are burnt out. Either they're disgusted, angry or looking to get out. One of them told me she couldn't wait to transfer. Another said this school was just as bad as P.S. #5. (To be clear, it's not.) All I know is that once Deja was gone, the whole class settled down.

The rest of my day was fine. I had the crazy third graders again after lunch, but this time the homeroom teacher not only stayed nearby, she also made them copy a list of how to show manners three times. And I received a few letters of apology from the kids who ran out of class.

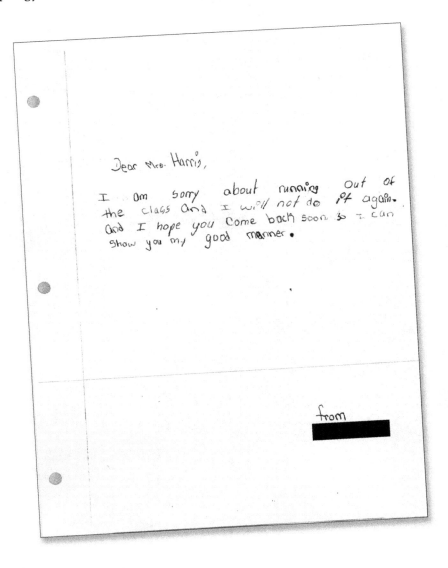

Dear Mrs Harris.

I am sorry that I was bad when you were in here. I will be good the next time you come in us. I will listen to you and respect you like I want to be respected.

From ████ ████

████ ████
1/17/002

Dear Mrs. Harris I'm sorry for running out the class room with out you. And not listening to you. I'm sorry I got smart with you. I hope you can come Back soon. I will Change My behavior.

I honestly didn't think any of these girls would care, but some of them seemed genuinely sorry. Even Little Miss Destiny inquired about whether I had read her letter or not. When I left, I thanked them all and wished them well. The homeroom teacher apologized again and told me to "be aware of what I was getting into" with teaching.

My next class belonged to the teacher who had ever-so-kindly dragged Deja out of the room. She had a large group, a mix of fourth and fifth graders. She told me they talked a lot, but would keep it to a dull roar. "Be tough," she said. The class went well. I enjoyed talking to them and helping out with their projects. They were in the middle of writing their autobiographies and today's assignment was to create the cover. Occasionally, one of them would get a little rowdy and I'd squash it immediately. I could because these kids were accustomed to listening to their teacher, and the possibility that I might "tell on them," was a strong deterrent. Of course, there's always one. *This* one climbed up on her desk and started dancing. When I put her name on the board, she got down immediately and tried to sweet talk me into erasing it. Fat chance, sister.

My last class was a racially diverse group of autistic children. The only additional instructions I received were, "Count the kids and make sure I bring back that same number I take." I was a nervous wreck. Lucky for me and the children, the teacher's aide agreed to stay with me. We took them next door to a huge, mostly empty but junky, room with big balls, baskets, an old, out-of-tune piano and some kind of weird swing contraption. It was sort of like a makeshift, indoor playground. The whole scene was sort of surreal. On one hand, the students seemed so fragile, yet they were also very rugged. Every time they rolled one of the giant balls, banged on the piano or swung on the swing, I was afraid they'd hurt themselves; but they didn't. Some of them approached me, holding my hand or just holding on to me for a bit before wandering off. At first, I tried to interact with them, but they seemed unaware of me; or perhaps they just couldn't communicate. I had no concept of their limitations and abilities. I was totally incapable of providing them with a meaningful educational experience. Yet, there I was.

I sat next to the aide who was both laidback and vigilant at the same time. They couldn't go anywhere. The door was closed. Still, every few minutes, I counted them. Sometimes they sat completely motionless inside the big balls or baskets for long periods of time. So motionless that I checked to make sure they were still breathing.

One of the girls seemed a little more lively and aware than the others though she still didn't speak.

"We don't think she's autistic at all," said the aide. "Her mother is either crazy or she has her in the program for money. Now [the child] is behind developmentally and mimicking the autistic students. They're trying to place her in learning-support classes to help prepare her for reintegration into regular classes."

As I sat there, counting the kids, I wondered why on Earth they would allow me to work with children with special needs? I don't have any training. I have no idea what to expect or what to do if there's a problem. This was just stupid. When the instructor returned, he said something like, "Tomorrow, when you come…" I quickly made it clear that I would not be there tomorrow. Head Start, here I come.

January 17, 2002 (Day 8 of 21)
Third day at P.S. #6

I was excited about working with small kids for two reasons: 1) I get a kick out of them. 2) I wanted to know if they were as out of control as the older children. Are these children starting off angry, hostile and undisciplined, or is that developing over time? Checking in with "Miss Fran," the Earth-Mother-like director of Head Start, I explained that I didn't really know anything about the program. She smiled, assuring me that I'd be "just fine." Plus, there was a classroom aide, which meant I wouldn't be totally on my own.

"We go by first names in Head Start: Miss Fran, "Miss Monica," etc. It's harder for the children to pronounce last names…and it just seems friendlier."

Knowing that Miss Clayvon would quickly turn into "Miss Crayon," I settled on Miss Clay. Directed to the room at the end of the hall, I met "Mrs. Dorsey," the classroom aide, and noted that she went by her last name. She was setting up breakfast for the kids and didn't really have time to brief me. So I sat back and watched the morning routine unfold: The parents signed in, while the kids hung their nametags on the board and said the number on their nametags. (Some kids were up to twelve. Others were only at four.) Next, the children signed in on a little piece of paper, either the first name or first and last depending on the child's progress. The parents were responsible for getting all of this done. They were invested in the process, from both a point of pride and practicality. They had to get to work. I bet a lot of them were practicing with their kids at home.

As I introduced myself, most parents asked if the regular teacher was sick. I let them know that she would be back on Monday. They regarded me suspiciously and politely glanced at Mrs. Dorsey who gave them the nod, "I won't let her screw up too much." That was good enough for them. The parents dispersed as the children settled in. Immediately, one little girl introduced herself, gave me a hug and informed me that everyone at her table wanted one, too.

"Don't let them suck you in," Mrs. Dorsey warned. "Some of them are very needy and they'll be hanging on you all day."

Ironically, they weren't hanging on me so much as giving me a run for my money. I had to ask them over and over to do or not do things. They were constantly hugging, pulling and hitting the other kids. They're only four so it wasn't that big of a deal, but when you're trying to do a counting lesson or read a story, it helps if half the class isn't rolling across the floor.

Mrs. Dorsey was the disciplinarian in the room. She reminded me of my great grandmother, no-nonsense but loving. She wouldn't let the kids act like babies. When they asked me to tie their shoes, blow their noses or open a carton of milk, Mrs. Dorsey informed me that they already knew how to do these things.

"They're just playing you for attention," she said.

I didn't mind being played, as long as I wasn't in the middle of teaching. Our volunteer grandmother, "Miss Nancy," was constantly being played. Whereas Mrs. Dorsey spoke once with the expectation of being obeyed (*and she was*), Miss Nancy fussed a lot and didn't pause long enough for the children to respond to her direction. Consequently, she wound up finishing up a lot of their chores; but she also provided valuable one-on-one time for the kids who were falling behind.

Though I was the "teacher" in the room, Mrs. Dorsey and Miss Nancy were in charge. They knew the kids and the routine, and I was happy to do as told.

"Okay, now you take the roll," instructed Mrs. Dorsey.

Gathering the children on the rug, I struggled to get them to sit still, be quiet and say "present" or "here" when I called their names. I was trying different approaches, finding my voice. They were so little and cute. I wanted them to take me seriously, but I didn't want to raise my voice or be too stern. Mrs. Dorsey and Miss Nancy didn't seem to have the same concerns.

"Sit up. Pay attention. *Listen to Miss Clay!*"

When I finished the roll, one of the kids threw up...a lot. I mean *a whole lot.* Mrs. Dorsey and Miss Nancy moved as far away as possible without leaving the room. Suddenly, I was in charge. I held this kid's shaking shoulders while he spewed all over the rug, the floor and himself. I was a bit annoyed. Earlier, I had pointed out that he was sick and should be taken to the nurse. Miss Nancy and Mrs. Dorsey both insisted that he was "always sick." After ten minutes of throwing up, I asked them again to take the child to the nurse. This time they did. From that point, I was the teacher, no quotes, in the room.

We read a story. We counted. We went to the bathroom, which is challenging in and of itself. I had twelve little girls. Some didn't want to go. Some wanted to go twice. Some didn't want to put all their clothes back on. All of them played in the water. Though I asked them to wait in line outside the bathroom when finished, they took off running down the hall. Hurrying after them, I ran into Miss Fran.

"Everything okay?"

"Oh yeah..." I gave her a confident nod. She smiled, somewhat skeptically (though perhaps, I'm projecting) and returned to her classroom.

While most of the kids were manageable, there were a few who wouldn't listen to anyone. Mrs. Dorsey eventually dropped off one little wild child with her aunt who worked in the cafeteria. Seemed this happened a lot. The little girl got to hang out with a bunch of ladies who fussed over her and she didn't have to do any work. How was this helping anyone?

Then there was a chatty little girl who started a shoving match. When I gave her a time out, she sulked and asked every minute or so if it was over. She also did the same thing during naptime, "Is it time to get up yet? Huh? Is it time?"

And finally, we had a sweet-faced boy who wanted to run and jump and hit. So, that's what he did, regardless of how many timeouts we gave him. Miss Nancy made some offhand comment about him needing "to be on Ritalin," but I could tell she felt bad about it afterwards.

"Sometimes they're just a little much," she said.

I understood. I still couldn't believe I had cursed at that boy at P.S. #5. But teachers are human. Teaching can be stressful. Even when the kids are four.

By the end of the day, I was anxious to speak with parents. The little boy's mother promised to speak to him and to get him to bed earlier. (Many, many problems can be cleared up with a good night's sleep. A cup of tea also works wonders.)

The little girl who kept asking the same question over and over? Well, it turned out her mother, a smiley, good-natured young woman, was intellectually challenged. When I explained her daughter's behavior, she responded, "I try. I tell her to be good. But she don't listen to me. I'll tell my mother."

Mrs. Dorsey confirmed that they both lived with the little girl's grandmother. I wondered if perhaps the little girl was combating the same challenges. Even if she wasn't, she was probably doing the best she could without a mother who could properly guide her. I hugged the girl and told her I knew she could do better the next day.

"Aw, it's a Kodak moment," her mother said and flashed another big grin.

Most of the parents had listened patiently and addressed the bad behavior right then and there. When I asked Mrs. Dorsey if there was any point in speaking with the wild child's mother, she responded, "Absolutely none."

I'm guessing this kid has a future that includes being dragged from classrooms.

January 18, 2002 (Day 9 of 21)
Fourth day at P.S. #6

I wasn't really sure what Head Start was about when I arrived. I thought it was a glorified babysitting program, but it's actually one of the most critical education programs in America. It socializes children to the classroom environment and teaches them basic skills like putting toys away, disposing of trash, learning to write their names, count and say the alphabet. But it also provides practical experience with listening to the teacher, playing nicely with others and having nice lunch conversation. It gives underprivileged kids a better chance of succeeding when school actually starts.

The parents I spoke to made sure their children participated more and behaved better the next day. We also had an early dismissal so some of the students, including the "Little Hugger", stayed home. Twelve kids are a lot easier to deal with than twenty. Plus, I knew the routine so I was able to be more effective. Quite a few of the boys, who barely said anything the first day, quickly clicked into the second day's lesson on opposites. And some of the girls, who were miles ahead socially, had difficulty grasping the concept. Generally, the kids were sweet and brimming with potential, though some of them were already using non-standard English. When I reminded them to say, "I am" instead of "I'm is," they got it. But who's going to reinforce this when they're not in school? And, sometimes, even when they are in school. A lot of teachers let the kids slide because they don't believe they can do any better. George W. Bush referred to this as the "soft bigotry of low expectations." I'm not certain about how soft it is, but it's definitely bigotry.

At the end of the day, I found myself chatting with parents again. This time, I had nothing but good reports. Even the little girl who kept asking the same questions over and over was like a new kid. My suspicion that she may have had some intellectual challenges disappeared. When it was time for her to leave, I thanked her for behaving so well and reminded her to listen to mommy. Her mother's big smile faded and tears fell from her eyes. She thanked me and the little girl threw her arms around me.

People often talk about how inner-city parents don't care and don't take an interest in their children's education. All of the parents I spoke with cared. A lot. Most of them thanked me, though I felt like I should have been thanking them since I had enjoyed their children so much.

As I waited for the last child to be picked up, Destiny, the smallest of the third-grade girls who had given me such a hard time, strolled into the classroom with her little brother in tow. She was surprised to see me and I was surprised to discover that she was Mrs. Dorsey's granddaughter. I tactfully let her know what a terror Destiny had been, though I did acknowledge she had apologized. Mrs. Dorsey chuckled and cooed, "I know you weren't misbehaving." And that little brat just snuggled up to her grandmother and grinned. I guess Mrs. Dorsey is only a tough guy when it comes to other people's kids.

Finally, I dropped the last little girl off to wait with the other kids in the Land of Late Parents. As I started out, Miss Fran informed me that I didn't have to leave.

"You can stay and clean out closets or something. But if you leave now, I have to put you down for a half day."

I hadn't taken a break the day before or that day and I was tired. I told her I was getting paid forty bucks a day, and she could keep the other twenty if she wanted.

Despite her attempt to pimp me for cheap labor, Miss Fran was very concerned about the public education system. We wound up in a deep discussion with a couple of other teachers and aides. Generally, they felt the main problem with the kids was poverty; after that, uninformed parents and, then, a school system that makes it almost impossible to expel problem students. Miss Fran had lots of ideas about how to get better results, such as funneling new school funds into reading centers. Children who aren't on grade level would stop regular school all together, and spend all of their time focusing on reading until they're up to speed. Seemed like a great idea to me. Kids who can't read tend to disrupt class.

They had also all heard about my encounter with Deja. She was one of theirs. They had worked very hard to get her on track, but her home life was difficult and, once she left Head Start, she was just another kid in a general classroom.

"General-ed. teachers don't have a lot of one-on-one time built into their schedules," explained another teacher.

Everyone I spoke with agreed that P.S. #6 was a lot better than it had been, but the principal's hands were tied when it came to dealing with problem students. It wasn't that she didn't believe in giving up on a child, so much as not being allowed to give up. I was new to the game, but it was pretty obvious to me that a kid like Deja needed special help. How obvious does it have to be before somebody does something about it?

P.S. #6: PERCENTAGE OF 5th-GRADERS
SCORING BELOW BASIC:[*,2,3]

2000–2001

Math } 91%   Reading } 82%

---

* Percentages are rounded.

> "Public School #7"

January 23, 2002 (Day 10 of 21)

Kindergarten to 12th Grade: Over 1600 students: 91.7% African American; 2.1% Asian; 1.7% Latino; 4% White; 0.5% Other.[1]

"*I* have to ask you this, Miss Harris. Did you choke 'Sunshine'? She says you choked her and slammed her head up against the wall."

The day began like any other subbing day. I arrived at P.S. #7 early, thinking three days, third grade, shouldn't be that bad. I'd have a chance to teach something other than art in a school near one of the more affluent neighborhoods in the Philadelphia area. When I told people where I'd be subbing, they all said the same thing, "Ohh...that's supposed to be a good school."

I ran into a teacher in the parking lot and asked how the kids were.

"Sometimes my kids are great; other times, they're pretty rough," he answered. "If I'm not being 'mean,' they don't listen. But being mean all day long, five days a week is draining me."

He escorted me past the metal detector to the office. "Found a volunteer on the street," he joked before heading on his way. For all they knew, I could have been just that. Still no request for I.D.

The principal signed me in: "Name? Social security number? Job number? Who are you in for? Thank God. You can pick your kids up in the yard at 8:25. Your room is "117", down the hall."

"That's it?" I asked. "No lesson plans, a class list...?"

"'The Coordinator' will be down to prep you," she responded, moving on to some other task.

I found the classroom, but it was locked. Luckily, the teacher across the hall, "Mrs. Hammond," volunteered to call the office for help. While I waited, she

> 99 <

briefed me on the situation I was walking into. The teacher I was subbing for wanted help with her class, an assistant or something. She stopped coming to work when they declined her request. Officially, she claimed to have had a car accident. Last year, she taught fourth grade and one of her students left a bag of feces on her desk. This year, she'd been "downgraded" to a third-grade class filled with problem students: one hit her in the head with a baseball.

"Woo-hoo," I thought. "Can't wait to meet these kids."

After locating them in the schoolyard, we joined the rest of the school in saying *The Pledge of Allegiance* and listening to morning announcements. I watched them closely as they twisted, giggled, whispered and eyed me suspiciously—nothing too out of the ordinary. Heading to the room, they became noisier and nosier.

"Keep it down. Yes you." They kept a lid on it, not yet sure just how far they could push the new lady. But once we were in the room, I had to ease up on playing tough. I couldn't do the roll without a class list. I didn't know the room procedures. There were books on the teacher's desk but no notes indicating what they might be working on. And you can't rely on the kids to tell you because sometimes they lie... just for the fun of it.

I needed to figure out what I was supposed to be doing before waging war for control. I stood at the back of the room flipping through textbooks and papers. Realizing that all of my attention wasn't focused squarely on them, the kids became louder and louder. A passing teacher stopped in to see if everything was okay. I told her I was trying to figure out which lessons the kids were on. She gave me an idea of "around about" where they should be. Then she decided to give me a lesson in classroom management. She firmly addressed the students, telling them to quiet down, face front and prepare for work. They quieted to see if she was saying anything of interest. She wasn't, so they resumed their conversations. A little taken aback, she quickly exited.

"Oh boy," I thought. "These kids are used to running the show." I guess that's what happens when the regular teacher hides out at home. Normal expectations don't apply. I took off my jacket and prepared for battle.

First thing I did was get them to make name cards for their desks. I learned all of their names fast and I used them every two seconds: "'Anastasia,' 'Malik,' 'Takia'...be quiet, sit down, turn around."

For me, teaching is very physical. I move around a lot. I use a lot of energy. I want the kids to know that at any moment, I could be standing right next to them. This helps keep the kids who are misbehaving (which was most of them) a little more focused. If they're doing something they aren't supposed to be doing, I get on their cases and stay on them until they stop. The problem was that so many of them were doing something they weren't supposed to be doing that getting on their cases seemed to be all that I was doing.

When "Mrs. Jones", a teacher from a nearby classroom, stopped in to check on me, the students were really showing out. She asked if I wanted to send some of them to her room. I felt a little bit incompetent fobbing off my students, but I got over it fast sending the most challenging student with her and reserving the option to send others if necessary.

"No problem," she said. "Just let me know. I'll come and get them."

I *wanted* to send at least ten students with her. Despite the 110% that I was giving, these kids were bouncing off the walls. Some did no work. Others talked constantly or wandered around the class. Then, there were those who called me over to show me every scrape and nick on their bodies. One kid was playing games on his cell phone. So I took it. I took a car, a bracelet, a necklace and a tennis ball (No point getting popped in the head today). These kids were ready for everything except learning. Why do parents allow their children to bring all that crap to school?

I was determined that we would get some work done. I tried to fill every vacant moment. Idle minds and all... We spelled out loud. We worked in their books. We got everyone up to the board. I had to give these little kids credit. A lot of them were capable of doing the work. They just didn't feel like it.

By 10:30 a.m., they were pissed with me. I had given them vocabulary words to study and use in sentences, and an assignment to look up the seven continents. I could be wrong, but they're in third grade. They should know Texas and Alaska are not continents, right? They felt otherwise...about everything:

"How are we supposed to know that?"

"That's too much work."

"We don't get homework."

"Yes, we do. But not this much."

"I don't want all this work."

"I'm not doing it."

"She mean."

According to my friend Nora, "If the children aren't referring to you as 'mean,' you're probably not doing anything."

Anyway, it was 10:30. Time for lunch. The kids were ready to go—if for no other reason than to get away from "all this work." But they were still cutting up. They'd quiet down; we'd start walking. They'd start talking and playing; we'd stop and stand. We did that several times before they picked up on the fact that lunchtime was evaporating. I wondered if this was against school policy. Did they have a right to a certain amount of free time? We didn't have personal freedoms in Catholic school, so I don't know.

By the time we made it to lunch, we had 30 minutes left. I quickly went to eat and recover from the first two hours of the day. Before I could finish my baked chicken leg and a yogurt, a lunchroom monitor came looking for me. One of the kids had ratted out the boy with the cell phone. I had given it back, making him promise to put it away because I was afraid it might "disappear" from the room. Little did I know, the school policy is to turn the phone in to security and inform the parents that they have to retrieve it. She handed the phone back to me.

I headed for the office, turned the phone in and swung back by the room to figure out what I was going to do with these kids for the afternoon. I wasn't quite as effective as I wanted to be before lunch, to put it mildly. By the time I flipped open a book, it was time to pick up the kids, and it was only 11:15. That meant I had over three and a half hours left to fill. God help me.

After lunch, the kids were even more hyped. Usually, school lunches consist of things like pizza, grilled cheese sandwiches, macaroni and cheese or a thin hot dog or hamburger on a bun. Don't carbs convert into sugar in your system? As I escorted the kids across the schoolyard, they ran like nuts—screaming, yelling, sliding on the ice. It looked like fun, but I wondered if they'd be able to rein it in and get back to work. Nope. By the time we got back to the room, they were acting up so much that Mrs. Jones stopped by to lay them out. It wasn't like I was being a pushover. They were just out of control. Nearly every teacher I came in contact with told me I had a "hard class."

The teacher next door told me he used to have eighth grade and he cried every day before work. Now, he has fourth grade and he doesn't cry, but "it still sucks," he said candidly. "I don't fear for my life, but this school is no walk in the park."

This man had been teaching for twenty-three years. This was only my tenth day. I clung to this rationalization as I stood by watching another teacher wrangle my students. Mrs. Jones was in full-on preach mode, telling the children how ashamed they should be. She also insisted that they write letters of apology to me for homework. The first time kids wrote letters of apology to me I was touched. This time, not so much. It's just more stuff I'll have to make sure they've completed. I'd rather they focus on real work. But Mrs. Jones was on a roll and they were listening. Amazing. They could shut their mouths to be told off but not to be taught. Maybe my voice wasn't loud enough or something, but I refuse to yell all day long. Though I must admit, Mrs. Jones wasn't yelling. She was naturally gifted with a booming voice.

"You're just behaving like this because Miss Harris is nice," she sermonized.

"I am not!" I wanted to protest. "I'm *mean*..." Honestly, I'm not sure that "mean" matters. The first boy I sent with Mrs. Jones had returned unchanged. In fact, I had to pull him off of another kid after lunch. When it was time to go to art, another boy told me he wasn't going because I had put a circle around his name on the board, indicating that I planned to call his mother. Of course, "he hadn't done nothin'," other than pick fights, act up, not participate, walk around the class, etc.

One of the things I learned at P.S. #5 (aside from the fact that if stressed enough, I will tell a kid to "sit the hell down,") is that you really cannot do everything—at least not all at once. I left this protesting child in the classroom with a girl who was sick and took the rest of the kids to art, which was no simple feat. They were running, pushing and playing in the halls. I managed to get most of them to art. I told the art teacher which of them should spend the period doing work instead of participating in a fun project. They were surprised. I guess they figured I'd be so happy to dump them that there wouldn't be any consequences. Double nope.

I went back upstairs, got the kids who were still playing in the halls, hiding in the classroom and the bathrooms and brought them down to art. Then I went back to get "Mr. Take-the-Circle-Off-My-Name" and "Miss Sick." I walked them to the principal's office. They kept the boy and called his mom and sent the girl to the nurse.

Finally having five minutes to myself, I raced for the bathroom...something I'm starting to view as a luxury. By the time I got back to the class, the girl was back. The nurse was "on break." She told the girl to come back at 1:15. What if this kid was seriously ill? And what about my break?

I told her to sit down and put her head down. She fell asleep immediately. I flipped through the math book looking for work. What I found was useful math scenarios like, "let's do a budget for a disaster." What is that? Shouldn't they be working on multiplication and division? I was barely able to find a page of review problems before I had to pick up the kids. On my way, I ran into the nurse who wanted to make sure I understood her office hours. I wanted to tell her what she could do with her office hours; instead, I told her I couldn't talk right then. I had kids to pick up.

Two. That's how many candy canes the art teacher had given out to well-behaved students. Out of almost 30. I would have been embarrassed but a) I had just met these kids; b) Apparently, she couldn't control them either and she knew them; and c) What was she doing trying to buy good behavior with month-old, stale candy canes? The kids aren't stupid.

Back at the room, I asked the kids to stop and wait quietly to enter. As they settled down, one lone straggler I'll call Sunshine came skipping down the hall. Why she wasn't with the rest of the students, I had no idea. What I did know is that she had been a real pill all day. I must have asked this kid to sit down, be quiet or pay attention 50 times. She had done nothing—even when I gave them time to complete their homework. And here she was skipping down the hall as though we had nothing better to do than wait for her...tra la la.

"Sunshine, get in line," I said. She headed for the end of the girl's line and I turned to the boys who were unexpectedly quiet. I asked them to enter the class, get out their skill packs and get to work. They were thrilled to go before the girls, so they headed in obediently. Just that quickly, there was a situation in the hall. A larger girl (a fifth or sixth grader) was arguing with Sunshine who was now in the middle of the line. When I asked what was going on, the older girl politely explained that she had seen Sunshine push her little sister who was now crying. Sunshine, of course, proceeded to scream and holler that she "didn't do anything."

The "Big Sister" was remarkably restrained considering that she seemed to be about two seconds from popping Sunshine in the mouth. As I tried to get to the bottom of the argument, both Mrs. Jones and Mrs. Hammond came to see about the ruckus. The boys were getting excited, trying to see what was going on in the hall. The Big Sister wanted justice for the "Little Sister." Sunshine was still insisting that she was innocent. I told the Big Sister she could leave, and we'd handle it from there. I sent the rest of the class inside to get to work. And they did.

In the hallway, Sunshine continued to perform. "She lyin'. I didn't push that little girl." (That little girl was several inches taller than Sunshine.)

"Then why is she crying?" I asked.

She shrugged in response.

I was happy to let Mrs. Jones and Mrs. Hammond take the lead since I had no idea how to deal with this child. Mrs. Hammond told Sunshine to take her hand off of her hip and to stop speaking so disrespectfully. Sunshine sucked her teeth and looked away, so Mrs. Hammond removed Sunshine's hand for her. Sunshine put it back on her hip, rolled her eyes and turned her back to us. Mrs. Jones turned her back around. They went back and forth this way for a bit. I could not believe the way this tiny little girl was brazenly sassing two veteran teachers old enough to be her grandmothers.

Suddenly, Mrs. Jones leaned in grabbing Sunshine's shoulder: "One of these days, I might get you in a room alone and let it be my word against yours." Sunshine's eyes widened. I'm sure mine did, too. I looked closely at Mrs. Jones. Her threat seemed more like a tactic to get the girl to fall in line than anything else.

Sunshine's response? "What'd I do?"

Mrs. Hammond intervened, offering to let Sunshine sit in her room while she ate lunch. I thought that was a good idea. It would give Sunshine time to cool out and give me time away from Sunshine. Mrs. Jones also offered to let Sunshine come to her room. I decided that Sunshine would go with Mrs.

Hammond, and I asked Mrs. Jones if she would take a couple of the boys for me. She was happy to do so.

I leaned inside the room, "You, you and you," I said to the three boys who were up and running around. "Let's go." I guess they thought I hadn't noticed. They marched past me grumbling and sucking their teeth. Last I saw Sunshine, she was still arguing with the two teachers.

Closing the door on the scene in the hallway, I took a deep breath and moved as many kids to the front of the room as possible. I began the math lesson and, miracle of miracles, the class started working. I had about 24 students at this point and we were clicking along. We did problems on paper first, then on the board. The students cheered when they got them right. When they got them wrong, we went over how to do them correctly. I had everyone's attention and disruption was minimal. I couldn't believe how well it was going. Suddenly, the door swung slowly open like in a cheap horror flick. There stood Sunshine, the picture of innocence, escorted by a woman I hadn't met before. Near as I could figure, Sunshine had refused to behave in Mrs. Hammond's room so she took her to the principal's office and the principal was sending her back to me.

I took a deep breath, hoping this kid would disappear, but she didn't. So I asked if she would behave now. She said she would. The woman smiled and headed back down the hall. I asked Sunshine to take her seat. She took her sweet time, touring the class like a celebrity, stopping at this one's desk and that one's... you know, to say a few words to the people.

"Sunshine, take your seat." Eventually she did, but as soon as I resumed the lesson, she was back up and walking around. The kids near her started talking and giggling. I asked Sunshine to change seats and she walked out. No warning. No, "Can I?" Just up and left. Even the other kids were surprised by this move. They started talking all at once; some jumped up to see where she was going.

"Sit down!" I yelled and they scrambled for their chairs. "And you better all be in your seats when I get back." I went after Sunshine. I knew I wasn't supposed to leave my class alone, but I didn't trust this little girl to wander the building unsupervised. Halfway down the hall, we passed a male teacher. I asked if he could take Sunshine to the office. Before I could explain that my class was unattended, he spat out, "No," and kept walking.

As I followed Sunshine down the hall, I could tell she wasn't sure where she was headed. "Keep walking to the principal's office," I said, a few steps behind her. By the time we got there, I was fairly upset. I approached the first person that made eye contact with me. "She walked out of class," I said calmly. "Don't send her back."

On the return, I half expected to see a few kids hanging out of the door watching for me, but I didn't. And when I stepped into the room, they weren't quiet but they were all in their seats. I thanked them for that and immediately went back to the lesson trying to focus through my growing irritation. Just as we starting to regain momentum, Sunshine popped up banging on the door.

"I want my stuff!"

Most of the kids shook their heads in disbelief, while the little boy who sat near the door started to open it.

"Do not open that door."

"I want my stuffff!" she screamed.

I gathered Sunshine's jacket, books and unsanctioned toys. Once again, we walked the hall to the principal's office. When we walked in, the same woman I had left Sunshine with before looked puzzled.

"She came back," I said.

"She must've snuck out," she weakly responded

I dropped Sunshine's stuff on the bench and headed back to class again. My head was pounding. Couldn't they provide a little support? I tried to will the frustration away as I reached the room, but before I could even pick up a piece of chalk, the same woman who had returned Sunshine the first time opened the door and asked me to step outside.

"The principal wants to speak to you."

"Fine," I said. I told her what I was working on with the kids and I left.

Some of the kids yelled after me, "Miss Harris, are you leaving?"

"I'll be back," I answered, despite the fact that I wasn't so sure. I couldn't control that little hellion and I had left my class unattended. Twice.

All eyes were on me as I entered. A woman waved me toward the back. I knocked on the principal's open door and entered. She asked me to sit down. That morning, I felt like she had barely seen me. Now, I had her full attention.

"I have to ask you this," she said. "Did you choke Sunshine?"

Never in a million years would I have guessed that's why the principal wanted to see me. I was so stunned. All of the anger that had been building in me evaporated. "No," I said calmly. I wasn't insulted. I wasn't angry. The idea was just so absurd.

She continued, "She says you choked her and slammed her head up against the wall."

"I did not choke that child," I said. "Or, slam her head against a wall."

She held my gaze for a second, then let out a sigh. "I'm sorry, Miss Harris. I had to ask." Then, after another second, she continued, "Would you still be willing to come back tomorrow? It's hard for us to get subs." (I wonder why.)

"I'll come back," I responded, "but we need to do something about Sunshine."

"Sunshine is not one of our problem kids," she said.

"She's been nothing but a problem all day."

Trying to smooth things over, she muttered something about calling Sunshine's mother.

"Can we call now?" I asked.

She hemmed and hawed about having a meeting to attend but, finally, she said I could call. I think she expected me to back down. I didn't. So she asked one of her assistants for Sunshine's home number, then began packing for her meeting. As soon as the assistant returned with the number, I dialed. I got Sunshine's mother on the phone right away. I told her I was subbing in her daughter's class and how poorly she had behaved. I also told her that she had accused me of choking her. She asked to speak to Sunshine. I called her into the office and handed her the phone. "Momma Sunshine" must have been talking a mile a minute because Sunshine could barely get a word in.

"I...I..." Suddenly, she burst into tears and blurted out, "Not her, the other teacher. The other one..." She listened a few seconds more and then handed the phone back. Momma Sunshine was on her way. I told her I'd be waiting in the principal's office.

The principal came back in to get something. She glanced at the teary-eyed Sunshine.

"Sunshine...?" I said.

"Not her, the other teacher."

"You knew I was talking about Miss Harris," the principal said annoyed. "You said she choked you."

"It was the other one," she said again. I asked if she meant Mrs. Hammond. Sunshine nodded.

Granted, I didn't know Mrs. Hammond from a can of paint, but she struck me as dignified and concerned—the kind of woman who leads by example. I couldn't see her choking a child. I explained that Mrs. Hammond had agreed to let Sunshine sit in her room for a while to calm down.

"No," Sunshine interrupted, "not her. The other one."

"Mrs. Jones?" I asked? She nodded. I hadn't left Sunshine alone with Mrs. Jones. This girl is just lying, I thought. And apparently the principal thought the same thing.

"I have to go," she said. The Coordinator will sit in on the meeting with you."

"The Coordinator?" I questioned. "The one who was supposed to prep me, but never showed up?"

The principal turned to one of her assistants, and told her to make sure the Coordinator was in this meeting. Then, she was gone.

I went back to the classroom to pick up my things. I noted that the kids weren't doing anything except sitting around chatting. I woke up one girl. Made others move to their appropriate seats. I glanced at this woman who was supposed to be monitoring the class and wondered why she wasn't doing anything. I told the students I had a meeting with Sunshine's mother.

"Do your homework. I'll see you tomorrow." As I was leaving, the woman followed me into the hall.

"Excuse me. I'm supposed to stay with the class?" She was a little upset when I said, "Yes."

"I'm a counselor. I'm not certified," she blurted out.

"Neither am I."

"Oh," she said, a look of fear in her eyes.

"My God," I thought, "they're not *that* scary."

As I waited in the principal's office, the absurdity of this situation picked at me. Today was my first day at this school and I had already been accused of choking a child and called a parent-teacher conference. Belatedly, I wondered how this woman would respond. Would she be upset? Angry? Would she be ready to sue, or worse, kick my ass? I know if my child told me a teacher choked her, I would be...I don't know what I'd be...but spittin' mad might come close to describing it.

Of course, the Coordinator was nowhere to be found when Momma Sunshine arrived. I decided to go ahead and start. It was immediately obvious that this woman didn't have a lot of money, or an excess of education. I jumped to conclusions: mostly of the she's-not-paying-attention-to-what's-going-on-with-her-kid variety. But I was dead wrong. She was so upset about the whole situation, she had to fight back tears. She was 28, had two daughters and, up until this year, Sunshine had no problems in school. But since they moved and Sunshine changed schools, this woman had been summoned to the school every other day to sit in Sunshine's class and watch her.

"I thought it was her teacher. I thought she just didn't like Sunshine. But now you're telling me the same thing. It's a different story."

As for Sunshine, she had morphed into this adorable, quiet, soft-spoken child who actually responded when I asked questions. No wonder her mother didn't believe the other teacher. I asked Sunshine if the work we did in class was hard. She said it was "really hard." I asked Momma Sunshine if her daughter was in the after-school program. She didn't know anything about an after-school program.

At this point, the Coordinator (who oddly enough reminded me of the Coordinator at P.S. #1) joined us. She had been teaching for 25 years and was very adept at handling parents; she was absolutely soothing. Sunshine's mother asked about the after-school program right away. The Coordinator explained that the program was for "middle-of-the-road students who could learn quickly enough to improve their performance on standardized tests."

One of the problems Momma Sunshine was having is that she didn't know the right questions to ask. So I tried to help. I asked if there were other services for which Sunshine might be eligible. And there were, but first Sunshine needed to be tested, which the Coordinator said would be done in the next couple of days. After that, they'd discuss options. The Coordinator then turned to Sunshine and helped focus her on what she needed to do to better her behavior.

Her mother seemed tremendously relieved, and promised to sit in for a while during class tomorrow.

As we finished up, the Coordinator turned to me, asking if I'd like to sub in the middle school. She said they had several vacancies. (I had already heard through the grapevine that several teachers had quit mid-year because they were so disgusted.) I declined.

"I love the middle school," she said. "We can beat on the kids and they don't go home and tell their mommies."

I looked at her like she was crazy, and I was pretty sure Momma Sunshine was looking at her the same way...not to mention Sunshine. The Coordinator just kind of chuckled, unembarrassed, then excused herself.

"Where's this other teacher?" asked Momma Sunshine.

As we started down the hall, I explained that Mrs. Jones had turned Sunshine around to make her look at us while we were speaking to her, but that it wasn't excessively rough. (And it wasn't.)

"Maybe she accidentally touched Sunshine's neck," I suggested.

"It was after that," Sunshine corrected me.

On our way, we ran into Sunshine's cousin. He immediately told his aunt that he had seen Sunshine "being bad" when she came into his class. I asked who his teacher was.

"Mrs. Jones."

But he didn't say that she had choked his cousin. I had no idea what to believe anymore. We continued down the hall, passing a few kids from my class. Some just looked at me; others spoke. At Mrs. Jones' door, some of my kids were lined up for the after-school program. When they saw me, they hugged me. I couldn't believe it. I was tough today; mean even. Still I got four or five hugs. Clearly, I'm not workin' this bitch thing right.

I introduced Momma Sunshine to Mrs. Jones who performed a song-and-dance number the likes of which I had never seen. She totally played on the woman's struggles. She talked about Sunshine's nice clothes, how pretty she was and how she had to turn the love she had for her mother into good behavior to make her mother proud. By the time she was done, she was talking Momma

Sunshine into giving her daughter another chance. A look of confusion washed over Sunshine's face.

I just stood there watching, not sure what to do. Finally, I walked away to go write down Sunshine's homework. I felt ill. I felt bad for Sunshine's mother because she's struggling to get her kid a decent education and doesn't really know how to accomplish this. I felt bad for Sunshine because she's struggling with her studies. I felt bad for Mrs. Jones because, as much as she seems to care about these kids, the strain of this job has warped her. I think maybe she did choke that girl. She's going to have to live with that. So will Sunshine. So will I.

January 24, 2002 (Day 11 of 21)
Second day at P.S. #7

All in all, I had better control of the class today but it was still pretty rough. Sunshine was much more like the sweet child she had been in the presence of her mother than the troublemaker she had been all day yesterday. I moved her to the front of the room to help her focus and worked with her during my free period. She was an angel, but that child can barely read. That's why she was constantly disrupting class. Unfortunately, by the time Momma Sunshine arrived, her daughter had given up and gone back to her old ways. I moved her to the back table along with three other little, chatty girls. Mother and daughter had a conversation and Sunshine cooled out again. Before leaving, Momma Sunshine wanted to know how they'd done on the homework, especially the seven continents. They missed Antarctica (which is understandable) but I was proud of them for trying.

During lunchtime, the terrified counselor from the day before and I struck up a conversation. I told her that, once upon a time, I wanted to be a child psychologist. She told me that it wasn't what she thought it would be. It was much more political and she wasn't sure she was going to stick with it. She also confided that the class I was assigned to had "a lot of kids with serious emotional problems or who had been left back." That explained why the regular teacher was hiding out at home. The other third-grade teacher, who had been sitting at the table in a zombie-like state, unexpectedly snapped into awareness.

"There are too many discipline problems for one class," she commented. Seeming on the verge of a serious problem herself, she shook her head and lapsed back into silence.

As the day progressed, I did my best to keep the students working and focused, but some of them were beyond my ability. Since calling Sunshine's mother seemed to work, I decided to try calling other parents. The first one seemed annoyed that I disturbed him. After my detailed account of how his son, "Eric," wouldn't listen, wouldn't stay in his seat and continually disrupted class, he told me to tell him that he'd take his PlayStation away. Eric took this for the empty threat it was and continued to bounce off the walls. In addition to being kind of hyper, Eric was also very bright. I doubt the class challenged him at all. So I tried making him my assistant. While he was at the blackboard helping me or working with another kid, he was great. As soon as I gave another student a turn at being the assistant, Eric, once again, became a problem.

Then, there was the "Wolfman," who was worse today than he had been the day before. And yesterday, he was literally howling at the ceiling. (I must admit, this weirded me out a bit.) Wolfman's hair was a mass of messy twists. His clothes were dirty. And he constantly argued and fought with the other kids. His desk was over four feet away from the other students (a huge red flag) and again, there was the howling thing. I left three messages for his mother: at work, at home and at his grandmother's. Not one was returned. In the meantime, I rose above my apprehension and kept his butt after school.

Next on my top-ten list was a child I'll refer to as "Lonesome Lauren." Every single number in her file was wrong or disconnected. I knew she was in the foster care system, but someone had to be responsible for her. She was a bright kid, but only did her class work when she felt like it. She wouldn't talk to me at all. She also didn't get along with the other kids. Being shuffled around from home to home probably didn't make for a happy-go-lucky kid, but Lauren was just straight-up mean.

Though no one explained exactly what the problem was, several people, including the counselor, warned me about a boy named "Daniel" who showed up on my second day. He seemed harmless; a little awkward, but bright. He struggled a little with his work not because of a lack of ability, but because, like so many kids in public school, he hadn't been taught. Daniel's speech, his clothes—everything seemed to be from some earlier time period, like the 1950s. He wore very neat and clean pants and shoes, not sneakers and jeans. His hair was cut close and I think he had a vest on over his button-down oxford. He enunciated when he spoke, as though English were his second language, though, I was pretty certain he was American. He also behaved fairly well though he was obsessed with calculators and had at least three. I thought perhaps people were overstating this boy's problems, but even older students passing him in the hallways referred to him as "that crazy boy." I wouldn't be totally surprised if one day he turned out to be a brilliant success or, if I believed everyone else, a bomb-toting mass murderer. His educational experience could very well be the deciding factor.

Mrs. Hammond took two of my students to the principal's office to call their parents. And, still, I had to send a few kids back to Mrs. Jones. I rationalized my decision as a choice to focus on teaching, instead of discipline, but the truth is I just couldn't handle all of these kids at once. Thirty fairly well-behaved kids are a challenge. These children were ridiculous. We weren't getting anything done. So I walked three of the boys, including Eric, down the hall.

The thing that struck me first about Mrs. Jones' class was that it was quiet. Second, she was sitting down. Third, the kids were working. Sure, part of it was that her kids were older, more mature; but they also probably had a healthy respect for the fact that this woman just might jack them up.

I asked if a couple of my kids could stay with her for a while.

"Sure," she said, barely looking up. She waved the boys over to the side of the room where they had to stand. I wasn't sure if this was cruel or appropriate. After all, the point was for them to have less fun than they seemed to be having in my class so they'd behave when they returned. I watched as they silently lined up.

"Thank you," I said.

She looked up. "I'll do better today," she said softly.

Yeah, she choked that kid. I nodded and turned to exit, glancing at the boys who were sporting their best puppy-dog looks. Part of me felt guilty as sin leaving them with her. The other part of me felt sad and frustrated that they wouldn't behave for me. I left them with her for about an hour. When I brought them back, they had calmed down considerably. Probably just happy to sit down.

I spoke to every parent who came to pick up a kid; I sent messages home through siblings; and I kept students after school—Wolfman for 45 minutes. When the other kids started leaving, suddenly, the kids who'd been acting up all day, weren't so tough and the tears started flowing. At P.S. #2, when Cliffortin cried because I put his name on the board for "being bad," I wanted to cry, too. Today, I was unmoved. If these kids don't develop some kind of discipline now, it'll just be that much tougher for them later. I told them to tell their parents they might have detention again the next day.

At the end of the day, I walked out with Mrs. Jones. I felt like I should say something, but what? "Don't choke any more kids." She didn't need me to tell her that. She knew. So we talked about controlling the classroom.

"When kids act up in my room, I call their parents. I tell them they have to come sit with them in the class. The kids straighten up fast. The administration doesn't like it, but I don't care," she said.

Could teachers really make parents come sit in the classrooms to watch their kids? I don't know but if this practice is instituted District wide, that'd be a lot of parents missing work. Or, a lot of kids getting their acts together real fast.

All and all, it wasn't a horrible day. At least no one had accused me of choking anyone.

January 25, 2002 (Day 12 of 21)
Third day at P.S. #7

I couldn't sleep, again, last night. Woke up at four a.m. trying to figure out which seats I could change to gain more control over the class and never fell back to sleep. Surprisingly, the children were enthusiastic about the changes. So I moved them around like little chess pieces, trying to hit upon just the right arrangement. I wanted it to be about learning, not who's acting up or hitting or talking. The changes were moderately successful, but I knew, with some students, the only thing that would help would be moving them out of the room altogether.

The day was long, made even longer by the fact that all of the sixth-grade teachers called out. All of them. Art, gym and classes of this nature were cancelled because those folks had to cover for the AWOL teachers. That meant no free periods for anybody. The little kids in my room were supposed to have "literature." I'm not sure how that's different from reading, but that's what we had instead.

I chose a play and gave out parts. Most of the kids loved it, including the follow-up Q & A. Sunshine couldn't follow at all, even when I stood right next to her and pointed to where we were in the story. The words on the page held so little meaning for her that it was painful to watch. I inquired several times about the testing she was supposed to receive, but no one could tell me when they would get to it.

As I ate my lunch in silence, I felt like it was nearly midnight though it was only 10:30 in the morning. The middle-aged man across the table intermittently stared, a smile dancing around the edges of his mouth.

"You the sub that choked the girl?" he finally asked.

"I didn't choke that girl!" I spit out.

He laughed, said he knew I hadn't.

"Is that what people are saying about me?" I asked.

"No," he reassured me, "they tell the whole story of how it was you, then another and another." He shook his head, gathered his things.

Did I need this? When he left, I put my head down and closed my eyes. I felt the way the other third-grade teacher looked yesterday: beat up and disgusted. The Sunshine situation really bothered me. When Mrs. Hammond and I finally spoke about it, she didn't have much to say other than warning me to protect myself.

"If I'm with a student outside of normal class times," she confided, "I keep my door open and I'm visible from the hall."

I thought back to working with Sunshine on reading during my free period and keeping Wolfman 45 minutes after school the day before. I guess he could have made up something about me, too. I took a deep breath and went to pick up the kids.

One of the lunchroom monitors directed me to pick up one of my kids from the waiting room. He had spit milk through a straw at another student. It turned out to be "Narada", a smart, sweet kid I liked a lot. He told me that it had been an accident. Maybe it was an accident; maybe it wasn't. It certainly wasn't malicious. It was something a kid would do. Tearing up, Narada told me he apologized to Wolfman. I gave him a little hug and told him to come on. As we passed the other third-grade teacher, I asked how she was. She punctuated her shell-shocked glare with a shrug. Truly, I felt her pain.

Narada and I arrived just in time to see Wolfman preparing to fight a student from another room. All of the other boys were gathered around cheering him on. Wolfman was bobbing and weaving for his fans. Two other boys were jumping in, slapping at the other kid, then jumping back behind Wolfman. I told them to break it up, which the kids in my class were quite willing to do. But the other boy was furious. He kept trying to get around me to get to Wolfman. I called to another teacher for assistance.

"Let them fight and get suspended," she yelled back.

I instructed Wolfman to return to the classroom and put my arm tightly around "Angry Boy." As I guided him across the yard to his class, I asked if he noticed all of those boys surrounding him. "You were about to get beat up."

"Do you know how many times I've been beat up?" he asked. "I don't care. I'm sick of it!"

As we reached his teacher, I explained what was going on. I expected her to take over, talk to him or something.

"Let him fight and get suspended," she replied.

Angry Boy pulled away from me, snatched off his jacket and ran back across the yard toward my class. I ran after him, yelling for my students to go in. They started moving in along with a couple of other classes. Angry Boy pushed through the crowd, hunting Wolfman down. I sent Narada to get the security officer. In retrospect, how bad could the fight have been? They were only third-graders. But I could feel the fury coming off of that boy. I really thought he might hurt Wolfman. Luckily, security arrived and dragged Angry Boy off somewhere.

When I arrived at the room, Wolfman was waiting outside, leaned up against the door.

"You are so lucky you listened to me for once, or you'd be with security right now, too," I said.

He grinned in response, as the boys explained that Angry Boy had hit one of their smaller (and more obnoxious) classmates. Wolfman had stepped in to protect him. I felt kind of proud of him but I still gave the violence-is-not-acceptable speech. Oddly, Wolfman was better today. Though his mother hadn't returned my calls, his hair was combed, his clothes were neat and clean and he was engaged. Every five seconds he was waving his hand in my face to read or go to the board. He was still talking a little too much, but he wasn't howling. I counted that as progress.

Getting back to work, I sent five students to the board to write down the continents. Two of them almost had all seven spelled correctly. The rest had five or six of them (that damned Antarctica.) We went over them again, then I sprung a quiz on them. They were surprised and excited. I gave out paper, moved desks, moved students, and personally invited half the class to remove stuff like calculators and textbooks from their desks. They never completely quieted down. They talked to me, to their neighbors. How come they don't know proper procedures for taking a quiz? What has their teacher been doing?

I put five math problems on the board, instructing them to copy all of them down before attempting to solve them. When I erased them, half the class cheered. The other half groaned. Most of them had ignored my instructions, but were fast enough to get the problems done. The others...oh well. As I was about to erase the next set of problems, Wolfman begged me to wait. I told him I'd give him ten seconds and started counting down, "10, 9, 8..." The whole class decided to join in loudly, "7! 6! 5!.." I couldn't believe how raucous they were. At least they were enthusiastic. Wolfman finished copying the problems a half-second before I erased them.

I was having fun. The kids were having fun. They were working and learning...then it happened. Someone had a calculator. I specifically told them "no calculators." I marked an "F" on the girl's paper and took it. (Too harsh? I hate cheating.) She boo-hooed; I mean she wailed. Had I known she'd carry on like that, I would have waited until the end of the class to put an F on it. My bad.

I called the office, and they assured me they would send someone to retrieve her. They didn't. By the time I called back, two others had been caught cheating: one copying the continents from his notebook, another looking up vocabulary words in the textbook—F and F again. They all vehemently proclaimed their innocence. (Didn't they see these coke bottles I was wearing on my face? I saw them cheating.) They cried, protested, ran around the room. Finally, I made the three cheaters stand in the hallway where I could see them. The others finished the quiz, but they were worked up and distracted.

I needed a few minutes to deal with the cheaters who, of course, were doing summersaults in the hallway. I assigned independent reading to the rest of the class, which meant they read out loud to themselves. All 30 of them. At once. It was maddening. And it sounded so much like talking, that after a while I guess they figured they might as well talk. So we had to stop that all together.

I was really annoyed with all of them, except the four kids who had been consistently well behaved for the last three days. I decided instead of pointing out who was misbehaving, I'd reinforce the good behavior. I invited the Fab Four to the back of the room to color. The rest I invited to get their readers out to do some work. Of course, they were upset about this turn of events but that was the point. Unfortunately, I chose a boring story. So once a student had a turn at reading, he or she went back to complaining about what we were doing. We finished the story, but they didn't make it easy for me.

The cheaters were still acting up in the hallway. Finally, I took them to the office myself. I was gone for three minutes and when I returned, there were three fights in progress. Daniel was chasing Lonesome Lauren because she slapped him in the face twice for accidentally bumping into her. He was furious, literally shaking with anger. Luckily for Lauren, her legs were much longer and she was able to stay ahead of him. He stopped chasing her when I intervened, but he continued to shake and fume.

Sunshine was trading punches with a boy whom she'd called a "f****t." He responded by punching her in the face. And the girl who had supplied the calculator to the cheater was outed. Seems others were outraged that she had been given the opportunity to color when she had aided and abetted. I was so disappointed; she was one of the best-behaved students in the class.

Somewhere around here, two security officers wandered by. I flagged them down, asked if they'd take the brawlers to the office. They took them all except Daniel, whom they escorted straight to the counselor's office.

The last three days had been...ridiculous. Since my time at P.S. #7 was coming to an end, I thought a conversation seemed to be in order. I told the kids straight out that they were considered one of the worst classes in the entire school. I thought they might be shocked.

Immediately (and somewhat unanimously), they responded, "It's the teachers."

There was one lone voice of reason among them. She was an incessant talker (her mother asked me what to do about this) but honest, "No, it's our behavior."

This admission brought forth a storm of candor. They knew they should do better; they just didn't.

I had stayed on these kids; constantly making them straighten up, behave, and participate. I spoke to parents—sometimes twice. And still, I had to have detention on my last day. One of the few students who showed remorse was the girl who had lent one of the cheaters a calculator. She was really a great a kid: well-behaved, polite, obviously smart, which is why the other kids picked on her. Though people like to pretend it's a "black thing," being really smart is not popular among a high percentage of Americans. She'll need the appropriate guidance to nurture her intellect and withstand the impending punishment from society at large as she matures. The sooner she puts this thing into perspective, the better. I wiped her tears, encouraged her not to allow herself to be dragged into other people's nonsense just to be liked and sent her on her way.

As I was dismissing the last of the students, the vice principal stopped by to tell me he called the parents of the kids who were fighting and told them they had to return with their kids on Monday. Then he asked me to stop by on my way out.

"Who'd I choke now?" I thought, but when I reached his office, he told me I was doing a great job and that he was pleased that I'd done work with the kids, instead of just playing games. I asked if he wanted me to mark the quizzes and send them back. He said no, but he wanted me to come back. I assumed he meant with the same class; and surprisingly, I was totally up for it. I really liked those little kids.

"We'll definitely have openings in sixth. One until June," he informed me.

I asked him if this was the sixth grade where all of the teachers had just stopped coming to work. He was surprised that I knew about this. He resorted to flirting; promised to support me, suspend students, if necessary. I thanked him for dealing with the fighters, but told him I wasn't certain that I'd want to come back to work with the sixth graders. I asked about the third-graders again.

"We're not sure what's going to happen there." He buttered me up some more, introducing me to the high school principal and vice principal. I thanked him and told him I'd think about it and maybe show up on Monday.

Sunday, January 27, 2002

My heart was racing and my head had been pounding all weekend. I wouldn't hesitate if it were for the third-graders, headaches, racing heart and all. If I had the time to work with those kids, figure out what they should be doing, I think I could help. But older, bigger kids that have already chased off their regular teachers? I don't think I can do it.

Monday, January 28, 2002

I didn't go. I went to the doctor. It's not my blood pressure but my heart rate is "speeding up and strong," according to my excessively thorough doctor. He's not sure about the headaches.

"My guess?" he said. "You hate your job."

It's not even a regular, full-time gig. How can it be affecting my health so dramatically? I feel so bad for teachers in the inner city. That's why they're calling out or walking out. They're probably sick or looking for other jobs or both. The only teachers who say they love teaching are the ones who don't teach full-time. They're in administration, teaching only a few classes or none at all. Or, they teach in the suburbs or at Catholic and private schools.

I don't think I'm going tomorrow either. I'm exhausted. I'm not sleeping. And I'm not actually making enough to cover my bills. Substitute teaching is the hardest job I've ever had. The only job I've ever had that paid less was working at Roy Rogers. I bet they're paying more these days.

Tuesday, January 29, 2002

Nora's back from Italy. She said the reason I've been having headaches is that I care. "If you really want to teach and want the kids to learn, it's upsetting," she commiserated. "That's why I had to go to Italy...to recuperate from subbing."

I decided to brush up on my copywriting skills and sign up with an employment agency. Clearly, teaching is not a long-term option for me. I called P.S. #7 to let them know I wouldn't be returning, but I couldn't get a human on the phone, much less the vice principal. I left a message. Moving on.

P.S. #7: PERCENTAGE OF 5th-GRADERS
SCORING BELOW BASIC:[*2,3]

2000–2001

Math } 64%   Reading } 60%

---

* Percentages are rounded.

> "Public School #8"

February 5, 2002 (Day 13 of 21)

Kindergarten to 5th Grade: Approximately 300 students: 96.1% African American; 0% Asian; 3.5% Latino; 0.3% White; 0% Other.[1]

*J*think I've had enough. Subbing has to be the most thankless job in America. I've been lamenting the plight of teachers, how underpaid, overburdened and unappreciated they are; how they're expected to work miracles under impossible circumstances. Today, I feel bad for the subs. I feel bad for me.

Again, I was in for an art teacher (do these people ever go to work?) at a school in the heart of North Philly (one of the most economically depressed areas of Philadelphia) near Temple University. I had been on the hunt for a progressive, little inner-city school with dedicated, happy teachers and well-educated, enthusiastic children. When I first walked into P.S. #8, I thought maybe I'd struck pay dirt. The school was old, but well kept. Children said, "Good morning." Teachers smiled. The Coordinator, an older, white man in a bow tie who called to mind the word "headmaster," greeted me, signed me in, prepped me and escorted me to class. No request for an I.D., but other than that, he was batting a thousand.

The hallways were decorated with bright, interesting art projects created by the students. The art room was big and messy; every inch jammed with books on Picasso and quilt making, works of famous artists and student projects in various states of completion. At least this art teacher did something when she was there.

As usual, there were no emergency lesson plans. Since Valentine's Day was approaching, I decided cards were in order. Most of the kids quickly put together something for their parents or grandparents, while a few romantic souls decided to capitalize on the spirit of the day. They didn't play games or try to be cool; they liked whom they liked and didn't like whom they didn't like. Still, offering up a carefully crafted, heart-shaped pledge of love in no way guaranteed that it would be accepted. I did, however, encourage the kids to at least be polite about it.

The special ed. classes moved along very quickly. There were only eight students in one class and four in the other. They focused and finished up, leaving me enough time to read them several stories. The second graders were rambunctious and talkative, but they got the work done. As I walked them to the cafeteria, they took off running. By the time they reached the lunchroom door, they were in trouble. One thing I'll say, the faculty and staff at this school stayed on top of the kids. I overheard a woman in the office talking on the phone with a parent. She was explaining that the principal wanted to discuss the child's attendance record.

"We don't have that kind of problem with the students here," she commented matter-of-factly.

And this was a first. All of the teachers and students have lunch at the same time. The lounge is filled with long tables that seat ten or more people at once. On the whole, the teachers seemed happy. They laughed and joked with each other, told stories about the kids. It felt like a community.

There were some minor gripes about administration, but the only real point of contention seemed to be that the younger teachers have been busting their butts for certification and the older teachers didn't have to take the exam. So there was a little resentment. "Some of these older teachers are not qualified," stated one of the younger teachers and not so quietly. "The exam should be retroactive."

She was probably right; however, there seemed to be a more pressing issue— out-of-control children with emotional and behavioral problems. It'd be much easier to evaluate teachers if the classrooms were under control.

Another nice thing they instituted at P.S. #8 was a program called Drop Everything And Read (DEAR). From 12:30 to 1:00 p.m., every day, that's exactly what they did. Pretty cool. For a half an hour, every kid in the school is engaged in silent reading...unlike at P.S. #7, where all the kids read out loud, at the top of their lungs, all at once.

My next class was a bunch of rowdy kindergarteners with four or five boys who were more interested in making war instead of love. They wanted to box. I called their teacher and told her to come get them. (She offered. I took her up on it.) The rest of the class made it through the assignment just fine. Afterwards, I was enjoying a free period when "the Headmaster/Coordinator" rushed in.

"You're supposed to be covering 306. Didn't anyone tell you?" he asked. (Wasn't that his job?)

"No," I said, dropping everything. I followed him across the hall to a mixed fourth and fifth grade class being taught by a student teacher ("Little Teach") from Drexel University. The Headmaster explained that since the regular teacher wasn't there, I would be the "official representative of the School District." I chuckled.

The class was supposed to be working on ongoing Junior Achievement projects. At a quick glance, they seemed to be having recess.

"So I just support her?"

"Yeah," he said before leaving. "Just be in the room."

Turned out "just being in the room" wasn't easy. The kids were so rude to this young woman. I didn't want to step on her learning experience, but I also couldn't sit by and watch her be tortured. At first, I tried unobtrusively quieting the students; but that didn't work.

Each student was supposed to give a report, but the class was so noisy we couldn't hear the girl who was speaking. She looked pleadingly toward Little Teach, who lectured the children about courtesy. They responded by ignoring her and trying to strike up conversations with me.

"So what are we going to do in art?"

I don't know how they know, but the kids always know which teachers are in and which are out.

Somewhere in here, Little Teach's supervisor "Big Teach" snuck in. She nodded in my direction, letting me know that she'd be observing. I nodded back. Seemed to be the polite thing to do. Within minutes, she turned to me aghast. Before she could say a word, I made it clear that I had just met these kids. I wasn't letting them run amok. They were ignoring me, too. The student giving the presentation stopped yet again.

"You are being rude," she told her classmates. "And I don't appreciate it." Her plea went unheeded.

Big Teach stood and walked to the front of the room, sporting her best "I'll-straighten-this-out" expression. This woman probably had a Ph.D. in education. She teaches the teachers. I sat back, ready to watch and learn. Unfortunately, the kids quieted for a few minutes to hear what the "new lady" had to say, then went right back to business as usual. I'm not sure how to appropriately describe the look on her face, but "as though she'd been smacked" probably comes closest. In my estimation, we had two options: keep stopping periodically to quiet them or shut the class down all together. But then the students who are behaving lose out. So, as the only black adult in a room full of black students, I stood.

"*That* is enough. Quiet down and pay attention."

It worked. They shut their mouths and I cued the student to finish her presentation. In the meantime, I also confiscated the remaining icebreaker puzzles some of them were still working on. Big Teach and I continued to tag-team the discipline: she stayed on top of the class overall; I dealt with individual students. And Little Teach struggled through the presentation portion of our show. Somehow, we hobbled through and most of the students had a chance to present.

There was one young man, a truly special case, who continued to laugh, talk, etc. When I asked him to be quiet, he claimed to have a headache.

"There's a note that says I can go to the nurse whenever I want." And he wanted to go right then.

I asked Little Teach if she knew anything about a note. She did not. I asked "Mr. Special" to wait until after class like the other students.

"But I can go anytime I want. Because of the headaches," he insisted.

The more I tried to quiet him, the louder he became. Since my presence seemed to be egging him on, I walked away. He proceeded to talk to me from across the room with no regard for the fact that class was still in session.

"So what's up? I can't go?" he pressed.

"You wanted people to be quiet while you were giving your presentation, shouldn't you do the same for them?" I whispered.

He became more insistent, practically shouting across the room. I looked to the other two teachers who seemed to be waiting for me to "do something." Exactly what I had no idea, but then I remembered something Nora had told me.

"Sometimes," she said, "when I'm dealing with a really bratty kid who won't listen and won't be quiet, I walk over to him and whisper in his ear, 'You are pissing me off. You better get it together.'"

What the heck? I walked over, whispered that in his ear and walked away. It sort of worked. He stopped shouting to me across the room, downgrading instead to mouthing that his head hurt, and gesturing for me to write out a hall pass. I was about to do it when I thought to check with the office. No one knew anything about a note. I explained that he had been behaving very poorly and sending him to the nurse seemed like rewarding him for bad behavior, especially since he hadn't mentioned this headache until I asked him to stop interrupting the class.

"Oh," she said. "We'll send someone up."

I glanced toward Mr. Special who mouthed, "What's the hold up?" He was rather surprised when the Headmaster showed up and escorted him from the room.

By the end of the period, Big and Little Teach were both shell-shocked and shaking their heads. They thanked me for helping and wished me "good luck" with an implied, "you're going to need it" before leaving.

I was really embarrassed that the children had behaved as they did, especially since I knew they knew better. They may have jeopardized the relationship this school has with a major university. Not to mention the young student teacher. She'll graduate and go on to teach but, based on this experience, perhaps not at P.S. #8 or any other inner-city school. And who could blame her?

Quite a few of the students were also upset and embarrassed and they said so, to no avail. (I'm convinced that positive peer pressure is a myth.) The other kids were ready to move on to art like nothing at all had happened.

"You embarrassed yourselves and me. Clearly, you have no respect for teachers and little regard for your education, do you think you deserve to have art?"

The kids who had behaved well, said no and the Loud & Rowdies, of course, said "yes."

Some of them shrugged it off; others thought I should cancel art. But one of the more courteous kids stood up and said that they didn't always act this way and she was mad because the people who were trying to work are being punished, too.

"We're sick of missing out," she said.

"It's not fair," others chimed in.

I was tempted to give them my mother's old standby, "Life isn't fair." Just so that little fact doesn't catch them off guard later. But the truth is life could easily be more fair, especially if people would get on board with the concept. I started writing the names of the L&Rs on the board. Usually, this move accomplished absolutely nothing, but I had to do something. As I wrote each name, the corresponding student laughed, feigned surprise or acknowledged that he or she had behaved poorly.

"Yeah, I was buggin.'"

They knew. Out of all of them, only one kid claimed to be innocent and he was one of the worst offenders.

A teacher I had chatted with during lunch overheard this discussion and stopped in to see what was going on. When I told her how they had behaved, she dressed them down and gave lunch detention to the students whose names were on the board. That bothered them a little. What bothered them a lot was finding out that they really wouldn't be having art. They were outraged, while the well-behaved kids were deliriously happy. For all the backtalk, the Rowdies were still kids and they were upset about missing out. Some complained. Some moped. Others cut hearts out of notebook paper, but it just wasn't the same. I had red paper and colored markers. Everybody likes colored markers.

"Mr. Innocent" was beside himself. He tried to provoke an argument. I ignored him. He angrily paced the floor. I asked him to have a seat. He tried to sneak art supplies. I got to them first. He told me he was leaving. I told him to sit down. He claimed he was a safety and had permission to leave early. The other kids busted him and the real safety left. Mr. Innocent started to walk past me anyway. I held out my arm and asked again that he take his seat. He smacked my arm down (which surprised me), then took a seat. By this point, I was tired and didn't feel like dealing with this; however, what kind of example does it set to let something like that slide?

"I'm going to report you to the principal."

"I don't care! You were picking on me... blah, blah."

As the kids lined up to walk out, two teachers passed by. I let them know what had happened and straight away they took the boy to the office. After I walked the other kids to the door, I headed to the office. By the time I arrived, that little jerk had claimed he hit me but "only in self-defense."

"She hit me first. I only hit her to get her off me." He actually repeated that nonsense to my face: "...to get her off me." He's buggin' was my first thought; then I realized no, he's just malicious. This time I wasn't shocked or hurt, I was angry. I actually had to give a statement. The security guard filled out an incident report and asked if I wanted to press charges. It would serve him right if I did, but as angry as I was, I couldn't do it. That's all he needs is to get caught up in the criminal justice system before he reaches high school. It's all over after that. Suddenly, I felt very sad.

The principal, a middle-aged African American woman dressed in a sporty jogging suit, was as supportive as she could be considering that she didn't know me from a can of paint. She said she had to investigate, talk to the other kids, which I understood. She did, however, suspend Mr. Innocent for three days. After she sent him home, we called his mother who said normally she'd take a teacher's word over his, but since I was "just a sub," she wouldn't take my word. Not the slightest bit ruffled, the principal told her that she would see her for a meeting on Friday. She sat back in her chair, sizing me up.

"The other young man the Coordinator removed from your class—did you tell him he was pissing you off? she asked.

"Yes," I said. "He was."

She chuckled softly. "Don't do that. He's very verbal. He'll tell his mother and she'll be up here complaining."

Honestly, I didn't care whose mother did what, but I nodded that I understood, even though what I really wanted to say is "for two cents, I'd tape his mouth shut."

She went on to tell me that the two boys I had run-ins with were not representative of P.S. #8. She suggested that I stop by the auditorium to listen to the school choir rehearse. As she walked me out of her office, I asked that she let me know what her investigation turned up. She agreed and also encouraged me to come back another time to sub.

"And that kid will be right here when you do come back," commented the security guard as the principal disappeared into her office. "He's always in trouble. But when parents are in denial, and 'others' (she nodded toward the principal's office) well...he'll be here."

She was right—if not the kid who hit me, another just as bad. Seems no matter where I go, there they are: these troubled and/or malicious kids who hold everyone back.

I peeked in on choir rehearsal for a few minutes, but I can't remember if they were good or not. They could have sounded like angels. I didn't care. I was sick of subbing. It was time to start looking for another job. In the meantime, I called into HERBS and forced myself to take another assignment. Sister Joan had mentioned the principal at P.S. #9 to me once before—said she seemed to be very good. We'll see.

P.S. #8: PERCENTAGE OF 5th-GRADERS
SCORING BELOW BASIC:[2,3]

2000–2001

Math } 62%   Reading } 67%

---

* Percentages are rounded.

> "Public School #9"

Kindergarten to Fifth Grade: Approximately 600 students: 98.8% African American; 0.2% Asian; 0.5% Latino; 0.3 White; 0.2% Other.[1]

J've tried to make sense of everything. Tried to look at my life and the experiences and opportunities I've been fortunate enough to have and figure out how to give back. That's what this whole subbing thing was about… but it's beating me down. The possibility that I'll get certified becomes slimmer and slimmer with each assignment.

Today, I'm at a school Sr. Joan from St. A's recommended. She met the principal at a conference and discovered they had very similar educational philosophies.

"I've never visited [P.S. #9] but perhaps you'll have a better experience at this public school."

I wanted to meet this woman who had impressed Sr. Joan. And I wanted to see the school I would have attended if my mother hadn't sent me to St. A's. So when the call came to sub for a science teacher at P.S. #9, I jumped at it. Frankly, I was relieved not to be subbing in art. I was beginning to question its value to kids who haven't mastered the fundamentals of reading, writing and math. If I had my way, I'd probably swap it (and music) for extra math and reading classes, especially in elementary schools where kids are struggling. Kind of ironic considering how much I love art and music. The first thing I ever wanted to be was an artist, however, my mother generously pointed out the obvious, "You can't draw, Clayvon." I was crushed, but she may have been right. Though I still think her opinion was based on her decision that I would become a doctor.

I arrived at P.S. #9 to find an unassuming, middle-aged white woman alone in the main office, answering phones and preparing for the day. She had almost finished checking me in before I realized she was the principal. Like Sr. Joan, she seemed no nonsense and determined, minus the air of serenity. Very matter of factly, she admitted P.S. #9 had a huge discipline challenge. She also warned me that my first class was "a handful." Apparently, the last sub had some difficulty keeping it, as well as the rest of the classes, under control.

"He let the kids get away with things," she said, implying that "things" had snowballed into "bad stuff." Without a word, he dropped the assignment. Probably because he was expecting to teach, not yell at kids all day long. I kept thinking back to P.S. #7. It took three days for me to start to calm down the big troublemakers, only to have three others sprout in their places. My expectations were pretty low. The principal cautioned me to be tough but call if I had any problems. Did I have problems? Of course. Was I overwhelmed? No. Any over-the-top problem students? Oh yeah. Any well-behaved kids? Quite a few. Outrageous incidents? One.

"The girls are good. The boys...they can be rough," the first homeroom teacher warned me. (I now understand that "rough" is code for violent.) The students filed in noisily behind the teacher with an NTA (non-teaching assistant) bringing up the rear. I'm always happy to see an NTA. And since I'd been warned twice about this class, I was particularly grateful to see her. NTAs lay down the law; they're the discipline in the room. But this woman timidly discouraged the students from misbehaving and steered way clear of the more problematic kids. "Maybe she's new," I thought.

There were specific instructions on the day's lessons. We began with a story about water conservation. I asked for a volunteer and told her she could pick the next reader. The room erupted in protests.

"The girls won't pick us," said one boy.

"We won't ever get a turn," complained another.

At least they wanted turns. And since the girls didn't deny these accusations, I made an addendum: the girls had to pick boys and vice versa. We made it through the story though we had to stop several times because of excessive chatter. After a short Q&A, we moved on to two pages of notes. I asked for two volunteers to give out the notebooks. Hands shot up. In keeping with the theme of fairness, I intended to pick one boy and one girl. I chose a boy and was about to choose a girl when I noticed a young man quietly and politely raising his hand to help. In a room full of children yelling, "Oo-oo! Me! Meee!" he stood out. His clothes and hair were neat. He wore cute little glasses. He looked like the model student. Obviously, he hadn't been causing any trouble because this was the first time I'd noticed him. So I chose him. (Later, I realized he'd been with his homeroom teacher for the first 20 minutes of class doing some kind of reading evaluation and had come in late.)

The two boys rose efficiently to begin distribution of the notebooks. Everything seemed to be under control, except for one young man who was roaming all over the room, making odd noises and becoming a bigger and bigger distraction. Without fail, the NTA avoided him.

Thinking she could at least watch the rest of the students for two minutes, I pulled "Wandering Boy" aside to calm him down. I noticed that the noise level jumped a bit when I turned away but I also heard the NTA asking the students to quiet down. Unfortunately, several kids immediately charged the two boys distributing the notebooks "to help." I turned back just in time to see the first boy in a tug-of-war with another kid and "Mr. Quiet and Polite" using one of the notebooks to smack the girl who was raiding his stack in the face so hard, he knocked her down.

I witnessed this myself and still couldn't believe it. The NTA seemed to be frozen in place. The two boys stopped in mid tug of war to gawk in amazement. I grabbed Mr. Quiet and Polite who was standing over the girl, clenching and unclenching his fists. The girl scrambled back to her seat, put her head down and cried. I looked to the NTA who finally snapped out of it and checked to see if the girl was okay.

Pulling the boy away, I could feel his heart beating furiously. He had gone from zero to livid in 10 seconds. Clearly, there was a problem here, yet no one had mentioned it. I understand not wanting to stigmatize a child but let a sub know! Damn. The other students were staring and commenting. Mr. Quiet and Polite was so upset, I was unsure how he might respond or how long he'd let me hold on to him. I hushed the other children and moved the boy around the corner, out of sight. He seemed...not calm but contained. I told him to stay right where he was, then I let go. He stood silent, his eyes lowered to the floor. As I picked up the phone to call the office, he abruptly stomped off down the hall back to his homeroom teacher. Who knows what he told her? But she came quickly, the principal not far behind. The kids, the NTA and I explained what had happened.

"He was fine next door with me," was his teacher's only comment.

Yeah, most kids are fine one on one. "How about a little warning!?" I wanted to scream at her. "The boys can be rough does not cover it." The girl seemed to be okay but said she had a headache. While the other teacher walked her to the nurse, the principal said she'd take Mr. Quiet and Polite...somewhere. To the accommodation room? Her office? How about home? Or, to therapy?

Just last week, an incident like this would have really rattled me. Not now. Once I knew the girl was okay and the boy had been removed, I continued the lesson unfazed. Perhaps, it's a matter of experience. Or, perhaps, I'm hardening. Can apathy be far behind? I started putting notes on the board. The kids were suffering from residual hype. They could barely focus. So I made it a race—practically erasing the notes before they could take them down. Kids like games so they dove right in. Must they always be tricked or cajoled? What happened to learning because that's your job as a student?

The principal figured I could use a little more support so another NTA showed up for the last 10 minutes of class. She parked herself in a chair and argued loudly with the kids who wouldn't stay in their seats. She was almost more of a hindrance than a help. At the end of class, I asked the first NTA if the kids were always like this.

"Always," she said. "The teacher wants more parents to come up."

She was a parent—not an NTA. That explained a lot. Like why she seemed to be in shock. She was. And why a lot of the kids didn't listen to her. She was So & So's mommy, and though that kept So & So under control, it didn't mean a thing to the rest of the students.

I hustled off to the auditorium to pick up my next class and found the principal near the back, keeping a watchful eye on things. She pointed out the fifth graders. Observing them for a few minutes, I could already tell which of them would be trouble. One young lady in particular exhibited a blatant disregard for the adults in the room. She didn't lower her voice though she wasn't supposed to be talking at all. And she encouraged other students to act up. I figured we were headed for a run-in; however, the vice principal, a hard-edged, no-nonsense man, offered to walk the students up with me and get them settled. As he marched them along, "Trouble Woman" refused to walk quietly or in line, so he sent her to his office. Problem solved.

Once the kids were settled in the classroom, he cautioned them to behave. Then, he left. They were a little rowdy and everything seemed to be a joke to them, but they were okay. These kids were about to graduate, most likely to a public middle school where it'll be very difficult to "incidentally" get a good education. And they don't have a clue. I was about to administer a practice standardized test when I discovered that there weren't enough test booklets. They didn't want to do any work anyway, insisting that the other subs just let them play games. They had been complaining for over 40 minutes and we still had almost an hour to go. I stopped the lesson.

"What do you want to do in life?" I asked.

"What?" came the response, along with a bunch of blank stares.

"What do you want to do?" I asked again.

"Not teach," came a bold response. "No offense, but teachers don't make any money."

I explained that I was there because I wanted to help. "That's why most people teach. And you look down on us because we make this sacrifice to help you?" Since they were momentarily silent, I kept talking, trying to make the link between good teachers, a good education, good jobs and a better life. What I was saying was so obvious, yet they weren't buying it...not until I told them I had written for television and connected doing well in school with having more opportunities. I gave them the spiel, the extended version. I told them where I had gone to school and what kinds of grades I had gotten. I told them about all the jobs I'd had from cashier and public relations manager to administrative assistant and TV writer. I told them about the shows I'd worked on or freelanced for, as well as about all the ones that had rejected me.

"You wrote for *Living Single?*" came the first skeptical question. I nodded.

"Which ones did you write?" asked another.

Not really expecting the kids to remember them (since they were about five when the show originally aired), I described my episodes. Not only did they remember my episodes, they informed me that one had been on last night (the magic of reruns). They got so excited. Questions were flying at me. How much money did you make? Which characters did you write for? Do you know Queen Latifah? We talked about working in fast food restaurants vs. corporate America, about student loans and how much I still owed, the importance of good credit and some of their own aspirations to be artists or rappers. As we were winding down, it still seemed that they were too caught up in the glamour aspect of entertainment. Again, I stressed that it's not all flashy cars and big houses, and that most people don't hit the mega big time.

"You work your butt off," I told them. "The hours can be horrific. It's very cut throat. You're employed one minute and the next you're not. And everybody... everybody is smart."

What did they do? They started clapping, which was certainly not the reaction I expected to my cautionary tale. I stood there just looking at them, not knowing what to say. Class was over so I dismissed them, but they gathered around me insisting that I sign autographs.

"I'm not special. I'm just like you. I grew up in this neighborhood." They made me sign anyway. It was ridiculous but, for once, I felt like maybe I had actually reached them.

Word of my brush with the glam life spread. On my way to pick up my last class, kids were whispering, staring and smiling at me. I felt rather conspicuous, like I had toilet paper stuck to the bottom of my shoe. In truth, I knew they were according me a certain respect based on the perceived importance of show biz. It was ridiculous that what I'd said was more valid because of it. Kids need to know how to read, write and count because these skills will help them take care of themselves and their families...not because of the promise of the bling. I did well in school because my mother expected me to do well. So did my teachers. And, therefore, so did I.

As soon as I hit the schoolyard that afternoon, I was greeted with, "I hear you're famous." I turned to find the no-nonsense vice principal smirking at me. Feeling a little silly, I tried to explain that I wasn't famous; I was just trying to make the connection between the importance of learning as much as possible and being successful later in life. Once I said the words "used to write for TV," he glazed over. I tried to explain that kids don't really respect teachers, but if they connected education to what they'll be able to accomplish later in life—

"Yes, subbing and being lunchroom matrons have to be two of the worst jobs," he said walking away and leaving me to inhabit "my place." I wasn't trying to insult him. I just believe that substitute teachers would be respected if teachers were more respected. And in a capitalistic society, that means teachers need to be paid (and to perform) like rock stars.

P.S. #9: PERCENTAGE OF 5th-GRADERS
SCORING BELOW BASIC:[*2,3]

2000–2001

Math } 50%   Reading } 60%

---

* Percentages are rounded.

Kindergarten to Fifth Grade: Approximately 400 students: 12.9% African American; 5.9% Asian; 4.2% Latino; 77% White; 0% Other.[1]

*Y*esterday, I called P.S. #8 to find out how the investigation into the incident with Mr. Innocent had gone. Everything was fine. The other kids confirmed that I hadn't attacked the boy. The principal also invited me to come back again. And I would have, but then she uttered the magic words:

"It's on HERBS. Try to call and get it."

"Try to call and get it?" I waded through all of the available jobs on the automated phone system—twice. The first time, it wasn't there. Halfway through the second round, I came across a personal message at the end of a job description:

"It's a wonderful school," the regular teacher purred. "You should have a wonderful day."

Did she say, "Wonderful?" I could certainly use a little bit of that. So, today I'm headed in the opposite direction of P.S. #8, to Philadelphia's "Greater" (read: "whiter") Northeast, which is as close to the 'burbs as you can get while still remaining within City limits. People speak of the schools in the Northeast as though they constitute the Promised Land. The kids, the classes, the teachers are all "great!" I wanted to see for myself.

I got totally lost and had to call for directions. It took almost an hour to get to the well-maintained and recently painted P.S. #10, but I made it on time. Walking in, I noticed a couple of white teachers looking my way. I started to say "hi," but they looked away and kept walking. "Hmm." Except for the rare miserable individual, teachers in Philly have been pretty friendly—black, white, whatever. But sometimes, being black in a predominantly white society means waiting to see how you'll be received. I was interested to see what P.S. #10 had in store.

The school doors swung open held by two young white students. I smiled and thanked them. They smiled back, a good sign. Inside, two more white students manned what looked like a metal detector. Clearly, they weren't expecting any problems if they've assigned this job to children, but I wouldn't want my kid doing it. I bypassed this operation and headed straight for the office. Before I could open my mouth, a woman behind the desk curtly informed me not to ask her anything because she didn't know anything. Taking her at her word, I greeted the other person in the office who turned out to be the woman who had given me directions. She wasn't quite as chatty as she had been on the phone, but she efficiently welcomed me and supplied me with emergency lesson plans and a cup of water for tea.

"If I need help?" I asked.

"Just dial six."

The school was very clean and nicely decorated. Student projects hung along the corridor leading to the (yes, I caved) art room. I noticed a man across the hall eyeing me. Recognizing him from the parking lot, I smiled and said "hello." He barely squeezed out a nod before turning away.

Unlike the art room at P.S. #8, which seemed more like a studio, this one was a regular classroom with tables covered in paper and neat stacks of supplies around the room. A yellow sweater draped over the teacher's chair caused me to take note of the fact that this school was not stiflingly hot. That alone probably made it easier for the students and teachers to focus.

A short way down the hall, I found the teacher's lounge, a tiny room furnished with a table, eight chairs, a bookcase, a soda machine and a window plastered with NRA stickers. "Hmm." I quickly heated my tea and oatmeal and beat it back to the classroom.

The emergency lesson plans were very specific: "Use only the crayons on the back table (which were pretty raggedy) and the paper on the blue box." Either supplies are tight in the Northeast, too, or she didn't want a sub dipping into the good stuff.

The project suggestions weren't quite as specific: "Have the students draw each other, or a cityscape or their hands...discuss." Contemplating the assignment, I didn't notice the second graders standing quietly in the hallway waiting to be invited in.

"Can they come in?" the teacher asked sweetly.

"Of course," I said jumping up to greet them. As they filed past, some smiled, others waved. I smiled and waved right back. There was one lone, little black girl in the class. I've been that lone black girl: in most of my college classes, in nearly every class in graduate school and, way too often, in the working world. It can be a lonely place. When she caught sight of me, her eyes widened. I smiled, gave her the black people's "you-are-not-alone" nod and watched her face light up.

(My friend Deidre once told me even though she's not black, she always nodded when she passed one of the few black people on the studio lot where she worked. "So they know that I know and...it's okay," she explained, which endeared her to me for life.)

When I introduced myself, the kids responded in sing-song unison: "Good morning, Miss Harris."

They chatted quietly and smiled at me as I roamed the room encouraging and helping them spell. "You shouldn't have any problems with them," their teacher had said. I've heard that before...but in this case, she was right. I didn't have a single problem with any of her students.

The student population at P.S. #10 was predominantly white; however, as the day advanced, I ran into a few more children of color. And, though I cannot recall a single comment or conversation about race, creed or culture from any of them, the white students were quick to distinguish ethnic affiliations.

"He's Russian so he doesn't celebrate holidays like Valentine's Day."

"I'm half Jewish and half Catholic so I'm drawing a Star of David and a Cross with my heart."

"I'm Italian and you know what?"

"What?"

"Last year my brother died. My mom was real sad..."

They told me if their parents were having money problems, getting a divorce or had re-married. You name it. They told me about it, even though I was a total stranger. I wondered how much they shared with the teachers they see on a daily basis. I also wondered why it's often so difficult to get black kids to open up at all. Later when discussing this with my mother, she said it was because "black children know they're not really free." They always have to be concerned about what people think, outside of their community especially, but inside it as well. It was definitely that way in the past but, these days, fewer and fewer people of color are inclined to accept the burden of representing an entire race. They are individuals first, with no responsibility to anyone other than themselves. I'm not sure if this is a good or bad thing.

There were also kids at P.S. #10 who didn't know how to respond to me, though they definitely seemed to be grappling with it. Out of the blue, a little white boy called me over to show me a black crayon.

"My daddy likes black because he's a plumber," then he smiled.

I smiled back, recognizing that he was trying to connect, and told him I liked black, too. He nodded as if this made sense to him and I moved on to the next raised hand.

There were a few kids…just a few…who didn't want me anywhere near them. They shrank in their seats as I approached. This behavior could be attributable to any number of things, from not knowing me to knowing very few black people, if any at all. I gave them their space while letting them know that I was there if they needed me.

As always, there were also a few problem students but far fewer than in most of the schools I've visited. I had been told to expect some special ed. students to be mixed in for art. On the whole, they had been very well behaved; however, there was a boy who randomly alternated between his regular voice and the voice of an elderly Jewish man. Perhaps, he was imitating his grandfather or another relative, but it was odd. He talked incessantly, cried when I didn't let him present his art project first and disrupted the presentations of other students. He even punched the little girl who sat across from him. Luckily, she wasn't hurt. When his homeroom teacher returned to pick up the class, I mentioned that I understood he was working under special circumstances, but he had behaved very poorly and hit one of the other students.

"Oh no, he's not special ed.," she responded. "He's just a handful."

If he were a black kid in the inner-city, he would have been labeled "in need of emotional and behavioral support." His teacher immediately sent him and another little boy who had been acting out to the back of the room to stand while the others lined up. Then she made them apologize. The other boy apologized right away. "Grandpa" stubbornly lingered before he was able to spit it out.

"Get in line," she said, shaking her head. Off they went down the hall, the students racing ahead of her.

There was one class that had more students of color than any other with two or three black kids and a couple of Korean, Indian and Middle Eastern kids. Like the first class of the day, the students in this class were particularly nice and I think the only one in the entire school with a black teacher. Seeing how warm and open most of these kids were made me believe that perhaps racial harmony isn't so far off. There were only a few kids who did not get along. Two African-American boys and an Asian girl really didn't seem to like each other. But once I moved her to a table with girls: one black and one white, she was fine. I think the boys were just getting on her nerves. I also separated the two boys from one another, moving one of them to a table filled with white boys. Right away one of them blurted out, "I don't want him at my table." Once I made it clear that it wasn't up to him, they all managed to peacefully co-exist.

During lunch, I stopped by the teacher's lounge. Not one of the four teachers spoke or nodded in my direction. Feeling unwelcome, I grabbed a soda and went back to the classroom. I wasn't inclined to break down any barriers today. That's something you have to be in the mood for, like a chicken cheesesteak. As I ate, I watched the children playing in the schoolyard. They ran, screamed and jumped, a scene reminiscent of many inner-city schoolyards—minus the broken glass and cracked cement. My eyes fell on a little boy wearing a yarmulke. He was jumping rope with two little girls. He wasn't very good, but he tried hard and, without him, there wouldn't have been a game. I was both touched by the sweetness of this scene and surprised that I had time to contemplate it. I wasn't "recovering" from my first classes. I was just eating my lunch. This day had been so much less stressful than the previous fourteen. This school really was different. Why? The kids seemed no smarter than the other kids I've met, yet they certainly were better behaved. I went in search of someone who could give me a little insight—the woman who had checked me in. As it happened, she was also the Accommodation Room supervisor.

"We don't have many kids coming through though," she informed me.

When I commented that the kids were very well behaved, she jumped in with, "And you want to come back right?"

"I was just wondering why that is?"

"We have good kids out here," she responded.

I'm sure my expression conveyed my thoughts, "And what? We don't in the heart of the city?" Realizing I wasn't buying this boloney, she offered another thought.

"Some principals have what it takes. People know they mean what they say, and there's follow through. There are consequences to actions but..." she quickly added, "we don't expel children. I've been here four years and I've never written a pink slip." (I wasn't sure if she was making a distinction between suspension and expulsion, but there was a District-wide ban on expulsion.)

"If we get a kid that hasn't come from a disciplined school," she continued, "they behave poorly; but after a couple of weeks, they fall in line with the other students and fit in."

Thinking about Grandpa and a couple of other kids I ran into that day, I knew that wasn't always the case. But expectations and consequences I'll buy. The teachers who told their students they expected them "to be good for Miss Harris," were definitely better behaved.

Dropping her voice to a confidential level, she continued, "There's another school I worked at. It's not such a great school," she said. "It has problems. And it's out here."

I knew it wasn't a matter of geography or a black vs. white thing. I'm black. From third to twelfth grade, I went to predominately black Diocesan and private Catholic schools. I was well behaved and so were the overwhelming majority of my classmates. Some people believe it all comes down to socioeconomic circumstances, but none of us came from wealthy families. My mother sacrificed to send me to Catholic and private school. And I certainly could not have afforded to go to Swarthmore College if they hadn't given me financial aid and a partial scholarship on top of what my parents paid and I borrowed. So I will never believe that because you're poor or working class, you automatically don't know how to behave.

On the whole, the kids at P.S. #10 were nice and well behaved. Were they rowdy? Very few of them. Any outrageous incidents? Not one. I didn't even have to shout to be heard because these kids were accustomed to listening to their teachers. Even if I didn't speak loudly, they quieted to hear what I had to say. Yes, there were some difficult, combative children; however, by the third time I said, "Have a seat," and started walking over, they sat down and closed their mouths. And all of the students did their work.

Later, I was telling Nora about P.S. #10. We talked about how much more productive the classroom experience is when you don't have to spend all of your time on discipline. She told me about a girl with whom she had gone to high school who was a model student.

"We didn't find out until after graduation that her father used to knock her down the stairs. The point is she didn't disrupt class," said Nora. "I don't understand why it's become acceptable to act out at school if you've got it rough at home. How is this helping?"

I agreed. Not because I think abused children should suffer in silence. (Clearly they need to tell someone and get help.) I agreed because for children who are abused, oppressed, poverty stricken or living under otherwise horrific circumstances, an education is frequently the only way out. If they're allowed to come to school and disrupt the learning process for themselves and others, they're effectively eliminating the best chance of escape for themselves and their classmates.

P.S. #10: PERCENTAGE OF 5th-GRADERS
SCORING BELOW BASIC:[*2,3]

2000–2001

Math } 13%   Reading } 13%

---

* Percentages are rounded.

February 11, 2002 (Day 16 of 21)

Middle School: Approximately 900 students: 96.4% African American; 1% Asian; 2% Latino; 0.4% White; 0.1% Other.[1]

*B*ack in the inner city, it was business as usual. I knew I was in for a treat when I called for directions and the woman asked repeatedly if I had been there before. She was probably trying to warn me, but I showed up anyway. For the first, I was asked to sign a form acknowledging that I understood their zero-tolerance weapons policy, which I thought was usually directed at the students. At the time, I didn't think anything of it. Later, I wondered if they'd had problems with subs arming themselves. They also asked on another form, "Are you willing to return?" It was way too early in the day to make that kind of commitment. So I left it blank. And still no request for I.D.

I was assigned to two seventh-grade classes that I shared with the teacher next door. Young and enthusiastic, he topped off his sneaks, baggy pants and tie with neat braids. His language was sprinkled with slang, which I'm certain lent a certain amount of "street cred" with the students. He seemed like a big kid himself, but one whose mission it was to keep the other kids on track. And that was pretty cool.

Our two classes switched back and forth all day long. By the time I'd get a group settled and focused, the 45-minute period would be up, the kids would switch and I'd have to start all over again. There was a disciplinarian and an NTA who were more than willing to yell at the kids when they went, as "Mr. Cool" put it, "buck wild" on me. And I needed all of that help, not just because the kids were buck wild, but because I'm tired of yelling. I'm not a drill sergeant, and behaving like one is stressing me out. So that's it. New policy. No raising my voice…effective today. I need to conserve as much energy as possible because

I have to be at my most alert all day long. At most jobs, especially those in corporate America, you have little built-in moments perfectly suited to spacing out, surfing the net or catching up on personal calls. Anyone who claims otherwise is a big fibber. With subbing...forget it. I'm expected to discipline and encourage at the same time. At any given moment, I may find myself in a contest of wills with at least three different students, if not an entire class. All while trying to make the lessons interesting and relevant in order to justify why the kids should bother to pay attention. When I shared how I was feeling with the disciplinarian, she said, "You're doing well. You're keeping them in the room."

Is that the most I can hope for?

The Coordinator had sent piles of extra work for the students. I got the distinct impression that she wanted to make sure they were kept busy. Unfortunately, "The Last Leaf" by O. Henry, a story about a young woman at the turn of the century stricken with pneumonia, was on tap. The students were bored out of their freakin' minds...or maybe that was me. I had never read this story and realized I'd have to settle for the gist since I had to help the readers, stop the talkers, flip to the page we were actually on for some and remind those who could read well not to taunt those who struggled. As usual, too many of the students were rude, unmotivated and/or undisciplined. I'm pretty certain I was called a "bitch" (I'm getting used to it). However, when I replied, "Excuse me? What was that?" the young lady insisted that she hadn't said anything.

I stopped halfway through the story to find out if they even knew what it was about. To my surprise some did; most didn't. Probably because they were not only ignoring me, but the assignment, as well. Over the course of the day, we tried journal writing, rewriting news articles, reading out loud and silently about the Caribbean and answering questions. None of it went smoothly. Some were trying, but with the others constantly talking and playing, the motivated students gave up.

During my prep (break), I ventured out to command central—the Coordinator's office. Other teachers, including Mr. Cool, were talking, photocopying or just hanging out. Apparently, this is also where students are sent when they get into trouble. I recognized a young man from homeroom, standing in the far corner of the office. In class, he sat apart from the other students and did nothing, not even the easy puzzle I gave out. It wasn't that he couldn't do it. I checked; he could read. He just didn't bother. His behavior deteriorated as the day progressed. He had just returned from suspension for touching a girl's breast. This time he told a girl to, "Shut up and suck his dick." Besides being appalled, I was grateful that I wasn't the one who had to deal with this incident. How are teachers supposed to handle stuff like this?

The conversation in the office was lively. Eventually the other teachers worked their way around to asking me how I liked teaching and what I thought of their school.

"It's too hard," I said. "There are too many problem students and the rest of the kids aren't a walk in the park."

Mr. Cool chimed in that middle schools are just rough, "but there are worse places than P.S. #11." The other teachers agreed, as did I.

"But," I said, "I just don't believe those 'worse places' should define the standard." I mentioned P.S. #10 out in the Northeast. Granted, it's a grade school and so more aptly compared with schools like P.S. #8 or #9. Nonetheless, there are higher levels of expectation in place and the children live up to them. They have no choice.

"They tried me there, too," I explained, "but they stopped short of really tripping. The same type of discipline and levels of expectation should apply at all schools. Anything less is just unacceptable."

They were insulted and, as is customary, I was shunned for my candor (neither the first nor the last time, I suspect). They suddenly had things to do or lunch to eat. Familiar with this scenario, I decided to head back to the classroom. As I prepared to make my exit, another teacher who had been photocopying during my blurt of honesty stopped me.

"You're absolutely right," she said quietly. "There are far too many kids with emotional, developmental and behavioral problems mixed in with the rest of the population. There are bunches of them, floating around disrupting classes."

She went on to explain that she worked with kids of "normal" intelligence who needed social and emotional support (a different type of special ed.), such as the young man standing in the corner. He had been in a specialized support class.

"Then, for some reason, he was 'mainstreamed,'" she said. "He's nowhere near ready to be mixed in with the general population or to attend high school."

She went on to say that she thought the epidemic of children of crack-addicted parents was over, but she suspected that there was something else going on now; some other drug parents were using that was affecting the kids, or maybe just alcohol.

"Whatever it is, the results have been overwhelming," she concluded.

I wasn't familiar with what she was talking about. All I knew is that I was suddenly feeling even more discouraged. By the end of the day, the kids who were both able and inclined had finished the assignments and finished them quickly. The others had been holding them back and trying my patience. I lost count of how many times I had to give the same directions, ask them to be quiet, to get started or to take their seats. And those communal tables, where the students sit facing each other...whose crazy idea was that? Each student needs his or her own individual desk that faces forward so they can focus. This type of collaboration doesn't work well in environments where they have discipline issues and students of such varying levels of ability and motivation.

One of the girls did nothing all day except chat with her tablemates and copy down the assignments in her pretty little appointment book. She never did the work, just neatly copied the assignment. After a while, I took her appointment book and told her she could have it back at the end of the class. That didn't go over well. She sat glaring at me, probably wishing all sorts of poxes upon me. (In keeping with the theme of "The Last Leaf.") Even one of her friends told her she was out of line.

"You are trippin'," she said, giving voice to my thoughts.

Before I left, Mr. Cool stopped by to chat. I told him about "Little Miss Appointment Book" to which he replied, "Yeah, she's just about a nut." He also listened patiently while I vented.

"Too many of the students did nothing all day long. Of the ones who attempted the work, many couldn't spell, left out verbs and what's punctuation?"

He understood, but declared he still liked teaching and loved P.S. #11 because the staff is great.

"The kids are off the hook," he admitted. "When they act crazy, I act crazy right along with them. They punch me; I punch them. But when it's time to get to work, they listen. Okay, maybe the first three years were really hard...the first year, I was in shock and depressed," he said, "but I got used to it."

"I think that's the problem," I commented, as gently as possible. He seemed to contemplate this thought for a few seconds…then, he gave me his number.

///

P.S. #11: PERCENTAGE OF 8th-GRADERS
SCORING BELOW BASIC:[*,2,3]

2000–2001

Math $\Big\}$ 61%   Reading $\Big\}$ 48%

---

[*] Percentages are rounded.

February 12, 2002

I'm determined to ride this thing to day 21...just to prove to myself that I can do it. I'm also still hoping to land at a school that I love, that gets it right. So, instead of waiting for HERBS to call me with assignments, I called it. Usually, I'm offered days at the same schools over and over. I wouldn't mind going back to a couple of them, but not most of them. Though the smaller kids are less of a threat, they can be just as trying as the older ones. Plus I don't like what I'm teaching. Perhaps if I liked the subject matter more, I'd enjoy it more and be able to convey that enthusiasm to the kids. Or, maybe I'm just delusional.

As I listened to the available assignments, I realized that I'm starting to recognize the names of some of the teachers. Either I've subbed for them or met them while subbing for someone else. (Mr. Cool will not be in attendance tomorrow.) Some teachers are just chronically absent, especially the "prep" teachers who have different students cycling through all day. Classes like art, gym and music seem to be less about enrichment and more about giving the regular teachers a break. I decided to try high school again. See if it's as horrible as I thought now that I have a little experience under my belt. P.S. #1 may have been an anomaly.

> "Public School #12"

High School: Over 1200 students: 72.3% African American; 0.8% Asian; 2.1% Latino; 24.7% White; 0.1% other.[1]

*N*early three months after my experience at P.S. #1, I finally got up the courage to try a three-day, high school assignment. The students were still bigger than me, but I'd like to think I'm less easily intimidated now. We'll see. As expected, there were school police and NTAs stationed in the hallways, and a metal detector at the entrance. There was also a state-of-the-art TV studio and a desktop-publishing center courtesy of a $300,000 federal grant. Otherwise, the school was old, worn and huge. Despite the fact that it's located in a predominantly white, working-class section of Philly, the student body of this school is over 70% African American, a high percentage of whom are bused in. In general—black, white, Hispanic, whatever—the kids struck me as underprivileged and unmotivated.

I started with an advisory of fairly self-sufficient but kind of rowdy eleventh graders. A lot of the students seemed just as grown as I am, so I found it difficult to think of them as kids who didn't know any better. When I asked if they were usually so rowdy, they said it was the regular instructor's fault.

"When you have a teacher you know will call your parents and stay on you, you act better," a young lady informed me.

"Teachers probably get sick of chasing down parents," I responded. "Students need to take some personal responsibility for their education. And kids who act up should be expelled."

"How are you gonna keep people from their education?" another girl asked, displaying an ingrained sense of entitlement. She expected access but didn't feel she should have to do anything to earn or maintain it. Interesting.

"If you were really interested in your education, you wouldn't be so wild and disruptive."

Next, I had a bunch of rowdy ninth graders who settled down enough for me to go through a worksheet they were supposed to complete. I only had to put two of them out. One dropped his pants and mooned the class on his way. The other was just disruptive and difficult. Once the two of them were gone, the class went more smoothly.

Despite Sr. Joan's sage advice, I now have a completely different attitude about kicking students out of class. At P.S. #2, I put one kid out and felt guilty about it the rest of the day. Now, I feel like it's my duty to provide the kids who want to learn with an appropriate environment for doing so. A conversation I had with a small group of students made me even more resolute. They complained that all of their classes were loud and rowdy.

"We're not learning anything and we want to go to college."

I told them to transfer. Straight out. They'd have a better shot at being prepared for and getting into college if they went to a better high school. Unfortunately, finding a good public school with open seats in Philly is a tall order.

I also had two eleventh grade classes that were in the middle of the writing section of the PSSA (Pennsylvania System of School Assessment). Eleventh graders across the state are taking this test. The students were supposed to have one hour to do each of the three essays. Instead of just giving the kids a three-hour block or three one-hour blocks to do the test, they decided to let them do the essays over four days during English class, which were each 50 minutes long, giving them an extra 20 minutes to...pass out booklets? When I questioned the "Section Coordinator," a very efficient and businesslike woman, she said the administration decided it would be done this way. It was her job to implement.

"Stand on their heads if necessary," she told me. "But make them do it. If they won't do it, send them to me."

At the beginning of class, three young men the size of linebackers came to me and asked if they could take the test in another teacher's room because "it'll be way too noisy in here to think." I told them I was planning for it to be quiet, but I let them go anyway. The fewer students in a class, the more manageable it is. As they headed down the hallway, I saw a middle-aged, African-American woman step into the hallway.

"We're comin' to your class," one of the boys said.

"Did you get permission? You're not coming down here without permission," she said sternly.

"We got permission." They all looked back at me.

"It's fine," I said.

"Okay then," she responded. "Get in here. Let's go."

As they hurried down the hall, I wondered how she managed to exert that kind of positive influence over the students. Probably just one of those people born to teach. Then, I laid out the rules for the remaining students: no talking, no cheating. Keep questions to a minimum. The class was fairly quiet, but students argued with me, flirted with me, let their classmates read their essays.

"I'm just trying to get some ideas," a boy explained.

"That would be cheating," I informed him and the girl whose essay he was reading.

"For real?" he asked.

"For real." I honestly think they didn't know. It's not like they're being exposed to proper test-taking procedures. They freely shared that they've been taking home notes and the essays, as well as passing on the essay questions to their friends before class. All of them didn't cheat, but I got the impression that a blind eye had been turned to those students who chose to do so. They were shocked when I made them turn everything in before leaving the room.

One of the boys refused to give me his test booklet. When I insisted, he screamed, "I'm sick of you subs coming in here tellin' us what to do!"

"You're not supposed to argue with a sub like that," one of the larger guys chastised as he snatched the smaller boy's test. "Just give her the test, man." He handed the test booklet to me, flashing a wink and a grin.

"I won't be here tomorrow," one of the girls told me. "So you have to let me finish." I gave her a few extra minutes then collected her test. This was ridiculous. When you take the SATs, you clear your schedule. You don't get extra time if you can't make it back after the break. You also don't get to do a little, stop, think about it, come back the next day and the next to finish up. The kids also swore up and down that they could use dictionaries.

"That's why the teacher has them out here," they reasoned.

They were so adamant and I was tired of arguing with them. So I let this one slide. Later, I read some of the essays out of curiosity and quickly realized that very few of them actually bothered to use the dictionaries. Most of the essays were riddled with spelling errors, in addition to being just plain bad. All except one. A young man had written about his first two years of high school, when all he did was get high and hang on the corner with his friends. Then he got sober and turned his life around. He's doing well now, wants to go to college and is trying to help his friend get off drugs. Without revealing who had written it, I commented that someone had turned in a very good essay about turning their life around, just to encourage him. He peeked at me from the back of the class, then huddled back over his notebook.

Suddenly, students were asking me to critique the essays they were working on. "Can you read what I've written and tell me what you think?"

"No. You're still working. That would be cheating."

The last two classes of the day were more fresh-out-of-middle-school ninth graders. The sixth period class was particularly difficult and disrespectful. I reminded them that they were no longer children and, if they weren't there to work, they should leave. Whereas the students in the other classes chose to work, the sixth period students wouldn't leave and wouldn't do any work, except for one boy who sat copying someone else's homework for another class. When I took it from him, he tried to intimidate me into giving it back. He stood, leaned toward me and yelled that I didn't have the right to take his work. Still, didn't give it back.

"I'm not doing shit then!" he screamed in my face.

"Don't," I calmly replied. (Being cursed and yelled at by children had definitely lost its shock value.) He continued to mouth off, as I checked the hallway for an NTA. I asked her to escort him out for cursing at me. She was supposed to bring me a pink slip, though I suspected from the very familiar, molly-coddling way in which she spoke to him, she'd probably opt to protect him from the big, mean sub. She never sent the pink slip and by the end of the class, he was standing outside of the room door cutting up, waiting for the rest of this supremely ill-mannered crew.

The last class was much better. Word had spread that they had a sub. So mercifully, a lot of them cut. The students who bothered to show up were a little rowdy, of course. One kid informed me right off the bat that he didn't do "sub work." Otherwise, they were pretty nice and we managed to get through the worksheet and start on their paragraphs.

On my way to the parking lot, I ran into a woman who had been at P.S. #12 for 30 years. I commented that she must like it. She asked if I meant P.S. #12 or teaching. I said both. She responded that she liked P.S. #12.

"Why keep doing it then?"

"I need the job...but I'm definitely ready to retire," she told me. She said things had changed a lot over the years, but the kids don't give her too much trouble because she's one of the disciplinarians. When I asked what they do about students who cut classes she said, "After the first five cuts, you get an in-house suspension." Five!? I never cut a class until college. And, even then, not much because I was afraid of falling behind. Never in graduate school because I wanted to make sure I was getting my money's worth. (I'm still repaying those loans.) I should've asked for advice on what to do with that sixth period class.

Later that night...

I finished marking the ninth graders' worksheets. Out of the 50 papers that were returned to me, only ten kids got at least a 70 or higher. The one kid who got all the answers right cheated. Someone from the previous class had marked the correct answers on the worksheet when we went over it. When I pointed this out, she swore she had marked the answers on both the worksheet and her paper. No one goes from being unable to answer a single question, to getting everything right in the last five minutes of class. That's what happens when you don't have enough copies for all the students.

The one kid who got nine out of ten right and didn't cheat was a gung-ho kid in the Army ROTC program. Most of the kids were getting one, two or four answers out of ten correct. The worksheet didn't seem to be that difficult, though even the regular instructor had selected one wrong answer on the quiz key. I wondered if I should give the quizzes back. They hadn't done very well; it might upset them. There seems to be a popular belief among some that the reason why inner-city schools are failing is that black people don't care about education; that we're stupid, lazy and have parents that don't care. While some of us do have difficult home situations, no one wants to fail—no one. But some environments make it nearly impossible to survive, much less succeed, whether you are black, white, Hispanic or other. Outside of the one kid who wrote the essay about giving up drugs, the rest of the white kids I came across were staring off into space, sleeping during class or goofing off. This school's motto should be "P.S. #12—Providing equal disservice to all."

As usual, Nora and I commiserated about subbing. The latest news: The parents of gifted children in Lindenwold, NJ were organizing to sue the School District because most school funds were going to children with behavioral and developmental problems. I didn't know if that was true; however, most of the attention went to them.

I mentioned to Nora that I was having problems with one of the classes. "I can't put fifteen students out, right?"

"Why not? Talk to the principal," she suggested. "That's his job. Let him do something. If he can't provide a little support, he's sorry. And you can go sub somewhere else. That's what I do. Can't back me up? I'm out of there."

February 14, 2002 (Day 18 of 21)
Second day at P.S. #12

Usually, I can get a feel for the type of teacher I'm filling in for by the way the kids talk. This one? No idea. Some said she was out a lot; others joked that she was dead. Some of the students said she was mean: yelled at them even when they were quiet; put them out when they weren't doing anything. Of course, they're never doing anything. That's even in P.S. #12's handbook for instructors:

"Don't ask pupils for feedback on the disposition of a case. Their usual answer is 'They didn't do nothing.'"

The ring of familiarity made me chuckle, but the attitude was pretty cynical. A lot of these kids really wanted to be heard. I'm sure they'd have more than a few comments about this instruction.

My first class of ninth graders wanted to talk or play games instead of doing work: "Can you put a long word on the board, and we can see how many words we can make out of it?" one of them asked.

"You can do puzzles at home. We should do real work at school," came my response, which I'm pretty certain elicited a: "She mean."

I returned the worksheets, graded. They need to know what kind of toll playing games in school is taking on their brains. For the most part, they were surprised by how poorly they had done. Some were ashamed. Others wanted to know if a 60 was passing. (Shouldn't someone have explained the grading system to them by now?)

One girl figured she hadn't gotten any right, so she was pretty psyched to get four out of ten. Suddenly, she was willing to take a stab at the two paragraphs I had assigned. In fact, most of them attempted to write something. Maybe all they wanted was feedback on how they were doing. I went from student to student, reading, correcting and making suggestions. Maybe one or two of them wrote about a movie or a family trip. Most wrote about pain, confusion, loneliness and the sameness of their lives. They talked about working as though they'd been doing it for years, and wrote about things kids shouldn't have to experience. Wouldn't it be great if school could be their safe place?

The eleventh graders were supposed to finish up the PSSA. The Section Coordinator and I went through all of the answer booklets to determine which kids were almost done and which were nowhere near to finishing. The students near to completion were supposed to stay with me. My instructions were to "sit on them until they're done." The others were supposed to go with the Section Coordinator and...what? Have as much time as they needed to finish? It's weird that they give all this extra time and break the test up over several days, reinforcing the low expectations ingrained in the system. At the same time, it's completely unreasonable to hold these kids to the same standards as students from more competitive schools.

Marching orders in hand, I gave it my best shot; but eleventh graders know right from wrong and have already picked a team. Their attitudes toward the test varied widely, from viewing it as extremely important to failing to see the relevance. Some didn't show up. A few I had to round up from the hallway. They weren't ducking the class or me; they just had other things to do.

A few of the guys wrote one paragraph for each of their three essays, despite the fact that they were supposed to write five paragraphs for each one.

"I'm done."

Normally, my response would have been, "Fine, thank you." (Blowing off a test is a choice.) However, since I had instructions, I insisted they sit back down and either write more or stare at the book until the end of class. A few of the guys argued with me, but eventually sat back down. One kid, however, refused.

"I don't have nothin' else to say. I can't write anymore," he said over and over.

Looking at his three very thin paragraphs, I could not in good conscience let him turn the test in.

"Come on," I negotiated, "just write one more paragraph for each essay."

"I can't," he insisted.

"Why? Why can't you write more?"

"'Cause I'm stupid," he said matter-of-factly, as though there was nothing more to discuss.

I looked at him closely, thinking maybe he was just saying this to get me off his back; but the tears forming at the corners of his eyes told a different story. He was six feet tall, over 200 pounds, and he was about to cry.

"I'm stupid."

"'Cause I'm dumb."

"I'm not smart. I need help."

"He's stupid."

"She's stupid."

"I'm just dumb."

Over and over again I had heard kids label themselves and others "deficient." What kind of school system allows children to believe they're stupid? At minimum, the schools I attended tried to empower me; to make me believe that I could change the world. Not every class and certainly not every teacher…but enough of them to matter, enough to make me feel that I mattered.

Yet here was another black boy at P.S. #12 who truly believed he was "stupid."

"You are not stupid," I said, though I knew being unprepared and struggling with that test served only to further demoralize him. I told him he could go to the Section Coordinator's room and have more time. He shook off the tears, gathered his things and obediently headed to her room. How many more of the students who cut or sat in their chairs staring at the ceiling felt exactly the same way?

Despite the disruptions, most of the students (around 20 in each class) had knuckled down and done the work, especially the young women. They sat hunched in their seats scribbling furiously from the beginning of class 'til the end. They were working hard, but halfway through the last class, they were interrupted by a very loud young woman who wandered in.

"I don't have to take the test because my mother signed a form saying I didn't have to." (Is that really an option?)

She pulled out a bag of popcorn and a soda, and started chatting like she was at the food court. The other students kept their heads down and said nothing. Probably trying to avoid trouble. Or, perhaps they've never experienced the luxury of a completely silent test room. They didn't know she was infringing on their rights, but I knew.

"Excuse me...Miss...get out."

"What? How you gone tell me to 'get out?'" she asked indignantly.

"Let's go. Now."

She started to protest but the other students backed me up.

"Just go."

"Take your ass outta here."

"You don't do nothin' no way."

She cussed us all and flounced out, while the rest of them got back to work. It wasn't much, but moving this girl along was the least I could do for the kids who were trying.

I spent most of my lunch period waiting to speak to the vice principal. She welcomed me and listened intently as I described the situation with the upcoming, sixth-period students. Thoughtful and intelligent though she was, this sista would have me believe that she was "shocked that this type of behavior goes on" at her school. We had a nice talk. She wanted to know all about my background and how I came to sub at P.S. #12. She also promised to send the

Coordinator of the Business Academy (a non-college-track program) to help wrangle the students.

When the sixth period bell rang, most of the students were lounging in the hallway or in and out of the bathroom. I stood at the doorway waiting for the help I was promised. Suddenly, an unsmiling man turned the corner and he was not pleased. He yelled for the students to get into the classroom and take their seats. Following the slow-moving children into the classroom, he reminded them that they had all applied and been accepted at P.S. #12 and into their respective programs.

"Consequently, you can all be expelled!"

While most of the students quieted down, the boy who had cursed at me the day before strolled in late and loud. I ratted him out immediately. The Coordinator took him and sent back a pink slip for me to fill out. I had plenty of time to take care of it since most of the students still refused to do work of any kind. I gave them paper to write on; they balled it up and threw it at each other. I asked them to at least keep it down so the four or five kids who were working could concentrate. Nope. I didn't even want to talk to them anymore by this point. Each attempt I made to engage them was met with even more disdain.

In the meantime, "Cursing Boy" snuck back up to class. "Uh...can I talk to you?" The Coordinator was fast behind him and even more unsmiling if that's possible.

"Get back to my office and stay there."

"But I need to talk to her," he kept saying. "Can I talk to you?"

"No." I responded. How many times did I have to repeat it? The Coordinator escorted him away, again.

The boys in this class gave me a hard time; the girls were far worse. I found myself engaging in a word-for-word battle with one young woman because I asked her to quiet down. She actually got up out of her seat and walked over to confront me. This was a bit too much. I knew if I didn't shut this down, there'd be more and worse to follow. She was about two inches shorter and twenty or thirty pounds heavier than me. I felt my eyes narrow as I leaned in and snarled in my most menacing, Philly-Whip-Ass tone, "Girl, you bedda get outta my face." Surprised, she backed away. "And get out."

She started to argue, but then took another look at the expression on my face and decided she was "leaving anyway."

"Then go."

She stomped toward the exit, mouthing off over her shoulder. She tried to slam the door, but I caught it.

"Exactly to whom do you think you're speaking?" I asked. "I am not one of your peers." Suddenly, standing by herself in the hallway, she had nothing to say. I looked for the NTA but didn't see her. So I shut the door and turned back to face the class.

I tried to continue helping the few kids who were doing work, but the others were still batting around paper balls, yelling and laughing. I'd had enough.

"Shut up! I yelled. "You are the rudest, most disrespectful and belligerent class I've ever worked with!" (So much for my week-old, no-yelling policy.)

"What's belligerent?" one of the less obnoxious boys asked. I pointed to the dictionaries.

"Ahh...she don't know what it means," cackled another.

"I know. If you want to know, look it up."

The first kid grabbed a *Webster's* and started searching. The others expectantly awaited the translation—no doubt to determine just how insulted they should be.

"How you spell it?" he asked.

I was pretty sure I knew how to spell it but I was certain they would clown me hard if I didn't. I dove in slowly, "B...e...l...l...i...i..."

"I got it," he shouted. "Waging war, carrying on war; belonging to or recognized as an organized military power protected by and subject to the laws of war." He stopped and looked up at me. I'm sure my expression said, "Hunh?"

"Ahhh!!! She don't know what it means!" cackled that same student. As they howled with laughter, I started toward the kid who was reading.

"Lemme see," I said reaching for the dictionary.

"Oh...it's more," he said sheepishly and continued reading. "Inclined to or exhibiting assertiveness, hostility, truculence or combativeness; an obnoxious, argumentative adolescent."

The laughter stopped as I maturely refrained from blurting out, "Ha! How you like me now?"

A few of them seemed to see my point; but most were pissed off because they "hadn't done nothin'" and I was "disrespectin'" them.

"No you're the ones who are disrespectful."

"Unh-uh," one of the loudest of the rowdy girls argued. "When you told me not to call you 'yo' or 'girl' anymore, I didn't. That showed respect."

"What would possess you to call an adult "yo" in the first place?" I asked. She just stared at me. I was so angry by this point I wanted to scream. I flashed back to a conversation I had with Nora. We were talking about classroom control and she said that sometimes you have to embarrass the kids; make them feel stupid in order to get them to listen. But too many of them already believe that. I took a deep breath and looked at them; reminding myself why I wanted to teach. "They're just children," I told myself. "They don't know any better and even if they did, they've been allowed to get away with this behavior for so long that it can't be easily undone."

Some of them realized how upset I was and tried to shush their classmates, but others were on a roll that would not be halted. They complained about subs "coming in and treating them bad, blah...blah..."

"I didn't do that," I pointed out. "I politely asked you to stop talking and get to work. You haven't done it yet!" They really didn't understand why I was so angry. "The reason you have a lot of subs is probably because you have stressed your regular teacher out by treating her so poorly!"

"No, she's out because she's sick," said one of the girls.

"People get sick when they're stressed out," was my reply. "I came here to help, and you've treated me with tremendous disrespect. You never know who a sub is, or when that sub might be able to help you or hire you down the line. You just don't treat people like this."

My tirade seemed to make a small impact or maybe it was the yelling. Whatever, they piped down—but several of them asked for more paper so they could write their two paragraphs on why they hate subs. I didn't care what they wrote, as long as they wrote something.

I stood in the front of the room, still angry, willing the minutes to pass more rapidly when one of the students asked me to read her paragraphs. I was expecting sub bashing but she had written about losing her two little brothers after a firebomb was lobbed into her home. She called it "an act of terrorism."

"Is this for real?" I asked.

She turned to the young lady seated next to her. "She thinks I'm making it up."

"No, I believe you." It was just that she seemed too matter of fact about it. My heart went out. I wanted to give her a hug but she didn't know me, and she wasn't some delicate little flower. She was kind of tough, looked older than she was. I gave her my condolences, which she seemed to appreciate. I asked how her mother was doing.

"Still upset," she said, then handed me another piece of paper, a sheet that had to be signed every day by each of her teachers to prove she had attended class. Given the situation, I'm not surprised she's been having problems making it to school, but at least she was trying.

The young lady sitting next to her also gave me a sheet to sign. And she *was* a delicate little flower; very well dressed and well spoken. While pretty much everyone in the room had on jeans or sweats, she was wearing a beige knit dress and matching overcoat with heels. I could see her easily fitting in at any private academy, or even as a freshman at Howard or Harvard.

"What happened?" I asked, signing her sheet.

"I stopped coming to school for a while," she answered vaguely.

"Yeah, for like a couple of months," said the other young woman.

Again, I asked, "What happened?"

"I don't know."

There could have been a thousand reasons, but if I had somehow gotten stuck in that school as a ninth grader...well, I wouldn't have cut. My mother would have killed me. But I definitely would've been begging her to get me out. There is no way I could have survived four years of P.S. #12. Parents must not realize how bad some of these schools are, or surely they would do something. Complain, volunteer, pick up a part-time job and send their kids to Catholic school. Something.

As I continued to chat with these two young ladies, the "Delicate Flower" told me she didn't like P.S. #12 or their regular English teacher because she put her out of class after a boy hit her.

"Does that make sense to you?" she asked.

"You didn't have to tell her that," interrupted one of her roughneck classmates.

Trembling a little, The Flower responded, "Huh?"

"You didn't have to tell her," she nodded toward me as if I were the enemy, "that about our regular teacher."

The Flower dropped her eyes and stopped talking.

I felt bad for this kid. I'd be gone in an hour, but she'd have to put up with this bully for the rest of the school year, perhaps the rest of high school. That's not something for which you can offer condolences.

As the end of class approached, one of the boys I argued with defiantly shoved his hastily penned paragraphs about subs at me. Something along the lines of "I hate subs because they think they know everything." I didn't take offense. I gave him tips to improve it. To his credit, he patiently listened until the bell rang and the class was over. These children are starved for attention, but nobody seems to be giving it to them.

As the class filed out, Cursing Boy was waiting outside the door, clowning around telling people he "got five on it," which meant he'd been suspended for five days. Though he wasn't talking to me, I remarked that maybe he'd think about that before he cursed at another substitute teacher. He smirked in response, compelling me to continue.

"When I first met you, I thought you were a nice young man but you treated me like crap. You were disrespectful and rude and I didn't appreciate it." I wasn't nasty. I wasn't loud, but I meant what I was saying.

Suddenly, he was apologetic. "I'm sorry."

"I don't want your apology. I want you to behave like you have some sense."

He stood looking at me, as though he was waiting for the punch line.

"Get away from the door," I said disgusted.

"I'm sorry," he said once more before I closed it. Why is it that some of these kids only respond appropriately after I put on the bitch hat?

I was so happy that class was over, until the next class told me two of the girls from the previous class had gotten into a fight. One smashed the padlock from her locker into the eye of the other girl, whose eye was now swollen shut. I immediately thought back to the roughneck telling The Flower not to tell me about their regular teacher.

"Oh God," I thought.

"She was bleedin'!" one of the boys gleefully yelled as he poked his head in, then disappeared back into the hallway.

The kids jumped up wanting to go back out in the hallway, but I wouldn't let them. I peeked out but didn't see anything. Continuing with the blow by blow, the same knucklehead ran back into the room waving around a lock like a show-and-tell piece.

"This is it! This is the lock!"

I examined it; didn't see any blood. "Put this back where you found it... thank you."

Eventually, I kicked him out all together. Once he was gone, the others got to work. Half the class was missing. I had about 17 students, which was manageable. Most of them were in the "Communication Corps," which meant they at least had an established goal of going to college. Sadly, they had done just as poorly on the quiz as the other class. The only difference was they seemed to take it harder. Mr. "I Don't Do Sub Work" was stunned that he hadn't answered a single question correctly. As I continued giving out papers, he picked up his bookbag and started walking ever-so-slowly to the door.

"Where are you going?"

"Out. Whatever I'm doing here...it's not working."

"Sit down. We have work to do."

He sat. This boy was bright, articulate, personable, but—according to the other students—he did no work whatsoever. He bragged that he had gone to a magnet school, which I later found out has a special focus on music and a poor academic reputation. (I had run into a few refugees from this school over the past couple of days, including The Flower. All of them bright and articulate.) So Mr. "I Don't Do Sub Work" should have been doing a lot better.

"What are you doing at P.S. #12?" I asked.

"I don't know," he said. "I hate it. I want to transfer to Central."

That was going to be tough. Central is one of the top schools in Philadelphia and only a few spots open up after freshman year. He'd have to submit a writing sample, standardized test scores, and if he hasn't been working, his transcript can't be great.

"If you want to go to Central, you have to do the work."

I felt like I was reaching him and some of the other kids in this class. There were about ten of them—black, white, Asian and Latino—who were open and willing, but they needed guidance and an environment that supports learning. I'm guessing they haven't been getting either of those things at this school, where most kids seem to be slipping swiftly through the cracks.

As we dove into the day's assignment, several of the kids wrote about how dangerous the school was. One girl wrote that it seemed wrong that there were four fights on Valentine's Day, a day about love.

Why would any level of violence be acceptable in any school on any day?

My assignment over, I stopped by the office to sign out and drop off the cut list. The vice principal waved me into her office and offered me a month-long assignment teaching ninth grade physical science.

"Writing...not science," I reminded her.

She insisted I "could do it" and that I'd have her support, as well as the support of the whole science department. This seemed ridiculous to me.

"Why not get a legitimate science sub?" I questioned.

"Because we never get black substitute teachers at P.S. #12. And there's a lot of conflict between the white subs and the students."

"Probably because the students treat subs like dirt."

"The subs talk down to the students, call them names," she replied.

I told her straight out that I called that sixth-period class rude and belligerent. (I am nothing if not honest.)

"No, I mean the subs call them stupid; tell them it runs in their families. Things like that," she said. "Or, they come with their newspapers, put their feet up and read. All they do is keep the students in the classroom. The kids aren't used to subs who actually try to teach."

"And why would they treat me any better if I take this assignment?" I asked.

"I'll introduce you as the new teacher. I won't tell them how long you're staying. Far as they know, you'll be there for the rest of the year. Think about it. Call me in the morning."

February 15, 2002

I've been trying to decide if I should accept this assignment at P.S. #12. As much as I think I'd enjoy working with the kids from that last period, I dread the thought of dealing with the crazy, sixth-period class. The vice principal said she'd transfer anyone who gave me a hard time to a different section. That would be one to two kids max. The rest, I'd be stuck with. I could use the steady paycheck since I haven't found another job yet. Every day, there are tons of available sub assignments, but some days I just can't do it. I cannot make myself walk into another potentially awful situation. If I take this assignment, I won't be able to casually take a day off when it gets to be too rough.

I'm not sure I have what it takes to instill students with discipline, love of learning and pride in their work and in themselves. The people who can are miracle workers, especially for children from economically depressed areas. I'm also not sure I want to put down roots in this school no matter how temporarily. I get involved. I take things seriously. First thing on my mind this morning was yelling at those kids, telling them they were belligerent. I felt ashamed because I let them push me and I lost my temper. Do I want to subject myself to that kind of environment on a daily basis?

Against my better judgment, I called the vice principal and accepted the job. We made plans for me to start Tuesday, go over the syllabus, meet the other science teachers, etc. She called back two hours later. The head of the science department had already given the assignment to someone else. She thanked me and said she planned to call me when another assignment came up.

I think I may have dodged a bullet.

P.S. #12: PERCENTAGE OF 11th-GRADERS *SCORING BELOW BASIC:*[*,2,3]

2000–2001

Math } 60%   Reading } 46%

---

* Percentages are rounded.

February 18, 2002

I've decided that I don't have it in me. Subbing is horrible; teaching doesn't seem much better. I want to help but I don't think I can do it in a classroom. I think I could help a lot of these kids one-on-one, even the rowdies at P.S. #12. Thirty at once is too many. I don't enjoy fighting and screaming all day and, most of all, the situation saddens me beyond belief. When I walk into these schools, I see nothing but wasted potential, environments too rugged for children to flourish in, burned-out teachers struggling under the weight of unreasonable expectations. This system is destined for failure.

February 19, 2002

Last night, shortly after seven, HERBS rang me with a two-day assignment at some school I've never heard of before. I intended to decline it, but I hit the wrong button, then panicked and confirmed it. Bizarre as that was, I wasn't locked in. I could just dial back in, cancel and look for another assignment. As soon as I hung up, the phone rang again. It was HERBS adding another day to the same assignment. I started to decline but then I thought someone else might pick it up not realizing that there were two other days that went with it. So I accepted, planning to cancel the whole thing at once.

For some reason, I found myself looking the school up. Not only was it a middle school (yuck) it was located in what used to be one of the roughest white, working-class neighborhoods in Philly. I flashed back to a story my mother had once shared about a friend of hers who had gotten a good deal on a house through his connections as a veteran. But all his new neighbors saw was his brown skin. So they beat him...to death. The man went all the way to Viet Nam and back, only to be killed near his own front door.

These days, the racial mix has changed, but the violent reputation remains. A morbid curiosity arose within me. What must this school be like? Since the start-date was a couple of days away, I decided to phone the next day and see if I could get a feel for the place. The woman I spoke with told me I'd be subbing in English language arts (good) with seventh graders (bad, very bad). The boy at P.S. #3 who threatened to "sock me" was a seventh grader. The class at P.S.

#5 with the girls who attacked two different boys, stomping and punching one until he had an asthma attack and giving the other a bloody lip. Seventh graders.

"Okay," I said and hung up even more resolved to cancel. Then, for some reason, I called back and asked how the kids were.

"They're okay. Pretty nice," the woman said. "But that's to me." Not a ringing endorsement. "Will I see you tomorrow?" she asked.

"Yes," came tumbling out of my mouth for some unknown reason. I hung up and sat wondering what the heck was wrong with me. At no point along the way here had I planned to actually take this assignment. Yet not only had I confirmed through HERBS, I also verbally committed myself. I decided I could make it through one day. Then, I'd tell them I couldn't come back.

> "Public School #13"

February 20, 2002 (Day 19 of 21)

Middle School: Nearly 900 hundred students: 34.4% African American; 5.3% Asian; 31.7% Latino; 28.5% White; .1% Other.[1]

*T*he next morning, as I drove past abandoned buildings and rundown houses and storefronts, I came upon a frightening school. "Oh Dear God, please don't let that be it," I thought. And it wasn't. But truthfully, my fears were not at all assuaged when I pulled up in front of P.S. #13—another huge, weather-beaten, graffiti-covered brick building with metal security grates covering all street-level windows. There were a few kids in the schoolyard laughing and talking. Noticing me right away, they nodded or spoke and pointed the way to the hard-to-find entrance. Inside, tons of students sprawled comfortably in the cafeteria. When I asked where the office was, they politely directed me. After checking in, I was sent to the office of the Coordinator, where a tall, harried white man in jeans and sneaks welcomed me. He explained that they took a team approach to dealing with the students. I was in for the third member of one of their teams. He gave me four stuffed folders, each marked Day I and a class schedule with a header that read: "[P.S. #13] Middle Magnet School." Magnet school?! Hunh? He hurried me down the hall to introduce me to my grade partners, the "GPs." "Ms. GP" was a very nice woman with biggish hair and jeans-and-jewelry glamour. "Mr. GP" was a plainspoken regular Joe with a good-natured sense of humor. Like most veteran teachers I've come across, they both had unflinchingly unsentimental attitudes toward teaching and children, but they offered to help me in any way they could.

Students flowed in and out of the classroom, running to lockers and the bathroom while I settled at the desk. When the bell rang, they were all in their seats. I briefly introduced myself, told them I'd be there for the next three days

(Why did I say that?) and that their instructor had left plenty of work for them to do. I passed out a packet of six worksheets on the finer points of capitalization.

"Let's get to work," I said in my most authoritative teacher's voice. And they did. In silence. I couldn't believe it. I stood at the front of the class watching them until it occurred to me that I could sit down. I never sit down. And since watching them like a hawk seemed unnecessary, I created an answer key for the work they were doing. The lesson seemed grade appropriate, a little challenging for them, but not hard. When I finished, I walked around the class to see how they were doing. They were fine. Even when they were really messing up, they were able to correct their mistakes with a little guidance. I'm not saying these kids were brilliant. I'm saying they were regular students; the way students were when I went to school.

They were so well behaved I had time to check out the room while I waited for them to finish. It was large, run down and kind of messy, but clean. A retractable partition separated it from Ms. GP's room. I could actually see and hear her through one of the seams. There were motivational posters and sayings hung around the room, "Choice. Not chance," as well as tips on writing. There were also test papers strung on a clothesline across the side of the room, almost thirty papers with a score of ninety or above. At least a third of them with a perfect hundred. We went over the worksheets, going up and down the rows for answers. Everyone participated; there was no backtalk or "I didn't get that one." And most of their answers were correct. When class concluded, they filed out in an orderly fashion, leaving me astonished.

Next, I had a prep followed by a lunch. I immediately went to Ms. GP's room. "So this is a magnet school?" She nodded and went on to explain that she, Mr. GP and the woman I was in for worked together. Their classes interacted: they taught each other's students and they backed each other up. Then, she invited me to have lunch with them, something that hadn't once happened since I started subbing.

We sat in the teacher's lounge, a big room with tables and a popcorn maker talking with a couple of other teachers. The main topic of conversation was some kind of vote going on in the teachers' union—something having to do with the impending state takeover of the School District. The general consensus seemed to be that this could not be a good thing.

We talked a little about the issue of discipline. I mentioned how well behaved my first class had been.

"Really? 'Shelly's class is usually kind of retarded," said Mr. GP. "Don't be fooled. Our kids can be difficult, too."

"But in comparison to places like P.S. #5?" I asked.

"The hallways at P.S. #5 are very long so they're hard to monitor."

I looked at him. "You really think it's the hallways?" After pausing, he conceded that there were "other factors obviously."

The next class wasn't nearly as miraculous as the first. The students were very talkative. I also caught three of them copying answers so I told them they had to leave. I asked them to return to Ms. GP's room. The boy went quietly and remorsefully. The two girls argued and insisted that they were going to the Coordinator's office instead. I didn't care where they went. The other kids were watching to see how I handled this, so I wasn't about to allow them to stay in the room and disrespect me. I followed them to the Coordinator's office to make sure they actually went. He wasn't in, so once again, I instructed them to return to Ms. GP. "Miss Sassy Mouth" argued with me while the other girl giggled. Another teacher overheard and came to assist. Ignoring her, Miss Sassy Mouth continued the backtalk. Somehow, I managed to get both of them down the hall to Ms. GP. As I started to explain how they'd been behaving, Sassy Mouth muttered, "shut up" under her breath, which is not only rude but cowardly. She didn't respond when I asked if she were talking to me. "Miss Giggly Mouth" just giggled.

Ms. GP spoke in very soothing tones, "Now, Miss Sassy Mouth, I think you owe Ms. Harris an apology." I've been here before, wasting time with one or two students while the rest are waiting. As I walked away, I heard, "She walked away. So oh well."

I returned to the class where the rest of the students were, for the most part, working. We had not a single problem for the rest of the period.

Once class was over, Miss Sassy Mouth slunk back in, "I'm sorry."

"I'm still going to fill out the demerit form," I responded, not certain that it would even matter to her.

"But I apologized!"

"I don't want your apology; I want you to behave. You'll have the opportunity to do better tomorrow."

She looked stunned. I guess she missed the part about the three-day stint since she'd been late for class.

As Sassy Mouth dejectedly slunk away, I thought back to my high school years. Each demerit we received caused a point to be deducted from our deportment grade—permanently. There was no starting anew until the next September. What's worse is that the deportment grade started at ninety-five, not one hundred because, "Nobody's perfect." In my four years at Cecilian Academy, I had heard only one student mutter "shut up" to a teacher. I have no idea how many demerits she received. (They were usually liberally dispensed for things such as incomplete homework, going up the down stairs or wearing summer penny loafers with the winter uniform.) What I do know is that she was no longer a member of our class when the next September rolled around.

The homeroom class returned for Social Studies. Since I hadn't read the chapter and there were no extra books, the best I could do was explain the assignment and give them tips for finding answers. This time, they were chatty but nowhere near as rowdy as the students I usually encountered. A lot of the chitchat was directed toward me. They wanted to get to know me. I told them if they finished up their work before the end of class, we could talk. A lot of them did. But quite a few didn't. Once I confirmed that it was okay for them to take the textbooks home, I assigned the rest of the chapter as homework for those who hadn't finished. At many of the schools where I subbed, taking home books is not allowed under any circumstances.

The last class was fine. They got to work right away and knocked out the worksheets with a minimum of chatter. Overall, it was a pretty nice day. I talked with Ms. GP on my way out. Again, I remarked on how well-behaved the kids were outside of the few troublemakers. She told me that, this year, they'd been blessed with very nice kids. And, the team had worked very hard to stay on top of the troublemakers.

"The kids you had problems with, we always have problems with, but we're working on them." She also told me she used to teach eighth grade but after so many years, she decided to give herself a break and drop down to seventh.

"This school is pretty nice but if you come back to sub, there's no guarantee you won't get one of our off-the-wall classes. I told the principal you were good and we should try to hang on to you. We have problems getting subs sometimes."

I wasn't sure if I wanted to be held onto, but I definitely wanted to come back the next day.

February 21, 2002 (Day 20 of 21)
Second day at P.S. #13

Of all the schools I've visited, this one has the greatest sense of community—kind of an all-in-together vibe, especially the second floor. The teachers were tight-knit and worked as a team. The Coordinator was constantly on the phone with parents and everyone knew one another. Today, on my way in, I got caught behind a school bus that was trying to turn onto a teeny-tiny street. Since I was only a couple of blocks from the school, I pulled over, parked and got out. As soon as I started down the street, I heard, "Hi, Miss Harris." I looked up to see a boy standing across the street waving.

Normally, this would have freaked me out. I hate to admit it, but I try to be as inconspicuous as possible with my parking in case a student gets really pissed off about being kicked out of one of my classes and decides to key my car or something.

Today, it seemed okay. "Hi, sweetheart," I responded.

A short while later, I was in the teacher's lounge, asking Mr. GP if there was any place close by where I could get a sandwich.

"Don't go to the store near where you parked," he said, "and be careful when you go back to your car." He consulted the kids who were popping popcorn to help raise money for student activities.

"What's the name of that other place a couple blocks down?"

"No, the best place is the one near where she parked," one of the boys answered and he was not the kid who said "hello." The others nodded their agreement. Everyone knew where I had parked. Philly is like that. It's a big small town. Everyone either knows you and just saw you somewhere, or knows someone else who knows you and just saw you. It's the polar opposite of Los Angeles where a person can work with you on a project, insist on giving you unsolicited feedback on your script and eyebrows, but deny knowing you like Peter denied Christ when your mutual hairstylist mentions your name.

While the fellows got into a fairly lengthy discussion about sandwich freshness and quality, Miss Sassy Mouth strolled in. She jerked, surprised to see me. I waved. She waved back. Having reached no consensus on the sandwich situation, Mr. GP asked the kids if one of them would run down to the cafeteria for me to see what they were serving today. And wonder of wonders, Miss Sassy Mouth volunteered. She was absolutely wonderful all day long. She was quiet, did her work...whipped through it as a matter of fact. I teased her asking if she disrupted class because she was really smart and got bored and needed something to do. She laughed and said, "No." But I still marveled at her complete 180.

The boy I kicked out yesterday apologized and had all of the work done that he didn't do yesterday. And Miss Giggly Mouth, well...she made a dramatic entrance, announcing to the whole room that she would be good today. Within minutes, I had sent her packing, again. The rest of the kids were on track. I'm not saying they were perfect, but I was much less stressed out than usual.

During lunch (tuna from the caf), I told Ms. GP and Mr. GP about Sassy Mouth's complete turnaround. They didn't seem surprised. Ms. GP told me that her mother was "out there" and that she had just been laid off, "which has an effect..."

"And she's schizophrenic," added Mr. GP

He said it so lightly I thought he was joking, but Ms. GP went on to explain that a lot of the kids were on meds.

"They call them EBS kids, emotional and behavioral support," she said.

"At least they're on medication," I commented. "Quite a few of the kids I've run across probably need to be, but aren't."

"You've got some of them in your class, too."

"Far fewer than usual," I retorted. "You guys have it pretty good at this school."

"The only special ed. we have is MG—mentally gifted. Again, that brought me back to the fact that P.S. #13 is a magnet school. I asked what that meant exactly.

"It means we get to pick our kids. They have to apply," said Mr. GP.

"So you can expel kids who really misbehave?"

"Nooo, you can't expel them," he continued. "We try to weed out as many discipline problems as we can before they get here...but we still wind up with some."

He also explained that selection is based on population. Since the surrounding neighborhood now has a large Latino population, so does the school. But from what I've seen, the school is very mixed, almost evenly between African-American, Latino and white students, with a few Asian and Middle Eastern students as well.

At some point along the way, I mentioned to the homeroom kids that we could talk at the end of the day if they finished all of their work. Sure enough they held me to it. There were three kids who were lollygagging, holding the whole class up. I decided to go ahead with the chat, but those who weren't finished could not participate and they had to finish the worksheets for homework.

Being a Harry Potter fan, I thought this would be a good place to start. The book franchise was going strong and the movies had made a big splash. Swiftly and unanimously, the students proclaimed Harry Potter lame. End of story.

"Can we talk about boys?" one of the girls questioned.

"Yeah, we want to talk about the girls," a boy declared. That seemed fair. There was mutual interest on both sides. I figured this would be okay (soooo naïve).

The conversation started innocently enough with the girls firing away. "We want to know why the boys take longer to mature."

"And why they're always commenting on body parts."

"And why, even though they say girls are boring, they're always in our conversations?"

A small, wiry Latino boy with a big smile and an even bigger personality raised his hand.

Standing, he declared, "Because boys like girls." Then, he sat back down.

We all laughed. Some of the boys shouted affirmations or patted this young man on his back for speaking up. I complimented him on his honesty.

"I want to know why the girls are so violent," one of the boys asked.

I wanted to know, too. I'm no shrink, but seeing two different boys get stomped by girls at P.S. #5 convinced me that young women are very angry.

"Because the boys play too much," said one of the black girls.

"And," added a Latina, "they touch us without permission."

The other girls solemnly nodded their agreement, as the boys quietly let this sink in.

After some reflection, "Mr. Personality" raised his hand. "I think girls mature faster because parents care more about girls. Boys are on the bottom of the pile," he said. (Boy is he going to be surprised when he gets out into the real world.)

While the girls reacted, strongly disagreeing with this statement, a small, wiry black kid raised his hand.

"Girls have curfews and parents want to know where they are all the time," he said. "Us...they just let us go." Again, the boys sat quietly.

After a few seconds, one of the girls muttered under her breath: "Girls mature faster because they have periods."

"That's not fair," the boys protested. "She's not speaking up so everyone can hear."

Since she didn't want to repeat it, I mentioned that I had once written in a story that girls mature more quickly because they have a monthly reminder that they're becoming women.

As the girls smiled and nodded, Mr. Personality blurted out, "Oh we have a reminder. About every two weeks."

As the boys bellowed with laughter, one of the girls boldly asked, "Are you talking about wet dreams?"

The classroom erupted in noise. We had to be disturbing the class next door, maybe even the ones down the hall. Plus, I knew I needed to steer this conversation into safer waters. I quieted them, threatening to end the discussion if they didn't keep it down. As they hushed each other and stifled giggles, I noticed a quiet, white kid who had told me his name was "Peace Sign." He'd said little else since, but now his hand was raised. I called on him, hoping he would change the subject. He did.

"Why do some women become lesbians?" he asked without a blush or stutter.

"Why do some boys become f*****s?!" the girls snapped almost in unison.

"Hey, hey...that is not an appropriate term," I interjected.

"Gay then...why do some boys become gay?" they quickly corrected.

Peace Sign and the other boys nodded their heads, seemingly satisfied with this non-response. Perhaps the question was less about sexual preference and more about equality between the sexes. These kids have been exposed to so much at such a young age. Of course they think Harry Potter is corny.

Not all of the kids were so outrageous. To my surprise, the tall, jock-type guys were very content to let the little fellows speak on their behalf while they quietly nodded in agreement. But all were interested; not a single student was staring off into space. They must not often have the opportunity for constructive discussion. Even after the bell rang, they wanted to stay and talk some more. I insisted they go home and when they asked if we could do it again tomorrow, I gave a noncommittal, "We'll see," and shooed them away. As the last student trailed out, the Coordinator showed up at the door.

"Everything okay?"

I could tell by the way he asked that it wasn't. We had been pretty loud. "Oh...talk time," I said. "They got a little excited, but it was okay."

"Talk time?" he repeated. "Yeah...let's keep that to a minimum. Have a good evening, Miss Harris."

February 22, 2002 (Day 21 of 21)
Third day at P.S. #13

These kids really made me laugh today. I abandoned that don't-smile-at-them thing a while ago. It's not me and I can't pull it off, unless I'm miserable. Then, I couldn't manage a smile if someone paid me. I had Mr. GP's kids first. They whipped through the assigned worksheets in record time, but I was ready. I asked those who were done to take out a piece of paper and write down eight lines from a rap song—radio edit, no cursing, no offensive lyrics including denigration of women and racial slurs. Or their own rap or poem, same rules. They got so excited, you would have thought I said I was handing out free college tuition.

"We're doin' raps!?"

"Can we put like a letter then dash, dash, dash for the rest of the word?"

"Can we substitute a word for a curse word?"

"Can we write more than eight lines?"

"What if you don't know any rap songs?"

"Can we do rock or alternative?"

As was inevitable, the kids burst into rapping like we were in some kind of hip-hop musical. It took a few minutes to get them back under control.

"We are not rapping. We are writing. Those who aren't finished shouldn't be concerned about what the rest of us are doing. Those who are finished need to close their mouths and stop disturbing the people who are still working because we aren't starting until everyone is done."

Shortly thereafter, everyone was done and the work was correct. One young black guy, a basketball player who usually slow-poked his way through every assignment, finished the worksheets and wrote down all of the lyrics to a song in about five minutes. Usually, I had to make sure this kid didn't nod off. Suddenly, he was wide awake and wanting to go first.

"Come on down," I beckoned.

He stepped confidently to the front of the room and took up what I can only refer to as a "rapper's stance," and had at it.

"This is by Jigga. If you know it, feel free to sing along."

"Who is this personable and engaged child?" I wondered while most of the students sang along. This kid was good. At the end, everyone clapped and cheered, including me. Then I asked him to put the first eight lines up on the board. While he meticulously executed this task, other students read from their original pieces: raps, poems about music and love. The students were not only polite and enthusiastic; they were downright supportive—clapping and cheering, especially for those who were nervous.

Next, we took a closer look at lyrics. Now, I consider myself to be a pretty hip chick. I listen to urban radio. I grew up black. I've got a working knowledge of slang. So even if I don't catch every word, I can figure out what a song is about. After reading a few of the lines written on the board, I realized that I had been fooling myself.

"Uhm...I need someone to translate."

They were happy to oblige but first they spent a good five minutes laughing at me and mocking my pronunciation and tone. Working our way through the eight lines, I think we were all a bit surprised by how far removed from standard

English rap has become. And while the kids were a little embarrassed to tell me that some of the lines referred to smoking weed, I was way more fascinated by the fact that even they had no idea what some of it meant. They're just singing along and thinking it's cool because somebody played it on the radio.

As much fun as we were having, I was trying to make a point. "Slang is all the way to the left and standard English is all the way to the right. And you need to be able to bridge the gap between them in order to move forward." I thanked them for their work, told them I had enjoyed my time with them and sent them on their way.

Next, I had the homeroom kids for social studies. They were still trying to sucker me into more talk time. First thing this morning, Mr. Personality had greeted me with "Why do some girls become prostitutes?"

"There are male prostitutes," I replied flatly. (I was ready today.) While he sat down and thought about that one for a while, I moved on to collecting homework. Honestly, I did not expect them to have it, but they all came through. Only one of them flaked and even she had the homework done by the beginning of class.

"So can we have a class discussion if we finish our work?"

"Sure," I responded, knowing they had way too much work to finish in a 45-minute period. Once I told them they could get started on their rap lyrics/poem for language arts class, that was it. Same outburst as the first group. Same momentary hip-hop musical interlude. I had to threaten to cancel it to get them to calm down and get back to work. One of my favorite students wanted to skip the work and get right to the rap. I tried to get her to focus, but she kept talking and giggling and disrupting the class. Finally, I said, "Stop it with all this playing around. What are you twelve?"

"Yeah," she answered.

Sometimes I forget how young they really are. "Well then..." I said reaching for a comeback, "act like it." She quieted and got to work.

During this class, I received a note instructing me to cover one of the eighth-grade classes during my prep. This meant I had only 30 minutes for lunch, but oh well, duty called. Since Mr. GP had taught these students last year, he walked me to the room.

"Ms. Harris," he loudly announced, "if any of them give you a problem, send them to me." Then, he left.

It still took me a while to get them working. As a matter of fact, they informed me that they were going to play cards. But this wasn't P.S. #5 and I wasn't in shock. I made them put the cards away and take out a piece of paper to write an original poem or rap. A few of them got right to it with no argument. Most of them, irrespective of race or gender, acted as though I had added, "if you want" at the end of my request.

"I'm not doing that," one of the girls commented behind my back.

"Then get out," I responded turning to face her.

"I said I wasn't doing anything," she quickly revised and pulled out some paper.

At least they have a fear of being put out. That's a good thing. It took a while but we finally got moving. I had a couple of people putting raps on the board while we listened to a few original pieces. One guy wrote down an entire page of an original rap, nothing offensive, fairly straightforward. A couple of others read poems.

Once the guys finished writing lyrics on the board, we began translation. The eighth graders were not as tolerant of my mispronunciations and lack of familiarity with the appropriate rhythm.

"Why you all stiff?"

"You mean why am I enunciating? You read it. Show me how it should sound."

Suddenly, he realized it was a little more difficult to read a rap than one would expect. I tried it again, still not to his complete satisfaction but he gave me a pass. By this time, most of them were engaged, but time was up. Surprisingly, the eighth graders weren't that bad; nonetheless, I was happy to scuttle back to the second floor. For all of their grown up questions, the seventh graders still had enthusiastic attitudes. The eighth graders just had a lot of 'tude.

Back with the homeroom kids for language arts, I had even more fun than I did with Mr. GP's kids. Like the first group, they were so excited they whipped through the worksheets in no time. And no one bugged me about talk time. A kid they all called Potter because he looked like Harry Potter and sometimes sat in the back of the room holding onto a ratty-old broom (yeah, I dunno) asked if he could write down the lyrics to an alternative song by a group called Linkin

Park, instead of rap. Then, he refused to get up in front of the class and sing. Even when the other kids cheered him on.

"Come on Potter, you got your new sneaks on!"

"Sears ain't doin' all of that," he retorted.

So they started cheering his best friend to take his place. "Okay," he said getting up, "but bear with me because I'm a moron." He blushed, as he took the same stance as the first kid at the front of the room. I thought he was going to sing, but he started rapping—different slang, unusual imagery instead of new use of language, but it was rap. When he finished, everyone burst into applause and cheers. By the time he sat down, he was so red I thought he might explode... in a good way.

We moved on to some original pieces, poetry and rap. Some folks we had to encourage by giving them a round of applause. (The rowdies tended to be the shyest about getting up.) I was surprised by how willing the kids were to participate. There were little, delicate girls doing the beat box and rapping and boys spouting love poems. The cool thing was the respect they showed one another. Everyone was cheered and applauded.

We closed out the class with everyone singing the theme song to *The Fresh Prince of Bel-Air*. (It's a Philly thing.) I really had a blast with these kids and I made sure to tell them so. I also told them how smart and talented they were, and that I wished them all the best. As they filed out, a couple said "goodbye," a few waved. Peace Sign stopped at the desk.

"It was nice to have you," he said looking up at me sideways.

And then, they were gone. But word had spread and the next class poured in, "We rappin'? We want to rap!!"

The last class went as well as the other two. I personally checked each student's work because they kept calling me over to get the go-ahead to start writing their rap or poem. But most of them were struggling with the section on prepositions, so we took a few minutes to go over it. Then, we moved on to the hotly anticipated rap segment.

The boy I kicked out on the first day could not wait. He was pacing and rocking.

"Calm down. Calm down." I kept saying.

"I can't! I can't!" he responded.

And I believed him. I didn't put him out though because I had a better understanding of his situation. I did, however, separate him from the other students. He was so worked up, he seemed on the verge of hyperventilating. Earlier, I'd spoken to the GPs about him. Every day, he talked nonstop, fidgeted and played. Often, I had to stand right next to his desk so he could get his work done.

"What's the deal with 'Robert?'" I asked, trying to figure out how to handle him.

"Poor-white-trash kid?" Mr. GP asked. "Yeah, he's trouble. Lives around the corner."

"This kid is black."

"Oh yeah, he's crazy," said Ms. GP.

I didn't know if he was crazy, but he was bright and sweet. Maybe all this kid needed was the right medication. I spoke to him in a calming voice and asked him to take a few deep breaths. Eventually, he calmed down enough for the class to proceed.

Though it went well and we had fun, there wasn't the same sense of support for all of the students in the room. They did not clap or cheer the rowdies who had given me a hard time, including Sassy Pants, despite the fact that she had been on her best behavior for the last two days. I insisted that we be polite and clap for everyone but the applause was tepid. These kids made it very clear that they did not appreciate having their classes disrupted.

As I said good-bye, I looked up to see five of the girls from the homeroom class at the door. They were waving and yelling my name. When the others left, they came in to hang for a minute. It's funny. These girls were the rowdiest in the entire class. I had to stay on them. One of them I put out almost every day. She didn't even get to participate in the rap exercise. And there she was saying good-bye.

"You gotta stop making things difficult for yourself," I told her.

"I know...I know...I am."

They joked around a bit. Wrote "Bye. Holla." (keep in touch) on the blackboard and signed their names. The gesture made me feel appreciated, something I hadn't felt at any other school. Then, I kicked them out because they were supposed to be in gym class.

"Hold it down!" I yelled after them.

"We will!" they yelled back. These girls were bright. I had great hopes that they'd outgrow the playing around. After all, they were only 12. And with P.S. #13 behind them, I think they've got a good shot at being prepared for high school.

The principal, the vice principal, the grade partners and the Coordinator—despite the talk-time mishap—all invited me to come back.

"Just call whenever you want to come in," they told me. "We always need subs."

I had such a great time, I knew if I returned I'd probably never leave. So, I decided to keep moving. If P.S. #13 could create a great learning environment for such a diverse group of students, there have to be other schools out there that can do the same, right?

P.S. #13: PERCENTAGE OF 8th-GRADERS
SCORING BELOW BASIC:[*2,3]

2000–2001

Math } 11%   Reading } 5%

---

* Percentages are rounded.

February 25, 2002 (Day 22)

Middle School: Approximately 1100 students: 44% African American; 8% Asian; 20.7% Latino; 26.6% White; 0.7% Other.[1]

*J*urns out, last Friday was my twenty-first day of subbing and I didn't even realize it. Somewhere around the third hour of the first day at P.S. #13, I stopped keeping track and the day slid by unmarked. However, after the first fifteen minutes today, I found myself counting the hours, once again. At least I have a big, fat pay raise coming. Ninety-five bucks a day. Woo-hoo!

I took this new assignment because a woman at P.S. #10 tried to convince me that her school is nice because they have "nice kids in the Northeast." (There are nice kids everywhere.) Inevitably she relented, confiding that P.S. #14 (which is also in the Northeast) did have "a little bit of a problem." I wanted to see for myself. So there I was, hoping that it wouldn't be too awful because it was a guaranteed week's worth of work with the same group of kids. However, when I arrived, the office administrator explained that they didn't actually have a week-long assignment. Since they always need subs but have difficulty getting them, they advertise week-long assignments, then float subs "as needed."

"We're giving you the best assignment we can today," she pleaded. "We also have a male sub and we're giving him the EBS (emotional & behavioral support) class."

No point complaining. I had classes to teach. Today, I was subbing for another absentee sub. Teachers, staff and administrators all told me this man had "no clue how to deal with kids." Most telling was the fact that he only spoke to four of the students in one of his classes: a Latina girl, an African-American girl and two white girls who all sat together. He communicated whatever he needed to say to "the four," who relayed the information to the rest of the class. The Coordinator, a friendly and talkative woman, also shared that "Mr. Only-

Speaks-to-'The-Four'" tells the kids to do whatever they want, then punishes them for misbehaving.

"And please, do any story in the reader except 'The Red Lion'," she asked. "He keeps doing it over and over and the kids are sick of it."

Sounded to me like the man had snapped. Not that the kids were angels. Outside of "the Four" and a few others, they were loud, rude and disrespectful. I didn't want to talk to them either, but no kid deserves to be treated like that. I kept thinking there must be a way to remake the students at this school in the image of the P.S. #13 kids. Of course, P.S. #14 wasn't a magnet school. Regardless of attendance records, behavior problems or level of ability, this school had to accept all kids from its neighborhood. Still, things were being overlooked; basic stuff such as requiring teachers to speak to all students in their classes. Or, making all students face forward. Yes, it's old fashioned; but here's what you deal with when the students sit in little chat clusters.

There was a sturdy, good-looking black kid who was acting out and talking a lot. When it was his turn to read, the kid next to him quietly pronounced the words. I'm talking five-letter, one-syllable words—like mouse. They probably figured I couldn't see what they were doing, since they were sitting with their backs to me. When he finished, I thanked him and moved on. Later, I quietly pulled him aside.

"You do not read well, but you could do better if you'd focus, work hard and stop playing around."

I wasn't trying to be cruel; he needs to be able to read. At first, he tried to deny it. "No...I can read...I..." but when he looked into my eyes, we both knew the truth. He nodded, sat down and stopped playing around. After that, his hand was up every few minutes for help. I did my best but the class was full of kids who needed attention. When I couldn't help, he copied answers from the boy sitting next to him. Then, another kid copied his answers. Who copies from someone who can't read? That's when I decided to turn the desks around.

Then there was "Sammy," a wiry little white kid who alternated between telling the other kids to "shut up and give the lady (me) some respect," and bopping around the classroom socializing and doing nothing. He was a fun, funny kid, the kind who grows up to be the fun guy everybody wants to have a beer with but nobody wants to hire. When I started sending the totally-out-of-control students to the Coordinator's office, which doubled as the "timeout" room, this kid asked to go.

"...because I don't read so good and sitting in the Coordinator's office will keep me out of trouble."

"You read fine," I countered, "but you need to practice more."

In response, he took to heckling a Latina girl who was trying to answer one of my questions. He kept yelling, "She don't speak English good. She can't answer."

Her English was fine. He was just harassing her. I asked him to stop, but every time she opened her mouth, he yelled out, "I told ya. She don't speak English good."

As she fought back tears, I turned to him and said, "She speaks English better than you do."

The class "ooed" and he laughed. "No she don't." Then he bopped over to the other side of the room where he continued to make jokes.

I came close to giving him exactly what he wanted, sending him to the timeout room. But from what I could see, he needed every possible minute in the classroom he could get.

"That's it." I finally said. "Sit down, close your mouth and pay attention. You're not going to the timeout room, but I will call your parents."

It took a few minutes, but he settled back at his desk and toned it down for the remainder of the day. Though I seemed to have won that battle, I felt like I was barely keeping the kids under control. Surprisingly, the Coordinator stopped by to tell me what a great job I was doing.

"Lemme tell you, I appreciate the fact that I don't have to come in every ten minutes to calm the students down."

I asked if she knew there was a kid in the class who could barely read.

"We've called his parents three times to set up meetings. Not once have they shown up. And Mr. Only-Speaks-to-'the-Four' keeps giving him passing grades."

One more basic thing: Teachers who give students passing grades when they don't deserve them, should be fired.

After school, one of the administrators pressed me about coming back. To be honest, I found it difficult to justify driving an hour to the "greater" Northeast to be disrespected by children when I can be disrespected closer to home. But everyone had been so nice that I didn't want to leave them hanging.

"Listen," she told me, "we've got another assignment coming up. I can guarantee that on Thursday, Friday and next Monday, you'll have the same seventh grade classes for English Language Arts. It's on the system. Call and cancel this assignment and pick it up."

"Pick it up." Here we go again. I called HERBS right then. It wasn't there.

"I just put it on," she assured me. "Try again later. It'll be there."

It wasn't; however, I did stumble across a kindergarten assignment with two aids only 20 minutes away in the lower Northeast. I snapped it up and cancelled the other. This was the first time I had ever dropped an assignment. To my surprise, I felt not the least bit guilty.

P.S. #14: PERCENTAGE OF 8th-GRADERS
SCORING BELOW BASIC:[*,2,3]

2000–2001

Math } 59%   Reading } 50%

---

* Percentages are rounded.

> "Public School #15"

February 26, 2002 (Day 23)

Kindergarten to Fifth Grade: in Northeast Philadelphia. Approximately 700 students: 80.1% African American; 0.3% Asian; 10.4% Latino; 8.6% White; 0.7% Other.[1]

This morning I scrounged around a rough and rundown section of the lower Northeast looking for a legal parking spot. I hit pay dirt about three blocks from P.S. #15 on a narrow, glass-and-trash-strewn street lined with dilapidated row houses. Hoping I wouldn't come back to a flat tire or worse at the end of the day, I asked a passerby if it was safe to park there...as though I had a choice.

"You put your club on and all, right?" she said.

"Yep." And I had, but there was no "and all." I don't have a car alarm. And suddenly I was feeling pretty stupid about that. The woman shrugged, kept walking. Tomorrow, I'll be early.

I signed in, picked up the key and opened the door. The room was a mess: raggedy books, chairs and tables disarrayed and three teachers' desks loaded with "stuff." I randomly picked one and dropped my bag. As I settled in, a 45-ish woman with a smoker's cough and one of Philly's more pronounced accents dragged in.

"Hi. 'Annie.' Can you move over to that other desk?"

While I relocated, Annie laid it out: The regular teacher had broken her foot back in November. Since then, she'd been in charge though she was only a literacy intern on her way to getting certified. She made it very clear that she and "Kathy," the teacher's aide, were running the show.

"We've had sub after sub after sub who either didn't want to stay or got long-term spots somewhere else or were just weird. The only reason we even need a sub is because legally, as an intern, I'm not supposed to be left alone with the students and Kathy is usually only in here through lunch."

The irony was that this woman had far more training than I do and folks have been quick to leave me in charge of thirty, forty kids at a pop. I figured three adults with a bunch of five-year olds should be cake. I'd just lay back, take my cues from them. Less stress for me, help for them, we all win.

"All you need to do is let me know how I can help," I offered.

Relieved, she asked what I wanted the kids to call me. Drawing on my two-day Head Start experience, I suggested, "Miss Clay." However, since Annie and Kathy go by "Mrs. Whatever-Their-Last-Names-Are," the kids quickly revised my name to "Mrs. Clay," which amused Annie to no end. Ground rules established, she poured out her frustrations as we headed to pick up the kids.

"They're not going to be ready for first grade. I'm doing my best but I don't know what I'm doing and she (referring to the M.I.A. regular teacher) won't return phone calls. We don't even sing kids' songs because I don't know any. You know the thing is...the only reason I decided to become a teacher in the first place is because I never had paid summer vacations before."

"Hmm."

In the schoolyard, the kids were lined up, ready to start the day. Black, white and Latino parents hovered, greeting Annie and waving goodbye to their little ones. As the latest and greatest in a parade of subs, the parents regarded me suspiciously. Not one of them made eye contact with me except a shockingly thin black woman who sort of hung back, away from the rest of parents. Deep circles sat under her eyes, which bulged a little, drawing attention to the yellowing whites. She was fidgety and uncomfortable in her own skin, desperately trying to conceal the signs of addiction with over-the-top enthusiasm.

"If you have any problems with "Ahmad," call me. I'll be right up here," she excitedly blurted out, placing her hands on the shoulders of a bright-eyed boy who could have used a comb through his hair.

I nodded and turned away as we headed in. For the most part, the kids seemed manageable. Of course, there are always a few to put you through your paces. In this case, their names were: Ahmad, "Wynton," "Shontay" and "Busy Brooke," who was constantly in motion. Then there was "Micah", who had been diagnosed with ODD, Oppositional Defiant Disorder,* which meant he did what he wanted, when he wanted. No exceptions.

"He's violent, volatile and very smart," said Annie. "Every other day I have to have him physically removed from class because he goes off."

Five years old and that out of control? I couldn't imagine, though I did get a little preview. He was yelling and pushing around little, innocent-faced Busy Brooke because she was sitting at the wrong table—not his table; just the wrong table. She stood her ground though; almost daring him to flip out. In fact, the more worked up he became, the more she settled in, observing him like some kind of behavioral psychologist. All that screaming and she barely flinched, even when he hit her. I expected Annie to do something but she pretended like she didn't see what was going on. I did, so I escorted Busy Brooke to her appropriate seat and tried to calm Micah down.

"I will not calm down. I will not sit down. I will not be quiet," he informed me.

"Hmm."

Annie gathered the children on "the rug" for the morning routine. I remembered this much from Head Start. After taking roll, collecting quarters for pretzels, etc., she grabbed a book and began to read. I'm sure the kids couldn't hear her because they were playing, yelling and laughing. Yet she continued as though she had perfect order. I found her behavior...I don't know...odd. And before I realized it, I had abandoned the "lay-back-and-let-Annie-lead" strategy. I clapped loudly, telling the children to pay attention. The few who didn't found themselves back at their tables, hands neatly folded on top. I don't know where it came from. Probably some Catholic-school flashback, but it worked. They were quiet; perhaps even in shock.

A short while later, a tall woman with a booming voice entered toting Dunkin Donuts coffee for Annie and herself. This was Kathy. I introduced myself and asked where I could get a cup of tea.

"No tea or coffee. Not even a soda machine in this school," she replied politely before dismissing me as "the latest sub."

---

*Oppositional Defiant Disorder (ODD) is diagnosed when a child displays a persistent or consistent pattern of defiance, disobedience, and hostility toward authority figures including parents, teachers and other adults.[4]

It was journal time anyway, which amounted to 20 minutes of coloring. I was kind of surprised. I thought journals were for writing, if not their deepest thoughts maybe some ABCs. But no, they just scribbled. Next came guided reading. Annie split the children into three noisy groups and assigned me to one of them. I managed to get the kids to say and spell "bear" and "bedtime," but they only vaguely recognize the one or two other words on each of the book's four pages.

I think I get how to help someone read better, but going from nothing to reading? I don't know how that happens. With me, one day it just clicked. The words made sentences and the sentences made a story: "Lisa and the Grump" to be specific. Yes, my mother sat with me every night helping me pronounce the words in my little reader, but I couldn't read. And then, one day, I could. Perhaps I was making progress all along and didn't realize it. Maybe whatever practice we give the kids will help them along.

Annie seemed to always be scrambling for another activity, which is a shame because the great thing about kindergarteners is their enthusiasm. You give them a piece of paper, and not only will most of them try to do the exercise, they'll decorate it, too. I think we should capitalize on that exuberance; spend more time on each exercise, go over answers and write them on the board. Annie insists that their attention spans are "too short for all of that." Yet, she'll sit them in front of the VCR for an hour-long cartoon.

Lunchtime belonged to Kathy, so I headed straight for the teachers' lounge to eat and eavesdrop on talk about the impending state takeover of the School District. Some of the teachers were concerned that profits would take precedence over learning. Others were worried about losing their jobs and pensions. They wanted to know what Edison, the private school management company slated to get a big piece of the pie, could come up with that hadn't already been tried. The newer teachers (including me) figured Edison couldn't possibly do any worse. From what I'd read, they have a pretty good record of instituting discipline, but fall short when it comes to pulling up test scores.

Inevitably, the conversation worked its way around to the fact that I was the latest in a long line of kindergarten subs.

"Why don't they hire a long-term sub and give those kids some stability?" questioned one woman.

"Maybe they don't want to pay the extra money," I commented. "After a sub is in a position for more than 30 days, the rate goes up."

"That and they're having problems finding people who want to stay," chimed in another woman. "Yesterday's sub claimed the kids 'had too much energy, especially Micah.'"

They all reacted. Turns out Micah had an older sister and brother in the school who were just as problematic. And they weren't the only ones. Each of them had similar stories of being ignored and disrespected on a good day, and cursed or attacked on a bad one. Suddenly, the topic shifted to corporal punishment—the teachers were in favor of it. They told stories about working in North Philly, which was predominantly black and considered very rough until Temple University embarked on its massive expansion project. The teachers claimed they had fewer problems with the kids in North Philly because many of the teachers were part of the community. They'd been working in the schools for twenty and thirty years and "didn't hesitate to hit the kids when they acted up," said one.

Another shared a story about a woman who had incredible control over her classes. Her secret: she carried a huge yardstick with her at all times.

"She used to beat the shit out of the kids," she said howling with laughter. "But she had taught their parents too so she had permission. Lots of teachers sent their problem students to this woman. Even if she didn't hit them, they would come back crying because they thought she would. It was great."

The other teachers chuckled. I didn't find it funny. It felt very uncomfortable to be sitting around with a bunch of white teachers[†] talking about beating black children. I commented that I didn't think the public would go for corporal punishment, but by this point they were waxing poetic about getting parental permission. Clearly, they were tripping. This is America—a country that enslaved and bred black people, that allowed biological experimentation on blacks in Tuskegee, Alabama and elsewhere, that continues to allow police

---

† There were no black teachers at P.S. #15 other than two women who had been coaxed out of retirement to consult on a part-time basis and me. That's a huge problem. According to a 2017 study, black students who have at least one black teacher between kindergarten and third grade are 13% more likely to enroll in college. And having two black teachers during this period could raise that rate as high as 32%.[5,6]

brutality, inequitable rates of incarceration and other routine practices of institutionalized racism. Black parents are not going to give blanket permission for white teachers, or any teacher for that matter, to hit their children.

Eventually, they got around to asking where I had subbed, then shook their heads as I rattled off the list.

"How was P.S. #1?" one of them asked.

"Not so good. That was my first day." They groaned in sympathy.

Another woman mentioned that several years ago, she had been working as some kind of teacher representative for the School District. One day, they sent her to P.S. #1. When she arrived, a guard warned her not to walk down a certain stairway because a teacher had been raped there.

"I turned around and walked out," she said. "No job is worth my life."

Someone pointed out that P.S. #1 now has school police. However, a short time after I had subbed there, my cousin Michael casually mentioned that he'd seen one of the school police officers "getting his ass kicked" by some boys... probably students...right on school grounds. Then he suggested that I find somewhere else to sub.

"I'm too old to be kickin' some boy's ass for messing with you."

So many people, mostly teachers, had warned me not to go back to P.S. #1.

"You're lucky you made it out without getting hurt," I've heard again and again. Though I'm glad I had a chance to see inside for myself, I'm not a glutton for punishment and I'm never going back.

The rest of the day flew by uneventfully. For the most part, I observed the routine: the teachers, the kids, Micah especially. He's a smart, industrious little boy who whips through his work quickly. When the other kids were coloring, he pulled out a piece of paper and practiced copying words ten times each. I gave him some new words to copy and told him how smart he was. I thought if I could make him feel comfortable with me, then the transition to a new sub would be less traumatic for both of us. Not only was he calm, he drew a picture for me. I think we'll be fine.

After walking the Ks (the kindergarteners) to the library for pick-up at the end of the day, it was time to head out.

"See you tomorrow," I said.

"You're coming back?" Annie asked, surprised.

(During lunchtime, one of the teachers confided that she has nodes on her vocal cords from yelling at the first graders so much. She's afraid to transfer because she doesn't know what kind of situation she'll end up in. Ditto for me. At least I know the kindergarteners won't be kickin' my ass.)

"Yeah, I'll be back."

Later, during my daily phone conference with Nora, we continued our lament of the appalling conditions in public schools. She's subbing in Jersey, one of the wealthier states in the union. Sometimes she's in poverty-stricken Camden, which is short on books and teachers and where, according to the January 12, 2002 edition of the *New Jersey Courier Post*, sometimes 87% of students at a given school score Below Basic proficiency—across the board. Other times, she's in places like Medford where the average cost of a home is over $330K.

"Clayvon, it's disgusting how much money this school has," Nora railed. "They provided me with a free, restaurant-quality lunch. They actually sent around a menu in the morning. I was subbing in gym and barely had anything to do. Thank God I had the *Times*."

"A free, restaurant-quality lunch?" I couldn't even buy a cup of tea at P.S. #15. More importantly, all of the kids couldn't have an afternoon snack because there weren't enough leftover fruit pies and fruit cups. The kids didn't complain. They just got a carton of milk and made do. No one cried about it not being fair. That's just the way it is. I bet the kids in Medford have enough snacks, books, teachers and whatever else they need. They're doing very well on standardized tests. According to that same issue of the *New Jersey Courier Post*, the following percentage of students in Medford elementary schools scored Proficient or Advanced (vs. Basic or Below Basic) in language, math and science:

Medford, NJ Schools:	
School	% Proficient and Advanced
Cranberry Pines E.S.	98.6
Maurice & Everett Haines	91
Milton H. Allen E.S.	90
Taunton Forge E.S.	93.8

Money matters.

February 27, 2002 (Day 24)
Second day at P.S. #15

The cool thing about this school is that the teachers talk to one another. Just hanging out in the faculty room during lunch, I've heard a lot. One thing is very clear: folks are looking for a way out. They can't take the lack of discipline in their classrooms. Some let the kids do whatever they want. Others scream all day long or use bribery. The science teacher told us she buys little metal rings by the bag and uses them to coax good behavior out of the kids.

"They get one ring to sit down, another to look at me while I'm talking, one more to participate. And a gold stamp that says, 'very good' on their foreheads to line up quietly. Otherwise, I can't get them to do anything, not even sit down."

I'll be honest. I thought she was pretty pathetic, especially since she was including all of the kids in the class where I was subbing. Some of them are extremely sweet and cooperative. They don't need to be bribed.

"I got 800 kids coming through my class," she said defensively. "I can't know all of their names and I certainly can't control them."

Somewhere around here, I'm guessing my accusatory expression settled into one of compassion. It's the art-teacher syndrome all over again. You're not with the kids enough to establish a relationship or develop even minimal control. I know what that feels like...consistent and overwhelming incompetence.

"I'm definitely not coming back to teaching next year." She was 51 and looking for another career.

A first-year, special-assignment math teacher was having her own issues. She was constantly getting kids who have been labeled "math deficient," but weren't.

"I don't know why this keeps happening. A lot of these kids are perfectly fine in math, but they keep sending them to me."

I thought it odd too, but my guess is that some of them are challenging so the teachers get them out of the classroom any way they can. Or, perhaps they're so overwhelmed that it's hard for them to keep track of whether it's Omar or Haseem who doesn't get that 2x2 and 4x1 are both 4.

"I've generally been in shock since I started about a month ago," she confided. "I don't think I can do it."

When she asked about the prospects of getting a job in the suburbs, the other teachers weren't particularly encouraging. Maybe they've been applying for the same positions. Or, maybe they're just planning to get out altogether. All Annie talks about is getting through this last year of certification so she can switch to "another career." I told her I didn't think this "other career" would be easy either.

"Whatever it is, it'll pay more and be better than teaching," she responded. "Teaching takes up too much energy. It's too political and I'm just worn out from dealing with the problem kids," she declared. "And it's just going to get worse. One of my friends has a child in her class with a tracheotomy," she continued. "Since she's the teacher, she has to clean out the kid's trach every morning. It takes an hour."

"What are the other kids doing while the teacher is cleaning out the trach?" I asked.

"I asked the same thing," said Annie. "You know what she said? 'How do I know? I'm cleaning the trach.'"

Everyone reacted with frustration and disgust. It's bad enough that school districts have been forcing kids with emotional and behavioral problems into general classes; now they're making teachers responsible for kids who have severe physical limitations as well. What if something happens? I was having the hardest time wrapping my head around the whole concept. Considering the devastating impact these students are having on the classroom, why would inclusion become the solution of choice?

"Special ed. teachers make more money and they have smaller classes," said Annie, who had considered that option. "But, if they get rid of special ed. classes, they get rid of the teachers, too."

There it was. It's always about "the dolla-dolla bill, y'all." Unfortunately, that leaves kids like Micah free to run unchecked through the system, sabotaging the learning process for himself and the rest of the students. Today, for example, he was particularly challenging. He came in angry and muttering to himself.

"I hate this place. I hate these teachers."

His voice was even different, low and raspy, instead of clear and high like a little boy's voice should be. I stood watching him for a few minutes, trying to reconcile this rambling little person with the reasonably calm, bright boy I thought I'd bonded with 24 hours earlier. Pulling him aside, I tried to encourage him to have a good day. He glared at me as though we'd never met. He also screamed, refused to listen, fought, fell out on the floor. I've never seen anything like it. At one point, he hid in the coat closet and held the door shut from the inside. Yanking the door open could have hurt him, so I walked away hoping he'd come out on his own.

A few minutes later, Annie asked me where he was. When I told her he was in the closet, she flatly replied, "We're not allowed to lock the kids in the closet."

Why would I think something like that was an acceptable option? Patiently, I explained that he had locked himself in the closet.

"Oh," she said. "He's not allowed to be in there unsupervised." Then waited for me to go and get him.

Luckily, he had finally let go of the doorknob. He was lying on the floor in the dark. I sat next to him and asked why a smart little boy like him would behave like this.

"I'm not smart. I'm stupid," he responded.

He just needs some attention and understanding, I thought. I took his hand and gently led him back to his seat. And he went. But shortly afterwards, I had to pull him off of "Shontay" (three times) because "She has the special pencil." Micah is a strong little boy who wears heavy, leather boots. It's not that I can't hold him or stop him, but when he's kicking and screaming it's hard to do it without hurting him...or getting hurt. Annie's been kicked several times... hard. So she's not inclined to tussle with him. Instead, she called for security officers who came in and threatened him.

"The cameras are on, Micah. They're watching you. If you don't behave, they're gonna take you to see the judge."

It wasn't just the security officers who were playing mind games with this five-year-old child, Annie was getting in on the action, too.

"And you know the judge can take you out of school."

I was horrified. Micah was clearly afraid. He fell to the floor, screaming and crying. The security officers picked him up and carried him out of the room. All of this in front of the other kids. Afterwards, Annie told me Micah was well aware of what a judge was.

"He's been before them. First when he and his five brothers and sisters were taken away from their mother, and again when they decided Micah should be allowed to go to regular school instead of being placed in a special institution. He's supposed to be taking medication," she commented. "But I don't think he is."

There were so many things wrong with what I'd just witnessed that I didn't know where to begin. With the judge's ridiculous decision to allow Micah to be in a general classroom in the first place? With the scare tactics used by Annie and the officers? Or, with the fact that this kid may not be taking the medication he so obviously needs? But since I'm only a sub with 24 days of experience, I decided to keep my mouth shut.

February 28, 2002 (Day 25)
Third day at P.S. #15

Hanging out in the faculty room today, I ran into Officer "Lena," i.e., one of the people who dragged Micah screaming from the classroom yesterday. Five-feet tall and somewhere in her late 40s/early 50s, Officer Lena struck me as the more compassionate of the two security officers. Without the slightest provocation, she began sharing stories about her experiences as a security officer for the School District. She told me about a stint at a "last-chance" school (so named because it's a student's last chance before being kicked out of Philly's public school system all together) in the Northeast. She said it was racially mixed but predominantly white when she left in the late 90s.

"Don't ever go there," she warned. "It's rough. Most of them aren't bad kids, but they're crazy. They're not even allowed to carry fingernail files."

Officer Lena had also worked at quite a few of Philly's infamous high schools, including P.S. #1.

"They're all horrible. The kids are in control. They don't bother to be discrete about selling drugs. They deal out in the open. Weed in the inner city. Pills in the Northeast."

She also warned me not to go into the fire towers in these huge school buildings.

"...not under any circumstances. That's where the students gamble, do drug deals and have sex." She said she arrived for an assignment at a new school and the principal immediately directed her toward one of the fire towers.

"I knew better and went the opposite way," she said before suggesting I stick to elementary schools because they're safer. (This I had already figured out.)

The day was draining. In addition to Micah, we had about eight other kids who were acting out. One of them, Wynton, was behaving so poorly that Annie took him next door to the first-grade class to cool out early in the afternoon. The kids wouldn't even listen to Kathy and she's the enforcer. One word from her and they usually settled down because she's tall and she's got three kids. So she really has that authoritative "mommy" voice down. Plus, if the students act up too much, Kathy makes them get their lunches last. They hate that. Annie thinks it's bad, but it works.

I wondered if the kids were so out-of-control because Kathy's sixteen-year-old daughter was visiting. She wasn't doing anything other than sitting quietly. I thought we should keep the kids who were misbehaving inside during recess. Ordinarily, Annie and I aren't allowed to split up. Today, she cleared it with the vice principal, who has a reputation for being flexible and concerned. (The principal was a different story all together. I had heard several times that she "couldn't care less about the school, the kids or the teachers.") Of course, Annie wanted me to stay in because she "can't stand being cooped up inside all day." More and more, I seem to be cast as Mean-old Mrs. Clay. When recess rolled around, Annie took the "goodies" out to play and left me to handle the kids who had been misbehaving.

So we sat. In silence. Ahmad, Busy Brooke, Shontay, "Jay" and "Michelle," who is usually very well behaved. They had plenty of time to imagine the fun the other kids were having without them. Their sad little faces and poked-out lips becoming sadder and pokier by the minute. I intended to talk with them about good behavior but, as usual, all of my attention was seized by Micah, who flipped out and flipped over several chairs and a table. Concerned that he might hurt himself or someone else, "Little Kathy" and I carried him over to the rug so he could stretch out and really dig into his tantrum. She's such a nice kid; strong and direct like her mother. She told me she had behaved exactly the same way Micah does when she was a kid—just for attention.

"Why?" I asked.

"I don't know. We did find out I have ADHD."

Today, Little Kathy was with us because she had been sent home from school for lateness and an incomplete uniform. She may have outgrown the tantrums, but she's still putting Kathy through it. Then, Kathy comes to work and gets put through it one more time by Micah.

I could not believe how strong that little boy was, or how relentless. He wouldn't stay on the rug. He crawled all over the classroom, rolled on the floor, tore through the coat closet. He twisted, pulled and kicked as Little Kathy and I carried him back to the rug...again. My shoulder and wrist are still aching. I got him to put his head down for a while, but then he started moaning and screaming. The other kids seemed a bit freaked out by his behavior. They weren't alone. This thing was getting old. It was time for some family intervention. Annie begrudgingly gave me the list of home numbers, insisting it wouldn't do any good. Granted, "Aunt Lizzie," who drops Micah off in the morning, did seem like an odd bird. I called anyway and aunty showed up. Not Aunt Lizzie, who's actually just a neighbor who drops off and picks up kids for a couple of bucks, but "Aunt Monica," a hardworking, no-nonsense sister in her 30s. And Aunt Monica feels that Micah's problem is that he's been coddled too much.

"I'm tired of coming up to this school," she fumed. "It's never for my kid. It's always for Micah or his sister or his brother."

After I explained how he'd been behaving, she took Micah to the girl's bathroom and spanked him. Then she directed the teary-eyed Micah to apologize to his classmates and to us. Annie was amazed. I'm not a big proponent of corporal punishment. I'm more inclined to torture a kid with an unending lecture, but Micah cooled out for the rest of the day.

Wynton was next. Annie refused to call his mother because, "She's hostile." Again, it was on me. I dialed. The woman wasn't hostile but she did launch into a diatribe about the principal suspending Wynton when other kids were bothering him. I told her I had personally seen her little boy knock down two different kids and spit juice into another child's hair just that morning. That's when she asked to speak to Wynton, who hung on the other end of my cell phone, saying nothing more than, "Un-huh, un-huh." Then he closed the phone and handed it back to me.

"What did she say?" I asked.

"She said, 'bye,'" he answered and strolled back into the classroom. (Yeah, right.)

When I called back, his mother claimed they'd been disconnected and asked me to call again tomorrow if he continued to act up. Wynton was better after the call, not good, but better.

Since I was on a roll, I also spoke to Busy Brooke's mother after school. I explained as gently as possible that her daughter couldn't write her letters, any of them.

"She is sweet (and she can be) but she's falling behind. If she doesn't catch up soon, she'll be playing catch-up for a long time to come."

An emboldened Annie punctuated the conversation with the fact that Busy Brooke had been wiping boogers on the other kids. It did need to be addressed, but I had kind of forgotten about it in the face of this child's inability to write her own name. As Annie stepped away, I asked the woman if she could work with her daughter at home. She said she did and would continue to do so. She seemed capable and open to suggestion. Why hadn't Annie spoken with her sooner? Before leaving, Busy Brooke threw her arms around me, gave me a big hug and probably wiped some boogers on my jacket.

Just to be clear, all of the students are not problematic. Some of them are angels. There's little "Gabrielle" who's smart, polite, well behaved and cute as a button. I'm trying not to get worked up about it but she's not well cared for. Her clothes are dirty and her braids need to be redone. My first day waiting with the kids, I noticed that her mother, who barely seemed old enough to have kids, breezed by, yelled her name and kept walking as Gabrielle ran to catch up.

When her mother swung through the second day, I introduced myself and told her what a great kid she has.

"Gabrielle is very smart," I said.

Barely slowing down, she responded, "I know." Then she giggled. "Psych. I don't mean to be like that. But she is smart. I know. We work on her letters and her reading at home."

As she continued on her way, I waved goodbye to Gabrielle, who smiled and scurried after her mother. Watching them cross away, I noticed her mother had on tight black pants, split high on the sides and high-heeled black boots. Today, as she swung by yelling for Gabrielle, I noticed she had on the exact same outfit, with the addition of a long, pink wig. That's when it hit me. Is this girl a prostitute? I forced my lips into a smile as Gabrielle sweetly waved goodbye.

March 1, 2002 (Day 26)
Fourth day at P.S. #15

I woke up feeling dizzy and nauseated. Being around these kindergarteners has finally gotten to me. They're always sick. At least three of them threw up this week; some more than once. I'm always the one wiping them off or walking them to the nurse. I thought about calling out but I knew the chances of them getting a replacement for me at this point were slim. Besides, I promised Annie and the kids that I'd be there for the whole week. So I headed out and got there just in time to meet the kids at the classroom door. "Mia", a little pigtailed pixie, ran up and threw her arms around me. Some of the others smiled and giggled, as though they were relieved to see me. Suddenly, I was feeling much better.

We also had a special treat planned. In honor of Dr. Seuss's birthday, the principal was scheduled to read to the kids at 9 a.m. We gathered the children on the rug and waited. At 9:30, Annie was dragging out her math lesson, hoping the principal would catch her in action and be impressed. To her credit, it was a good lesson. She had the kids counting and identifying money. By 10 a.m., she had switched to reading them a book but they were getting pretty antsy.

"Remember, be on your best behavior," Annie kept reminding them, "because the principal can throw you out of school."

Enough was enough. I strolled down to the principal's office and politely inquired if we should keep the children gathered on the rug or if the principal would be coming later. One of the ladies in the office told me that she'd be there in 10 minutes. Ten minutes later, a large blond woman in a gray dress, pearls and a tall red and white striped hat swept dramatically into the room. The kids reacted as though the Cat in the Hat himself had appeared. They were awed to silence. Even Micah was fairly cool, which leads me to believe that he's a bit more in control than people think. The principal did have to ask him to be quiet and to stop erasing the blackboard while she read. These antics were mild in comparison to the norm, but Annie died a thousand deaths with each of his missteps. Apparently, she'd been reprimanded for her lack of control over him. Finally, the principal authoritatively ordered Micah back to his table. He didn't go, but he did stop interrupting and sit down. The principal accepted this compromise as a victory and finished the story.

Later in the day, Micah's legal guardian, "Aunt Val," stopped by. I told her he'd been better since Aunt Monica's visit.

"Monica doesn't play with Micah," she said. Then she re-confirmed what Lizzie and Monica both told me. "He does not act out at home the way he does at school."

Either all of these women are lying or this kid is playing us for fools. I called Micah out of the room so that Val could give him the "I'm-checking-on-you" speech. But this gentle woman punctuated her remarks with a tender smile that scared no one, including Micah. He shot back his most winning grin and beat it back to the class.

Sometime in the early afternoon, I was summoned to the office and invited to stay for another two weeks since the regular teacher had extended her medical leave again. I happily accepted and Annie thanked me for staying, but she didn't want to tell the kids in case I changed my mind. I told her I didn't foresee any reason why I wouldn't be able to be there, so it should be safe. As far as I could tell, the kids had no discernible reaction whatsoever.

While the first half of the day passed uneventfully, the remainder did not go as smoothly. Wynton missed the principal's visit because Kathy had taken him next door to stop him from repeatedly kicking Busy Brooke. Granted, she probably wasn't completely innocent in all of this, but kicking? My latest conversation with his mother went pretty much the way the first had gone, with her promising to talk to him.

In general, the Ks (kindergarteners) were quite rambunctious today. Part of the problem was that we broke from the routine with the principal's visit. Also, as Annie shamelessly admitted, she has no classroom management skills. She's usually scrambling to figure out what we're going to do next, which means the kids have a fair amount of idle time. Plus, it was the beginning of the month. So Annie had changed the seat arrangements to give the Ks a chance to make new friends. Such a sweet idea...in theory. In practice, it produced a lot of arguing, hitting and running around the room.

I tried to calm them down so we could focus on the alphabet and writing their names, but it wasn't going well. Then Annie found out her house had been robbed. She was frantic. Before leaving, she blurted out that I should make every person picking up a kid sign for them.

"Cover your ass. If you're not sure, ask the kid who the person is. You just never know."

Appreciated though it was, Annie's advice merely added to my anxiety. What if I let one of the kids go off with some nut who isn't related to them? Or, more likely, some nut who is related to them? That, combined with the fact that Kathy was gone and I was alone with 32 hyped-up kindergartners, set my nerves on edge.

The Ks seemed to have one collective thought: "She can't watch all of us at the same time."

I was determined to get them settled into an activity, but they wouldn't cooperate. Next thing I knew, one or two over here were fighting. Two or three over there were chasing each other. They were testing me and I had no intention of failing. It's easier to control them in a confined area, so I called all of them to the rug where they continued to hit, argue and push.

"Ahmad, Shontay, I will definitely be speaking with your parents."

"Okay-okay. I said, 'okay'...okay?!" responded Shontay.

"You're not supposed to say 'okay' to a teacher," said "Keeshaun," one of the brightest and best-behaved boys in the class.

"You're right," I said. "And you are all mistaken if you think you're going to run around the classroom and act up on me. You know how to behave and I expect you to do so."

Micah, who had been fairly low-key during all of this, was starting to get worked up just as the other kids were calming down. I pulled him aside and reminded him that he behaved for the principal and his aunts, so he could behave now.

"I'm not stupid, Micah. And neither are you. So cut it out."

"I am stupid," he responded.

"No, you're not," I said and turned away. He immediately announced that he was "the smartest boy in the class," sat down and closed his mouth.

I made them all sit there until they were still and quiet. I thought back to conversations with Sr. Joan and decided to lay out my expectations. They looked bored. I told them we wouldn't be having the special Dr. Seuss cake since they had behaved so poorly. They didn't care.

"What about snacks?" one of them asked.

"No snacks either. Not today." I felt a little bad about that; however, I do not believe in rewarding bad behavior. We didn't have time anyway. It had taken me so long to get them under control that it was time to go home. Then, I thought about the kids who are always well behaved, regardless of what their classmates do. I told those five (out of thirty-two!) they could take a fruit pie with them, which is normally not allowed. (I've been told that extras are thrown away at the end of the day. No, I don't know why.)

By the time I got the kids to the library for pick-up, we were ten minutes late. I opened the library door to a bunch of grumbling parents, introduced myself and explained that Annie had to deal with an emergency. Then, I asked them to sign for their children and also told them that most of the kids had been very poorly behaved today. As each person signed for a kid, I quickly gave a little feedback. Most of the parents were patient and cooperative; a few grumbled.

One man groused, "Sounds like all the kids were out-of-control today." I understood the insinuation; Annie wasn't there and I couldn't handle them. But I wasn't taking the blame for the children's poor behavior.

"There were five kids who were very well behaved all day," I replied just as Keeshaun's grandmother stepped up to sign for him.

"Keeshaun was one of them."

"As always," his grandmother chirped. Then she grabbed Keeshaun's hand, threw her head up and strutted off.

The man shot me a look, then jerked away with his son trailing behind.

Next, Ahmad's Mom stepped up. I asked if she could wait so we could talk. Needing shelter from the nasty looks the other parents were shooting her way, she politely asked if she could wait inside. And despite Shontay's, "Okay! Okay?" I told her stepfather that she had been giving me a lot of grief. He said he'd tell her mother and three minutes later she was standing in front of me. When I asked her to wait inside, she squeezed past, snidely commenting, "Too many subs at this school. That's the problem."

I was doing my best to provide some continuity until the regular teacher returned and this woman was trying to blame me for her daughter's behavior?

"That's not the whole problem," I snapped, turning to look at her. She dropped her eyes and quietly took a seat.

Most of the parents asked about their kids before I could say a word. Even older brothers and sisters wanted to know how their siblings were doing. "Jorge's" grandfather desperately wanted to talk to me but he didn't speak English. And in the face of this crowd, every word of Spanish I had ever learned somehow escaped me. So I smiled, handed over his grandson and turned away.

Finished with the rest of the parents, I spoke with Shontay's mother first. Immediately, she started telling me how sweet her daughter is. And she does have a very sweet demeanor, but I have to tell her three or four times to do everything.

"When I try to direct her, she smiles, covers her face and yells, 'Noooo!'"

"That sounds like her," the woman admitted, dropping the pretense. "I work too hard to take care of Shontay for her to be acting up. I'm going to talk to her."

I could tell she was embarrassed, so I also mentioned that Shontay had given a quarter to another kid so she could get a pretzel too, which was very nice.

"I try to give her fifty cents or dollar so she doesn't have to see other kids having things she can't have, but that's going to stop if she doesn't straighten up." She gave me her number and told me that she's always home Wednesday, Thursday and Friday afternoons. She also promised to check back in next week.

"Please do," I said. We both knew this was serious. Shontay had failed kindergarten last year. They promoted her to first grade but she wasn't ready for it. So they sent her back. She's the oldest kid in the class but she's very immature and stubborn. How much is being sweet going to help if she can't master kindergarten?

Finally, I turned my attention to Ahmad and his mother. Though she may have been struggling with addiction, I tried very hard to show this woman the same respect and courtesy I gave the rest of the parents. She brings her son to school every morning and picks him up every afternoon. Every day, she tells us to call if we have problems with him. And he is a piece of work, but in a class dominated by Micah and Wynton, Ahmad was slick enough to fly under the radar.

"I wish you had called," she immediately began. "Ahmad's father was home today."

After I explained that I couldn't leave 32 kids by themselves to make a phone call, we spoke at length about her son. To my surprise, she lectured him about being respectful and made him not only apologize, but look me in the eye while doing it.

"We will be talking to Ahmad," she said. "His father, his grandmother and his uncles."

She gave me two numbers to call if I had any more trouble. Then she made Ahmad promise to do better. She also asked if she could come by the classroom to check on him. I told her she was welcome any time. Whatever issues she may have been having, right then, she was stone-cold sober and very concerned about her boy.

On my way back to the classroom, I stopped by one of the other kindergarten classes. Though I was doing my best, I felt like a failure. Maybe I had been too stern or not stern enough or I don't know. I shared my crazy day with the other two teachers, who nodded knowingly and claimed to have even more problem students in their class.

"How can you take it?" I asked.

"I can't," answered one of them with astonishing candor. "I think I'm going to have a nervous breakdown. I don't know how I'm going to get through the rest of the year."

"My doctor says I've had a mild stroke," the other responded.

I looked at these two intelligent, capable women and asked the obvious question. "Why are you still here?"

"I love working with kids," came the reply. The other nodded in agreement.

Feeling the despair washing off of them, I shook my head. Given their circumstances, a mild stroke and a pending nervous breakdown, I'd be looking for other employment. Pension, good works and bills be damned.

March 4, 2002 (Day 27)
Fifth day at P.S. #15

Yesterday, the city's most respected newspaper, *The Philadelphia Inquirer*, released its "Report Card on the Schools," a comprehensive, multi-page spread that listed statistics and standardized test scores for fifth, eighth and eleventh graders from the region's public, private and Diocesan schools. Other than a handful of elite schools, the results for Philly's public schools were pretty devastating. I expected the faculty room to be abuzz with chatter. It wasn't. The teachers were uncharacteristically quiet. I thought perhaps they were ashamed; I'm ashamed and I'm pretty new to the teaching game. Still, I feel acute personal responsibility because I'm supposed to be teaching.

"Anyone see 'The Report Card on the Schools?'" I asked, hoping to stir up some conversation.

Some nodded, acknowledged that P.S. #15 had done poorly, then dropped the subject.

"How poorly?" another asked.

"40 percent of the fifth graders scored below basic proficiency in math. 74 percent scored below basic proficiency in reading," I volunteered.

"Well we did well in math," another commented.

"40 percent of the kids? Below minimum proficiency?" I questioned.

"That's good?" the first-year, special-assignment teacher spat out.

The other teacher shrugged and looked away. Perhaps she was thinking compared to 74 percent Below Basic, 40 percent isn't so bad. But it is. 74 percent below basic in reading is nearly unfathomable for a school in an industrialized country. I see it every day and I still don't get it. Reading is so much more fun than math. The books have pictures. There are talking dogs and rainbows and whatever else can be imagined. Reading is the key to everything, including math.

Reportedly, the principal commented that the kids in this school aren't capable of doing much better even under the best of circumstances. I say, she should be fired. These scores don't reflect the children's ability to learn. They reflect what they've learned. And that's not much. I don't know how anyone connected with teaching in Philly's failing public schools can feel anything other than shame, frustration, anger or despair. Yet from the shadow of those wretched test scores, a ray of encouragement emerged. One of the first graders from next door came over to read to the kindergarteners. We happily turned over story time to her and she did a wonderful job. There she was: a little exception to what was passing as the rule. The Ks were enthralled. They leaned in, elbows on knees, chins in hands, carefully listening to every single word.

Later, "Mark H.," one of our smart little cookies, asked if he could read to me. No doubt to show me that he could read nearly as well as the first grader. When I finished gushing, he said, "And I'm going to get you a Valentine's card next February."

"Mark, you'll be in first grade by then," I responded.

"Oh...I forgot," he said, flashing his charming smile.

I was grateful for these few bright spots. Otherwise, our days seemed to be filled with disappointment and frustration. Annie says Mondays, in particular, are bad.

"They spend all weekend doing what they want at home and come in all hyped up and have to be constantly reminded about appropriate behavior."

I thought it could also be, "Yippee, back to school where we can do whatever we want." Whatever it is, it feels like starting all over again. Micah was bad but still borderline okay for him. Wynton was kicking, hitting and ignoring us, as usual. I've called his mother twice and he hasn't improved. Today, he came in with a brand new box of crayons. A reward for his bad behavior? A bribe to do better? Surprisingly, he did share his crayons with the boys at his table, proving that he's not completely awful. But when Mia tried to borrow one, he knocked her out of the chair. And even though Busy Brooke no longer passes boogers (thanks to Mom's intervention) and was nowhere near Wynton's crayons, he knocked her down too, just for kicks and giggles. Then he punched "Jay" in his stomach hard enough to make him cry and Jay is not a wussy little boy.

This time, I went in search of a pink-slip to write him up. I'm hoping the vice principal will follow through and suspend him.

On a positive note, one of the parents called us. She was aware that her son, "Kamal," had been "having some bad days" and she wanted to know how he was doing.

"I spanked him this morning," she explained, "because I found him standing on the corner like he had no intention of going to school."

"He's five," I wanted to say. "He's too young to be walking himself to school." Instead, I focused on the issue at hand. "He won't do his work (which isn't like him) and he's been fighting."

She gave me her new telephone number, said she'd talk to him and would be popping by to check on him. Annie was not quite so enthused.

"We don't want them just coming up here," she said. "When Gabrielle's mother wanted to come observe, [the regular teacher] made her get a child abuse clearance (which takes 4-6 weeks). She got it, sat in here about an hour, then left."

"Maybe she didn't feel welcomed. Don't you think making her get a clearance to sit in on her child's class is a bit extreme?" I asked.

"No, we don't know what kind of people they are."

Everyone thinks that schools need more parental involvement. It's probably the most highly touted solution for inner-city schools. Yet there was Annie trying to put the kybosh on it and telling me that the regular teacher did the same thing.

"That's ridiculous," I said, as she continued. I could kind of understand the hesitation with a few of the students' parents. But all of them? And even if Ahmad's Mom can be a little unnerving, she's on the case. He was better today. After school, his father—a clean-cut, clear-eyed young man—picked him up. He made a point of introducing himself and asking how Ahmad was doing. He'd been better, but I encouraged him to stay on him.

"You know it," he said smiling down at his son.

Then there was "Jorge's" grandfather, again staring at me expectantly. I finally managed to put a few sentences of Spanish together; told him Jorge was a good boy, but he needed to pay more attention when we do work.

"Gracias," he said grabbing my hand to shake, "muchas gracias." He was so grateful to get that little bit of feedback, how could Annie not want to involve the parents? Look at how it's going without them.

Since I only had two weeks left with the kids, I've been pondering what I can do to best be of service. The Ks spend the majority of the day listening to stories, watching cartoons, coloring and playing. Stuff they can certainly do at home. Maybe they should be learning something in school. Writing the alphabet, sentences, whatever they can handle. I had been encouraging the kids toward "word" work before. Now, I'll be pushing it like their futures depend on it—because they may.

When I laid out my shiny new ideas for Annie, she responded in her typical manner, "Knock yourself out."

March 5, 2002 (Day 28)
Sixth day at P.S. #15

Micah tortures all of us in turn. This morning, as Annie read to the class, he mocked her so loudly we couldn't hear her. "Ba, ba, ba..." he taunted, like one adult might say "blah, blah, blah" to another. Annie asked him to stop... once. He got louder. So she went back to reading and ignoring him. We had already shipped Wynton next door to curtail his morning hitting, kicking and spitting. Why should we put up with nonsense from Micah? I really couldn't take it anymore.

"Boys and girls, who's being bad?"

They all turned and pointed, "Micah!!!" He got very angry and started to cry.

"See Micah," I reprimanded. "No one thinks what you're doing is funny."

"What are you laughing at?" Annie snapped at the kids who giggled.

In retrospect, while my approach may not have been the most sensitive... or mature, for once we had a fairly peaceful morning. Unfortunately, as the day wore on, Micah fixated on Kamal. I separated them several times; but when we dropped the kids off for math class, Micah literally jumped on Kamal and started beating him. As usual, Annie turned and walked away as though she hadn't seen anything. The math teacher looked to me pleadingly, as she tried to restrain Micah. I didn't feel up to dragging him away or hunting down security, so I brought Kamal back to the room with me. I felt terrible that he had to miss math because of Micah, but he seemed quite content to sit in the room and work on his fractions in peace. I, on the other hand, was quite disheartened.

It's not just the Micah situation. Annie and I seem to be butting heads more and more. I strongly feel that the kids need to do more work. She thinks they need to have more fun because they're only in kindergarten. Annie (and Kathy) give the Ks kudos for misspelled words, or "inventive spelling" as it's termed in Annie's graduate classes. "I KN RD" means "I can read." I give them kudos for trying but I also teach the kids how to spell the words correctly. I had phonics. It works up to a point; then you just have to know how the words are spelled.

"That's the way you spell 'school'?" Gabrielle asked, pointing to the word I had written on her paper.

"Yep," I answered, noting her confused glance toward Annie and Kathy. If I had to guess, I'd say she was wondering, "Should we tell them?"

I understand the theory behind inventive spelling. Kids have to start somewhere, and gradually they build to the appropriate means of spelling and writing. But from what I've seen, the kids aren't building so readily. What "I KN RD" really means is, "I can't read or write or spell." That's a problem.

Why not push them to do better, instead of assuming that they can't? There are at least nine or ten kids in this class who are very bright, well behaved and completely unchallenged by the little bit of work Annie gives them. Two-thirds of the way through the school year, and there are also five or six kids who don't know their ABCs. Annie calls them the "low-end" group. I'm starting to think she's just a low-end teacher. And her low-end expectations are robbing these children of a good start to their education. Everyone needs to know how to read.

Today, I officially started working with the ABC-challenged kids. If I can at least teach them the alphabet over the next two weeks, then maybe reading won't be such a mystery. We started where everyone begins...with the alphabet song. (The other kids wanted to join in, but Annie was working with them on advanced coloring or something.) To be honest, I may have underestimated this challenge. Busy Brooke is way too hyper to get much done. She can say her ABCs, though once she gets started, it's difficult to make her stop. Give her a piece of paper and, within seconds, she has covered it in something resembling Sanskrit. "Kenny" routinely skips letters of the alphabet. "Juan" wastes all of his time whining about having to do "extra work." "Dena" couldn't keep her eyes open because her mother had a party...on a Monday night. And Jorge, my little ESL student, is so quiet and shy that I can't tell if he's actually singing the ABC song.

None of them can write the alphabet, even a little. Not one. Not even ABC. For a minute there, I considered abandoning this group to focus on the more advanced students to help push them further ahead. Or, maybe even the in-between kids, like Shontay (who's been much more diligent since the talk with her mother). But I'm afraid that if the kids who are struggling with the ABCs don't get some extra help now, first-grade won't go well and it's all downhill after that. So, it's me and the slackers.

Wynton returned to class at lunchtime. As soon as he finished eating, he started up again and we still hadn't heard about his suspension. So I took him to the vice principal's office, a large classroom with a huge conference table. Kids were everywhere: standing, in chairs against the walls and lined up down the table. At the head sat the vice principal, a tall African-American woman in a suit. She had a notepad and a call list she was working down. In between calls, I informed her that we were still having problems with Wynton.

"Oh yeah," she said. "I called you guys about him this morning around 7:30."

I reminded her that we start at 8:15, as she took Wynton off my hands.

"I'll put this into motion right away," she said delicately referring to the suspension. So Annie and I were both a little surprised when hours later Wynton's mother showed up at the library to pick him up.

"I'm Wynton's mother," she said scanning the faces of the kids. "Where is he?"

Looking back and forth between Wynton's mother and me, not a syllable escaped Annie's lips. I looked at this short, wide woman with braids and couldn't see what it was about her that struck such a chord of fear in Annie.

"He's in the vice principal's office," I offered. "He's been suspended."

"No one called me," she replied flatly.

It's weird to tell a parent that her six-year-old child is so out-of-control that he's been suspended from kindergarten...again. I didn't know what else to say and Annie was on mute, so we stood awkwardly silent for a few seconds.

"Where's the office?" she finally asked.

I volunteered to show her, but as we reached the opposite side of the room, Annie sort of snapped and started yelling out random things.

"He punched Jay in the stomach. He spits juice at the other kids! He's always kicking and hitting!"

Wynton's mother stopped and turned to face Annie, who by then was encouraging the librarian to chime in.

"Tell her...tell her how he behaves!" The librarian turned away, clearly wanting no part in this outburst even though she complains about Wynton every single day. I understood Annie's frustration and anger. This woman seems to be letting her kid run wild; but since we finally had her attention, I didn't want to waste it by pissing her off.

"I'll fill her in," I offered, hoping Annie would calm down. After locking eyes with Wynton's mother for a few seconds, Annie managed to get a grip and turned her attention back to the other children.

On the way to see the vice principal, I tried to discuss Wynton's behavior; however, his mother was fixated on picking up her other son from his second-grade class. So that's where we headed. When we arrived, the teacher was standing at the front of the room, yelling at the top of her lungs for the students to be quiet and get in their seats. I knocked but no one noticed, so we opened the door and walked in. Kids were yelling, playing, running around the class; two boys were fighting. Wynton's brother was on the floor, crawling around the room until he stopped short in front of his mother.

"You think that's funny?" she calmly questioned. He jumped up, as she instructed him to get his things. She glanced disgustedly toward the teacher, who had stopped yelling by this point and stood frozen at the front of the room. (Embarrassed perhaps?) She said absolutely nothing. I don't even think she made eye contact with Wynton's mother.

Back in the hallway, another teacher approached and informed this woman that her older son had walked out of class today and wouldn't come back. I wasn't sure if she meant the one crawling around on the floor or if this was another kid she was talking about.

Wynton's mother responded with something like, "Uhn-huh."

I would have been beyond mortified to find my son crawling around a classroom on all fours. Maybe she was in shock. Maybe she thinks we're incompetent. I couldn't tell and she wasn't saying.

She turned to me. "Wynton left his new hat at school yesterday. It's orange."

"You need to talk to the vice principal. We can get the hat after." When her older son finally emerged from the classroom, he quietly followed as I led them down the hall. Since the vice principal was on the phone, Wynton's mother insisted that we go look for the hat. She gestured to Wynton who hopped down from the chair, seemingly undisturbed by the events of the day and followed.

As we walked to the classroom, it occurred to me that this woman might leave without talking to the vice principal. So I gave her some feedback on Wynton's behavior in as calm and objective a manner as possible. Her response?

"Wynton should know better."

As opposed to her other kids, who clearly did not? I looked at Wynton. Like his mother, there was no discernible expression on his face. There hardly ever was. I found the orange hat in the closet and handed it to his mother. Having exhausted my repertoire, which was limited to honesty, I again suggested that she see the vice principal. Though we headed in that direction, she said it didn't matter because she was transferring her kids.

"Do you really think that will help their behavior?" I asked.

"Oh yeah, it'll help all the way round."

As we stopped at the office, the vice principal was still on the phone. Wynton's mother waved to get her attention. "I'm transferring them anyway," she called out.

The vice principal put her hand over the receiver, "All of your children?"

She nodded and the vice principal gave her a "go with God" wave and moved on to the next child. As she strolled casually down the hallway, offspring in tow, I felt frustrated that I couldn't reach her, yet hopeful that I might never have to lay eyes on Wynton again.

Later, as I shared the day's events with Nora, I realized that my cake assignment was anything but. Even if Wynton didn't return, Micah is still there and he and Annie have this weird, co-dependent thing going on. Either she's letting him do whatever he wants, or she's calling security and terrorizing him with "seeing the judge." She doesn't want to push the kids to do more work, even though she says they're behind. She's afraid of the parents and doesn't want them involved. None of it makes sense to me.

Nora maintains that if paychecks and requirements for teachers were higher (similar to professions of other college graduates) they'd get a whole different caliber of people applying for positions.

"Your friend Annie doesn't know what the hell she's doing."

"Neither do I," I pointed out.

"Yes, but you're not incompetent. Teaching is often the last resort for people who can't do anything else."

Harsh as this observation was, it wasn't totally unfounded. There are a lot of good teachers, but there are also quite a few who do not have the temperament or intellectual where-with-all to be effective instructors. Many—good, bad or indifferent—fail to hold their own career choice in high esteem. When I tell teachers that I used to work in TV and that I have a friend who subs and has a law degree from Harvard, they can't imagine why we would let go of careers like that to teach, especially to sub. Honestly, we're starting to wonder ourselves, but I'm pretty sure it started with a naïve and misguided notion that we could make a difference.

March 6, 2002 (Day 29)
Seventh day at P.S. #15

We're not sure if Wynton is actually transferring but he's gone for now. Last time he was suspended for sticking a safety pin into another student. This time, he's out for at least three days…three, whole Wynton-free days. I guess the vice principal takes these things a little more seriously than the principal. On the whole, I've noticed that the white teachers and administrators tend to be less inclined to demand good behavior. I can't figure out if it's because they don't feel the kids can do any better, or if they feel sorry for them. Even when black teachers feel sorry for the kids, they still expect them to do the work and behave because they know that an education is pretty much the only thing standing between them and a really hard life.

Nora summed it up in her unique style: "Okay, you're poor. Your brother's truant and they're getting ready to take him from your mother who's out of work. That's awful. But do you really want to be illiterate on top of that?"

That's why this situation with Micah is so upsetting. Sometimes, I think if I'm tougher on him, stop letting him get away with murder, maybe he'll settle down and spend his energy on learning and playing instead of manipulating and flipping out. But he's wearing me down. He takes up so much time and energy. My arms are literally aching from trying to stop Micah from repeatedly throwing "Lebron" to the floor over a computer Lebron had first. Annie continued reading to the kids as though nothing was happening, but the kids were focused on Micah. What kind of effect does this situation have on them? Most of the kids do not like being around Micah. Some of them think he's "crazy." They told me so...quietly because they don't want him to be mad at them.

Today, I called security. Fortunately, they were able to come right away. Officer Lena and her partner dragged Micah from the classroom kicking and screaming.

"He comes in worked up every day. Every. Damn. Day." I lamented to Kathy when she arrived.

"He's like that all the time."

"No," I said. "He's worse in the morning."

"I wonder what goes on in the evening," she responded.

Later, when Micah returned, he was sullen and withdrawn, sequestering himself to the toy dressing table in the corner. Officer Lena told us it took a half an hour for him to calm down; the same amount of time it took for him to work himself into another frenzy. Annie, Kathy and I agreed that we shouldn't send him to science class, especially since the teacher was barely able to control the students.

After we dropped the rest of the kids off, Annie disappeared and I returned to the classroom where Micah was calmly and articulately taking Kathy through his evening of playing games, eating dinner and watching TV. (Sometimes he really is the loveliest child imaginable.)

"Then I go to bed," he said.

"And you go to sleep?" Kathy asked.

He started to shake his head "yes," but then emphatically declared in a singsong voice, "No. My brother talks and talks and talks and talks and keeps me up."

Kathy and I exchanged a questioning glance. She asked if he wanted to take a nap.

"No."

We both encouraged him to put his head down and rest.

"No."

Finally, we gave him some of the work he missed due to the hissy fit. He got right to it as Kathy and I spoke quietly, both wondering if the key to this kid's behavioral issues could possibly be as simple as getting a good night's rest. I know I'm pretty to the left when I haven't gotten my seven and a half hours.

I strolled over to the office where I called Aunt Lizzie. I shared Micah's revelation about his brother keeping him up at night. She said she'd "take care of it," which I assumed meant she'd pass the info along to the real aunts. She gave me the impression that she wanted to get back to her soaps but I insisted she speak to Micah.

I couldn't hear what she was saying though I'm pretty sure it was the standard "you-know-better" talk. He responded rather formally, "Yes...yes... okay...yes...good-bye." When he hung up, he flashed a big grin and raced back to the classroom. He was an angel until the other kids returned; then it was back to the status quo. Just before afternoon recess, Annie told him if he could get his "behaviors" together for five minutes, he could carry the bag of toys outside. I pointed out that I'd already given the bag to "Michael", which set Micah off on another crying jag.

In the face of his histrionics, Annie said, "Well, I did say if he could get his behaviors together for five minutes..."

Usually, I defer to Annie. (Once she finishes her student teaching, she'll be a certified teacher, while I have been subbing now for twenty-nine days and may as well have gotten my credentials from a cereal box.) This time, however, I was very aware that the eyes of all the little people were upon us. I could feel their anxiety. Even worse, I knew Michael was two seconds away from disappointment. Something he never brings into our lives.

"No," I said very firmly. "Michael is good all day long, every day. He's taking the bag."

I glanced at Michael, who was trying to contain a triumphant smile; then at Micah, who after momentarily toning it down to hear the final outcome, reached way down deep inside to pull up a wail that would have shaken our eyeballs from their sockets...if we hadn't headed out to play.

After school, when Aunt Lizzie came to pick up Micah, she asked if he had been any better after she spoke to him. She was not pleased with my response.

"I'm sick and tired of having to come up to this school for him," she sputtered, which was odd, because as far as I knew, she hadn't come up. Not when I called. She spoke briefly to Micah on the phone. That's about it. But I guess she wasn't getting paid extra to field calls from the teacher.

I'm starting to resent spending so much time dealing with Micah myself. He's well fed, well dressed and clean. He also seems to get a fair amount of attention. He's one of the brightest kids in the class. He's ahead of most in terms of vocabulary and reading, but his behavior is totally out of control, as is the behavior of his brother and sister. On any given day, one or both of them will be standing unrepentantly outside of their classrooms, having been kicked out for inappropriate behavior. Do all three of them have Oppositional Defiant Disorder? Or, are they spoiled, manipulative children?

In contrast, Gabrielle, with her dingy clothes and unkempt hair, is a joy to be around. When one of the kids spilled grape juice on her shirt (which had finally been washed) she took it better than I did. I rushed her into the bathroom and tried to get the stains out without completely soaking her shirt, but they wouldn't budge. The thought that she'd have to wear this grape-juice stained shirt for the rest of the week pained me. Finally, in frustration, I said, "Ask your mommy to wash your shirt again."

"I wash my own clothes," she told me.

"Your mommy taught you to use a washer and dryer?" I stupidly responded, wondering how this little girl could reach the buttons and knobs.

She looked utterly confused and shook her head, "No."

"Then how do you wash your clothes?"

"In the tub," she responded as though it should have been obvious.

I felt weak. This beautiful, five-year old child was washing her own clothes by hand in a bathtub. Suddenly, her dingy clothes seemed amazingly bright. Clearly, she's not coming from the best of family circumstances. Still, Gabrielle is one of the smartest, most well behaved and pleasant students in the class. Why is she doing so well while Micah isn't? He isn't the only kid in the class who's the child of an addict (ex or otherwise) but, outside of Ahmad, the others are much better behaved. Annie says it's a matter of contact. Their mothers aren't allowed to see them. Other members of their families have custody. I guess Micah's mother is still around. Ahmad lives with his mother who's trying but the jury is still out. It's all so complicated and I am so far out of my depth. All I wanted to do was teach.

March 7, 2002 (Day 30)
Eighth day at P.S. #15—Lunchtime

I am so freakin' mad right now. I tried to work with that little group of ABC-slackers again today. Busy Brooke was out, which I thought would help since she's usually so distracting. Right now, these kids don't know what a "d" looks like unless I point it out. I figured I'd keep rolling from guided reading right through gym. (I'm not even sure why they call it gym since the guy just reads stories in a nearly incomprehensible accent that for some reason captivates the kids.) Get a little extra time in with the kids. A ratio of five or six students to one teacher is a huge luxury and they wasted it.

Despite the fact that Jorge barely speaks English, he's the only one of them who tried. The others...ugh. We were out in the hallway working on the letter "k." I struggled to get them to write "key" and "Kenny." You'd think by the time we got to "king," they would have been on a roll. All they had to do was write k-i-n-g...but no, they wouldn't do it.

"I can't dooo it. I can't dooo it," Juan whined over and over.

"Juan, I'll spell it for you, k...i... Juan, write k...i...okay just the k..."

"I don't know howww..."

There was a big freakin' "k" at the top of the page. This was the third "k" word. He had already written Kenny and key. How could he suddenly not know what a "k" is?

"I don't know howwww...I can't dooo it..." he and Dena were both practically chanting.

Other kids wanted to work with me; were actually upset that they couldn't be in the ABC group with Mrs. Clay. But these kids...geez. I persevered, asking them to give me another word that begins with "k."

"Uh...G?" Dena volunteered. I looked at her not comprehending where that could have come from.

"No Dena, a word that begins with "k," like key, king, Kenny. Like the words we've just written."

"E?" she offered.

Kenny started giggling, I think because Dena was just so wrong. Then Dena started giggling. All I could hear was Annie's assessment of Dena ringing in my ears.

"I think there's some mild retardation there."

I suspected that Dena's problem might be that she doesn't really try anything other than my patience. None of these kids wanted to do squat. And once the "gym" guy showed up, that was it.

"That's not fair," Juan whined repeatedly. "We have to do extra work and they get to have fun. It's not fair."

No, being illiterate is unfair, I wanted to say, but I was tired of fighting with them. So I took them in for "gym."

"How are they supposed to catch up if they won't do the work?" I harangued Kathy. "They don't even know their ABCs. That's so basic."

She agreed, but she's a veteran and able to detach. I am absolutely haunted by the futures I envision for these children. So I push and they push back. I stepped out of the classroom for five minutes. When I came back, one of them had pulled the elastic cord out of my souvenir Olympic jacket, and wrapped it around the leg of the chair where it was hanging. This was the reward I got for caring and for trying to teach these little buggers something. I was just done.

Later that day...

I eventually calmed down but I was determined to get to the bottom of it. After the gym guy left, I asked the children if they had seen anyone playing with my jacket. They looked at me as though they were suddenly unsure of what I meant by "jacket." (They had just spent a half an hour enraptured by a man who barely speaks English; yet, they were looking at me as though I was speaking in tongues.) I pointed to my jacket and the elastic cord wrapped around the chair.

"Did any of you see someone playing with my jacket?"

Kenny nodded his head, "yes."

"Kenny, you saw someone?" I asked hopefully.

Deer, headlights, the whole nine. He seemed absolutely shocked that I called his name. Kenny is quiet and fairly well behaved, other than that I don't have a sense of him. I take the blame for that. During my first week, Kenny was getting over ringworm, so I kept my distance. I didn't even want him near the other kids because I figured the more of them exposed to it, the greater my chances of getting it. I'm a little squeamish about stuff like that. Ringworm and lice particularly skeeve me out so I wasn't taking any chances. I walked Kenny to the nurse's office every time his bandage fell off. Finally, I insisted (with the full backing of the nurse) that his mother take him home and not bring him back until his doctor faxed over a note saying he was past the contagious stage. It wasn't personal. I just wasn't up for an outbreak.

In addition to Kenny's unconscious nod and Kamal's declaration ("I saw, too.") we had a little random blaming for fun and spite. Eventually, I narrowed it down to two suspects and two credible witnesses: Juan and Ahmad, the former; Kenny and Kamal, the latter. I sat them down and kicked my investigation into high gear.

"Kenny, did you see someone playing with my jacket?"

He nodded and timidly pointed, "Juan."

Juan's eyes widened but he didn't say anything. Kenny smiled shyly at me, then cut his eyes toward Ahmad, his smile fading. Ahmad shot back a grimace, causing Kenny to shrink but rugged little Kamal spoke up without hesitation.

"Ahmad...I saw him. With Juan."

Ahmad balled his fists, ready to pop Kamal. Since I was standing there, he opted to cry instead. Then, he claimed that Kamal was the one who was playing with my jacket. Noting the look on my face, he quickly switched to blaming Micah. That was a better strategy, except that if it had been Micah, all of the kids—especially the girls—would have told me by now. As we continued our chat, Juan "slipped."

"I only pulled one side and Ahmad pulled the other."

"So you admit you were messing with my jacket?" I asked.

"Nooo," clarified Juan. "I said that's what they probably said."

"Who are 'they,' Juan?"

He took a deep breath and held it. Taking the fifth, I think.

I decided to put this squarely in the laps of the people who owned it: the parents. Ahmad continued to boo-hoo while Juan seemed to be contemplating the situation, looking for the appropriate spin for the padres. Annie and Kathy thought Ahmad was innocent.

"He wouldn't cry if he was guilty," Annie said. "He'd just be smug."

They've known him longer so I decided to hold off on calling his mother. Then Annie suggested that perhaps it wasn't a good idea to call Juan's father either.

"I get the feeling he might give Juan a pop," she said, motioning as if she were about to backhand someone. Kathy stared at her in disbelief.

"Juan's father beats him?" I asked. "You know this?"

"No, but you know..." Annie said, not bothering to finish her thought. "It's up to you."

I had met Juan's father. He drives one of the daycare vans. He seemed pretty nice and very responsible. I decided not to base my decision on some ignorant stereotype of Hispanic men residing in Annie's head and called. Juan's father was at the school within ten minutes.

"Did you mess with your teacher's jacket, Juan? Tell me the truth," asked "Poppa Juan."

"No, Daddy." Juan responded, his eyes wide and unblinking.

"See," his father said, "he doesn't lie to me...and he never, ever lies to his mother...let's call his mother."

I've caught Juan in quite a few lies, including this one. It amazes me how many people really don't know their kids from a can of paint. I listened as he explained the situation to his wife. Then he put Juan on the phone.

"No, Mommy." Juan said softly with the same wide-eyed, unblinking stare.

"See... he never lies to my wife. Never."

I'm sure my expression was pretty wide-eyed too. What could I say?

We were about to drop it, when Juan added (for emphasis I think), "I didn't really do it, daddy."

"What do you mean, you didn't really do it?" his father shot back.

"I didn't really do it," Juan repeated softly once more before clamming up again.

His father seemed at a loss. "We'll talk about this later at home."

"Okay, Daddy." Juan calmly said and strolled back into the room. He didn't appear to be afraid or worried about what might come "later." Actually, he seemed confident, like he had the situation firmly in hand.

Since the opportunity presented itself, I brought up Juan's tendency to space out during lessons and give us a hard time about doing his work. We'd had a previous conversation about Juan's struggles with the alphabet. Poppa Juan assured me that they were working on the ABCs. He had made flash cards and everything.

"It's hard for me to get him to pay attention sometimes, too. But he's getting better."

"Good," I answered. Again, what could I say?

Later in the day, we took the kids out for recess. They ran around the schoolyard screaming like...kids. All except for Micah, Juan and Ahmad. Micah had been fairly quiet all day, which was the first indication that he wasn't feeling well. After punching one of the girls, he plopped down on one of the benches to wheeze and blow his nose in peace.

"She's a bitch," I overheard Ahmad comment, no doubt in reference to me though he wouldn't admit it. I thought a little bench time was warranted, which I'm sure made him love me all the more.

Juan, on the other hand, spent his playtime following me around the yard, interjecting at every opportune moment, "I didn't really do it, Mrs. Clay." It's hard not to like Juan. He's one of the smallest kids in the class but he has a huge personality. With his angelic face, gold jewelry and moussed-up 'do, he sort of reminded me of a kindergarten-size version of Prince or a life-size boy doll that comes with a matching denim outfit.

After a half an hour, I suggested to Annie that we take the kids in and do some work.

"Why? It's kindergarten, they should have some fun," she replied. "Besides, if we stay out another half an hour, then take them in, give them a snack…we're done."

I suggested we at least teach them how to play an organized game like dodge ball.

"Knock yourself out."

I didn't need her help. Playing dodge ball in the middle of a semi-busy Philadelphia street is not only a tradition; it's a rite of passage. Once, when I was a kid, we shut off our street for an all-day block party and street cleaning. The adults challenged the kids to a game of dodge ball. We were in the middle; they were on the ends. I was sliding around unnoticed, managing to stay far away from the path of the ball 'til my mother got into the mix. Unlike the other adults, she wasn't about to take it easy on us. She played like it was a competition sport. Once she got going, the other adults stepped it up, too. Suddenly, we were hiding behind each other, running, jumping and dodging as we tried to escape the hurtling ball. They mowed us down unmercifully. There wasn't a single one of us left standing at the end. It was sooo much fun! Not teaching these kids how to play would be depriving them of their Philadelphia heritage.

I took it easy on the Ks since it was their first time. I put the smallest kids (including Juan) on the ends with me so they wouldn't get hurt. And the rest of the Ks were in the middle, screaming, laughing and running every time the ball came within three feet of them. I was having just as much fun as they were, when suddenly I heard over my shoulder, "Maybe we should head in."

"We're in the middle of the game."

"Yeah, I was just thinking we could go in, get the snack started…"

I knew what this was about. Shortly after Annie vetoed the idea of going in to do work, all of the other kindergarten teachers took their kids in to do work. We were the only class still in the yard and that didn't look good. Heaven help Annie if the principal caught us.

"We're going to finish the game first," I insisted. While we continued to play, Annie nervously watched the doors. Every time someone exited the building, she nearly swallowed her tongue. I let her stress for a bit, then I wrapped up.

Back inside, I took Micah to the nurse because he seemed to be getting worse. Then I took Ahmad to the office to call his mother. I told her about his language and the jacket incident. She said she'd see me at dismissal. One of the male security officers overheard and made Ahmad apologize to me. He did it but he was completely unrepentant.

With about an hour to go, I figured the day couldn't possibly get any worse. That's when Dena showed me an old sore on her arm.

"This is where my mommy accidentally burned me with her cigarette."

"Has that happened before, Dena?" I asked.

She nodded, "Yes."

I looked more closely at the bruise on her lip. When we asked her about it earlier in the day, she said she'd fallen. When I asked again, she said the same thing, which made me believe her about the cigarette burn.

When I told Annie, she pulled Dena aside and examined her legs and arms.

"No bruises," she observed, though she did have quite a few old scars. Annie concluded that we didn't have enough proof to do anything. "You have to be sure with this kind of stuff."

I was upset. Annie was upset. We stood staring at each other feeling helpless. "Maybe that's why she can't focus on her ABCs."

"They never teach you how to handle this stuff in graduate school," Annie responded.

I'm not even through my second week and I'm worn out. It feels like I've been at this school for months. I'm way too involved for a sub. I need to take a step back. I was planning to ask Gabrielle's mother if I could give her some clothes today. All last night, I thought about how I could position the offer so it wouldn't sound like charity or pity or like I was accusing her of being a bad mother. But Gabrielle was absent today, giving me just enough time to reconsider and mind my own business. Yep, taking a step back, gaining some perspective, being less involved...it all sounded like a very good plan.

March 8, 2002 (Day 31)
Ninth day at P.S. #15

Today was not horrible. We found out that Wynton's mother had made good on her threat and transferred all of her children out of P.S. #15. I'm sure it was my imagination, but it seemed that teachers all over the school had a little more spring in their burdened steps. I know Kathy and I were pretty giddy; and Annie, who is blessed with a naturally morose disposition, was walking around the classroom singing to the kids. I have never seen her so happy or motivated. She even suggested we tell the other kids Wynton was kicked out for bad behavior. Seemed reasonable to me. I'm constantly harping on the importance of consequences but Kathy was hesitant.

"Sometimes kids come back."

They'd been down this road earlier in the school year, when another little troublemaker moved away. Annie wanted to use him as an example, but the regular teacher wouldn't let her.

"That kid never came back," Annie argued. "He was long gone and we could have used it to our advantage. This is an opportunity."

I was torn. On the one hand, we were struggling to establish authority over a bunch of five year olds...well really one five year old. Showing Micah that behaving badly could lead to expulsion might go a long way toward making an impact. But if Wynton returned and told the other kids we hadn't actually kicked him out, they'd never believe us again.

Annie's point was that we needed to do something about the Micah situation and I agreed. In fact, I had already spoken to the vice principal about this very thing. Turns out she's just as fed up with his special status as we are. She thinks we need to be firmer about the behavior we will and will not tolerate; unfortunately, it's difficult to lay down the law when you have no way to enforce it. I explained that we needed a consequence for his bad behavior; some kind of plan for putting a stop to it before the entire learning process grinds to a halt. That's when she informed me that we could send Micah to the Accommodation Room. What!? I didn't even know they had an Accommodation Room.

"That's because normally, we don't send the smaller kids there," she explained. "In Micah's case, I'm willing to make an exception."

Though Annie thought this was a good plan, she still felt using Wynton as example would give us extra leverage. Ironically, this was the first morning that Micah didn't come in raving. Two of his aunts walked him all the way to the classroom door and warned him to behave. He started off fairly well. By journal time, he was slamming his book on the table over and over, stopping the other kids from doing their work. At first, they giggled along, pulling their hands away before he smashed their fingers. After about five minutes (literally) they weren't giggling anymore. They were getting that anxious look they get when playing with Micah isn't fun anymore. I asked him to stop a couple of times. He ignored me, giving me the opportunity to enact Operation Preemptive Timeout.

We moved the other kids to different tables and called for security. Unfortunately, the vice principal hadn't mentioned our new time-out system to the woman who answers the office phone. Instead of sending one of the officers, she set about a game of 20 questions.

"What's he doing exactly? How long has he been doing it? Did you ask him to stop? Do you really need security...?"

I'm sure she just couldn't wrap her head around why three grown women couldn't handle this kid. If I were on the other side of this classroom door, I'd be wondering the same thing. I insisted and a few minutes later, the two security officers arrived to find Micah still slamming his book down on the table over and over and over. Granted, this behavior wasn't nearly as bad as it has been, but the goal was to stop it before it reached that point.

Once he was gone, the rest of the Ks settled down and got to work. The next half hour passed quietly and productively; then it was time to pick up Micah. I have no idea why he's become my responsibility, but he has. So I made my way to the Accommodation Room, which was about the size of a walk-in closet. I got the impression it wasn't used very often, despite the fact that the school has such a serious discipline problem. Officer Lena and another woman sat gently lecturing Micah while he listened attentively. He seemed to be evaluating what they were saying against his prior behavior and making mental notes about the changes he'd make. He's such a likable, engaging boy...when he isn't torturing us.

By the time we reached the room, Annie had gathered the Ks on the rug. Kathy busied herself on the other side of the room, wanting no part in the falsehood that was about to be perpetrated.

"Did anyone notice that Wynton isn't here anymore?" Annie asked pointedly. Some of the kids nodded. Others seemed to be wondering who this Wynton fellow might be. Annie looked to me for support. I gave her an encouraging nod and she plunged ahead.

"Know what happened?" she dramatically asked. "He was kicked out of school for his bad behaviors."

Some of the kids looked a little worried. Others looked toward Micah. Bright boy that he is, Micah had already clued into the underlying implication that he could be next.

"I don't care if I get kicked out," he announced, then became very quiet.

As Annie drove home the concept of expulsion, I suspect each and every kindergartener took her words to heart. I felt dishonest but anything that improves the classroom environment has to be a good thing, right? All of the kids were on their best behavior for the rest of the day, including Micah who was still quite subdued. Annie took advantage of his toned-down demeanor and benched him during recess for "roughhousing." He wasn't doing anything the other boys weren't doing, but I think she called herself cracking down. At every turn, she threatened him with a visit to the Accommodation Room.

"We shouldn't threaten him," I suggested, "even if he is acting up. It'll lose its effectiveness." I think he should just look up and find himself there, like he's been beamed up.

No Wynton. No Juan (scheduled absence). No Busy Brooke (absent). And a subdued Micah. I felt a bit like singing myself. The class was under control. The kids were calmer. We were getting more work done. Even the kids in my little group of ABC Slackers were doing better, including Dena. I found myself enjoying the kids more; seeing them for the amazingly forgiving, honest and generous people they are. Gabrielle had five sparkly, new pencils, which she opened and dumped into the box of crayons and markers for everyone to use. How often does she get new pencils? Or, new anything for that matter? Not very. Yet, she didn't hesitate to share.

The kids aren't just generous with each other. Over the past two weeks, they've offered me cookies, chips, juice, lollipops and drawings. What had I given them? Nothing. That needed to change. All I had was my recently purchased box of Girl Scout Thin Mints. When I say I love these cookies, I mean the mere thought of them makes my heart beat faster. I'm allergic to chocolate and wheat. Still I'll treat myself to a box, which I freeze and slowly eat over the course of a couple of months.

As I started offering them up, the kids seemed amazed. Maybe because they see me as more of a disciplinarian; the one who keeps them in from recess and talks to their parents when they're bad. Or, maybe they just recognize me for the Thin-Mint-hoarding sister I am...who knows? The point is they inspired me to share. And they all seemed to pick up on the value of these little chocolate treasures. All except "Sophia", who gave her cookie to Gabrielle because she doesn't like chocolate (weirdo kid) and Dena who needed clarification:

"Can I still get a snack?" she questioned.

"Sure," I responded. Fair question. Who trades one cookie for a whole pie?

"Okay," she said, grabbing for one of the delicate wafers. "Thank you."

Micah and Ahmad both tried to act like they didn't see what was going on. Probably because they didn't expect to get a cookie. I did take my time making my way to that side of the room. They sat very still, watching me out of the corners of their eyes. I was wondering if they'd even accept a cookie from me. We were all relieved once the offer had been extended and accepted.

Today was pretty alright.

March 11, 2002 (Day 32)
Tenth day at P.S. #15

The teachers at P.S. #15 had an "in-service day," which meant classes were dismissed at noon. It also meant Kathy and I would only be paid for a half-day of work. She was upset. I was exhausted, so I didn't mind. Plus, I'm still freeloading off my mother and my salary has risen to a whopping $95 a day before taxes. A half day's pay of $47.50 still puts me ahead of the forty bucks a day I was making.

We did very little work between 8:30 and 10:30 a.m. At least six kids were absent, including Micah. One woman actually took her kid back home after she found out that classes would be dismissed at noon. Maybe it's easier to keep them home than to make arrangements for someone to pick them up in the middle of the day, but this was still bizarre to me. I was never allowed to stay home from school unless I was sick. Once, when I was in high school, we had a horrific blizzard on the last day before Christmas break. I'm talkin' snow drifts up to my shoulder. We only had a half-day of classes, which I pointed out to my mother.

Her response: "Don't you have a final?"

"Yes."

"Well...you better get going."

Off I went, through the bitter cold and ice. Instead of the usual forty-five minutes, it took two hours to get to school and it was closed. I was a frozen, shivering mess. Thankfully, the nuns let me, and the one other girl whose parents were far too committed to education, in to use the phone.

"Can you come get me?" I pleaded as my mother (who, mind you, didn't go to work) sleepily answered the phone. "School is closed."

"Clayvon," she said in an exasperated tone, "I can't drive in all that snow and ice."

"It took me two hours to get here."

"Well..." she said, "you better get going."

Anyway...Annie was in ultra kickback mode so she let me do the morning lesson, which is still playtime for some of the kids. When Annie does the lesson, I do a lot of shushing and shuffling kids around to calm them down. When I do the lesson, I'm lucky if she stays in the room. Today, we focused on "B is buh, buh, buh." We said it over and over in a sing-song manner so it would sink into their little noggins. (I learned this from Annie.) Then I asked for words that begin with the "buh" sound and wrote them on the board so the kids could see what they look like. Most of the kids were offering up "ball," "bat" and the like. Mister-Michael-Perfect-Manners, however, broke out with "butterfly." Butterfly! Three whole syllables. I actually choked up.

Annie read the kids a story. As usual, she was struggling to keep them quiet and focused. I contemplated not helping since she doesn't help me, but it's so unfair to the kids who are trying. So I pitched in and helped settle them down. Then came journal time, a.k.a. Annie's drink-and-a-drag break. While I worked on spelling and writing with the students, she sipped coffee and disappeared for her morning smoke. Overall, the kids weren't too bad, though Ahmad tried to make up for everyone else's fairly decent behavior by loud-talking and commandeering another boy's pencil because it was bigger. I sent him to the corner, then joined him for a chat.

"Why do you think I'm always on your case? Do you think it's because I'm just mean?" I fully expected him to say, "yesss," dragging it out for effect as the Ks tend to do, but he surprised me.

"No, because you want me to be good."

"Why do I want you to be good, Ahmad?"

"So I can learn," he responded matter-of-factly.

Sometimes I feel really guilty about being so strict with the children. The fact that he understood gave me a bit of comfort.

"Look Ahmad," I said, "it's not fair to you or the other kids when you waste class time. You know what you're supposed to be doing. You're a smart boy. There's nobody in this class smarter than you."

"Not even Micah?" he challenged.

Annie and Kathy are always going on about how smart Micah is and "... if only he could get his behaviors together..." So all the other students think Micah is the smartest kid in the class. He's not the only smart kid and we need to be more mindful of the self-esteem of the rest of the students.

Looking Ahmad squarely in the eye, I answered "Not even Micah."

He smiled wide and promised to do better. And he did...for a while. Then something or another happened and Kathy kicked him out of class.

Annie reappeared toward the end of the journaling session and walked around complimenting the "pretty coloring." It's really a shame. Most of the kids really do get that they should be writing words or sentences, but they need help. A slow, quiet day like today presented a great opportunity to give each kid a little extra one-on-one. Kathy helps when she can, but she's usually cleaning up the class, returning milk crates and putting together the kid's homework during this time.

"These kids are behind. They're not going to be ready for first grade."

That's Annie's mantra. I don't get why she doesn't get that they won't be ready because she's not preparing them. Mark H. is reading on a first-grade level, but he doesn't write a single word during journal time because coloring is easy. With a little encouragement, he could make great progress. His parents are definitely motivated, God bless them. His mother brings him to school every morning. His father picks him up every afternoon. They're intelligent, thoughtful people who inquire about his progress every single day. Both of them have mentioned that if their son can't do something easily, he just gives up or falls apart.

"One Saturday," said Mark's father, "I just made him practice putting on his own clothes...all day."

"Good," I responded.

Mark H. told me himself that he "always likes to be first or next" and that he likes "other people to do things for him." Though I was impressed with his ability to articulate these thoughts, kindergarten seems to be the time when kids should be learning to do things for themselves. We shouldn't let him get away with coloring all the time when he can write. Since we had fewer kids than usual and Annie was rushing to read yet another story, I decided Mark H. should keep working on his sentences.

"You make me so sad," he complained in his adorable little voice.

"You make me sad, Mark, because you're not doing your work."

With encouragement and a little assistance, he finally wrote, "Superman is my buddy. And we fly together."

Sounded like the beginning of a story to me. Who knows what this kid could achieve if he's challenged in the right way?

March 12, 2002 (Day 33)
Eleventh day at P.S. #15

Life just sucks. Then you become a teacher. Or, worse, a sub.

The day started bright with promise. Two of our parents made good on their pledges to "pop in." We hadn't even started the morning lesson when I noticed Ahmad's Mom hovering around the doorway, hoping to be invited in.

"I just wanted to check on Ahmad," she said almost apologetically.

"Come on in," I said. "He's over there."

Despite the fact that she really caught him off guard, Ahmad seemed pleased to see her. She, on the other hand, was not so pleased to see how chatty he was during class time.

"Pipe down and pay attention to your teachers," she said. "Learn somethin'."

Annie monitored the scene with suspicion, but I was happy to have the support as long as she wasn't high. And she didn't seem to be. She was there for only a few minutes and Ahmad straightened up immediately. After she left, I noticed him staring at me: One eye closed, his head cocked to the side and an inquisitive grin on his face.

"Yessss?" I teased.

"Did you call my mom?" he asked.

"Nope," I responded, shaking my head. "She just showed up."

I'm not sure he totally believed me until she just showed up again in the afternoon. This time, he wasn't so pleased and when she directed him to pay attention, he sort of smirked. Why did he do that?

"Boy, I know you're not giving me attitude. I'll wipe that smirk off your face..." and on and on.

I could feel Annie bristling. It wasn't like this is what I had in mind either. Luckily, she didn't stay long. By the time she left, Ahmad was sitting quietly, his usual evident amusement tidily stowed away. There are a lot of things I could say about this woman, but that she doesn't care about her son isn't one of them. I'm sure there are other things she could have been doing, but there she was checking up on him. How many parents actually do that? Maybe Ahmad figured that out too because he was pretty well behaved for the rest of the day. Or, maybe he was just scared to death she would pop up again. Either way, it was working.

Juan got busted, too. Poppa Juan dropped by to check on his pride and joy. He beckoned me into the hallway to ask how his little boy was doing.

"About the same. Not paying attention. Not really doing his work."

"I'm still working with him at home," he assured me. "Okay then...thanks."

He was about to leave, but I insisted that he come in. What's the point in parents stopping by if their kids don't know they were there?

The kids were on the rug facing Annie as she read a story. It quickly became apparent that Juan was off in his own world, as usual. He wasn't paying attention to the lesson; wasn't engaged on any level. In fact, he was distractedly playing with two quarters. Poppa Juan was a bit taken aback.

"Juan," he whispered trying to get his son's attention without disturbing the whole class. "Juan."

Juan turned, surprised to see his father. His eyes widened a little but he didn't say anything.

"Put those quarters away and pay attention."

Juan fumbled with the quarters, not so much because he was nervous but because he just didn't seem to want to put them away.

"Juan...give me the quarters."

Reluctantly, Juan handed over the quarters.

"And turn around. Pay attention," his father whispered.

Juan flashed him the same bored expression he usually reserves for Annie, Kathy and me followed by, "I need a tissue, Daddy."

"Listen to your teacher, Juan."

"But Daddy, I need a tissue," he insisted.

Poppa Juan turned to me, apologetic, "Do you have any tissues?"

I offered one from my personal stash, which he quickly handed to his son. Juan quietly blew, dabbed his nose gently and held the tissue out for his father to retrieve.

He took the tissue from Juan and once again told him to turn around and pay attention. Juan sighed and turned toward Annie.

Poppa Juan shot me a look, clearly hoping that Juan was now on track. Annie showed the kids a picture in the book and asked, "What color are the mittens?" Hands shot up all around Juan, who seemed to be completely unaware that a question had been asked. His father was crushed.

"Juan, come here."

Juan calmly rose and strolled over.

"Why didn't you raise your hand to answer the question?"

"I was gonna," came Juan's response.

I could tell this man had no idea what to do. That made two of us. I wasn't even sure what the problem was. At least now, his father knows. He sent Juan back to the rug, thanked me and quickly exited.

At the end of the day, after all the kids had gone, Poppa Juan came looking for me. He told me how upset he was by what he'd seen.

"I called my wife and told her. She's upset, too. All I can think is that he's the only boy in the house and he's spoiled. Maybe he thinks he doesn't have to work for anything. So I took all his toys and video games and locked them up. He's going to have to show me that he's working hard before I give them back."

I felt bad for Poppa Juan. It's hard to hear that your kid is deficient in any area. Over the last two weeks, he found out that his kid fibs and spaces out in school. Better to address these problems now than at the end of the year when Juan flunks kindergarten. Overall, I thought the parent visits were very productive.

My little ABC group was also doing better. I didn't really know what I was doing, but 20 extra minutes a day seemed to be helping. I used whatever tools or worksheets I found around the class and made up others. Nothing complicated, just fill-in-the-missing-letter exercises for the majority of the kids and copy the letters for my little group. They all seemed to enjoy the worksheets, especially Busy Brooke, whom I'd just about given up on. For the first time, she was able to copy A, B, C, D and E so that they really looked like A, B, C, D and E. I was so excited that I hugged her and told her what a good job she had done. Unfortunately, she got so excited her whole body started shaking and she completely reverted to her usual scribble. Nevertheless, this was a great day for Busy Brooke, and such a far cry from yesterday when she told one of her tablemates that he "smelled shitty."

I was feeling pretty good about things. With access to the Accommodation Room and the Wynton story firmly in place, staying on top of Micah seemed a little easier. He wasn't quite as out of control. Even Annie said the class "wasn't as horrible as it had been." The kids were calmer. We were getting more work done. Parents were more involved. Then, I glanced toward the classroom door, where I saw a familiar expression of disdain pressed against the glass.

"Nooo…" I said, drawing the word out unconsciously. I rushed to the door, just as he jerked away. Snatching it open, I saw Wynton and his whole friggin' family, rounding the corner on their way to the principal's office. Back in the classroom, Annie and Kathy both wanted to know what was going on. We huddled together as I whispered the bad news in as casual a manner as possible.

"I just saw Wynton. What's he doing here?"

"Oh no," said Annie, crestfallen. "Why did we use that story? Why did we tell them Wynton got kicked out for bad behavior? Now, we're gonna have to eat it."

"Wait a minute. Let's not panic," I interjected though that's exactly what I was doing. "Maybe they'll say no; maybe they won't let him come back."

"They have to take him back," explained Kathy. "They can't say no if this is his designated neighborhood school."

"I knew better and I used that story anyway," Annie moaned.

I thought it was a good idea, too. I wanted her to hammer it home even more. "Maybe they're picking up records or something," I suggested, still in denial despite the evidence at hand.

Kathy just shook her head. She has too much class to say, "told ya so." Besides, we were upset enough. Just as we were starting to gain some momentum and control, that mean little boy might be coming back. I refused to give up hope until we knew for certain. By the time I returned from lunch, we knew. His mother wasn't able to get her kids into the school that was going to "help them all way round." So they're back. All of them.

Annie was desperately trying to figure out what she was going to tell the kids to explain Wynton's sudden reappearance. I was trying to figure out how my life had taken this unforeseen turn when I noticed a pile of potato-chip crumbs on my desk. Yesterday, there was a Cheeto. I tossed it, thinking the kids must play at the desk when I'm not in the room. Then I saw Keeshaun offering Annie some chips.

"Keeshaun, did you leave these chips for me?" I asked.

His face lit up with a smile and he nodded his head. Such a great kid. He hasn't caused an ounce of trouble or concern in the two weeks I've been here. He's smart as a whip, mannerly, gets his work done and looks for more. It's kids like Keeshaun that drew me to teaching. I cannot believe that something as basic as being able to learn in a peaceful environment is such a rare commodity in the inner-city. I thanked him for the chips and a few minutes later, I noticed another pile on my desk.

That afternoon, as I walked the kids back from math class, they saw Wynton lurking in the hallway. Most had no reaction, but I couldn't imagine they were pleased to see him. All of them, except Micah and Ahmad who giggled and waved, had been kicked, pushed or spat upon by this child. There's no way he should be allowed to return. But there he was.

"He wants to come back," I said laying the groundwork for whatever lie we'd have to tell next.

When we got back to the room, I told Annie that the kids had seen Wynton in the hallway, so we needed to say something.

"I'm ready," she said.

I have to give it to Annie, we gathered the kids on the rug and she stepped up and dealt with the situation.

"Some of 'youse' probably saw Wynton in the hallway," she said, pausing for a few seconds. "Well…he wants a second chance and Mrs. Clay and I said okay because everyone deserves a second chance, right?"

As most of them half-heartedly nodded their heads, Annie and I exchanged a look. How proud were we? Lying to a bunch of kindergarteners.

March 13, 2002 (Day 34)
Twelfth day at P.S. #15

Having recovered from yesterday's emotional setback, I was determined that Wynton's return would not undermine the progress we'd made. And to his credit, he started off the day making a conscious effort to behave. I tried to be warm and welcoming; take the new-slate approach. Annie immediately started with the threats: singling him out by name, warning that if he acted up, "he could be bounced again." (As though he'd been bounced before.) Not that it mattered; neither approach worked.

We began the morning with a word bee. Starting with the letter A, we worked our way through the alphabet. For the most part, the exercise went well. Most of the children were able to come up with at least one word that begins with "A." We did have a few surprises though. Loquacious Ahmad went out on his first try, as did our resident genius Micah who sobbed and screamed so loudly we couldn't continue.

"AHHHHHH!!!!" he shrieked

I had 31 other kids I was trying to work with, Micah screaming in my ear and Annie standing across the room staring off into space.

"AHHHHHH!!!!" he continued.

"Annie, can you please get Micah?"

"AHHHHHH!!!!" he screamed even louder.

"I'll try," she said, not moving an inch. She lifted her finger ever so slightly and said just barely loud enough for us to hear, "Come 'ere, Micah."

Relieved that someone was finally acknowledging his tantrum, he went straight to her, bawling as though I had somehow personally and maliciously prevented him from saying "apple." Right around this time, Kathy arrived... shortly followed by Officer Lena and her partner who stopped in specifically to check on Micah. With all of that attention focused on him, he quieted pretty quickly and the rest of us were able to get back to work.

The last three standing were Mister-Michael-Perfect-Manners, Gabrielle-the-Golden-Child and Mark (I-always-like-to-be-first-or-next) H., who eventually disqualified himself by calling out answers. As much as Michael wanted to win, Gabrielle wanted it more. I had said they could use the words posted around the room, if they could read them. Gabrielle shocked me by reading "hippopotamus." Michael wanted to use the word "koala." He could see that it started with a "k," but he wouldn't take the chance. "Kenny," he finally blurted out, but Gabrielle pounced back with "kitchen" and Michael was done. As the rest of the kids gave them a big hand, Michael dejectedly moseyed back to his seat, while Gabrielle stood basking in the glow of her victory until long after the applause had died. I had never seen her so happy.

All of the kids were fine during journal time, except Micah who flipped out again.

"AHHHHHH!!!!"

I have no idea why or how it was resolved, but Kathy handled it.

By the time we walked the kids to science class, Micah, Wynton, Ahmad, Kamal and Lebron were rolling around the hallway fighting and playing. When we came to pick them up, the science teacher had pink-slipped Wynton again for knocking one kid out of a chair and hitting another. He should have been suspended again, but that didn't happen. (I'm guessing the principal handled it this time.) By the end of lunch, Wynton was throwing things, fighting and behaving like a little hellion. It was time to separate. He put up a fight as I steered him toward the door, but once we reached the hallway, he stopped struggling, shoved his hands in his pockets like a little old man and adopted a look of casual boredom.

I took him next door to the first-grade class, which was team taught by two energetic and organized young women who didn't take any crap off the kids. They have the only classroom on the floor that seems to be under control.

"He knows where his corner is," one of them responded. Sure enough, he went right to it.

When kids are sent to our room for punishment, I don't make them stand in the corner. They do work and I help them with it. Watching Wynton stand defiantly in the corner made me realize that all of the personalized attention I lavish on the kids visiting our class may be inspiring repeat offenses. One day, a little boy was sent to our class after he exposed himself to his classmates. I spent a little time working with him and the next time he saw me in the hallway, he ran up and threw his arms around me.

"What's that about?" his teacher asked, retrieving him.

Not knowing what to say, I shrugged. Some of the kids are so starved for attention that if you show them the least bit of kindness, they latch on. However, bonding with me does not encourage them to behave in their regular classrooms. We may have to start offering "corner time" as well.

To our dismay, the first-graders had an assembly so Wynton was returned a short while after I'd dropped him off. I decided to let him finish his corner time in his own room; see if that had any effect on his behavior. But he wouldn't stand for us. In fact, he slid down to the floor and stayed there. Feeling sorry for him, I was about to invite him to rejoin the class when he started making a loud humming noise.

"Hummmm. Hummmm. Hummmm."

I asked him to stop. He ignored me.

"Hummmm. Hummmm. Hummmm."

I reached out to touch his shoulder and he flinched, sinking down in the corner even more. He was afraid that I'd hit him. In that moment, I felt tremendous compassion for this boy. Is he beaten at home? Is he acting out as a result of child abuse?

"I'm not going to hit you, Wynton," I promised, which encouraged him to straighten up...and resume humming.

"Hummmm. Hummmm. Hummmm."

That was it. I grabbed his hand and headed back toward the first-grade room.

"They not there," he calmly reminded me.

He was right. I knew there was no point in trying to talk to him. "They not there," is the most this kid has ever said to me. I tried the Accommodation Room next, but it was closed. That left me with the last resort: the other kindergarten class with the one teacher who's had a mini-stroke and the other who feels as though she's on the verge of a breakdown. I hated to do it. They always seem so overwhelmed, sending two or three kids a day to our room. Plus our kids like going over there because they get to play and color, which is not much of a punishment. But, as I dropped Wynton off, I met their new aide—a fortyish black woman who, unlike the two teachers, seemed neither overwhelmed by nor afraid of the kids.

"Please make sure he doesn't play, color or have fun of any kind," I requested.

"You got it," she replied.

"But if you have any problems just bring him back."

"Won't be any problems," she responded looking at Wynton. "Right?"

For the first time ever, I saw the faintest flicker of concern cross this boy's face.

With Wynton gone, I hoped the class would regain some order. Several kids were now acting out. Lebron in particular was having a bad stretch. When I first arrived, he was bullying Mark H. and not listening. After I spoke to his mother, he chilled out. In fact, he came in the next day and insisted on reading a book to me. He did such a nice job, we let him read for the entire class. He'd been pretty good since then but, suddenly, he was back to knocking down Mark H. like it was his vocation.

Annie says when you get rid of one bully, another rises to take his place. Once Wynton left, Lebron became a bully again. I think it's because he sits with Micah now. Micah gets to do whatever he wants, so why shouldn't Lebron? I didn't have a lot of time to ponder the situation though because Annie took two markers from the box at Micah's table.

"AHHHHHHHHHHHHHHHHHHHHHHHHHHHHHHHHHHHHHHHHHH!!!"

She stood less than a foot away from Micah, holding the markers and picking at her nails, while he screamed.

"AHHHHHHHHHHHHHHHHHHHHHHHHHHHHHHHHHHHHHHHHHH!!!"

Inevitably, she looked up to find me staring at her as if she were completely out of her mind. She sauntered over to explain.

"I just want to see what happens if we ignore him altogether."

"AHHHHHHHHHHHHHHHHHHHHHHHHHHHHHHHHHHHHHHHHHH!!!"

The other kids at Micah's table looked as if they were about to burst into tears, Lebron included. Moving them helped but they were still upset. All of the kids were upset.

"AHHHHHHHHHHHHHHHHHHHHHHHHHHHHHHHHHHHHHHHHHH!!!"

A full fifteen minutes later, he showed no signs of relenting. I tried to keep the other kids focused on work, but they were putting their hands over their ears, saying that Micah was making their heads hurt.

"Annie, we need to call someone," I said.

"No. It's a reflection on my classroom management skills if we keep calling for help. Plus which," she continued, "they may not come when it's a real emergency. One of the subs before you called security three times in one day because he couldn't handle Micah. The third time, they didn't come and that was the time he was kicking me over and over."

"AHHHHHHHHHHHHHHHHHHHHHHHHHHHHHHHHHHHHHHHHHH!!!"

As I started for security, Annie stopped me saying she was "trying something else." She had enlisted the services of an out-of-control second-grader who had been exiled to our class for the second time in one day. The last time, he sent his teacher back down the hall with, "Bye you fuckin' smelly bag." (Who talks like that in this day and age?) At Annie's urging, this kid scrambled around after Micah who was crawling all over the room trying to escape him. He didn't touch Micah but who knows what he was saying to him. After all, Annie promised that if he could get Micah to quiet down, she'd let him play on the computers instead of standing in the corner. She watched with what appeared to be amusement as I called the boy off and Micah returned to his empty table complaining that his head hurt.

With all the madness of the afternoon, I forgot about Wynton until the end of the day. When I brought him back, he was shocked to find the rest of the kids cleaning up and getting their jackets. I don't know what to do about Micah or Wynton, and I don't want to deal with Lebron on top of them. So after school, I spoke to his mother and let her know that we would pink-slip him the next time he knocked down another kid.

"You really don't want a pink slip in Lebron's file. He's smart. He might be able to get into a magnet school one day, but not if he has a bunch of discipline issues on his record."

"I don't know what's gotten into him lately," she said. "I wish things were like they were in the good old days, when teachers could hit kids." (What? Was she offering to let me beat her child?)

"We cannot hit the kids, but you can spank him or take away his toys."

"I try not to do that. Once, Lebron and his sister were fighting and she scratched him. The old teacher called child services...over a scratch...and I know she must have told them a lot because she called at 12 and they were at my house by 12:15."

Why do grown folks have conversations like this around children? They're little, not deaf. I sent Lebron to wait with the other kids, as his mother continued to explain that "nothing came of the investigation, but now she's afraid to spank him and he knows it."

Lebron is a beautiful little boy; always clean and immaculately dressed. I've never seen so much as a hair out of place. He is extremely well cared for. Something I cannot say about all of the kids. Even if I believed her, there was nothing I could do about that situation. So I focused on the problem at hand.

"You need to get your son under control now because later will be too late."

We agreed that she would make time to come up to the school and sit in the class, as well as instituting some kind of discipline at home. We finished speaking just as Annie urgently beckoned me over.

"Clayvon, this is Micah's mother," she said catching me completely off guard.

I was so stunned to see this woman in the flesh that I didn't even say, "hello." Luckily, Annie had plenty to say about "how sick Micah is" and "how the nurse said he couldn't come back to school until he's better..." (a blatant lie) Annie babbled as I took note of this woman's expensive clothes and professional demeanor. She looked nothing like the negligent, drug-addicted parent I had been imagining. I wanted to shake her and scream, "Do you know how messed up your kids are? You've got three in this school, each one worse than the next. WHAT ARE YOU DOING??!!!!"

Based on the way she was looking at me, I figured my feelings were pretty evident.

"He had a bad day," I squeezed out, trying to be civil.

"He did?" she responded, as though she'd never heard this type of thing about a child of hers before.

"Every day is a bad day with him," Annie jumped in. "Tell her why you went off today, Micah..."

Of course, Micah was all innocence and light as he always is around members of his family; and, at this particular moment, he was beaming.

"Markers!" blurted out Annie. "Because of markers, he screamed for 15 minutes straight..."

When Annie finally stopped talking, the woman nodded and walked off with her son in tow. I don't know if she was concerned, embarrassed, didn't believe us or just didn't care.

March 14, 2002

Yay! No school today! I needed to take care of some personal business, so I played hooky. I planned to let the office know in advance so they'd have time to get another sub, but Annie and Kathy insisted that I call out. They don't believe the regular teacher is coming back next week, and they don't want to take a chance on the office folk replacing me with another sub. Kathy will be there in the morning with Annie and they'll get the prep teachers to cover the afternoon. They both assured me it would be fine. Honestly, I wouldn't mind staying longer. Most of the kids are so sweet. If we could just figure out what to do about Micah and Wynton...

"Boy, did these kids miss you!" exclaimed Annie. "Where's Mrs. Clay? Where's Mrs. Clay?"

I have to admit that was pretty nice to hear, but then she ruined it by telling me how good they had been while I was gone. Not that I wanted Annie to be tortured...I just sort of expected it.

"So they're perfect when I'm not here? They must hate me."

"Nooo," Annie assured me. "They had a very fun day, lots of coloring time and recess in the yard. Plus which, the first graders put on a show for K through second. They sang songs and our kids sang along..." (Translation: "We did no work of any kind.")

I was bummed that I missed the show but while I was gone, I had a revelation that I wanted to spring on Annie.

"I think we should separate Micah from the rest of the kids. They shouldn't have to sit with him and put up with his nonsense."

Annie was a little taken aback. "Everyone will want to move then."

"So just say 'no' to the others."

"He can't sit by himself," she said weakly.

"Half the time he refuses to sit with the other kids anyway," I countered logically. "He sits at that little dressing table in the corner. We could make that his permanent spot."

"He can't sit by himself," she repeated emphatically, probably somewhat shocked that I'd even suggest such a thing.

I understood her point of view. Isolation is a tough sentence for a child, maybe even borderline cruel. The alternative is to allow Micah to continue his reign of terror. When it's the good of the one vs. the good of the many, I think we have to go with the many. And deal with the one in as humane a way as possible. Annie didn't want to talk about it at all, so we dropped it; however, I had every intention of revisiting it before the day was out.

The morning went smoothly. When journal time rolled around, the kids got right to work. I didn't have to remind them to focus on writing instead of coloring. They were eager to show me their work and get help making it better. My badgering...I mean encouragement...was finally paying off. The stickers I started giving out probably didn't hurt either. The kids were amazingly well behaved throughout the day, even with the prep teachers. So good, in fact, the librarian hadn't made enough "I-was-good-in-library" bunnies and flowers. She'd given out all she'd made and promised to deliver more later. When Annie and I picked up the kids, they displayed them with pride, some taking special care to point them out.

"See, Mrs. Clay," crowed Jay. "I was gooood."

Nothing, however, shocked me more than seeing Wynton slowly strut by, chest puffed out, waiting for someone...anyone...to notice his flower.

"Wow...Wynton! Good job!" I exclaimed as the corners of his mouth turned up into a slight smile. I honestly thought it couldn't get any better, but then Michelle held out her bunny to me.

"Yes, Michelle. It's very nice."

"No...I'm giving it to you," she said in her little chipmunk voice and stuck it on my shirt.

As far as I had been able to tell, this child was barely aware of my presence. She never chatted with me. She barely responded when I spoke to her. Even when I threw her out of the word bee for calling out, she said nothing. Yet there she was, making my day with this random act of kindness. I was so touched. We were both cheesing pretty hard. Next thing I knew, Busy Brooke had rushed over and slapped her ripped flower on my shirt, "Here!" By the time we reached the room, she had changed her mind and ripped it back off. Then she slapped it back on again. Then she ripped it off again.

"Keep it," I finally said, as she went to slap it on again. She seemed surprised, but ultimately really okay with the decision.

As I headed to lunch, proudly sporting my yellow bunny, I noticed Gabrielle was upset.

"What's wrong?" I asked.

"Nothing," she said, turning away.

It hadn't escaped me that she didn't have a bunny or a flower. "Are you upset because you didn't get a bunny or flower but you were good in the library and you're always good in the library?"

Tearing-up, she slowly nodding her head.

"Gabrielle, don't be upset. I know you were good." The tears gushed, as she fell against me.

"You can't always count on other people to notice that you're good, Gabrielle. Be good for yourself. If you know you're good, that's all that really matters. Okay?"

She nodded again, the tears disappearing. When I returned from lunch, she was on a mission.

"Can you draw me a flower?"

I drew my prettiest flower, but it wasn't what she wanted. She wanted a big one, like the ones the librarian had given out. We borrowed Ahmad's, I thought to trace, but she looked at it and drew her own version.

"Can you write 'I was good in library?'" she asked, then grilled me about my spelling. "That's how you spell good...with two Os?" (Annie and Kathy and that damned inventive spelling.) I nodded. She wanted scissors...then tape. And she didn't settle down until she had her own do-it-yourself flower adorning her shirt.

As I contemplated this amazing child, the class phone rang. The woman from the principal's office informed me that today was my last day because the regular teacher would be back on Monday. "Click." I felt as though someone had just kicked me in the stomach. Everyone...everyone said the regular teacher wasn't coming back. Everyone was wrong.

"We've been here before," Kathy pointed out.

"I don't believe it," chimed in Annie. "They'll let you go. Then she won't show up and we'll be up the creek again...trying to get a decent sub. Give me your number," she insisted. "Just in case she doesn't show up. You never know."

But sometimes you do. I gave her my number but I knew my time with them was over and I was very sad. I hate goodbyes, so I decided to try to focus on making the most of my last day with the Ks. As Annie marched off to the office for "confirmation," I raised the subject of separating Micah with Kathy.

"...it's just not healthy. Michelle doesn't want to sit with him and Lebron is following in his footsteps. He needs to be moved."

Kathy agreed, but she also was concerned about isolating Micah. Luckily, he was absent, so we were able to talk to the kids who sat with him. Michelle told us straight out that she didn't want to sit with him, so Kathy moved her to another table right then. Lebron, who idolized Micah, and "LaToya", who's absent a lot and a little unaware of what's going on around her, wanted to stay. I don't think either of them should be allowed to make that decision.

Kathy was still contemplating the issue when Annie returned.

"They're saying she's definitely coming back Monday. I'll believe it when I see it."

"I moved Michelle," Kathy informed her. "She doesn't want to sit with Micah."

"Oh…" Annie responded, "yeah… I was thinking about that. When Micah comes back, I'm gonna move him to a table with Wynton. Let them kill each other."

Kathy and I exchanged a look. That wasn't the solution we had in mind. And in fairness, Wynton had been astonishingly well behaved today. All the kids had been. And not because they were coloring and playing all day, not while Mrs. Clay was still in the house.

Inevitably, recess rolled around. I'd been promising the kids we were going to have relay races and today was the day. I had little flag pins to give to the winners. Everything was going great. The kids were having a ball. The girls were standing off to the side, awaiting their next race. The boys stood in two lines that stretched back to a set of big, metal doors leading to the basement of the school. We'd had about two races, when someone pushed open one of the doors from inside, hitting a couple of the kids. When they realized what they'd done, they closed it just as quickly, causing a couple of the boys to lose their balance and fall forward. Suddenly, Keeshaun screamed out. His hand was caught between the two closed doors. I was by his side in seconds, but the doors lock automatically and I didn't have keys to anything.

"Annie…open the doors!" I yelled.

"I don't have keys for this door!" she yelled running over. "What are we gonna do?! What are we gonna do?!"

"Open the side door."

"What's that gonna do!?" she screamed, panicked.

"I can run through and open the doors from the inside."

"Oh…" she said, quickly unlocking the other door.

Keeshaun was crying so hard by this point, I thought his whole hand might be broken. I ran at full speed through the corridors and down the stairs, pushing open the doors. Only one of his fingers was actually caught, but it looked pretty bad. The tip was smashed. The skin was broken. He was a mess. We were a mess.

"Try to calm him down," Annie instructed. "The principal will have a fit if she sees him."

"Who cares?" I thought trotting Keeshaun off to the nurse for all the good it did. Despite his mother's expressed consent over the phone, the nurse couldn't give him anything for the pain.

"District policy," she lamented.

Keeshaun sat quietly whimpering and waiting for his mother while I held ice on his finger. Naturally, the principal, whom I'd seen maybe twice since my arrival, just happened to stop by the infirmary right then. (There must be surveillance cameras somewhere.)

"What happened to your finger?" she questioned Keeshaun.

"I was waiting for my turn to race...and the door opened...and my finger got caught," he stammered tearfully.

"It was an accident, honey. You'll be okay," she responded with the warmth of a toenail clipper. Then turning to me, she said "Why don't you leave him with the nurse and go back out to the schoolyard. The intern isn't supposed to be alone with the kids."

I gave Keeshaun a hug, reassured him that he'd be okay and left. Back in the schoolyard, Annie was still pretty worked up. She was already bringing the kids in.

"He's okay," I assured her, "but the finger looks bad. I think the tip might be broken."

"Thank God you were here," she responded. "I couldn't think. I was just panicking. I was imagining the worst. When you ran in to open the door, the only thing I could think was that I should have gone because now I was gonna have to pick up the finger."

It was right then that it hit me. Maybe the principal's attitude might be less about District policy and more about Annie policy.

"This is going to be her excuse to not let me take the kids out for recess any more. She just started letting me take them out again since I lost one of them."

"You lost one of the kids?"

"Mark H. wandered off," she explained. "I couldn't find him. His mother found out and called the School District to complain."

"Definitely Annie policy..." I thought, then I offered, "Just blame it on the sub."

At the end of the day, I gathered the Ks on the rug for the last time. It felt like I'd been working with these kids for three months, instead of three weeks. The thought that I would never see them again literally triggered a pain in my heart. I told them how much I enjoyed teaching them but that I wouldn't be there next week, expecting some of them to cheer, or at least smile. They didn't. Not even Wynton or Ahmad. They just sat there looking at me. I thought maybe they didn't understand what I was saying, until some of them jumped up to hug me. Annie cut our goodbye session short by calling the kids to get their bookbags and coats. It was just as well. I was overcome with sadness.

Amid the flurry of activity, I pulled Gabrielle aside. I felt like I needed to say just the right thing to help her stay on track.

"Listen, Gabrielle, you're smart. You have to go to college. You have to find a way to get there. If you always get good grades, you may be able to get a scholarship...or you could go into the army. Unless we're at war. Then don't go, okay?"

She nodded, not in a "I-don't-know-what-Miss-Clay (she stopped calling me Mrs. Clay when she found out I wasn't married) is-babbling-about-so-I'll-just-nod" way. But in a way that made me believe this five-year old child is just waiting for her body to catch up with her soul's wisdom and understanding. At minimum, she's a kid who's smart enough to figure things out quickly. I hugged her and sent her off to get in line.

Today, as we walked the kids to the library for pickup, Annie let me take the front of the line. Usually, she insisted I take the back to keep an eye on Micah, Wynton and the rest of the cut-ups. Walking with the girls was nice. They chatted animatedly, asking if I still had the pictures they drew for me.

"Of course."

"Where?" Michelle wanted to know.

"On my wall," I fibbed, not wanting her to think they meant any less to me because I keep them in a drawer.

The kids understood that I wouldn't be waiting with them anymore, so when we reached the library door, most of the girls hugged me goodbye. The boys sort of paused next to me so I could tickle them or ruffle their hair.

"You be good," I heard myself saying over and over. Truthfully, as upset as I was, I couldn't manage much more.

Annie was pretty perfunctory. She thanked me for my help, once again reiterated that she might be calling me if the regular teacher didn't show up and that was that. I closed the door behind them and stood watching through the glass as the Ks scrambled for seats. One terrific thing about five year olds—they don't dwell.

After making sure Keeshaun had been picked up, I headed out. On my way, I ran into Kathy.

"You were the best sub," she said, hugging me. "Take care."

Getting into my car, I marveled at how nice my last day had been. Other than Keeshaun's accident, it had been what I had imagined teaching would be. Then it hit me. Micah was absent...and he'd been absent for the last two days. As a result, everyone was less anxious and the environment was calmer. There wasn't a single fight. Even Wynton, whom I thought was the most uncooperative little boy in the world, was suddenly kinder, gentler and being rewarded for good effort and good behavior. This realization just reinforced what I already knew. Micah does not belong in this class. It's not doing him or anyone else any good. He needs therapists. He needs specialized teachers. He needs more than a general classroom can give him.

This assignment had been much more difficult than I expected. I'm not sure I made any real difference. I made changes but that's not the same thing. I tried to institute more order, make the environment calmer, make the kids do more work, make Annie do more work. If nothing else, I think I helped establish higher expectations. My little ABC slackers didn't make the great leaps of progress I hoped for, but we made some. Today, Kenny sang the whole alphabet song, including "LMNOP," instead of just "LMOP." I couldn't believe it. He broke into a huge grin and sang it all over again.

Jorge wrote almost the whole alphabet without peeking and finally got up the courage to sing loud enough for me to hear his mistakes and correct them.

And Juan finally understood what I meant when I said, "If you can sing the ABCs, you can write the ABCs."

Busy Brooke also made a little progress. We were working on Ms and Ns, and lo and behold she produced two totally recognizable letters. I got excited. She got excited. Then she couldn't make any more Ms or Ns. I tried moving on to "S," but she was way too hyped. This time, instead of giving up and moving on to the next kid after five or so minutes, I held my hand over her eyes and guided her hand in the shape of an S.

"I can do it! I can do it!" she kept insisting.

But she couldn't. Time after time she scribbled something completely illegible. I kept guiding her hand until she calmed down enough to feel what the pencil was doing. Suddenly, she was covering her paper with Ss. I was so proud. More importantly, she was proud of herself. Yet, as amazing as I thought this breakthrough was, I knew even if I stayed, I had no idea how to get her to the next level. She needs someone who's trained to deal with dyslexia, hyperactivity or whatever learning challenges she may have. The longer it takes for her to get the help she needs, the longer it will take to catch up. The school was supposed to schedule testing for learning disorders, but three-quarters of the way through the school year nothing's happened. I see the frustration in her mother's eyes, but she needs to stay on these administrators until they get it done because doing her daughter's homework every night isn't the answer.

The morning of my last day, Mark H's mother asked me if there was anything I thought she should be doing (like I'm an expert). Mark H. was one of the brightest, most articulate kids in the class, but he needs to be guided and pushed. For what it was worth, I told her she should probably make him do as much as possible for himself. She nodded, grateful for my "professional" opinion. Looking back, I wish I had said the glaringly obvious: "Get him out of this school!" Who knows how long it'll take her to figure it out. She doesn't know that you can walk through the hallways of this and so many other schools and see teachers or security dragging screaming and cursing kids out of classrooms. She doesn't know that Micah holds her son's class hostage. She doesn't know that many of the administrators are burned-out or checked-out, and that the teachers just want out. This type of environment will ruin the best of children, even a great kid with good parents like Mark H.

P.S. #15: PERCENTAGE OF 5th-GRADERS *SCORING BELOW BASIC*:[2,3]

2000–2001

Math $\}$ 40%   Reading $\}$ 74%

---

‡ Percentages are rounded.

PART 2

Update on the Schools

My mission in life is not merely to survive, but to thrive..."

—Dr. Maya Angelou
Author, Activist, Poet

> Between Then & Now

*A*fter my three-week stint with the kindergarteners, I went on to complete 30 assignments ranging from one day to two months at 25 different schools. At nearly every one of them, the story was the same: classrooms being held hostage by a few students who continuously disrupted the learning process; all students missing out on valuable learning because part (and sometimes all) of my time, attention and energy was focused on trying to keep the children who needed extra support focused and working or, at least, in their seats. It was beyond difficult and, at the end of the school year, I decided to return to corporate America.

As the years passed, I often thought about the children I'd met. I had high hopes for the students of P.S. #10 and P.S. #13, but for so many others, I could imagine no bright futures ahead. In particular, I worried about that last group of kindergarteners, wondering how they were and where they were. I imagined that most of them advanced from grade to grade together, inevitably graduating from fifth and landing together in the same middle school. How much of their elementary education had been lost because of the extra time and energy teachers were forced to devote to "managing" Micah and those who would follow in his footsteps? How far behind were they all on day one of middle school? Were they at all ready for high school when the time came? Was college even an option? Had they missed out on a quarter of the education they otherwise would have received and needed? Or, was it more like 50%?

Would any amount of lost education be acceptable for a child you love?

Though I had left subbing behind, I followed the progress of the schools I visited over the next fifteen plus years. Just by keeping up with this small sampling, I learned quite a bit about the issues and trends affecting the School District of Philadelphia (SDP) and public schools all across the country. A lot has happened, especially in Philadelphia. There have been four education superintendents, three mayors and a statewide cheating scandal on standardized tests. Not to mention where it all began for me, with the takeover of Philly's public schools and inevitable disbanding of the state-controlled School Reform Commission

(SRC), seventeen years later in June of 2018. Whether or not the SRC left the District in better shape than they found it is still up for debate. What is clear is that they returned it to local control along with a balance sheet still deep in the red and buildings in desperate need of repair and environmental remediation.

Since the Fall of 2012, the SDP has been under the steady leadership of William Hite, Jr., Ed.D., an educator who seems to be as fiercely committed to financial accountability as he is to academic improvement. Just one year after his arrival, over 4000 District employees, including 1900 teachers and aides, administrative staff, nurses and all vice principals in the system, were laid off in an effort to meet a $300 million budget shortfall.[1] School counselors also took a big hit, leaving the District with more school police than people trained to provide the psychological and emotional support many students need.[2]

Hite, along with the now-defunct School Reform Commission, closed and consolidated schools that were under-enrolled and low-performing. He also targeted some of Philly's most dangerous schools with funds and programs designed to improve safety, engagement and environment. In fact, in the 2014-2015 academic year—only three years after Hite's arrival and for the first time since 2001—there were no schools from Philadelphia on the state's List of Persistently Dangerous Schools.[3] While some credit must be given to the District's head-on improvement efforts, there are those who claim this achievement was largely due to the underreporting of violence instigated by high-level pressure, a charge that predates the arrival of William Hite.

The new Superintendent also went toe-to-toe with Philadelphia's powerful Federation of Teachers—freezing salaries for over five years. To his credit, Hite declined at least one $60,000 bonus in a show of solidarity, though some still insist he was hired to disempower the teacher's union specifically and clean house generally.[4] As funding has loosened over the last few years, vacant positions are slowly being refilled, though according to some, often with people from outside of the District who start at higher salaries than those whose salaries were frozen. In June 2017, the SDP and the teachers' union finally came to a $395 billion agreement that included retroactive pay for teachers. Unfortunately, this left the District $245 million short of the necessary funds to finance the deal, a position the SDP has found itself in again and again.[5]

Progress at last?

Acknowledging the disparity in educational opportunity plaguing Philadelphia's ethnically and racially segregated communities, Superintendent Hite identified providing access to quality schools in all neighborhoods as his #1 goal. Though he has a vision and a plan, progress is slow, something Dr. Hite has publicly acknowledged in the past. However, the SDP's *Action Plan Update 2018: Progress + Priorities* focused exclusively on the positive—part of an effort one insider commented to "change the narrative about the SDP." Still, progress is progress and the SDP has some accomplishments to be proud of, including[6]:

- The highest graduation rate in over a decade: 72%[7]
- Academic progress that is improving faster than the state average
- $100M of long-term taxpayer money saved through high-interest debt refinancing
- One million new books distributed to all K-3 classrooms
- 70 classrooms modernized with state-of-the-art technology
- PSSA reading gains in every grade from third through seventh, with third-graders posting the largest increases
- Over 3800 certifications earned by CTE (Career & Technical Education) students, qualifying them for post-graduation jobs (though there have been complaints that graduates hoping to join the local electricians' trade union still didn't have enough credits)
- Sufficient confidence in local leadership to dismantle the School Reform Commission and return control of the District to Philadelphia

All good news, great news in fact. Sadly, the *Action Plan Update* failed to mention a couple of things:

- 79% of students are still testing into the Basic Proficiency and Below Basic Proficiency categories in Math and 61% are still testing into the Basic and Below Basic categories in ELA (English Language Arts) on standardized tests (more on this later)[8]
- 12,000 necessary building repairs throughout the District with a whopping price tag of $4.5 billion[9,10]

- A five-year backlog of 9,000 environmental problems that include rats, roaches, mold, cancer-causing asbestos and high levels of lead in peeling paint and school drinking water[11]

In July of 2018, *The Philadelphia Inquirer* and Philadelphia *Daily News* (along with help from anonymous SDP staff members) exposed dangerous and ongoing environmental conditions in its Pulitzer-prize winning series, "Toxic City: Sick Schools." Shortly afterward, the state of Pennsylvania and the City of Philadelphia announced $15.6M in emergency funds for an aggressive summer clean-up of 57 of the city's most "environmentally dangerous" schools.[12] By the end of the summer, only six of those schools had been completed. Five months later, the December 2018 SDP *Building Improvement Update* noted that 75 mold remediation projects, 17 asbestos abatements and 6 paint and plaster projects had been completed, though it didn't say exactly how many schools were completely hazard free. Thirty-eight more projects were in the queue and expected to be addressed over the next twelve to eighteen months.[13,14]

Crumbling plaster and broken tiles, the main sources of asbestos fibers in classrooms, have been commonplace in even the best of Philly's public schools for decades. As I subbed in one of the City's best, plaster dropped from the ceiling and onto a student. She brushed it off, shook her head and got back to work.

In November of 2019, *Good Morning America* anchor T.J. Holmes interviewed a woman who had taught in one of the District's premier schools for the last decade. Recently diagnosed with mesothelioma, an asbestos-related cancer, she is now in the process of suing the District, which had not made teachers, staff and parents aware of its presence in their school.

Lead is also not a new issue. In 2016, the *Guardian* reported that thirty-three U.S. cities were using unreliable water testing methods like those used in Flint, Michigan, which could "underestimate" the amount of lead in drinking water. Among the major cities named in this report were Chicago, Boston, Detroit, Milwaukee and Philadelphia.[15] While subbing, I occasionally came upon signs warning those who could read not to drink from school faucets.

According to experts "there is no safe level of lead exposure for children," but elevated levels have been linked to a long list of medical problems, including the limitation of proper brain and nerve development, reduced IQ and behavioral problems:

> "Numerous studies link elevated bone or blood lead levels with aggression, destructive and delinquent behavior, attention deficit hyperactivity disorder (ADHD) and criminal behavior." [Wright et al. 2008; Braun et al. 2006; Needleman et al. 2004; Needleman et al. 2002; Nevin 2000; Bellinger et al. 1994].[16]
>
> —Centers for Disease Control

The diagnosis of ADHD, in particular, is on the rise throughout the country, nearly doubling from 6.1% of the U.S. population in 1997-1998 to 10.2% by 2015-2016. That's about two times higher than average world rates[17] but still lower than PA state averages, which rose from 8.2% in 2003 to 11.1% by 2011.[18] I'd be interested to know what the ADHD rates are specifically for children attending classes in Philadelphia's decrepit school buildings. As remediation slowly continues, I think we have to question whether a significant percentage of the behavioral issues witnessed in classrooms every day and routinely blamed on poverty, parents, screen time, etc., are at least partially related to lead in the city and school environments.

In December 2018, the *Philadelphia Notebook* reported on Dr. Marilyn Howarth of the University of Pennsylvania's Center of Excellence in Environmental Toxicology testimony before City Council. She supports expanding Philadelphia's Building Construction and Occupancy Code to include protection from lead exposure in schools.

Said Dr. Howarth, "The most recent data from the Philadelphia Department of Public Health reveals 6.2% of children (2400 every year) have elevated blood lead levels, more than twice the national rate of blood lead elevations of 2.5% and much higher than the 3.7% of children in Flint Michigan at the height of the water crisis."[19,20]

Following up with Dr. Howarth, I learned that the 6.2% stat is based on fewer than 30% of the city's children being tested at the recommended ages of one and two years old. So the real rate could be significantly higher.[20]

"Philadelphia should require universal blood lead testing of all children age one and two since almost every Philadelphia child is at risk."

Dr. Howarth also supports testing for older students, especially when they exhibit symptoms that correspond to elevated lead levels. Though she labeled deteriorating paint in homes as the #1 source of "...lead exposure for most children," in her December 2018 comments, she also identified Philadelphia's soil, water service lines and schools as additional contributors. Since there are no studies on the impact of lead in the school environment, Dr. Howarth used the Environmental Protection Agency's risk assessment approach and considered the sources of lead exposure that Philadelphia children experience to conclude that "the exposure to peeling lead paint and the resultant dust in schools poses a significant hazard to children every day."[20]

She recommended the following: inspection and certification of schools by the Philadelphia Department of Public Health for all student-occupied buildings, testing of all drinking water sources and removal of those that are unsafe, timely remediation and stabilization of damaged and deteriorating paint, as well as protection for students while this work is taking place.[20]

According to the notes she provided, Dr. Howarth's closing remark to City Council was: "We urge you in the strongest terms possible to pass this legislation that will be an important first step in preventing the dumbing down of Philadelphia children by lead exposure."[20]

> Perhaps it's time for mandatory, in-school testing of lead levels for all SDP students.

In March of 2019, Governor Tom Wolf announced the Restore PA Plan, a set-aside of $4.5 billion to restore PA's infrastructure and prepare for 21st-century opportunities. Among other things, the plan will target the cleanup of contaminants, including lead-based community hazards throughout the state. Funded by a "commonsense tax," the four-year program kicks off in 2020. Note that the $4.5 billion the governor is dedicating to upgrading and cleaning up all of Pennsylvania is the exact same amount the School District of Philadelphia needs to repair, upgrade and eliminate toxic contaminants from its school buildings.[23] In the meantime, local leaders, including state Senator

Vincent Hughes and Philadelphia Federation of Teachers President Jerry Jordan, formed a coalition to more immediately secure $170M in emergency funding to address cleaning, maintenance, pest control, asbestos removal and lead paint stabilization in Philadelphia schools.[24]

Though the City, State and School District are finally taking steps toward remedying the environmental hazards that plague Philadelphia schools, there's still a lot to be done. According to the *Philadelphia Inquirer/Daily News*, more than 80% of Philadelphia schools (including charters) have some level of "dangerous asbestos," and 90% of the District's 300 plus buildings were built before 1978, when lead paint was banned.[11,21,22] With that in mind, let's take a look at standardized testing.

› A Word on Standardized Testing

*T*he following section provides brief updates on each of the 16 public schools and one Catholic school I wrote about in the first part of this book. Several of them are now closed. Some have been converted to charter schools. A few have improved or at least maintained, while others have lost ground. Along with each update, I am also including the percentages of students who continued to test into the bottom category of PA's standardized tests (PSSAs) each year.

Back in 2002, *The Philadelphia Inquirer's* "Report Card on the Schools" listed the test scores from the 2000-2001 school year, exposing just how poorly Philadelphia students were doing. The results were staggering with 70, 80 and sometimes 90 percent of scores in each grade tested falling into the Below Basic Proficiency category.[1] For consistency, I have continued to keep track only of Below Basic scores for each grade that was originally tested. Just as a reminder:

PSSA scores fall into four categories:[1]

1. Advanced
2. Proficient
} Where all test results should be

3. Basic Proficiency
4. Below Basic Proficiency
} Where most test results actually are

Those who interpret "proficiency" as being able to read and do math on grade level viewed these test results as failing marks for both the students and the schools. Former Assistant Secretary of Education Diane Ravitch clarified in *Reign of Error, The Hoax of the Privatization Movement and the Danger to America's Public Schools,* that although proficiency doesn't translate into "on grade level," Below Basic Proficiency does indicate "a weak grasp of the knowledge and skills being assessed." Roughly, it would equal a D or below.[2] Either way, it was bad and it shook Philadelphia's education community to its core.

The Inquirer stopped publishing their annual "Report Card on the Schools" quite some time ago. I, however, continued to track PSSA scores through the 2017-2018 school year. (Test results for all PA public schools are available on the Pennsylvania Department of Education website.) I am certain that some will claim that by including test scores here, I am validating high-stakes testing, which has been criticized for demonstrated cultural bias, poor formulation and built-in failure rates, as well as for being based directly on books that many schools simply cannot afford to purchase.[3] Others will complain that I'm focusing solely on Below Basic Proficiency rates when the real goal is for students to achieve Proficiency. There are also those who will say test scores are only one small piece of the puzzle. Even the SDP now uses a combination of factors (academic achievement/test scores, attendance, climate and college and career readiness) to "grade" schools.[4] While this is all true, Philly's test scores still indicate a huge problem that persists nearly 20 years later.

Interestingly, test scores had been on the upswing for many Philadelphia schools until the 2014-2015 school year when PA—along with many U.S. states—adopted the more challenging Common-Core aligned State Standards. They "define expectations for what students should know and be able to do by the end of each grade."[5] The Common Core is not only supposed to ensure that every child across the U.S. is truly college and/or workforce ready by the time they graduate, but also to ensure equity. In other words, it's supposed to make certain that we do not provide Blake at suburban School A with a comprehensive and challenging education, while Zilin and Malik at inner-city School B barely get the basics year after year, and Becky and Juan at rural School C get something altogether different.

Along with the more rigorous and, hopefully, more egalitarian curriculum came more rigorous testing. Philadelphia's students were not expected to do as well on the test and many did not, not just in Philly but across the state. Dr. Hite addressed the results in an open letter to the SDP community.

> "Not surprisingly—given the more rigorous standards and skills assessed—preliminary results show that across Pennsylvania fewer students scored proficient or advanced in both English Language Arts and Mathematics on the new PSSAs. Our performance on the new PSSAs mirrors these statewide trends..."[6]

—William Hite, Superintendent
School District of Philadelphia

Dr. Hite wrote that a major transition of this sort would take time and require "investments in teacher training, curricular materials, student tutoring, and other support." He also emphasized that the District was still in the process of aligning its curriculum and resources to meet the new standards.

When I first began subbing in 2001, the PSSAs were given in fifth, eighth and eleventh grades. The *No Child Left Behind* law was implemented during that same year and, soon after, annual testing was required in every class of every grade, every single year. In 1997, standardized testing was a $263-million industry. According to USinflationcalculator.com, these same tests should have cost around $388M in 2014. Instead, the industry had ballooned to $2.46 billion.[7] Perhaps it's time to figure out how to redirect some of those funds back into actual instruction.

Though some may favor the elimination of standardized assessments all together, we have to be practical. Most institutions of higher learning still require test scores. More jobs now include testing along with applications. Not to mention, until we stop pretending that all schools are operating on a level playing field, testing is one of the only means by which we are able to actually demonstrate that they are not. As you read the following updates, you can decide for yourself whether or not test scores matter.

> Update – Public School #1

*Y*ears ago when I subbed at P.S. #1, there were 1900 students enrolled. Fifteen years later, there are fewer than 800 and a truancy rate that hovers around 25%. In 2011, P.S. #1 was re-designated as a "Promise Academy" and flagged for "irregularities" in standardized test taking.[1] In 2013, it experienced an influx of students from a closing rival school that, like P.S. #1, had made the state's List of Persistently Dangerous Schools two years in a row.[2,3] Specifically because these two student populations were combined, P.S. #1 became one of 20 schools to receive money from a $730,000 multi-year grant from the Philadelphia Foundation. The funds were earmarked for training and support services designed to "reduce violent incidents, decrease suspensions and establish a school-wide culture of acceptance and respect."[4]

In 2015, P.S. #1's top administrator received the prestigious Lindback Foundation Award for Distinguished Principal Leadership. In response, he commented to *Newsworks.org* that he was "especially proud of the school's progress when it comes to graduation and attendance rates during the transition." Both, he seemed to feel, demonstrated a growing sense of accountability among students and staff that he hoped would translate into a better academic reputation for P.S. #1.[5] Shortly thereafter, he resigned his position and relocated to another state.

PSSA scores for P.S. #1 had been consistently abysmal, with a high percentage of students (50%, 60%, 70% or more) testing into the Below Basic Proficiency category.[6] But, in 2012, PA switched to the subject-specific Keystone Test for high schools. P.S. #1 students began scoring a bit better with fewer students (30%, 40%, 50%, etc.) testing into Below Basic.[7] It has been suggested that the reason for this improvement is that the Keystone Tests are based on material that the students are taught vs. the PSSAs, which are based on general knowledge all students are expected to have acquired.

I had the opportunity to speak with a teacher who currently works at P.S. #1. He agreed to share his thoughts anonymously. My first question, of course, was how is P.S. #1 today?

"It's dangerous," said "Teacher X". "Any school with a metal detector at the front door is sending a signal that there's the possibility for all kinds of violence."

He went on to tell me that there's an official police office in the school building, and normally seven or eight uniformed officers with badges and handcuffs (but no guns) on duty during the course of the day. Along with school deans, they encourage students to get to class instead of wandering the hallways. There are also usually three or four police cars waiting outside the school at the end of each day: two at the front and two more posted at the ends of the street to discourage fights from spilling over into the surrounding neighborhood.

"There are a lot of fights. Pretty much every day. Thursday, there was a fight. I was told there were ten girls involved in it. I don't think there was a fight yesterday. I think, on Fridays, a lot of kids leave early and go home. In my room yesterday, a Friday, ten kids were late to second period and six were absent. That's pretty good. Last period, there are thirty-four kids on roster, which is [over the limit] and I have another class with forty-three. One student was on time and five were significantly late. The rest were absent. Six out of thirty-four showed up."

Regarding the high level of truancy at P.S. #1, Teacher X added, "Maybe they'll show up the first couple of weeks or months, then they stop coming. You start mailing letters...calling...but the phones are disconnected. We call all the time. All the teachers. It's part of our job. I never would have imagined that we'd have to spend so much time calling parents and mailing letters."

He also said that some of the parents have just given up.

"They'll tell you, 'Look, I've done everything I can. I don't know what to do. He's eighteen years old. He's going to do what he wants.' That's that."

Turning back to the safety issue at P.S. #1, Teacher X commented that they are really understaffed. "We don't have enough people circulating in the hallways... deans or behavioral specialists...[or] in the building to make things work."

He also pointed to "the building itself," as another hazard. Originally designed for several thousand students, now different wings are cordoned off, but students still use them for fighting, selling drugs and having sex.

"There are so many places for these kids to hide."

He also reported that heavy reliance on substitute teachers and the proliferation of cell phone use have also had negative influences on school culture:

"A lot of the bullying happens and [information] starts circulating with the press of a few buttons. Suddenly, everybody will just leave class and go watch a fight and videotape it with their phones. It happens frequently."

Wondering if the grant to enhance school climate has made a difference, I asked if he had seen any changes over the last couple of years.

"One positive thing is that there are less hall walkers. [A few years back], the second floor was like a shopping mall. Kids walking around like zombies, staring into phones, waiting for the next fight. It was ridiculous."

I mentioned that I pulled the *Safe Schools Report* for PA and the School District of Philadelphia, and though the number of reported violent incidents was significantly lower than a couple of years ago, the numbers were still staggering. For the 2015-2016 school year, the District reported 4,889[8] violent incidents vs. 8,062[9] reported in 2011-2012. (The number of incidents reported statewide in 2015-2016 was 42,968[10]). In comparison, the reported incidents for P.S. #1—only 53[11]—seemed reasonable until I realized that it averaged out to be at least one plus violent incident during every single week of school.

"I promise you," Teacher X responded. "The numbers are much, much worse. There is a lot of pressure to not report these things, and administrators report as little as possible. I know that. They sweep as much stuff as possible under the rug because their jobs are on the line. It's way higher. I know that. They lie. They lie. They lie."

Switching gears, I noted that P.S. #1 is a Promise Academy. "What does that mean?" I asked.

First he laughed, but eventually said, "What that means is they get a bunch of money from wherever that comes from so they can fund after-school programs and enrichment programs. That money disappeared [long ago] but they kept the name. I think because it sounds good. Now, we're part of the Turnaround Network. That's the new thing. There's all these failing schools in Philadelphia, and we're one of the top 10 failing schools. So they call us a Promise Academy, which means they make [the teachers] do a lot of professional development during the summer. It's paid…but I don't see how it's helping. Most of the kids are dropping out...I don't see new books. I haven't gotten supplies for a year. [We don't have] the things that keep kids around like theater, performing arts, etc. We have basketball, football and track. That's it."

Teacher X also explained that the professional development sessions focus on topics such as "how to deal with kids who've been through trauma; how to use a grade book in the way [the School District] wants us to use it, or [being] lectured. It just feels like a lot of this stuff is meant to prop up a bureaucracy... just keep the funds circulating rather than helping the kids."

When asked what he thinks would help the kids, he quickly answers, "Well... engaged families. That would be the first thing. Second, if they had communities that were engaged, as well. I think the culture of these kids is a combination of prison culture and white-trash culture," which he feels promotes neglect of education, promiscuity and glorification of violence through music.

"It can't get any worse than that. It's such a norm that to deviate from that norm would alienate you if you're a part of that norm...the inner-city black community we serve. It's so destructive. No one talks about that stuff though, or we're not supposed to."

When asked if any of the students take school seriously, he admitted that there are students who want an education.

"Yeah...and I feel bad. We're letting these kids down. And the schools are letting them down. And their classmates are pulling them down. I definitely have some kids, more than some, a lot of kids that are really good...we do have kids going to college. I'm painting a pretty bleak picture but we definitely do have some successes with these kids."

Teacher X attributes the achievement of these students to the values and aspirations instilled at home. For the rest, it's a different story.

"I think the problem is by the time these kids get to high school, they're already so far behind; reading on a fourth-grade level. And teachers are under enormous pressure to raise these test scores because that's what their evaluation and the school evaluations are based on. It's really hard to negotiate that. The teachers wind up looking like they're not doing their jobs and they're failing the kids. The administration looks like they're failing the teachers and the kids. The school is labeled a failing school..."

He was quick to add that he feels the teachers at P.S. #1 "know their stuff" and are doing the best they can with very little.

"Some are stronger in certain areas than others. There's a lot of stuff I need to work on, but for the most part, the teachers are very serious about what they're doing."

Eventually, our conversation turned to charter schools, which Teacher X says are not helping.

"I looked at a recent report on charters at a few random schools. They were a few percentage points lower than the average public school. It's a wash. Maybe there are some great ones, but…you get a kid mouthing off, acting out, fighting and they get kicked out of charter schools. And they all come to us. All of them. We have to take them. You'll have 20 students in your class who need emotional support, but no aides. None."

He also addressed his frustration over the School District's drive to decrease suspension rates.

"If you want to decrease suspension rates, you've got to increase them first. Big time. But it's like they don't understand that. They just want happy numbers."

The final word from Teacher X on the progress of P.S. #1?

"I don't feel like we're turning around at all."

UPDATE – P.S. #1 (CONT'D)

Proficiency Exam Scores Reported for P.S. #1 (11th Grade)

Remember: Higher Percentages = More Students Failing the Test
Lower Percentages = More Students Passing the Test

Percentage of Students Scoring **BELOW BASIC** Proficiency[*]

PSSA Results:[6]		
2001 – 2002	Math: 51%	Reading: 61%
2002 – 2003	Math: 71%	Reading: 65%
2003 – 2004	Math: 80%	Reading: 64%
2004 – 2005	Math: 82%	Reading: 60%
2005 – 2006	Math: 84%	Reading: 52%
2006 – 2007	Math: 73%	Reading: 65%
2007 – 2008	Math: 83%	Reading: 54%
2008 – 2009	Math: 76%	Reading: 67%
2009 – 2010	Math: 63%	Reading: 56%
2010 – 2011	Math: 56%	Reading: 49%
2011 – 2012	Math: 72%	Reading: 61%
Keystone Exam Results:[7][†]		
2012 –2013[‡]	Algebra: 50%	Literature: 38%
2013 – 2014	Algebra: 50%	Literature: 30%
2014 – 2015	Math:[§] 50%	English:[§] 38%
2015 – 2016	Algebra: 40%	Literature: 25%
2016 – 2017	Algebra: 65%	Literature: 48%
2017 – 2018	Algebra: 56%	Literature: 41%

[*] Percentages are rounded.

[†] Philadelphia high schools switched from the PSSA to the Keystone exam, which adheres to the more rigorous PA Core Standards.

[‡] Stricter testing security implemented statewide.

[§] Keystone results spreadsheet identifies subjects as math and English, instead of algebra and literature.

> Update – Public School X

*A*fter several more visits to P.S. X, I came to understand just how hard P.S. X's principal, faculty and students had worked to turn the school around. The level of enthusiasm and school spirit demonstrated by all was touching; however, the conversion of nearby K-5s to K-8 schools caused admissions for P.S. X, a middle school, to dwindle. In June of 2011, P.S. X graduated its last class.

Principal "Williams" shared, "Though there had been discussions about converting P.S. X to a K-8, the District inevitably decided that P.S. X would close and one of the new K-8s would take over our building."

It is believed by some, the former principal included, that P.S. X's hard work and noteworthy progress—demonstrated by improving test results and consistent achievement of Annual Yearly Progress goals—were discounted, while the school taking over its building was favored because its principal had personal ties to the District's Regional Office.

Just out of curiosity, I took a look at PSSA scores for the other school, which I'll call P.S. "Y." With significantly fewer of their students testing into the Below Basic categories for reading and math, P.S. Y's reported scores were better than P.S. X's[1*]:

	P.S. Y/7th % **Below** Basic Math	P.S. X/8th % **Below** Basic Math	P.S. Y/7th % **Below** **Basic** Reading	P.S. X/8th % **Below** **Basic** Reading
2008-2009	9%	20%	14%	15%
2009-2010	9%	50%	9%	38%
2010-2011	8%	28%	19%	26%

Interestingly though, when the PA test cheating scandal broke, P.S. Y was implicated in all three of the years investigated. P.S. X was not named in connection with cheating at all and, with the exception of the 2009-2010 school year, the number of P.S. X's students testing into Below Basic was still well below the average for most Philly schools during this period.[1,2]

Another issue that may have played a part in P.S. X's selection for closure was the School Performance Index (SPI). This formula was used to determine which schools would be closed, converted to charter or renewed. According to a *NewsWorks* article, the system was labeled "faulty" after two years and discontinued in 2012, with SDP officials acknowledging that they had no idea how many school had been affected in the process.[3]

UPDATE – P.S. X (CONT'D)

PSSA Scores Reported for P.S. X (8th Grade)[4]

Percentage of Students Scoring BELOW BASIC Proficiency[*]		
2001 – 2002	Math: 52%	Reading: 56%
2002 – 2003	Math: 60%	Reading: 49%
2003 – 2004	Math: 33%	Reading: 29%
2004 – 2005	Math: 24%	Reading: 27%
2005 –2006	Math: 31%	Reading: 36%
2006 – 2007	Math: 36%	Reading: 35%
2007 – 2008	Math: 13%	Reading: 15%
2008 – 2009	Math: 20%	Reading: 15%
2009 – 2010	Math: 50%	Reading: 38%
2010 – 2011	Math: 28%	Reading: 26%
2011 –2012	**~ School permanently closed ~**	

---

[*] Percentages are rounded.

> Update – St. Athanasius Catholic School

*C*hange has also come to my grade school alma mater over the last 15 plus years. In addition to a second computer lab and after-school classes in French and robotics, St. Athanasius (St. A's) also has new leadership. Rev. Joseph Okonski (pastor) and Andrea Tomaino (principal) both demonstrate a sincere pride in the school and its students, while also acknowledging room for improvement. Needless to say, I was stunned when a site called *GreatPhillySchools.org* rated St. A's a "5" out of a possible "10."[1]*

It's been decades since I was a student at the school and the education landscape has changed dramatically, but I seem to recall being fairly well prepared for high school. When I approached Rev. Okonski about this rating, he alerted me to the fact that there had been "some issues" with the way St. A's and other Catholic schools had been rated. He readily agreed to let me take a look at the school's standardized test results, but also suggested I speak with the principal to gain more insight. I explained that I would be writing about St. A's in my book but that I could use a code name, like Catholic School X.

"Why?" he asked. "It is what it is. If we find out we need to do better, then we'll focus on doing better."

Not 24 hours later, I received a text from Rev. Okonski confirming a school tour and a sit-down with the principal. When I arrived at her office, Ms. Tomaino, who's been with St. A's for over 17 years (the last four as principal) wasted no time diving headfirst into the *GreatPhillySchools.org* controversy.

"The formula they're using to convert our scores seems to be a bit of a mystery," she said, explaining the frustration she and other Catholic school principals from the Northwest region of the city have had. "The test that St. A's takes is a national, norm-referenced test (the TerraNova)," she continued. "It's not gauging whether or not each student passes or fails the test (as on the

---

* *GreatPhillySchools.org* was created by the Philadelphia School Partnership, a nonprofit organization that has awarded millions of dollars to Philadelphia's charter, public, private and Catholic schools. Their mission is to improve outcomes for low-income students and respond to the demand of families by expanding access to great schools.[2]

PSSAs) but how they did in comparison to the other students taking the test nationally."

The mean average or the "norm" for the majority of students across the U.S. is in the 50% range. That doesn't mean that 50% fail or 50% pass. The "mean average" literally means 50% is the average score on this test for all students taking it.

"We're trying to meet with them [*GreatPhillySchools.org*]" she continued. "We're working with Sister Edward down at the Archdiocese" to get the matter sorted out.

Though I understood we were talking about two different types of tests, I still wanted to know how St. A's students were doing in the era of high-stakes testing.

"Test scores are primarily used to track student progress from year to year, especially in reading and math. And to track any deficits in instruction. Did this class do well on the standardized math test one year and not so well the next? And then, why? Where is that weakness coming from?" she explained. "We don't put a lot of pressure on our students. Some school districts do a lot of test preparation. We do that within our daily lessons…but we don't teach to the test. It's just another evaluation tool. And that's what we tell our students. You come in. You do your best. That's all we can ask for."

She logged on to her computer and started pulling up TerraNova scores. "It's only been in the last four years or so that we've been keeping computer files," she commented.

Older test results had been stored in boxes and milk crates around the school, which we both wound up digging through, though we didn't find as much as I was hoping for. For the scores she did have, it seemed the school's seventh graders were pretty much falling in around the 50th percentile with the majority of U.S. seventh graders taking the same test.[3] But as for how to compare these scores with the Below Basic Proficiency percentages that I had been tracking on the PSSAs, I had no clue. I made a note to reach out to Sister Edward.

Generally, *GreatPhillySchools.org* is an extremely useful tool. You type in a school name, click submit and get an easy-to-understand 1-10 overall score, as well as 1-10 scores in math, reading, safety, attendance and, for high schools, the percentage of college-bound students. In a huge, financially strapped school district like Philadelphia's, where parents and students are struggling to determine their best options, there is definitely a need for it. The problem is that the site's formula for determining ratings has come into question more than once.

Some have questioned the weight they assign to each different component of the score: Attendance and percentage of college-bound students count for 30% each, safety accounts for only 10% and reading and math scores are worth only 15% each, which allows high schools with low standardized test results to achieve higher ratings if attendance and the number of graduates going to college are high.[4] Similarly, some schools with historically stellar reputations maintain the same high ratings despite recent test scores that indicate they've slipped. For example, there's a school near the expensive, downtown section of Philadelphia which, according to its 2015-2016 School Progress Report (SPRs), received an overall designation of 43%, placing it in the "watch" category (2nd to lowest). This score was primarily the result of steadily declining achievement results (44%, 35% and 33% over three years) and low progress scores (39%, 45% and 30%).[5] (More on SPRs later.) Yet according to *GreatPhillySchools.org*, this school is still one of Philly's best, while the Catholic grade schools in the Northwest section of the city were assigned nearly the exact same mediocre rating.

Sister Edward Quinn, Assistant Superintendent for Curriculum, Instruction and Assessment for the Archdiocese of Philadelphia, which governs all of the City's Catholic schools and churches, broke it down for me:

"What happened is that they [*GreatPhillySchools.org*] took the testing from a charter school that used both the TerraNova and PSSAs. However, we learned that the TerraNova edition they used was not the same as the TerraNova edition that we use. We are using an edition that is much more rigorous with constructed response, which requires the students to actually write out answers, whereas the one used as a model was multiple choice, which can just be a guessing game on the part of the student."

That was problem number one. Problem number two surfaced when Sr. Edward contacted CTB, the company that publishes both the PSSAs and the TerraNova to discuss the situation.

"We spoke to executives and psychometricians [the scientists who develop and interpret standardized tests] who were very strong in their opinion that we were trying to compare apples and oranges. And that we really could not justify equivalence of these tests, nor could we obtain equivalent scores. We wanted to be cooperative," said Sr. Edward. "We wanted to provide our data [and] be able to share what we had done with the public, but we could not come to a consensus about the methodology they were using."

Inevitably, *GreatPhillySchools.org* agreed to replace the ratings they assigned for the Catholic schools that chose not to participate with N/A, as it does for many private schools. Sr. Edward has encouraged Catholic school principals to report their results on their own websites under "points of interest."

She acknowledged that the Archdiocese could have chosen to use the PSSAs; however, they deliberately chose the TerraNovas so that they would be able to "assess their students within a national context, which supports a broader base of learning."

Time was also a serious consideration for choosing the TerraNova over the PSSA. "The testing itself for the PSSAs takes nineteen hours[†] out of instructional time," she continued. "And the way we've structured our TerraNova testing is that [it] takes a maximum of five hours. We don't want testing to be an interruption to instruction.

"We are also very strong in the opinion," she continued, "that students should be prepared for testing by what they do day-in and day-out in the classroom. We do not take time aside before the standardized testing to prepare them specifically for the standardized testing... We use the data to improve instruction through professional development, instructional programs and improvement of course elements."

The approach seems to be working.

"In the year 2002, our mean scores in the city of Philadelphia were at the 32nd percentile. In 2016, our mean scores were at the 62nd percentile"

"Which means...?" I asked.

"Looking at the national rankings," said Sr. Edward, "back in 2002, our students were performing better than 32% of the nation, whereas in 2016, they performed better than 62% of the nation."

---

† In August of 2017, PA Governor Tom Wolf and PA Secretary of Education Pedro Rivera announced a 20% decrease in the length of PSSA tests for grades three through eight, which could result in two fewer days of testing for some students. The goal was "to reduce stress" and place more emphasis on learning.[6]

An across-the-board improvement of 30 percentage points in fourteen years is incredibly impressive, but I wanted to know specifically about St A's which, based on the statistics we were reviewing, was not achieving at the same level. Sr. Edward explained that they have "examined the data and see that math [in particular] is an area that needs to be strengthened. Use of the data allows us to look forward to increased growth."

But looking a little more closely at the numbers for St. A's over the last six years, she added that another important reason the Archdiocese chose the TerraNova test is that it measures both anticipated and achieved scores for individual students. She pointed out the scores for a few students in each grade that were significantly lower than the grade average, yet the scores were still higher than what these students were supposed to be capable of achieving.

"… if I look at St. Athanasius and I can see that obtained scores are exceeding anticipated scores, I say something good is going on in that school," commented Sr. Edward.

Sr. Edward's insights brought me back to the discussion with Ms. Tomaino. Another change that has recently come to St. A's is an increase in the number of special needs students enrolled in the school.

"Right now, we have between five and eight kids per class who are pulled out for remedial help," she told me. "We're looking into pull outs of five to six students per class for advanced instruction as well."

Since there are schools within the Archdiocese specifically geared toward students with disabilities, St. A's previously had a policy of no admittance for students with special needs.

"In the past, the principal and school counselor would sit down with parents and say, this is not the best environment for your child: the classroom sizes are too large, and he or she will not be able to get the individual attention they need to do their best. And parents would either withdraw the students or, sometimes, insist that they stay here anyway."

These days, both Rev. Okonski and Principal Tomaino have a different viewpoint.

"If people want to send their kids here, we have a moral obligation to take them," said Rev. Okonski.

This sentiment is echoed by Ms. Tomaino, "What's the alternative?" she asked. "[P.S. #9] where a child committed suicide not long ago because he was bullied? Today, we say, 'This is what we can do to help your child and this is what your responsibility in this will be.'"

The principal went on to say that they create a team for each student with a diagnosed disability, which includes a psychologist, a speech therapist, one of three guidance counselors, remedial reading/math instructors, a school nurse, an administrator and classroom teachers who work with the parents. Together, they develop an education plan that delineates an approach vs. the specific measurements outlined in public school IEPs (Individual Education Plans).

"We will provide accommodations for students with special needs— changing seats, allowing them to take a break and go for a walk when needed, device assistance, etc. Curriculum will be modified if it is determined by the team to be appropriate, but ultimately, parents have the final say."

I asked if the increase in special needs students has added to classroom disruption, or in any way affected the orderly nature of the school.

"We'll take students who may have had difficulty in their last school settings, but we will not take students if their records indicate that they have disruptive disorders. However, sometimes we wind up admitting students who have gone undiagnosed, then…we do our best to help them."

"What happens if you can't help?" I asked.

"In all honesty," she replied, "most students who transfer in do thrive because of the structured, caring, nurturing environment, [combined with] support from parents. They do not want their child to be unsuccessful here and be required to return to their previous environment. So I see more support with school work and behavior. Students are not asked to leave if they are trying their best and cooperating with school policies and procedures."

Ms. Tomaino's final comment was, "I would sooner have a child enrolled at St. Athanasius School who was a slow learner with a good heart than a genius with a disrespectful, uncooperative attitude."

True to her word, toward the end of the 2017-2018 school year, Principal Tomaino and Rev. Okonski made the difficult decision to have two of their students finish out the year working at home with the understanding that they would not be able to return to St. A's in the fall.

Said Rev. Okonski, "We had ongoing discussions with the students and their parents but, in the end, we determined that they just were not able to comply with our school policies."

UPDATE – ST. ATHANASIUS (CONT'D)

Mean Normal Curve Equivalent: St. Athanasius School (7th Grade)[3]

As compared to all students taking the TerraNova nationwide with 50% being the average score.[‡]

2010-2011	Math: 48%	Reading: 52%
2011-2012	Math: 49%	Reading: 53%
2012-2013	Math: 44%	Reading: 51%
2013-2014[§]	Math: 37%	Reading: 47%
2014-2015	Math: 46%	Reading: 53%
2015-2016	Math: 43%	Reading: 53%
2016-2017	Math: 41%	Reading: 51%
2017-2018	Math: 48%	Reading: 50%

‡ Percentages are rounded.
§ The Archdiocese of Philadelphia adopted the more rigorous PA Core Standards.

> Update – Public School #2

*I*n the years following my brief visit to P.S. #2, it landed in the national spotlight. First, for distinguishing itself by dramatically improving results on the PSSA between 2009 and 2011. Scores jumped over 50 points in both reading and math during this period. Education experts, policy makers, and teachers were particularly thrilled because whatever they were doing at P.S. #2 was working, regardless of the fact that 90% of students were disadvantaged with 25% identified as special needs. Both the school principal and superintendent of the SDP were praised and upheld as examples—until a few teachers came forward, anonymously accusing the school of ongoing, organized, administration-sanctioned cheating. Unfortunately, these allegations turned out to be true.[1]

During this same period, 52 Philadelphia public schools, as well as others throughout the state, were accused of "assisting" the test-taking process: from prepping students with information about what would be on the test to physically changing their answers.[1] In response, the Commonwealth of PA instituted greater security measures for standardized test taking in 2012, causing scores to dip dramatically across Pennsylvania.[2]

If you take a look at the scores for P.S. #2 listed at the end of this chapter, you'll see that the number of students testing into the Below Basic Proficiency category began to decline in the 2008-2009 school year, with their best scores reported in 2009-2010. Though even in 2010-2011, they were still doing well in comparison to many other PA schools. However, the year following the allegations of cheating, the number of students at P.S. #2 who were testing into Below Basic—which in essence is failing the test—climbed back up to 49%, just about where they were in 2007-2008. Test scores were not available for 2012 when the tighter security measures were implemented but, in the following year, 57% of P.S. #2's eighth-grade students scored Below Basic in reading, while 68% scored Below Basic in math. In 2014, when the tougher common-core aligned tests were implemented, the number of students testing into the

Below Basic category increased to 61% for reading and 96% for math…96%! That means nearly the entire eighth grade "failed" the math section of the test.[3]

During the same year, *The Philadelphia Inquirer* conducted an investigation into the underreporting of violent incidents in Philadelphia schools. Again, P.S.#2, which had previously been on PA's Persistently Dangerous Schools list, then praised for incredible improvement between 2008 and 2010, came under fire. Teachers anonymously accused the school administration of discouraging the reporting of violent incidents, including students cursing at the teachers, throwing things and fighting. The *Inquirer* reporting team labeled it "active suppression of information that would reveal how violent Philadelphia schools really are."[4]

P.S. #2 narrowly escaped closure in 2012. It survived mostly due to protests from parents and support from a State Representative who testified that closing the neighborhood's elementary, middle and high school all at the same time would have a "devastating effect".[5] In 2016, P.S. #2 was designated as part of the School District's Turnaround Network, which often means drastic changes in faculty, staff and, hopefully, in achievement and culture as well. It should be noted that P.S. #2 had been designated a Promise Academy in the past, but budget shortfalls left P.S. #2 without the extra financial support it had been "promised."[6,7]

UPDATE – P.S. #2 (CONT'D)

PSSA Scores Reported for P.S. #2 (8th Grade)[3]

Percentage of Students Scoring BELOW BASIC Proficiency*		
2001 – 2002	Math: 73%	Reading: 63%
2002 – 2003	Math: 61%	Reading: 51%
2003 – 2004	Math: 65%	Reading: 45%
2004 – 2005	Math: 58%	Reading: 47%
2005 – 2006	Math: 58%	Reading: 44%
2006 – 2007	Math: 51%	Reading: 37%
2007 – 2008	Math: 52%	Reading: 49%
2008 – 2009	Math: 34%	Reading: 25%
2009 – 2010	Math: 16%	Reading: 12%
2010 – 2011	Math: 31%	Reading: 26%
2011 – 2012	Math: 49%	Reading: 49%
Stricter Security†		
2012 – 2013	Math: unavailable	Reading: unavailable
2013 – 2014	Math: 68%	Reading: 57%
More Rigorous Testing‡		
2014 – 2015	Math: 96%	ELA:§ 61%
2015 – 2016	Math: 98%	ELA: 48%
2016 – 2017	Math: 92%	ELA: 87%
2017 – 2018	Math: 98%	ELA: 72%

---

* Percentages are rounded.

† Stricter testing security implemented statewide.

‡ School district adopted more rigorous PA Core Standards.

§ New PSSA test switched from reading to English language arts (ELA) to reflect the greater range of skills being tested.

> Update – Public School #3

fter my very negative experience at P.S. #3, I was rather surprised by the progress it seems to have made over the years. Previously labeled one of the lowest-performing schools in the city, the number of eighth-grade students who had been testing into the Below Basic Proficiency (or "failing") category for math and reading has declined. It dropped from 39% to 29% Below Basic in reading, and from 55% to 33% Below Basic in math during the first year of its downsizing and conversion to a Mastery Charter School. Even while PA was embroiled in the cheating scandal, P.S. #3's scores continued to improve, reinforcing the legitimacy of its progress.[1,2] Based on this, Mastery was given the go-ahead to expand P.S. #3 to include a high school.

With seventeen schools and counting, Mastery is Philadelphia's largest charter operator. It specializes in "turning around" low-performing schools by establishing safer environments and greater emphasis on discipline, student achievement and college prep.[1] They've been condemned by some for a less than stellar success rate; while others point out that they took on some of Philadelphia's most challenging schools and made progress. In Mastery's early years in Philadelphia, they produced dramatic results that caught the attention of both Oprah Winfrey, who reportedly donated $1 million[3] and President Barack Obama, who commented:

> "...in just two years, three of the schools that Mastery has taken over have seen reading and math levels nearly double...in some cases, triple...One school called [P.S. #3] went from just 14 percent of students being proficient in math to almost 70 percent. Now...and here's the kicker...at the same time academic performance improved, violence dropped by 80 percent..."
>
> —*2010 Address to the National Urban League*[4]

Mastery's critics have pointed to its high student turnover rates (reportedly 42% for P.S. #3 during the first four years of its conversion to a charter) as a major part of its success. Students who could not or would not comply with the contract all students and staff are required to sign agreeing to conform to Mastery's approach to teaching and discipline, found themselves in search of another school.[5] The strictly enforced Mastery education model includes a longer school year, longer school days and an academic program that, until recently, had been narrowly focused on "mastery" of reading, writing and math, along with support for the development of social and emotional skills.[6] Mastery also employs a three-tiered discipline system that includes old-school demerits and detention, as well as "hearings" for serious offenses like fighting, which can result in expulsion.[7] Meanwhile, most of Philly's public schools are "strongly discouraged" from suspending and expelling students. District schools are obligated to enroll any child within their "catchment area" [neighborhood] that applies, regardless of their track record.[5]

Mastery Schools' CEO Scott Gordon takes the accusation that they pick and choose their kids very seriously. He commented in a *Philadelphia Public School Notebook* article:

"There's a huge sensitivity internally…because we're accused of it all the time. But that is not our culture. We have a moral obligation [to educate these students] as any school does, but particularly a school that is doing turnarounds."[7]

This "moral obligation" was put to the test in the Spring of 2017, when *Philly. com* reported that Mastery students from different campuses (including P.S. #3) had teamed up and were actively provoking daily fights with students from another nearby school. One incident resulted in the principal of that other school being seriously injured as he tried to separate students. To Mastery's credit, Gordon and the principal of P.S. #3 were said to have paid a visit to the other school to personally apologize. They brought with them a basket of get-well cards for the injured principal from other Mastery students, who were described as "horrified by the event."[8]

Despite earlier impressive gains, when the tougher PA Core-aligned PSSAs were introduced in the 2014-2015 school year, test scores for P.S. #3 declined, along with most schools across the state. While P.S. #3's English Language Arts scores dipped a little, their math scores plummeted, jumping from only 11% of their eighth-graders scoring Below Basic Proficiency to 66% in the first year, and then 87% scoring Below Basic in the second year of the new tougher test.[2]

On the high school end of things, P.S. #3's Keystone* scores were more encouraging and ranged between 52% (Advanced/Proficient) in Math and 68% (Advanced/Proficient) in English,[9] which is reportedly higher than both PA state and School District of Philadelphia scores. Another high note for P.S. #3 was its 2015 graduation rate, which was 94%—a full 10 percentage points higher than the state average.[10]

In addition to annual standardized tests, Philly public and charter schools also receive annual School Progress Reports (SPRs) from the District.[†] These reports rate each school based on achievement, student progress, school climate and—for high schools—college and career readiness. Based on these scores, schools receive an overall number between 0% and 100% that identifies which Tier it belongs to.[11]

SCHOOL PROGRESS REPORT TIERS

Model (75-100%)	High scores; among best in the city
Reinforce (50-74%)	Several areas of strength, with targeted assistance should improve steadily
Watch (25-49%)	Some areas of solid performance; overall, needs intensive support to improve
Intervene (0-24%)	Low performance; requires immediate attention and assistance

P.S. #3 fell into the "intervene" category with an overall score of 20%. In fact, the vast majority of Mastery's middle and high schools are in the "watch" or "intervene" categories,[12] along with at least _75%_ of all District and charter schools in Philadelphia.[‡13]

---

* Keystone Exams are subject-area tests given in high schools only. Though implementation has been delayed, all PA students will soon be required to pass the Keystones in order to graduate.

† School Progress Reports can be found at PhilaSD.org.

‡ Though 75% of schools fell into the bottom two performance tiers, during that same timeframe, more than 50% of district schools and most charter schools increased their scores. Most schools also made progress in school climate, which includes safety and engagement. "The District is not where it needs to be [but] it [is] important to celebrate growth." –William Hite, School Superintendent, as quoted on *PhillyNews.com.*[12]

Mastery's setback also coincided with its switch to a more conceptual approach to teaching vs. their previous focus on "procedure and practice." According to *Newsworks.org*, Mastery is re-tweaking their instructional approach to blend the two methods.[14] Scott Gordon posted a response to the *Newsworks.org* article that addressed Mastery's weak standardized test results.

> "...struggling schools are identified as potential Renaissance Schools [Promise Academies for charter schools] because they consistently score in the bottom 10 percent or 20 percent of all Philadelphia schools prior to a turnaround. In 2016, 100 percent of Mastery Renaissance schools open one year or more are now rated in the top 50 percent of all 301 public and public charter schools in Philadelphia on the state's recently released School Performance Profile (SPP)..."[14]
>
> —Scott Gordon, Mastery Schools CEO

As you'll see later, landing in the top 50% of public schools in Philadelphia may not be the accomplishment we'd expect. Still, the one thing that cannot be denied is the incredible shift in school culture that Mastery creates. Students previously thought to have no chance of attending college are conditioned to reach for and, in many cases, attain that goal. In years past, Mastery students have won over $20 million in scholarship money with some being selected as prestigious Gates Millennium Scholars. This success is celebrated during their annual "college signing day" when Mastery high school students gather to acknowledge and support over 400 seniors who have been accepted at institutions all over the U.S. It's like an academic version of the NFL draft. To experience the enthusiasm and pride for yourself, check out the five-minute YouTube video *Mastery's College Signing Day*. It will put a smile on your face.[15,16]

UPDATE: P.S. #3

PSSA Scores Reported for P.S. #3 (8th Grade)[2]

Percentage of Students Scoring BELOW BASIC Proficiency[§]		
2001 – 2002	Math: 86%	Reading: 63%
2002 – 2003	Math: 74%	Reading: 47%
2003 – 2004	Math: 79%	Reading: 54%
2004 – 2005	Math: 58%	Reading: 48%
2005 – 2006	Math: 66%	Reading: 49%
2006 – 2007	Math: 55%	Reading: 39%
2007 – 2008[¶]	Math: 33%	Reading: 29%
2008 – 2009	Math: 12%	Reading: 16%
2009 – 2010	Math: 14%	Reading: 13%
2010 – 2011	Math: 8%	Reading: 15%
2011 – 2012	Math: 18%	Reading: 23%
Stricter Security[**]		
2012 – 2013	Math: 13%	Reading: 17%
2013 –2014	Math: 11%	Reading: 15%
More Rigorous Testing[††]		
2014 – 2015	Math: 66%	ELA:[‡‡] 20%
2015 – 2016	Math: 87%	ELA: 19%
2016 – 2017	Math: 79%	ELA: 18%
2017 – 2018	Math: 83%	ELA: 16%

§ Percentages are rounded.

¶ School downsized and converted to charter school. (Note huge decrease in percentage of students scoring Below Basic Proficiency over next three years.)

** Stricter testing security implemented statewide.

†† School district adopted more rigorous PA Core Standards.

‡‡ New PSSA switched from Reading to English Language Arts (ELA) to reflect the greater range of skills being tested.

> Update – Public School #4

*T*hroughout the years, the SDP has been both underfunded and, at times, mismanaged. In an ongoing effort to cut costs, a report on building usage was commissioned. The conclusion was that there were at least "70,000 unutilized seats in their nearly 300 buildings."[1] As part of the resulting consolidation plan, P.S. #4 was closed at the end of the 2011-2012 school year and its remaining students were transferred to other neighborhood schools. The reasons cited for its closure were the high cost of needed building repairs, continuing poor academic performance and low enrollment that left P.S. #4 at only a third of its capacity.[1]

UPDATE – P.S. #4 (CONT'D)

PSSA Scores Reported for P.S. #4 (5th Grade)[2]

Percentage of Students Scoring BELOW BASIC Proficiency*		
2001 - 2002	Math: 49%	Reading: 49%
2002 - 2003	Math: 48%	Reading: 50%
2003 - 2004	Math: 81%	Reading: 66%
2004 - 2005	Math: 45%	Reading: 63%
2005 - 2006	Math: 41%	Reading: 52%
2006 - 2007	Math: 53%	Reading: 77%
2007 - 2008	Math: 27%	Reading: 54%
2008 - 2009	Math: 45%	Reading: 65%
2009 - 2010	Math: 27%	Reading: 41%
2010 - 2011	Math: 40%	Reading: 60%
2011 - 2012	Math: 24%	Reading: 48%
~ School permanently closed ~		

---

*Percentages are rounded.

> Update – Public School #5

*O*ver the years, P.S. #5 demonstrated a very slow and intermittent decline in the number of students testing into the Below Basic Proficiency category in math and reading. In 2003, it was named to Pennsylvania's Persistently Dangerous Schools list. In addition to solidifying P.S. #5's reputation as one of the most violent schools in the city, the "persistently dangerous" designation also meant that school administrators had to develop a safety plan and offer parents the option to transfer their children to other schools.[1]

In September of 2009, P.S. #5 stopped accepting new students. The remaining 59 seventh-graders were given the option of applying to another middle school or transferring to the high school next door to finish up their final year. The official reasons cited for P.S. #5's closure in SDP reports were "declining enrollment, failure to operate at capacity, excess capacity at the adjacent high school, increasing capacity at other neighborhood feeder schools and, perhaps most importantly, its academic performance or "failure to achieve Adequate Yearly Progress for five consecutive years in a row."[2] There was no mention of the incredible risk this dangerous environment posed to both students and teachers.

UPDATE: P.S. #5

PSSA Scores Reported for P.S. #5 (8th Grade)[3]

Percentage of Students Scoring BELOW BASIC Proficiency[*]		
2001 - 2002	Math: 80%	Reading: 60%
2002 - 2003	Math: 81%	Reading: 64%
2003 - 2004	Math: 71%	Reading: 51%
2004 - 2005	Math: 66%	Reading: 63%
2005 - 2006	Math: 71%	Reading: 64%
2006 - 2007	Math: 65%	Reading: 58%
2007 - 2008	Math: 56%	Reading: 53%
2008 - 2009	Math: 57%	Reading: 44%
2009 - 2010	Math: 49%	Reading: 40%
~ School Permanently Closed ~		

[*] Percentages are rounded.

> Update – Public School #6

*I*n 2002, P.S. #6 had the dubious distinction of being the seventh worst performing school in the District. That same year, it became the first Philly school to be converted to a "neighborhood charter school," a model in which students are assigned to the school based on where they live vs. admission by lottery or application. Since then, it has been managed by a private company that aspires to help both its students and families in need. P.S. #6 offers counseling and other services, including a health center for students and adults who live in the area. Viewed by many as one of the first "real" community schools, P.S. #6 serves a high percentage of homeless and transient students in addition to area students.

Fifteen plus years after I first subbed at P.S. #6, it seems to still be solidly mediocre at best. On the 2015-2016 PSSAs, nearly 60% of its fifth-grade students scored Below Basic Proficiency in both English language arts (ELA) and math. The percentage of fifth graders at P.S. #6 who have been "failing" the test has fluctuated (seemingly randomly) between 24% and 56% with no scores quite as low as those achieved before the conversion to a neighborhood charter: 65% Below Basic in reading and 85% Below Basic in math.[1] According to the official 2015-2016 School Progress Report, P.S. #6 earned an overall score of 32% out of a possible 100%, along with a "watch" designation that persisted through 2018.[2,3*]

Still, P.S. #6 has a history of strong community support. In 2016, students, staff and parents cheered and applauded when the School Reform Commission voted to expand the school. While P.S. #6 is by no means academically stellar, it is respected for providing what is perceived as a safe school environment with a low tolerance for bullying.

UPDATE: P.S. #6

PSSA Scores Reported for P.S. #6 (5th Grade)[1]

Percentage of Students Scoring BELOW BASIC Proficiency[*]		
2001 - 2002	Math: 85%	Reading: 65%
2002 - 2003[†]	Math: 66%	Reading: 50%
2003 - 2004	Math: 51%	Reading: 46%
2004 - 2005	Math: 43%	Reading: 49%
2005 - 2006	Math: 46%	Reading: 46%
2006 - 2007	Math: 24%	Reading: 38%
2007 - 2008	Math: 37%	Reading: 39%
2008 - 2009	Math: 27%	Reading: 54%
2009 - 2010	Math: 27%	Reading: 53%
2010 - 2011	Math: 54%	Reading: 59%
2011 - 2012	Math: 27%	Reading: 31%
Stricter Security[‡]		
2012 - 2013	Math: 42%	Reading: 54%
2013 - 2014	Math: 37%	Reading: 48%
More Rigorous Testing[§]		
2014 - 2015	Math: 45%	ELA[¶]: 26%
2015 - 2016	Math: 59%	ELA: 56%
2016 - 2017	Math: 52%	ELA: 37%
2017 - 2018	Math: 62%	ELA: 29%

---

[*] Percentages are rounded.

[†] Converted to charter school.

[‡] Stricter testing security implemented statewide.

[§] School district adopted more rigorous PA Core Standards.

[¶] New PSSA switched from Reading to English Language Arts (ELA) to reflect the greater range of skills being tested.

> Update – Public School #7

A few months after the installation of Superintendent Hite, 43 schools—including P.S. #7's high school—were identified for merger, co-location or closure. The goal was "to create efficient use of school facilities that aligns programs and resources in ways most beneficial for the students." The initiative would also have saved the financially struggling District $28 million dollars.[1]

In response, teachers, students, administrators, parents and community activists from all over the city protested, pleaded and testified to save their neighborhood schools. While most—if not all—of the schools slated for closure were a long way from providing students with an optimal education, parents did not want their children traveling far away from home, through unfamiliar and/or unsafe neighborhoods.

In the end, the School Reform Commission reduced the number of closings to fewer than 25, which included fourteen schools that were on the City's "Persistently Dangerous" list. Though P.S. #7's high school was not on that list, it had still suffered a significant number of violent incidents. The high school was closed, leaving behind an elementary school still struggling to regain its footing in the aftermath of PA's standardized-test cheating scandal.[2] The number of fifth graders testing into the Below Basic Proficiency category hovered around 50% or higher. But in the 2009-2010 and 2010-2011 school years, P.S. #7 earned its best scores ever with only 19%-26% of fifth graders testing into Below Basic in math and reading.[3] Unfortunately, these scores also coincided with a report that over 83% of P.S. #7's test responses had been erased and changed to the correct answers, presumably by teachers and/or administrators.[2]

UPDATE – P.S. #7 (CONT'D)

PSSA Scores Reported for P.S. #7 (5th Grade)[3]

Percentage of Students Scoring BELOW BASIC Proficiency[*]		
2001 – 2002	Math: 68%	Reading: 55%
2002 – 2003	Math: 74%	Reading: 55%
2003 – 2004	Math: 77%	Reading: 59%
2004 – 2005	Math: 35%	Reading: 49%
2005 –2006	Math: 44%	Reading: 64%
2006 –2007	Math: 46%	Reading: 58%
2007 – 2008	Math: 33%	Reading: 43%
2008 – 2009	Math: 27%	Reading: 51%
2009 – 2010	Math: 15%	Reading: 26%
2010 – 2011	Math: 19%	Reading: 19%
2011 – 2012	Math: 30%	Reading: 54%
Stricter Security[†]		
2012 – 2013	Math: 38%	Reading: 44%
2013 – 2014	Math: 52%	Reading: 72%
More Rigorous Testing[‡]		
2014 – 2015	Math: 78%	ELA[§]: 48%
2015 – 2016	Math: 84%	ELA: 53%
2016 – 2017	Math: 82%	ELA: 43%
2017 – 2018	Math: 82%	ELA: 32%

[*] Percentages are rounded.

[†] Stricter testing security implemented statewide.

[‡] School district adopted more rigorous PA Core Standards.

[§] New PSSA test switched from reading to English language arts (ELA) to reflect the greater range of skills being tested.

P.S. #8's standardized test scores have bounced up and down over the years. One year, the percentage of fifth graders scoring into Below Basic Proficiency was very high. In the next two years, there would be notable improvement only to once again be followed by significantly high numbers. With 67% of fifth graders testing into Below Basic in math and a shocking 91% testing into Below Basic in reading during the 2008-2009 school year, rumor had it that P.S. #8 was headed for the chopping block.[1,2] It was spared this fate when then SDP Superintendent Arlene Ackerman selected P.S. #8 to be converted into a Renaissance Promise Academy, an internal, turnaround-model she developed to provide additional funding and programs for "traditionally under-resourced schools,"[3] including:

- A highly structured academic program with emphasis on reading and math
- Saturday school, summer academy and an extended school day[4]
- After-school athletics, enrichment and extracurricular activities
- Specialized services for children with social, emotional and behavioral issues[5]
- And replacement of at least 50% of its faculty, which for P.S. #8 turned out to be 20 out of 21 teachers[6]

The year it became a Promise Academy, P.S. #8 delivered its best PSSA results in 15 years with 0% of its fifth graders scoring Below Basic in math and 25% scoring Below Basic in reading.[1] In fact, according to an SDP study, in the first 18 months of the Promise Academies, they—along with their Renaissance Charter School counterparts—were making significantly greater gains than regular Philadelphia public schools.[4] Unfortunately for P.S. #8 and the other Promise Academies, the extra funding dried up after only one year when sweeping budget cuts were implemented by the state of PA and Superintendent Ackerman was forced to resign.[7] Though other chronically underperforming schools were designated as Promise Academies over the next few years, the gains P.S. #8 and the other schools in this network made evaporated as budgets were slashed again and again. The only remaining component of the Promise Academy model became the replacement of staff at the beginning of the conversion.[4]

This familiar, one-step-forward-two-steps-back pattern actually began back in 2002 when the state took over the SDP and established the School Reform Commission (SRC) to oversee it. In addition to "turning over 45 elementary and middle schools to private managers," the SRC "implemented wide-ranging and ambitious reforms in district-managed schools." Some were "restructured," which meant that a minimum of 50% of their teaching staffs were replaced and they received extra funding and resources (just like Ackerman's Promise Academies).[8]

Five years afterwards, the Rand Corporation, a nonprofit research organization that studied the progress of Philadelphia schools, concluded that although the number of elementary and middle school students who "achieved proficiency" had increased substantially during this period, the results for the privately managed schools were no better than the regular District-run schools. In some cases, they were worse. Schools that were restructured under District supervision and given additional funds "had the most significant gains."[8] The program was working…until the state of Pennsylvania cut the District's budget, stripping away the extra funding the schools needed to maintain the progress they were making.

Flash forward to March of 2016 when the School District announced the "turnaround" model, another program for low-performing schools that had:

- Two consecutive years of "intervene" status
- A negative three-year average of student growth
- A School Progress Report (SPR) "achievement" score in the intervene category[9]

Of the fifteen schools assigned to this new framework, eleven were original Promise Academy schools, including P.S. #8*, which at the time had an overall SPR score of 14%, an achievement score of 1% and a progress score of 0%.[9,10]

---

*In addition to being designated as part of the Turnaround Network in 2016, P.S. #8 was also named one of the "most rundown" SDP schools in 2017.[11]

Schools selected to participate in the new Turnaround Network,[†] once again, receive increased funding, more individual student attention, smaller class sizes and specialized staff. Though the similarities to previous efforts to overhaul low-performing schools are obvious, the current District Superintendent stated in a press release that funds had been secured for at least the first two years of the program and the goal is to graduate schools out of the network within three years.[9]

---

† As of February 2020, the SDP Turnaround Network seems to have been renamed the Acceleration Network and P.S. #8 is still a member[12]

UPDATE – P.S. #8 (CONT'D)
PSSA Scores Reported for P.S. #8 (5th Grade)[1]

Percentage of Students Scoring BELOW BASIC Proficiency[‡]		
2001 – 2002	Math: 62%	Reading: 41%
2002 – 2003	Math: 47%	Reading: 33%
2003 – 2004	Math: 24%	Reading: 36%
2004 – 2005	Math: 50%	Reading: 53%
2005 – 2006	Math: 33%	Reading: 63%
2006 – 2007	Math: 50%	Reading: 65%
2007 – 2008	Math: 70%	Reading: 85%
2008 – 2009	Math: 67%	Reading: 91%
2009 – 2010	Math: 14%	Reading: 52%
2010 – 2011	Math: 0%	Reading: 25%
2011 – 2012	Math: 15%	Reading: 46%
Stricter Security[§]		
2012 – 2013	Math: 37%	Reading: 56%
2013 – 2014	Math: 29%	Reading: 48%
More Rigorous Testing[¶]		
2014 – 2015	Math: 58%	ELA[**]: 31%
2015 – 2016	Math: 71%	ELA: 46%
2016 – 2017	Math: 52%	ELA: 31%
2017 – 2018	Math: 50%	ELA: 32%

[‡] Percentages are rounded.
[§] Stricter testing security implemented statewide.
[¶] School district adopted more rigorous PA Core Standards.
[**] PSSA test switched from reading to English language arts (ELA) to reflect the greater range of skills being tested.

> Update – Public School #9

*T*o this day, P.S. #9 strikes me as the typical Philly public elementary school. It's bad, but not bad enough to garner any special notoriety or to push it to the front of anybody's intervention list. Though not specifically implicated in the standardized test cheating scandal that rocked the whole state, the number of P.S. #9 students testing into the Below Basic Proficiency category mysteriously jumped from 16% and less to 30-48% after stricter test taking security was implemented in 2012. When the tougher Common-Core aligned tests went live in 2014-2015, P.S. #9's ELA numbers improved slightly, while the number of fifth graders testing into Below Basic for math jumped from 49% to 79%, and then to 89% in the following year.[1] Despite a School Progress Report overall score of only 15% and an official "intervene" status,[2] the 2016 Philadelphia School Reform Commission voted to expand P.S. #9 from a K-5 to a K-8, a decision reportedly based on the urgency of ridding the neighborhood and the School District of the incredibly poor-performing middle school that P.S. #9 fed into.[3]

In May of 2017, all eyes were on P.S. #9 as they dealt with the startling suicide of one of its fourth graders. According to reports, the boy came home from school and told his mother that he had had "the worst day ever." He went to his room where she later found he had hanged himself and left a note naming those who had bullied him. His mother's heart-wrenching comments were picked up by news outlets across the city, "...I just want to know what made yesterday the worst day ever for my child."[4]

Sadly, within the next week, this senseless and shocking tragedy played out again as two more SDP students committed suicide and one other attempted it, but survived.[5,6] In response to this shocking news, the District released a statement explaining that it had "communicated with principals, counselors, teachers and parents about how students can best handle situations where they feel intimidation, loss of power or depression." The City of Philadelphia's Suicide Response Teams from the Department of Community Behavioral

Health/Intellectual Disability Services provided consultation and support to the students and staff at the affected schools.[6] I witnessed this effort firsthand during my return visit to P.S. #9. A trained school psychologist discussed the link between bullying and suicide with a group of elementary students. Only one of them expressed discomfort with the topic, while the rest seemed open and receptive to what she had to say.

According to the Centers for Disease Control (CDC) National Youth Risk Behavior Survey, Philadelphia students are "in-line" with the national suicide average and less likely to be bullied at school than students in other cities. What's troubling though as you delve deeper into the survey, is the revelation that Philly's students are almost twice as likely to skip school because they feel unsafe in the building or on their way to or from school.[7]

A while after the story of the suicide at P.S. #9 broke, I ran into an old family friend and her two granddaughters at a picnic. The older one is a student at St. Athanasius (St. A's) and the younger one attends P.S. #9. Though we hadn't officially met, the younger one approached to ask if I had made the cookies. When I said, "Yes," she responded, "You did a good job."

Noting how forthright this little girl was, I asked my friend if I could talk with her granddaughter about her experience at P.S. #9. A couple of weeks later, they came over for—you guessed it—cookies and a chat. It didn't take long for her to tell me what she didn't like about P.S. #9 and why.

"There's a lot of kids that don't do what they're actually supposed to do. They bully people and stuff like that."

She went on to tell me that she had been bullied, too, and though she tried to fight back at first, she eventually told her teacher who told her to tell the principal. When I asked if she felt safe at school, she hesitated, but then said, "Yes. The last couple of days, people didn't mess with me."

"How about before that? Did you feel safe then?"

"Not really," came her quiet reply.

I hesitated to bring up the suicide, but I forged ahead (with permission) mentioning the little boy's name and asking what happened.

"I heard that he hung hisself in a cubby hole."

When I asked why, she explained matter-of-factly, "People were bullying him."

"Do a lot of people get bullied?" I asked.

"Not anymore. After that incident happened."

I asked how they handled it at school, if they had talked about it.

"Not the kids," she responded. "But the teachers talked to the students. And they had a little candle thing with pictures and stuffed animals…I guess it was like a little funeral with a picture."

When asked if the vigil made her feel better, she answered, "A little bit."

Despite the fact that she's optimistic about the upcoming year, she told me that she'd rather switch to another school, like her sister's.

"I heard the kids are a lot more behaved and don't bully a lot."

Checking in with "Big Sis", I asked if there was bullying at St. A's.

"Half and half," she said. "'Cause one minute [kids] want to be your friend. The next, they're bullying you. Things are better now but when we were younger, the ones who were meaner tried to hurt people."

I wasn't surprised by her answer. Kids can be mean. I was bullied when I went to St. A's, but bullying wasn't quite as extreme or public as it is today. Plus, once the teachers and parents got involved, that was the end of it. When I asked if the teachers and the principal try to help, she smiled and said, "Yes. Very much."

She went on to say that she would rather stay at St. A's than transfer to another school.

"I like my friends and the classes and I feel safe because they have a gate around the school and cameras that let them see if somebody is trying to trespass."

What stood out to me is that, unlike her little sister, she perceived danger to be outside of school vs. inside the school.

"Do you know about the stuff that happens at your sister's school?" I asked.

"Only one thing. This boy was being bullied so much he hung himself."

"What did you think about that?" her grandmother asked.

"I was sad for his parents and family," she answered. "And that those kids are that mean."

My friend sat quietly contemplating what her granddaughters had shared, while they went in search of more cookies. After a few minutes, she commented that she doesn't often have the younger of the two and it never occurred to her to talk with her about what had happened though she had been "flabbergasted."

"Fourth grade. How did he even know how to hang himself?"

Despite the seriousness of the incident, she doesn't think that the suicide has affected her granddaughter.

"If it has, she's covering it up real well."

I wonder how many of P.S. #9's students are covering up real well.

UPDATE – P.S. #9

PSSA Scores Reported for P.S. #9 (5th Grade)[1]

Percentage of Students Scoring **BELOW BASIC** Proficiency*		
2001 – 2002	Math: 68%	Reading: 56%
2002 – 2003	Math: 68%	Reading: 52%
2003 – 2004	Math: 33%[†]	Reading: 30%
2004 – 2005	Math: 15%[†]	Reading: 29%[†]
2005 – 2006	Math: 13%	Reading: 18%[†]
2006 – 2007	Math: 19%	Reading: 24%
2007 – 2008	Math: 9%	Reading: 21%
2008 – 2009	Math: 2%	Reading: 16%
2009 – 2010	Math: 9%	Reading: 10%
2010 – 2011	Math: 13%[†]	Reading: 16%[†]
2011 – 2012	Math: 30%[†]	Reading: 48%[†]
Stricter Security[‡]		
2012 – 2013	Math: 30%	Reading: 51%
2013 – 2014	Math: 49%	Reading: 46%
More Rigorous Standards[§]		
2014 – 2015	Math: 79%	ELA:[¶] 50%
2015 – 2016	Math: 89%	ELA: 39%
2016 – 2017	Math: 91%	ELA: 37%
2017 – 2018	Math: 84%	ELA: 20%

---

* Percentages are rounded.

[†] Big jump in test results.

[‡] Stricter testing security implemented statewide.

[§] School district adopted more rigorous PA Core Standards.

[¶] New PSSA switched from Reading to English language arts (ELA) to reflect greater range of skills being tested.

> Update – Public School #10

*I*n 2011, P.S. #10 was selected as one of four schools invited to participate in Arts Link, a four-year program that "helps students learn math and science through visual arts."[1] Funded by the U.S. Department of Education and administrated through the Philadelphia Arts in Education Partnership, Arts Link worked with teachers to create lesson plans that integrated art across the school curriculum. Over the next four years, achievement at P.S. #10 and the other selected schools was tracked alongside similar public schools that were not participating in the program. By year four, the Arts Link schools had significantly lower absences and suspension rates and significantly higher science and math PSSA scores.[1] The makeup of the student body has also changed since my first visit. Today, P.S. #10 is more ethnically and racially diverse, with non-white students accounting for over 40% of enrollment.[2]

Though it does not have a top-tier "model" status on the School Progress Report yet, P.S. #10 has landed solidly on the "reinforce" tier with an overall score of 69%.[3] Note that the number of students testing into the Below Basic category held steady through the cheating scandal and the switch to more rigorous PA Core-aligned PSSAs.[4] Given the solid progress, it's no surprise that P.S. #10 was named the top most improved public elementary school in Philadelphia in 2017.[5] Unfortunately, it was also prominently featured in *The Philadelphia Inquirer/ Daily News* 2018 "Toxic City. Sick Schools." series where it was reported that a student was hospitalized and seemed to have suffered permanent neurological damage after eating chips of lead paint found in his classroom.[6]

UPDATE – P.S. #10 (CONT'D)

PSSA Scores Reported for P.S. #10 (5th Grade)[4]

Percentage of Students Scoring BELOW BASIC Proficiency*		
2001 – 2002	Math: 22%	Reading: 27%
2002 – 2003	Math: 32%	Reading: 26%
2003 – 2004	Math: 21%	Reading: 21%
2004 – 2005	Math: 19%	Reading: 21%
2005 – 2006	Math: 15%	Reading: 22%
2006 – 2007	Math: 10%	Reading: 20%
2007 – 2008	Math: 3%	Reading: 10%
2008 – 2009	Math: 6%	Reading: 16%
2009 – 2010	Math: 2%	Reading: 15%
2010 – 2011	Math: 8%	Reading: 16%
2011 – 2012	Math: 9%	Reading: 16%
Stricter Security†		
2012 – 2013	Math: 10%	Reading: 17%
2013 – 2014	Math: 11%	Reading: 19%
More Rigorous Testing‡		
2014 – 2015	Math: 14%	ELA:§ 6%
2015 – 2016	Math: 22%	ELA: 19%
2016 – 2017	Math: 16%	ELA: 6%
2017 – 2018	Math: 24%	ELA: 4%

* Percentages are rounded.
† Stricter testing security implemented statewide.
‡ School district adopted more rigorous PA Core Standards.
§ New PSSA test switched from reading to English language arts (ELA) to reflect the greater range of skills being tested.

> Update – Public School #11

*T*he effects of PA's test cheating scandal reverberated throughout Philadelphia and across the country. Based on copies of School District Test Security Reports acquired and reported on by *WHYY/NewsWorks* in partnership with *The Notebook* (and posted online for anyone who was interested), at least 25 schools were flagged for "irregularities" (the alleged continuation of cheating) in 2012—*after* the scandal was exposed and stricter security measures were implemented. The vast majority of the infractions were minor in nature—forgetting to cover up posters on the walls, letting students who were finished play with calculators, not noticing right away that a few students had tests and test booklets that did not have matching serial numbers. A few were a bit more serious: allowing students to carry their own tests to the next proctored room, leaving a test out on a desk in the open, encouraging students to double-check their answers after they had turned in the test and allowing students to whisper and trade scraps of paper.

Based on the memos, it seemed that when the monitors pointed out the problems, most schools took steps to correct the issues right away.[1] Only one school—P.S. #11—was alleged to have continued with active and open cheating, as well as a general disregard for input from the District-assigned test monitors.[2,3,4] Like P.S. #3, P.S. #11 was under investigation in 2012 and, because of the extent of the cheating in previous years, subject to extra test-taking scrutiny. Unlike P.S. #3, the teachers and administrators at P.S. #11 reportedly did not cooperate with the monitors.

District monitors assigned to P.S. #11 reported issues that included providing students with correct answers. Instead of cracking down on these issues, administrators at P.S. #11 formally complained that the monitors interfered and demonstrated a "lack of professionalism." The first monitor was relieved of her duties and disciplined. The second monitor, the head of the District's test security program, was fired. Both of their reports were ignored and the matter was dropped.[2,3,4]

Though Philadelphia was pretty hard-hit by the cheating scandal, the situation was not unique. During the era of No Child Left Behind when continued low standardized test scores could mean firings, conversion to charter or closure, similar issues arose across PA, as well as in Atlanta, Arizona, Washington D.C., Texas, Ohio, California, Chicago, etc. In fact, the *Atlanta Journal-Constitution* completed an in-depth investigation that concluded "200 of the 14,700 districts nationwide had suspicious test scores."[4] In Philadelphia, the cheating, in addition to damaging the psyches and confidence of the students, also invalidated the real gains that some schools made and distracted from the continuing impact of chronic underfunding. A University of Pennsylvania study determined that underfunding played a big role in the drop in test scores across Philadelphia during that same year:

"On the statistical side, this study finds that the 2012 budget decreases experienced in Philadelphia schools significantly contributed to the decline in test scores, even when controlling for [taking into account] cheating."

—James R. Sadler, *No School Left Uncorrupted: How Cheating, High-Stakes Testing, and Declining Budgets Affected Student Achievement in Philadelphia*[5]

Perhaps that's one reason why very few teachers and administrators were held accountable, despite the fact that cheating efforts were so extensive.[3] In December of 2015, the *Philadelphia Public School Notebook*—which teamed up with *WHYY/NewsWorks* to bring the test cheating scandal to light—reported that of the 140 PA teachers and administrators initially under investigation, only 23 were disciplined and only five faced criminal charges.[6,7] Some of the educators implicated in the scandal retired. Others were transferred, promoted or just left to continue in their positions. Investigations were closed with no explanation or follow up, and in many cases, schools and their personnel were cleared despite hard evidence of cheating.[3,8] Some have speculated that the questionable follow-through on this issue is directly tied to a lack of funds available for the investigation. Others believe PA's Dept. of Education just wanted the whole mess to go away. So it did.

On the 2015-2016 School Progress Report, P.S. #11 received an overall score of 7% and 0% for achievement.[9] Interestingly, the same year during which the tougher PA Core-aligned PSSAs were introduced, 171 parents of children at P.S. #11 (about 1/3 of its students) opted out of standardized testing.[10] Over 4,000 students across PA plus another 115,000 in New Jersey opted out of testing in the 2016 school year. 640,000 U.S. students skipped the standardized tests all together.[11]

It's not new news that parents, teachers, administrators and countless education experts oppose the extreme testing that now governs U.S. public education. Many are convinced that the only thing being taught is the test, while others are concerned that poor test scores are being used as an excuse to close public schools and open for-profit charters.[12,13] In response, parents and teachers are actively organizing and providing instructions and forms to opt-out. Some students have taken advantage of the ability to opt out for religious reasons; others simply refused to take it.[10,11,13]

UPDATE: P.S. #11 (CONT'D)

PSSA Scores Reported for P.S. #11 (8th Grade)[14]

Percentage of Students Scoring **BELOW BASIC** Proficiency*		
2001 – 2002	Math: 52%	Reading: 38%
2002 – 2003	Math: 44%	Reading: 34%
2003 – 2004	Math: 25%	Reading: 26%
2004 – 2005	Math: 21%	Reading: 20%
2005 – 2006	Math: 16%	Reading: 14%
2006 – 2007	Math: 16%	Reading: 13%
2007 – 2008	Math: 21%	Reading: 20%
2008 – 2009	Math: 17%	Reading: 11%
2009 – 2010	Math: 14%	Reading: 10%
2010 – 2011	Math: 16%	Reading: 10%
2011 – 2012	Math: 31%	Reading: 19%
Stricter Security†		
2012 – 2013	Math: 30%	Reading: 23%
2013 – 2014	Math: 47%	Reading: 32%
More Rigorous Testing‡		
2014 – 2015	Math: 83%	ELA:§ 28%
2015 – 2016	Math: 83%	ELA: 28%
2016 – 2017	Math: 91%	ELA: 44%
2017 – 2018	Math: 93%	ELA: 20%

* Percentages are rounded.

† Stricter testing security implemented statewide.

‡ School district adopted more rigorous PA Core Standards.

§ New PSSA test switched from reading to English language arts (ELA) to reflect the greater range of skills being tested.

> Update – Public School #12

*B*ack in 2001 when I first visited P.S. #12, it had over 1200 students and a reputation for violence.[1] By 2011, it had made PA's list of "Persistently Dangerous Schools" two years in a row.[2,3] Though P.S. #12 had worked itself off of the persistently dangerous list by 2012[4], enrollment had dropped significantly and by 2016, there were fewer than 600 students.[5]

P.S. #12 has also not fared as well on the PSSAs as it did in 2001.* Generally, over 50% of its eleventh graders scored Below Basic Proficiency in reading and math between 2003 and 2012. Oddly, during the 2010-2011 school year, only 5% of them scored Below Basic in writing, while 53% scored Below Basic in reading.[6] Despite this inconsistency, P.S. #12 was not implicated in PA's 2009-2011 cheating scandal. In 2012, when PA high schools switched from the generalized PSSAs to the subject-focused Keystone exams, there was an immediate and significant decrease in the number of eleventh graders testing into Below Basic.[7]

Although P.S. #12 has had a decades-long reputation of violence and low academic achievement, it has been hailed for recent progress. Much of this recent success is attributed to a smart, career and technical education (CTE) focus that includes visual arts production, business technology and health sciences. Strong leadership has also played a key role. After four years as assistant principal and only two as principal, P.S. #12's top administrator received the prestigious Lindback Award for Distinguished Principal Leadership.[8] Soon after, in 2016, the school was awarded a grant from Philadelphia School Partnership worth over $1 million to support its ongoing transition.[9] Promoting a high rate of college acceptance and attainment of industry certifications by its students,

---

*I had returned to corporate America by the time PSSA scores for 2001-2002 (the year during which I first subbed) were released. P.S. #12's results were shocking. Not because they were poor, but because I expected far worse. Yet, there it was in black and white print and confirmed on the official PSSA website: 44%, 38% and only 23% Below Basic in writing.[1] Months later, I ran into a teacher who worked at P.S. #12 and, of course, the first thing out of my mouth was how well they had done on the PSSAs in comparison to many other schools. Without hesitation, he replied that the scores in the paper were "considerably better than the real ones."

P.S. #12 seems to be on the verge of a breakthrough. Yet, official SDP School Progress Reports from 2015-2016 and, more recently, 2018-2019 place P.S. #12 in the lowest possible performance tier—"intervene"—with a score of 0% in achievement.[5]

UPDATE – P.S. #12 (CONT'D)

Proficiency Exam Scores Reported for P.S. #12 (11th Grade)

Percentage of Students Scoring BELOW BASIC Proficiency[†]			
PSSA Results[6]			
2001 – 2002	Math: 44%	Reading: 38%	Writing: 23%
2002 – 2003	Math: 68%	Reading: 55%	
2003 – 2004	Math: 57%	Reading: 43%	
2004 – 2005	Math: 62%	Reading: 57%	
2005 – 2006	Math: 52%	Reading: 41%	
2006 – 2007	Math: 55%	Reading: 46%	
2007 – 2008	Math: 68%	Reading: 51%	
2008 – 2009	Math: 73%	Reading: 62%	
2009 – 2010	Math: 83%	Reading: 62%	
2010 – 2011	Math: 58%	Reading: 53%	Writing: 5%
2011 – 2012	Math: 62%	Reading: 55%	
Keystone Exam Results[7‡]			
2012 – 2013[§]	Algebra: 29%	Literature: 17%	
2013 – 2014	Algebra: 24%	Literature: 13%	
2014 – 2015	Math:[¶] 21%	English:[¶] 13%	
2015 – 2016	Algebra: 20%	Literature: 11%	
2016 – 2017	Algebra: 44%	Literature: 47%	
2017 – 2018	Algebra: 44%	Literature: 40%	

† Percentages are rounded.
‡ Philadelphia high schools switched from the PSSA to the Keystone exam, which adheres to the more rigorous PA Core Standards.
§ Stricter testing security implemented statewide.
¶ Keystone results spreadsheet identifies subjects as math and English, instead of algebra and literature.

> Update – Public School #13

*J*admit it. I have a soft spot for P.S. #13. Of all the schools I visited the first time around, this one was my favorite. And that included a later visit to one of Philly's most prestigious schools. The seventh graders I taught were considered "economically disadvantaged," yet they defied the stereotypes. They were smart. They were enthusiastic. They knew how to behave in a classroom environment. Along with their teachers, they exhibited a true sense of school community. A lot seems to have changed between then and now.

In 2005, P.S. #13 was selected along with thirty plus other District schools to develop more intensive programs for gifted students. Though there were a few different formats, P.S. #13 had been assigned to "emerging scholars,"[1] a curriculum that uses research-based practices to demonstrate real-world application of classroom knowledge. Unfortunately, budgets came up short and it was never implemented; however, P.S. #13's ambitious principal found a way to incorporate elements of the program by having students meet twice a week to explore and discuss topics from global warming to poetry.[2]

In 2008, P.S. #13 received one of the highest forms of recognition possible when it was named a No Child Left Behind Blue Ribbon School by the U.S. Department of Education. Along with this honor, P.S. #13's principal was acknowledged for outstanding leadership. All of this attention was the direct result of achievement on PA's standardized tests. Looking at the scores listed at the end of this chapter, we can see that very few of the students were testing into the Below Basic Proficiency category in math or reading but here, it's the flip side that's so impressive. From 2004 to 2008, the number of students testing into the Advanced category skyrocketed: 29% to 77% in reading and 13% to 67% in math.[2] By 2008, 96% of P.S. #13's eighth graders were scoring Proficient or Advanced in reading, while 93% scored Proficient or Advanced in math.[3] Students who entered fifth grade scoring low were scoring much higher by the time they graduated.[2] As a magnet school, P.S. #13 can pick and choose its students to an extent. Even still, these results were outstanding.

P.S. #13's principal credited the school's success to "tremendous students" and a great teaching staff that had seen very little turnover in 40 years. He also cited moving beyond mastery of fundamental concepts to more critical thinking and analysis, supplementing his teaching staff with high school teachers who were able to elevate the level of middle school instruction and employing Cooperative Learning strategies.[2] P.S. #13 was considered one of Philly's "Vanguard" schools, receiving Keystone, Annual Yearly Progress and Best Practice awards. Then, in the summer of 2010, the principal abruptly retired, though according to at least one long-time staff member, "He was pushed out." She declined to say why or by whom.

In 2011, P.S. #13 was implicated in PA's cheating scandal. Unlike other schools accused of cheating, the evidence against P.S. #13 was confined to one school year (2011) one grade (eighth) and one subject (math),[4] which likely means that only one teacher was cheating. I wanted to believe the best of P.S. #13, but I found myself wondering about their past achievements. So I took a closer look at their PSSA scores.

P.S. #13 Grade 8[3]								
	% Advanced Math	% Proficient Math	% Basic Math	% Below Basic Math	% Advanced Reading	% Proficient Reading	% Basic Reading	% Below Basic Reading
2007-2008	66.8	25.9	6.3	1.0	76.7	19.5	3.4	0.0
2008-2009	55.2	30.0	12.2	2.6	78.3	19.6	1.7	0.0
2009-2010	57.8	29.1	9.2	4.0	84.0	13.6	2.0	0.4
2010-2011	58.8	30.6	9.3	1.4	78.7	17.1	3.2	0.9
2011-2012	60.2	29.3	6.3	4.2	81.8	17.1	1.1	0.0
2012-2013	48.0	30.0	14.0	8.0	70.0	21.0	7.0	2.0
2013-2014	57.0	24.0	11.0	8.0	47.0	31.0	16.0	7.0
2014-2015	8.5	27.1	47.3	17.1	16.3	65.9	16.3	1.6
2015-2016	5.0	19.0	39.7	36.4	9.9	64.5	22.3	3.3

P.S. #13 was implicated for cheating in the 2010-2011 school year. When tighter test taking security was implemented in 2012-2013, scores began to decline. By the second year of tighter security, students scoring into the Advanced category had declined by about 12 percentage points in both reading and math.[3] Eighth-grade math scores in the Advanced category rebounded in 2013-2014, but dropped another 23 points in reading. Scores plummeted in the 2014-2015 school year when the tougher standardized test was introduced and continued to dip during the 2015-2016 school year. The SDP assigned P.S. #13 to the "intervene" performance tier with an overall score of 22%, an achievement score of 26% and a progress score of 0% out of 100%.[3,5] Despite these dramatic swings, the number of students at P.S. #13 testing into Below Basic was still much lower than most of Philly's public and charter schools.

What caught my attention is that P.S. #13's test scores had started to decline before the switch to the tougher test. Did that mean they were cheating all along and tighter security exposed this? Or, were they suffering the effects of different leadership? How about those teachers who had been there for 40 years? Had they retired when the other principal left? Was the school suffering the effects of ongoing budget cuts? P.S. #13's 2016-2017 School Progress Report placed it back on the "reinforce" performance tier with a 51% overall score: more than double the previous year's score. Then in the 2017-2018 school year, P.S. #13 once again dropped to the "watch" tier." How on earth could a school that seemed to be going so right, suddenly go so wrong?[6,7]

UPDATE – P.S. #13 (CONT'D)

PSSA Scores Reported for P.S. #13 (8th Grade)[3]

Percentage of Students Scoring BELOW BASIC Proficiency*		
2001 – 2002	Math: 16%	Reading: 6%
2002 – 2003	Math: 20%	Reading: 8%
2003 – 2004	Math: 5%	Reading: 5%
2004 – 2005	Math: 5%	Reading: 4%
2005 – 2006	Math: 3%	Reading: 8%
2006 – 2007	Math: 4%	Reading: 2%
2007 – 2008	Math: 1%	Reading: 0%
2008 – 2009	Math: 3%	Reading: 0%
2009 – 2010	Math: 4%	Reading: 0%
2010 – 2011	Math: 1%[†]	Reading: 1%
2011 – 2012	Math: 4%	Reading: 0%
Stricter Security[‡]		
2012 – 2013	Math: 8%	Reading: 2%
2013 – 2014	Math: 8%	Reading: 1%
More Rigorous Testing[§]		
2014 – 2015	Math: 17%	ELA:[¶] 2%
2015 – 2016	Math: 36%	ELA: 3%
2016 – 2017	Math: 41%	ELA: 1%
2017 – 2018	Math: 38%	ELA: 1%

---

* Percentages are rounded.

† Implicated in cheating for eighth-grade math.

‡ Stricter testing security implemented statewide.

§ School district adopted more rigorous PA Core Standards.

¶ New PSSA test switched from reading to English language arts (ELA) to reflect the greater range of skills being tested.

› Update – Public School #14

I have to admit, when I subbed at P.S. #14, I was underwhelmed. Like P.S. #9, P.S. #14 was not a good school, but it also wasn't topping anybody's worst of the worst lists. Somewhere around 2007, the middle school was closed and treated to a $25 million makeover. It re-opened in the 2009-2010 school year as a special admission, arts-focused high school that requires good grades, good behavior and an audition for acceptance.[1,2]

According to reports, the founding principal was instrumental in integrating arts throughout the curriculum, establishing a wide variety of extracurricular activities and promoting participation in team sports for female students.[2] So far, the new high school has fared much better than the previous middle school with only 8% of eleventh graders scoring Below Basic Proficiency in reading and 20% in math.[3] But, as with most public schools throughout Philadelphia, budget cuts reportedly had a huge impact, causing the loss of teachers and administrators, the elimination of classes outside of core requirements and book and supply shortages.[4] Unlike other schools where I subbed, P.S. #14 has not been struggling with violence and low achievement. It held steady and even improved during the switch over to the Keystone exams in 2012, with hardly any P.S. #14 eleventh graders testing into the Below Basic category in math or English.[5]

P.S. #14 is doing well by pretty much everyone's standards. Even though it slipped to "watch" in the achievement category on the District's 2015 and 2016 School Progress Reports, it still managed to maintain an overall performance tier designation of "reinforce."[6] In 2017, P.S. #14 was nationally ranked by *U.S. News and World Report*—#85 out of all PA high schools, which earned it a bronze award.[7] If, during my first subbing experience, you had asked me how important the arts are to academic achievement, I would have said "not very." Clearly, I was wrong.

Update – P.S. #14 (Cont'd) PSSA Scores Reported for P.S. #14

Percentage of Students Scoring BELOW BASIC Proficiency[*]

PSSA Results[3]: 8th Grade		
2001 – 2002	Math: 52%	Reading: 39%
2002 – 2003	Math: 42%	Reading: 37%
2003 – 2004	Math: 28%	Reading: 26%
2004 – 2005	Math: 27%	Reading: 31%
2005 – 2006	Math: 32%	Reading: 28%
2006 – 2007	Math: 25%	Reading: 21%
2007 – 2008[†]	Closed	
2008 – 2009[†]	Closed	
PSSA Results[3]: 11th Grade (School Re-opened)		
2010 – 2011[‡]	Math: 19%	Reading: 8%
2011 – 2012	Math: 20%	Reading: 7%
Keystone Exam Results[5§]:		
2012 – 2013[¶]	Algebra I: 2%	Literature: 1%
2013 – 2014	Algebra I: 2%	Literature: 1%
2014 – 2015	Math:[**] 2%	English:[**] 0%
2015 – 2016	Algebra I: 1%	Literature: 0%
2016 – 2017	Algebra: 1%	Literature: 1%
2017 – 2018	Algebra: 1%	Literature: 2%

[*] Percentages are rounded.

[†] Lower grades phased out. School closed, renovated and converted to arts based high school. First year, ninth and tenth graders only.

[‡] First year for eleventh-grade students.

[§] Philadelphia high schools switched from the PSSA to the Keystone exam, which adheres to the more rigorous PA Core Standards

[¶] Stricter testing security implemented statewide.

[**] Keystone results spreadsheet identifies subjects as math and English, instead of algebra and literature.

> Update – Public School #15

*F*or many years, the neighborhood surrounding P.S. #15 has been rough and rundown. For example, in 2016, a nearby shooting caused the school to be placed on lockdown.[1] But after decades of low performance, P.S. #15 was taken over by Mastery Charter Schools in 2010, giving it a fresh start along with fresh paint, repairs, etc.[2]

The year before Mastery took over, 1 out of 5 students was suspended and very few students tested into the Proficient category for reading.[3] In fact, 68% of fifth graders tested into the Below Basic Proficiency category in math and 83% tested into Below Basic for reading. But starting in 2010, P.S. #15 began to make progress. The previous numbers dropped by 30 points in reading and 38 points in math.[4] Attendance was up 3%. Enrollment was up 7%. And all of this took place in the first year of its conversion to a charter school.[3]

Like many Mastery schools, P.S. #15 is known for having enthusiastic and caring faculty and staff that actively engage with parents and the community. In the 2015-2016 school year, it received an SPR climate score of 64%, nearly placing it in the top tier for school environments. Unfortunately, academic progress does not appear to be moving along quite as swiftly. While fewer of P.S. #15's fifth graders have been scoring Below Basic in English Language Arts on the new tougher PSSAs, more are scoring Below Basic in Math,[4] and recent School Progress Reports have consistently placed the school in the second to last tier—"watch."[5,6]

UPDATE – P.S. #15 (CONT'D)

PSSA Scores Reported for P.S. #15 (5th Grade)[4]

Percentage of Students Scoring BELOW BASIC Proficiency*		
2001 - 2002	Math: 55%	Reading: 54%
2002 - 2003	Math: 55%	Reading: 69%
2003 - 2004	Math: 55%	Reading: 57%
2004 - 2005	Math: 41%	Reading: 62%
2005 - 2006	Math: 31%	Reading: 57%
2006 - 2007	Math: 36%	Reading: 66%
2007 - 2008	Math: 35%	Reading: 60%
2008 - 2009	Math: 38%	Reading: 69%
2009 - 2010[†]	Math: 68%	Reading: 83%
2010 - 2011	Math: 30%	Reading: 53%
2011 - 2012	Math: 21%	Reading: 54%
Stricter Security[‡]		
2012 - 2013	Math: 21%	Reading: 41%
2013 - 2014	Math: 41%	Reading: 47%
More Rigorous Testing[§]		
2014 - 2015	Math: 57%	ELA:[¶] 8%
2015 - 2016	Math: 58%	ELA: 24%
2016 - 2017	Math: 58%	ELA: 20%
2017 - 2018	Math: 58%	ELA: 17%

* Percentages are rounded.
† Converted to Mastery Charter School.
‡ Stricter testing security implemented statewide.
§ School district adopted more rigorous PA Core Standards.
¶ New PSSA test switched from reading to English language arts (ELA) to reflect the greater range of skills being tested.

PART 3

$$1+1=2$$

Back Inside the SDP...
15 years later

We keep it a secret, but if parents knew their children were sitting next to kids who are emotionally disturbed—running around the classroom, calling people 'pussy'—I think there would be an outcry."

—Anonymous Teacher
School District of Philadelphia

> Back in the Saddle

*W*hen it comes to the School District of Philadelphia, there has been a wealth of in-depth reporting and an abundance of press releases, statistics and statements issued from the SDP itself. All addressing its progress or lack thereof. I wanted to see for myself if, over 15 years later, the schools were any better. So, despite the fact that I swore I'd never do it again, in August of 2017, I "allowed" myself to be recruited for a substitute teaching position. All I did was glance in the direction of the Kelly Educational Services booth at the District's back-to-school event. Before I knew it, I had a brochure and the name and number for one of their supervisors.

Kelly took over the staffing of substitute teachers for Philadelphia's public schools after Source4Teachers, another staffing firm, was terminated in 2016. Like the District itself, Source4Teachers could not keep pace with Philly's high teacher absence rate (twenty percent of them same-day callouts) while also finding enough long-term substitutes to fill 400 vacancies. After a year of chaos, the District hired Kelly based on its previous experience with large, urban school districts.[1]

I am happy to report that the requirements for substitutes are now more stringent and more clearly defined. The supervisor I spoke with walked me through the entire application process in about two weeks. Kelly requested an application and transcripts along with the usual background checks and child abuse clearances, just as the SDP had my first time out. But they also required a résumé, personal references and registration with the Pennsylvania Department of Education, in addition to proof that I completed eight mandatory hours of online training on conflict resolution, emergency procedures and the protocol for suspected child abuse. And one-on-one interviews and fingerprinting to check with the FBI database were conducted in-office on orientation day. Glancing around the room, I didn't notice anyone who seemed to be obviously questionable. Everyone appeared to be neat, professional and raring to go. Even my own feelings of dread were slowly turning toward excitement.

The entire assignment selection process is now online, though there's still an annoying automated calling system if you're into it. I was not and quickly checked "do not call," though sometimes they still did. Usually at the crack of dawn during periods of high need, such as Mondays, Fridays, bad weather days, good weather days and, of course, when the Eagles won the Super Bowl (Go Birds!) The starting salary is $126/day for uncertified subs, quite a bit higher than the $40/day the District offered back in 2001. For uncertified subs who work their way into a long-term assignment (which kicks in on the twentieth consecutive day in the same classroom) the daily rate is $200 per day. Kelly also offers free online training classes to help subs develop better classroom skills. There are scheduling Coordinators, local staffing supervisors and long-term assignment Coordinators available to help you find the right gig or to address any questions or concerns. This time, I didn't feel quite so unprepared or on my own.

During this second outing, from September 2017 to June 2019, I completed almost 60 different assignments at more than 50 different schools. I had the chance to visit most of the schools where I had previously subbed, as well as a bunch of new ones. My assignments included long-term and one-off assignments, as well as one gig that got me banned from a school. (Since you're wondering...)

The principal of a particular second-tier special admission school and I had a difference of opinion about why his students were crawling around the floor, flipping off the lights, fighting, screaming and ignoring the assignments they were supposed to be completing. He excused their behavior, blaming their regular teacher for not leaving enough work to keep them busy. But since most refused to do the work in front of them—and other school personnel who were asked to give me a hand either quickly declined or just didn't show up—I figured it was more likely that his students interpreted the presence of a substitute as an invitation to behave like jerks. His own students confirmed my suspicion.

"I feel sorry for you," one of them blurted out upon seeing my unfamiliar face.

I felt sorry for me by the end of that day. Still, I hoped that a talk with the principal would help us come up with some ideas that would benefit his students and the substitute teachers he so frequently needed. Unfortunately, "Mr. Man's" response was to explain how much "better" his kids were than the kids "out there in other schools." But having met some very lovely students "out there," I responded that I hadn't seen any evidence of that.

"Well, if you feel that way about it, don't come back," he barked.

I guess "okay," wasn't a strong enough reaction, so as an afterthought he followed me to my car and continued to harass me.

"I'll call Kelly...have you banned from the building..."

Needless to say, I was feeling a bit uncomfortable by this point. I responded as I normally would to some stranger fussing and following me. I said nothing, slid into my car and locked the doors. Finally, he got the message and backed away. As I watched him walk back toward his school, I couldn't help but wonder why he thought making excuses for the kids would benefit them, especially when they get out into the real world. He did indeed call Kelly and they "deactivated" me while investigating his complaint. I wrote my statement—the District is big on statements—and turned it in. Two days later, I was reactivated with the understanding that I would not be able to return to a school I had no intention of ever subbing at again. It was a win-win for everyone...except his students, who most likely still do not know how to behave when they have substitute teachers.

Anyway...I subbed in North, Northwest, Northeast, South and West Philly, etc., as well as Center City and surrounding well-to-do areas. I subbed in the inner city and in the more suburban areas of Philadelphia; in predominantly black and/or Hispanic schools and predominantly white and/or Asian schools; in elementary, middle and high schools; and in first- and second-tier magnet and special admission schools, as well as many struggling neighborhood schools. I focused on general education, but also accepted several assignments in special education: life skills, autistic support, emotional and behavioral support (EBS), as well as integrated inclusion classes with a high percentage of EBS students. The most challenging were the EBS inclusion classes. The most enjoyable and impressive were the life skills and autism support classes, which were small and focused exclusively on the specific needs of the students. The kids were well behaved, cooperative and intent on getting their work done. And there was always additional adult supervision. I also took assignments in the administrative offices of a few schools. (It's amazing what you can learn just by keeping your mouth shut and doing your job.)

My assignments ranged from half days to an on-again, off-again, long-term teaching position at P.S. #7. (You remember P.S. #7. The school where the third-grader accused me of choking her. Then, said it was another teacher and another who, shamefully, probably had choked her.) Back in 2001-2002, I learned that one or two children with uncontrolled or unaddressed emotional, behavioral or learning disabilities can tear down the education process, derail classmates and make the most enthusiastic teacher rethink his or her career choice. Though I had come to this conclusion the first time around, having the opportunity to observe one class over the course of an entire school year was eye-opening.

> Public School #7, Back...and Back Again

October-December, 2017
P.S. #7—Return Visit #1

*A*bout a month after I resumed subbing, I took a four-day assignment at P.S. #7. I was very interested to see how time had treated this school. Little did I know this four-day gig would turn into a recurring assignment that stretched over the entire school year.

Arriving a little early, I signed in and sat waiting for over an hour as people walked back and forth, talking in low voices about "breaking up the class" and "addressing behaviors." From what I could tell, there was another substitute in the mix...but what I wanted to know is, "What happened to the regular teachers?" Finally, the "Principal" walked me down to room "110," which up until recently had been the art room. If I had to guess, I'd say it hadn't been cleaned in about three years. It was huge and filled with junk. There were no desks of any kind, but there were several raggedy, wooden tables. In the back of the room, water dripped from the rusty faucet of a paint-stained sink that leaked into an old, dirty bucket on the floor. Nearby, a pipe stretched from the ceiling down through a hole in the floor. Someone had layered old carpet samples around the pole to cover the hole, I think. On the other side of the room, stacks of flat, dusty cardboard boxes filled the corner. At the front, there was a broken SMART Board, an old file cabinet and a wall-to-wall chalkboard thick with drawings, dust and dirt.

Suited-down and, I suspect, a bit embarrassed, the Principal grabbed a container of wet wipes. "I can help you clean up," she said.

Knowing that her time would be better served dealing with the teachers and parents waiting to speak to her, I replied, "You've got people waiting in the office. Can you just send someone to help me?"

Relieved, she scurried off and, a few minutes later, a Muslim sister showed up. She introduced herself as "Miss A," a member of the Climate team—the folks in charge of safety and discipline. She took a quick look around and proclaimed she had "very bad allergies" and couldn't deal with the dust.

"Maybe the cleaning staff could help?" I suggested.

"They don't do everything. You know...all types of cleaning," she responded.

I didn't know. My grandmother had worked on the engineer's team at a public school for over a decade. She and the women she worked with kept that school spotless. And on the few occasions she brought me along, I helped. Even today, it's still one of the more well-maintained schools I visited. Figuring I was on my own, I asked Miss A if she could please just get me some plastic bags and a broom. But a few minutes later, she returned with bags and brooms (plural) and pitched in like a champ. We stripped the room, sorted through piles of junk, moved tables and wiped them down, swept, put useful supplies in the front closet and threw out the ripped up paper, dried out markers, etc. We taped poster paper over the area with the dripping sink and the big hole in the floor then blocked the whole section off with tables. We had been working for about an hour when Miss A's boss, an unsmiling and unhelpful man, stopped in to tell us that ready or not, he was "bringing the kids."

"Can you give us another 20 minutes? We still need to clean the boards and get the boxes and other trash to the dumpster. We could use a little help," I hinted politely.

"Boss Man" offered a few more minutes and pitched in by sending some students to haul the cardboard to the dumpster. Miss A and I quickly finished cleaning out the coat closet and wiped down the window sills. The blackboards and the inch-thick chalk dust would have to wait. We overloaded a large trashcan and stacked several filled trash bags next to it just in time to hear desks scraping along the hallway floor.

Suddenly, Miss A pulled me aside and showed me the list of students.

"Look, you don't want this kid in here," she said noting 'Student X.' "Trust me. Or, this one, 'Trouble A to Z.' He's out of control, but better than X. And this kid here can be a handful..." She stopped talking just as Boss Man directed the first students into the room.

Heeding Miss A's advice, I politely approached.

"I was wondering if it would be possible for him not to be in this room?" I said, pointing to Student X's name on the class list.

Shooting Miss A an annoyed look, he responded, "If he's on your list, he's on your list."

"I was hoping he could not be on my list," I responded as tactfully as possible.

"I'd have to discuss it with the Principal," he said, clearly irritated by the request.

"Okay," I smiled. After all, if this kid is that much of a problem, shouldn't he be with his regular teacher...whenever she returns?

A few minutes later, Boss Man ushered in the remaining students. Thankfully, Student X was not among them, though Trouble A to Z was front and center. I lined the kids up in rows facing forward and introduced myself. I made it clear that I was not their regular teacher but I'd be there for the rest of the week. I have to say, most of these kids were pretty...awesome. Sweet, smart and cooperative, though they talked nonstop and giggled just as much. (Third grade.) Even Trouble A to Z—who had a tendency to walk out of class and run the halls when the mood struck—was on his best behavior. I immediately got them to work reading essays about whether or not dodge ball should be banned at school. (In Philadelphia? Huh.) When the Principal popped in to check on us, we were having a lively pro and con discussion. She said it was the best she had seen the class since school started.

Later that day as I headed out, the Principal quizzed me on the other schools where I had subbed. After answering, she stated rather than asked, "You don't want a long-term assignment." When I shook my head no, she charmingly asked me to consider a little, teeny-tiny two or three week assignment, "just until 'Regular Teacher' returns." I promised to give it some thought and over the next few days, made a point of finding out exactly what was going on. Here's what I learned. Initially, there were two, third-grade homerooms: One run by the "Grade Lead," an experienced senior teacher who had thirty-four students. This class was under control but it had more than the allowed number of students. The other class was also over the limit, but it was under the direction of a first-year teacher, who was struggling. Groups of her students, mostly boys, roamed the hallways: fighting, playing, hiding, whatever. And she let them because, otherwise, they'd be in her classroom doing the same thing. The Principal decided to turn the two classes into three with 27 students in the Grade Lead's room and 20 students in each of the other two classes. Less pressure on the teachers; more individual attention for the students. Everybody wins.

The day before Regular Teacher arrived, "New Teacher" went out on medical leave and Regular Teacher had no choice but to take on the entire out-of-control class. By the end of her second day, Regular Teacher also "went out on some kind of leave." Since then, the class had been cycling through substitutes until the day I arrived, when New Teacher's class was split between another Kelly sub and me. Though I can neither confirm nor deny either way, it was suspected by many that these two teachers weren't so much sick...as sick of the problem students. New Teacher, in particular, had been tried and accused by her peers:

"Those kids haven't been learning a thing. And that medical leave...bullshit."

Several of the teachers claimed they tried to help New Teacher, but she wasn't "open to it." I can only say that teachers, cafeteria workers and aides whose names I didn't even know went out of their way to encourage and support me. The Grade Lead was particularly awesome. Since there was pretty-much nothing in room 110 when I arrived, she walked me down to New Teacher's room to "go shopping" for workbooks, storybooks, text books and, most importantly, teacher editions because they have the answers. She explained to the other sub and me where the kids should be, and volunteered to share her upcoming lesson plans. I suspected, and it was pretty quickly confirmed, that her class was much further ahead than ours. So it didn't seem fair to skip the kids ahead, which meant it was on us to develop our own lesson plans. Though we initially agreed to share the teacher editions, the other sub eventually told me I could keep them because she "wasn't using them anyway."

Despite the fact that I was in over my head, I have to admit I was having fun. The kids and I were getting along great. Most of them did their homework and were eager to learn and participate. Though chatty and silly, they were generally well behaved, as long as I kept them away from the other half of their previous class. This wasn't easy since they had breakfast, lunch, recess and gym together every day. And, every day, there would be some kind of fight or roughhousing that ended with one of the kids in my care crying or hurt. Even the kids who were a "handful" were settling in, mostly I think because I didn't hesitate to call their parents. On any given day, you could find me after school in the office on the phone. And, for the most part, the parents were lovely—engaged, supportive, cooperative people who put an immediate stop to whatever problem I was having. Even the parents who did absolutely nothing in response to my calls were at least polite.

Trouble A to Z was getting a little better. He liked me and he knew two key things: 1) I would text or call his father on the spot if he mouthed off or acted up too much. 2) If he left the classroom, I would lock the door. Eventually, he stopped walking out without permission. Of course, sometimes I put him out because he wouldn't leave the other students alone, or he wouldn't do his work, or because he was crawling around in the closet or across the floor. Baby steps.

Spurred on by kindness and encouragement from the "Fabulous Senior Teachers" at the school, I agreed to stay a couple of weeks more since Regular Teacher hadn't yet returned. Once again, I was fantasizing about getting certified and becoming a real teacher. Then, in the space of one conversation, everything changed. New Teacher returned and though she told me she was "fine" with the way her class had been split, she convinced the Principal that she had been given all of the behaviorally and/or academically challenged students. Her solution was to re-split the class and give almost all of them—including Student X—to me. Recognizing a disaster in the making, I suggested that now might be the time for me to bow out. I had been trying to provide continuity for the 110 kids because I really, really liked them and wanted them to have the best shot at keeping up with their work. But since they were about to give me a bunch of new students who didn't know me from Adam and probably didn't want to be in my class, I figured any sub would do. And I said so.

"We don't need any sub," the Principal insisted. "We need you. Other subs are not going to call parents, check homework, give quizzes and make the work meaningful..."

I knew I should've just gotten up and walked out right then. I didn't know those other kids or their parents, but I knew Student X because he had made himself known to me. Every single day, sometimes twice a day, this handsome, well-dressed and articulate little boy came to the room, snatched open the door and yelled, "Hi, Miss Harris!" or just looked around to see what we were doing. Then he slammed the door closed, rattling the glass. One minute he was tackling me with a hug in the hallway, the next I'd be pulling him off of one of the students in my class. The thought that I would have to deal with this little boy all day, every day made me shudder.

Whatever the Principal was saying wasn't working, but then she uttered the magic words, "As educators…" I heard nothing beyond that. I was mesmerized by the fact that she had referred to me as an "educator," a title that carries so much dignity and responsibility. I caved, all the while knowing that I was just a big, fat sucker.

That afternoon, I broke the news about "the switch" to my class. Some were happy they were staying, a couple were happy they were leaving while four ("Kevin," "Kurt," "Janelle" and "Jaloni") refused to go, even after I pointed out that I would not be there permanently.

"Uhn-uh. We're not going," said Kevin.

"Nope," said Kurt.

Their parents were also adamant because 1) a boy in the other class kept threatening Kevin and 2) Kurt was finally starting to show an interest in school. Janelle and Jaloni figured if Kevin and Kurt didn't have to go, neither did they. New Teacher was both surprised and disappointed, but she agreed because she didn't want to "argue with parents." She then proceeded to cherry-pick from the other 110 kids who were supposed to stay with me, though she agreed to take Trouble A to Z.

"We're friends," she said. "I can handle him." Translation: "The Principal told me that under no circumstances can X and Trouble A to Z be in the same room…so I'm giving X to you."

In the end, I had three new hall runners, including Student X, as well as a couple of girls who were going through difficulty at home that left them hyper-emotional, distracted and distracting. Originally, I thought perhaps two kids in the class had ADHD. After the switch, it seemed like four or more had some form of it. It was harder to quiet them, harder to get them to focus and even harder to get them to do homework. Meanwhile, the four who insisted on staying with me continued to shine: Kurt and Kevin made sure I knew about anything that I didn't know about from how pretzel day worked to who took my pen off the table. Despite her shyness, I could always count on Janelle to have the right answer and the right attitude. And sweet, GQ Jaloni was always the first to help with anything. Homework done, well rested, smiles on their faces, these kids were excited about school and loved to learn.

Then there was Student X, who just so happened to be suspended for what was described as "beating the crap" out of another student. New Teacher transferred X and the kid he beat up to my room. I had two days to establish a relationship with all the new kids before X returned. I focused on the next biggest troublemakers first: "Hard Harry," a rough and tumble, street-wise kid who couldn't sit still and "Mean Marshall" who alternated between being talkative and sarcastic and just plain sullen. Both were X's buddies and, often, his primary targets. Marshall was the recipient of the infamous beat-down that finally got X suspended. No matter what I wanted Marshall to do—quiet down, sit down, get to work—I normally had to make the request at least three times, then debate the merits of what I wanted him to do. But once he got to work, he was fine and among the first to volunteer answers. When he was right, which was often, wow. His face lit up like the sun.

While Marshall was challenging, Harry was just difficult. The day of the switch, he tried to shove his desk into my knees as he dragged it down the hall because I was in his way.

"Move," he commanded.

"Look, I know you don't want to switch classes, but I'm glad you're here," I said. "This is your opportunity to start over."

"I hate this class. I don't want to be in here," he responded that day, and nearly every day after. Then he pushed past me into the room.

Starting right then, when Harry and Marshall walked out of the room, they got locked out and I called the office and their folks. I stayed on their cases about not doing homework, not paying attention, not staying in their seats, etc. The next day, we started all over again. I called their guardians right from the classroom. By the time X returned, his two buddies were no longer hall runners. He stood holding the door open, yelling for them to "Come on!" But they didn't budge. So off he went, to recruit his buddies who were still in New Teacher's class.

It took about two weeks to calm this class down. During that time, Kevin, Kurt and Jaloni began to get dragged into arguments and fights with some of the new boys, especially X. I called the office for help, but by then, I understood that neither Boss Man nor his team members would do anything other than tell me to "write it up." Miss A tried to help as much as possible, but at a certain point and with certain kids, mostly the boys, she steered clear. So I stuck with calling parents and on a few occasions had lunch detention. But while I made sure the kids got their lunch, I sometimes didn't get mine.

"Don't start that," one of the Fab Senior Teachers advised. "Take your lunch. It may be the only break you get."

She was so right. One day, I had lunch detention, my prep was cancelled and I never had the chance to eat or go to the bathroom...all day. Plus, lunch detention was more effective with the boys. They hated missing recess. The girls were often content to eat their lunch quietly in the room with me.

Though I was making slow progress with the other students, no matter what I tried, the end result with X was that he did what he wanted when he wanted: fighting, hitting, kicking, cursing. He ignored the adults around him, including me, and physically bullied and emotionally berated the other students. Every day, we struggled for control of the room. I know how ridiculous this sounds... battling with a nine-year-old...but the other kids were so intimidated by him, that if he spoke, they turned their attention to him, whether I was teaching or not. Not out of disrespect for me, but fear of him. I had started reaching out to X's family while he was still on suspension. His grandmother promised that they were working with him and that she would personally talk to him again, but nothing changed. The arguments, the fights, the bullying continued and Kevin was one of his favorite targets. One day, after X and Harry wound up in the office for fighting with each other, I had the chance to speak to them separately.

"Harry, why are you in the office again? You could be a leader, but you keep fighting, keep giving me a hard time, not doing your work. Why?"

"'Cause," he said quietly, "I don't want to be in your class."

"Well, hang in there for a minute. I think you're going to get your wish." (Regular Teacher had to come back sometime, right?)

Then, I spoke to X. "Can you please tell me what the problem is? Why are you behaving the way you do?"

"I just like to have a lot of fun," he said, matter-of-factly.

"But why do you keep fighting with everyone...and picking on Kevin?"

"I just hate Kevin a little bit," he said with complete candor.

"Why?"

"I don't know...it started last year. I just do."

"And you hate Kurt and Harry and Marshall a little bit, too?

"Harry...yeah," he said.

"What about Marshall? I thought you were friends."

"We are."

"Then why did you beat him up?"

X shrugged, "He got on my nerves."

The STS (Student Therapeutic Services) program seemed like the next logical step. STS workers, formerly known as "Wraparounds," were a phenomenon I encountered during my first outing as a sub. They sit in the classroom with students for all or a portion of the day, every day to help that student stay on track. We all had our fingers crossed that X's mother would sign off on it and she did. Turns out he had been in the program when he was in first grade. Unfortunately, no one was available right away. So he had to wait...and we had to wait.

In the meantime, Awesome Grade Lead offered her class as a timeout space.

"Are you sure?" I asked, grateful for the line she was throwing me.

"Oh yeah," she responded. "X and I are old friends. I can handle him."

He hated going to her class, I think because he no longer had a familiar audience. But hate it or not, when he started disrupting my class, I picked out some work for him, made sure he had a pencil and shipped him off for a visit. I often needed assistance to get him over there, but at least it gave the other kids and me a little break.

When report card time rolled around, the Principal asked New Teacher and me to distribute them together since we had both contributed to most of the students' grades. From noon until six p.m. of the first day, we sat in my freezing room, waiting. (We eventually moved to her room because it was warmer.) Only about half of the parents showed up over the three days, but it went fine and it gave me a little time to organize my room better and to get to know New Teacher a bit. Soft-spoken, young and idealistic, she was one of those people who always wanted to be a teacher like her mother. She loved kids, especially talking with them about their hopes, dreams and problems. Not in her wildest imaginings had she anticipated the reality of teaching in a failing, inner-city school. Though the kids liked her, they didn't necessarily listen to her. Maybe she wasn't convincing when she stomped her foot and screeched, "Stop it!" Maybe they could smell the youth and inexperience wafting off of her. Or, the privileged softness. Either way, nearly every day seemed to bring some new and shocking occurrence for which she was unprepared, especially when it came to how much the boys in her class fought. Even the sweet ones had become more prone to violence and she blamed all of it on X. I didn't disagree. I saw him working his way through the boys in my class—testing his ability to bend them to his will. He was now my "concern" and I was more than a little salty about it, especially when his mother showed up, angry and upset.

"Why was he switched from New Teacher's class if there's no STS person in your room?" she asked.

I turned to New Teacher who sat staring out the door like this situation had nothing to do with her. And I guess it didn't, not anymore. So I answered as positively and honestly as I could:

"The initial class was divided to address a number of discipline problems, and to see to it that all of the students receive the attention they deserve. Since X was having so many behavior issues in the other class, it was decided that he should be moved into this one. Though we had hoped this would give him a fresh start, we're still having the same challenges."

I went over his report card, which was pretty bad, and explained that his behavior was negatively impacting his own education, as well as the education of the other students. When I finished, she was on the verge of tears.

"I don't know what to do," she blurted out. "I'm sure by the way he behaves you think he has no structure or discipline at home, but he does. When I get calls from school, I put him on punishment; I take away his PlayStation. He doesn't care. He hasn't been outside since school started. I don't want him thinking this is what life is...being punished. He's in counseling...if this STS thing doesn't work, I'm going to have to send him to military school or something."

Folks, including me, always want to blame the parents, but this woman seemed reasonable and she seemed to be trying. I felt her frustration and pain, but I didn't see how I could help. Before leaving, she promised to see to it that his homework was done and to talk with him again about his behavior. I had high expectations for the changes I'd see after this productive, face-to-face meeting.

The next day, he was soooo much worse, alternating between ignoring me and accusing me of "lying on" him. As he stormed toward the door, I instinctively reached out to stop him, but he snatched away.

"Don't touch me!" he raged. "Or, I'll tell my mother you put your hands on me!"

I looked around the room at the other students who, as usual, were riveted—eyes wide, mouths open. But this time, I also saw the stress on their faces, which probably mirrored my own.

"Go," I finally said. And he did, violently slamming the door behind him.

"I can't do this," I thought. "This kid is going to hit me or hurt one of the other students. Or, God forbid, make me snatch him up." I took a deep breath, then reshuffled the desks away from the door since I expected X to slam it and shatter the glass any day now.

After school I went to see the Principal again. I had been asking every other day when Regular Teacher would be returning.

"I'm not sure." "I haven't heard." "Soon, I expect."

"Can you call her? Please?" I begged.

"I have to be careful," she confided. "Calling her too much during an approved leave can be made to seem as though I'm 'harassing' her," she said making air quotes.

"I'm the one being harassed," I wanted to say, "by a nine-year-old."

Over the weekend, I thought about it and prayed about it and decided not to accept another renewal. I needed to get back to my tour of the District anyway. But before I had the chance to break it to the Principal, she told me Regular Teacher would be back on Monday. I was so relieved. This was the best possible solution for everyone involved. Clearly, this woman would have a better idea of how to deal with this child than I did. The Principal insisted I wait until Friday, my last day, to tell the students. I felt like a traitor keeping this information from them, but she said they'd no longer listen to me if they knew I was leaving. So I waited and tried to present the news in a positive, upbeat fashion. A couple of them cheered, but most of them were shocked and upset. Ironically, X was the first to raise his hand.

"I'll miss you, Miss Harris," he said matter-of-factly.

I returned the sentiment to him and the rest of the students, though Kevin, Jaloni and a couple of others were absent so I didn't have a chance to say good-bye to them. I tried to make that last day as much fun as possible. We had the Room 110 Olympics...math problems, a spelling bee, chalkboard drawing, water bottle flipping, prizes, etc. We ate lunch in the room and, surprisingly, most of the class came, including Harry, Marshall and some of the kids from New Teacher's room. (Even X and Trouble A to Z stopped by, though they had opted for schoolyard recess instead.) We danced and talked and hung out on the big blue ABC rug for which I had traded two raggedy tables.

"This was the best day ever," said one of the girls.

For me, it was saddest. Starting over with the new kids had been tough, but I was so happy I had the chance to get to know them. They were a very cool bunch and I expected to miss them all a lot. At the end of the day, as it often happened, I couldn't get them to go home. They wanted to hang out, talk, do more backflips on the rug...but I knew parents were waiting. So I walked them out, hugged them good-bye and headed to the office to turn in my key.

Something—I don't know what—had happened during gym and X had been sent to the office. There he sat. Back on the bench and way too comfortable with it.

As I started for the door, he jumped out to scare me. "Boo!" I shook my head and smiled. (He likes to have a lot of fun.)

"X, maybe try to be nicer to your classmates and listen a little better, okay?"

He nodded, throwing his arms around me, "Bye, Miss Harris."

December 20, 2017
P.S. #7—Return Visit #2

Though I continued to visit other schools, I found myself missing the 110 kids way more than I expected. Then, out of the blue, I received a call from Janelle's grandfather.

"She just wants to hear your voice," he said, handing Janelle the phone.

"Hi, Miss Harris," she said in her polite little voice. "I miss you."

"I miss you, too. How are things going with Regular Teacher? Is she nice?"

"She is...but she's been absent a couple of times. So we had to go back to New Teacher's room. That didn't go so well."

I was surprised. I hadn't seen Regular Teacher's absences on the system, which meant they weren't planned...maybe not even listed if she was waiting until the last minute to call out.

"Maybe I'll come by and check on you guys. Okay?"

"Okay," she answered, smiling through the phone.

As usual, there were several open assignments at P.S. #7. I took a one-day in a special ed. class down the hall from 110. I figured I'd be able to kill two birds with one stone. I could check on the 110 kids and also have a chance to see what this standalone special ed. class was like. That morning, I swung by breakfast early to surprise the kids. Both 110 and New Teacher's students tackled me with hugs and "I miss you's," which seemed to surprise both New Teacher and Regular Teacher. Jaloni was so shocked to see me he couldn't talk, but eventually I got a smile and a hug from him. In my travels around school that day, I quietly peeped in on 110 a couple of times and stopped in once to say a proper "hello" to Regular Teacher, who had the students well in-hand and working.

I asked how she was doing with X who happened to be out that day.

"Fine. I can handle him," she said. "I just write him up...at least 10 times already."

"Yeah, I couldn't handle him," I confessed, surprising her. "I'm glad you're back. I did my best, but they really need you."

Though I had a few stolen moments with 110, I spent the majority of my time with the students from the small, self-contained special needs class. It was a life skills class that focused on self-care, writing and using the internet. The very competent teacher's aide knew what needed to be done, so I followed her lead and helped out where I could. There were four adults in a room of 12 students, including one who could not communicate at all. I recalled seeing this child during my previous visit. She'd often slide down to the floor in the hallway and stay there until one of the teachers or other students got her up and moving again. I expected to see more of that type of behavior, but (and I hate to admit it) these kids were generally better behaved and calmer than the 110 kids. Apparently, they thought so, too.

"Those kids you used to have..." one of them commented, "they're bad."

"That one kid's been banging on that locker for like an hour," another said referring to a kid making all kinds of noise in the hallway.

"He's in New Teacher's class," I corrected.

They nodded, realizing their mistake, just as "Bang-Bang" himself stormed through the class in search of one of the STS workers. I knew this kid. During the time of "the great split," New Teacher was planning to transfer him to my room, as well. When he found out, he flipped out.

"I hate this fuckin' school!" he screamed, throwing something against the wall before he took off running down the hall.

I echoed his sentiments, "Uhn-uh. Not him, too. No."

Based on these reactions, she "decided" he could stay with her and I tried to steer clear of him at all times. Today was no exception for me, but one of the truly patient STS workers spoke with him at length. Apparently, all of the locker banging was the result of missing perfect attendance because he had a doctor's appointment one morning. Even though he was better by the time they finished talking, he still refused to go back to New Teacher's room. Instead, he set about roaming the hallways.

In general, my day in special ed. was lovely. We did journal writing and internet research. They had art class, lunch and a few other exercises, all without anyone walking out of class or flipping out. Later, we went to a holiday party sponsored by a local group of corrections officers. The festivities were exclusively for special needs students, kindergarteners and first-graders. There was pizza, candy, games, prizes and fantastic gifts like jeans, coats, bikes and tablets. This was a day completely without stress, and I honestly don't think it had anything to do with the party. Normally, there is one special ed. teacher, one special ed. aide, one nurse and one STS worker in this class. That's one specifically trained adult for every three students. These kids were well cared for and doing fine.

January 16, 2018
P.S. #7—Return Visit #3

A staffer from Kelly called to see if I was available. Regular Teacher had put in a request for me! As usual, I was missing the kids something terrible, so I jumped at the chance.

"But," she went on, "after this visit, you will have reached your limit for subbing in this particular class without getting a long-term sub permit. It's a hundred dollars...I'm not sure it'll be worth it considering you don't know if you'll ever be in that room again."

Hmm.

Though I knew this might be the last time I saw the kids, I was excited and so were they. After the love-fest died down, the first thing I noticed was that the desks were now arranged in little clusters, like almost every other classroom in the District. And Jaloni was sitting with X and Harry! The next thing I noticed was that Jaloni seemed to have had a complete personality change. He was argumentative, quick to anger and spending all his class time goofing off with his table mates. Before the end of the day, he had physically attacked two different boys. In the first incident, he and Kurt were arguing...nothing new. But then Jaloni jumped on him—quite new—and they both went down. Somehow, Kurt wound up on top, punching like a pro—also new. I broke it up pretty quickly, but I was stunned. Here were two of my shining stars brawling in the hallway. I honestly didn't know what to say other than "Stop it!" And they did. Thank God.

Later, Jaloni was talking with a new boy in the class, a handsome and articulate young man who liked soccer. Next thing I knew, Jaloni had him in a headlock. The new boy wasn't hurt. He seemed to think they were playing, but he didn't see Jaloni's face. He was trying to hurt that kid. This time, I pulled Jaloni aside and asked what was going on. He had no answer.

"Look, you have to make a choice about the type of boy you want to be. Do you want to be Jaloni who fights and argues? (He shook his head.) Or, do you want to be well behaved, smart, fun Jaloni?"

"That one," he answered, wiping away a tear.

"Then be that," I responded, making a mental note to call his mother. Looking up, I saw X watching and smirking. "Do you want to sit with X and Harry?" I whispered.

When he shook his head "no," I suggested he talk to Regular Teacher.

"I did," he said.

"And?"

"She said I could move, but... (He sighed.) Can you move me?"

I wanted to, but out of respect, I asked him to wait for Regular Teacher's return. Looking back, I realize he didn't want it to seem like he didn't want to sit with them. Being harassed by them would be a whole lot worse than being on their team. I had blown it.

Overall, I was disappointed in the kids. All of them. Even Janelle, though she was still the best behaved of the group. They were right back where they were just after the re-split: loud, overly talkative, unfocused and taking way too long to get their work done. And I told them so.

"But I still love you," I added.

They smiled and giggled, taking my comments in stride, until I explained that I had hit the limit for subbing in their class and wouldn't be able to come back anymore. This was the one and only time I remember them walking out at the end of the day in complete silence. No hugs. No "I'll miss you's." Just silence.

January 30, 2018
P.S. #7—Return Visit #4

My next visit to P.S. #7 was courtesy of Awesome Grade Lead who had a funeral to attend. I was happy to help out considering what a lifeline she'd been for me. Plus, it gave me a chance to check on the 110 kids who were very happy to see me until they realized I wasn't in for them and Regular Teacher was out "again."

Awesome Grade Lead's class was known for being one of the best in the school. For me, they were fairly well behaved though louder than normal. Despite her many warnings, a few of her kids chose to act out while I was on duty. One boy was pulled out of lunch and sent home by the Principal. (I have no idea what happened but she was fuming.) And a fight broke out between two of her best students: one, a former hall runner turned straight A student; the other, one of Awesome Grade Lead's most trusted. To be honest, "Miss Trustworthy" started the fight, but she was completely unprepared for the level of anger and emotion that erupted from the other girl. The class came to a screeching halt while I tried to calm her down and keep them separated. Some of the kids were helping me; others were cheering them on to fight. Inevitably, I sent Miss Trustworthy to New Teacher's class and called an STS for help with the other one. The sad thing is that both of these girls were very sweet...but together. Not so much.

Throughout the day, as I ran into teachers, they either whispered to me or brazenly yelled down the hallway, "Please come back." I figured they just wanted me to pick up one of the open assignments, until one of the Fab Senior Teachers pulled me into her room, closed the door and broke it down.

"Regular Teacher is here two days a week at most and even then she's asleep at her desk. No one knows what's going on other than that the kids aren't learning anything."

The last time I came, I heard nothing but good reports. Now suddenly, she's completely messing up?

"I'd love to help out," I responded, "but I can't handle X on an ongoing basis."

"He has an STS worker now. And there's a parent volunteer in the room."

"Two other adults, plus me? Hmm. Still, I can't assign myself..."

"Talk to the Principal," she said. "Maybe you can work something out."

Later in the day, X's STS worker brought him to Awesome Grade Lead's class so she could keep an eye on him and another student at the same time. Or, maybe he was kicked out of his class. Either way, there he was. And though he had work to do, mostly he just watched and yelled out to me intermittently during the lesson:

"Hey, Miss Harris."

"When are you coming back to our class, Miss Harris?"

"I like your hair."

Other than that, he was kind of mellow. And when his STS worker left the room, he went with her.

"This could work," I thought.

As I headed out at the end of the day, I swung by the office to speak to the Principal. She explained that Regular Teacher was approved to be out as much as she needed to be for the next month or so. She said she'd love to have me back but she wasn't sure when Regular Teacher would be out. None of this made sense to me. How is she supposed to cover her classes if she doesn't know when her teachers will be there?

"If she calls out, call me," I offered.

We made a plan. She'd call me by 7 a.m. and I would do my best to be there by the start of classes at 8:30ish. I figured two or three days a week would be fun, plus I'd be bumped up to $200 a day and I could use the money. All I needed to do was pay for my emergency long-term permit. I promised to call her when all of the paperwork was completed. But I got a call from Kelly two days earlier than expected telling me my permit was approved and that they needed me at P.S. #7 right away. Regular Teacher had stopped showing up all together.

February 7, 2018-March 26, 2018
P.S. #7—Return Visit #5

No one was happier to see me than New Teacher, who often had both classes when Regular Teacher was out.

"It's too much," she said, handing over two day's worth of assignments. "Glad you're back."

Though the kids were happy to see me, they were excessively talkative, undisciplined, unaccustomed to getting and doing homework, unaccustomed to listening and completely incapable of walking in a straight line. They argued and hit each other constantly. Half of them no longer had math books, notebooks or pencils.

What the hell?

Even more disturbing were the changes in Jaloni, Janelle, Kurt and Kevin— the four students who had insisted on remaining in the class with me instead of returning to New Teacher's room. Distracted and agitated at best, none of them seemed like the happy, enthusiastic students I left behind. Jaloni was still sitting with X and Harry, still following their lead and still miserable. Immediately, I made everyone turn their desks around to face front. In the process, I separated the three boys. Just like that, Jaloni was free and the blame was all mine. It took a couple of weeks and several conversations, but he began to return to the smiling, chatty, helpful kid I first met.

Inarguably the best student in the class, Janelle seemed lost—unfocused, unengaged, lethargic. One afternoon, I found her standing at the classroom door, just staring out into the hallway; something X, Harry and Marshall were inclined to do. I was accustomed to telling them to sit down, but Janelle? She wasn't the best student because she always had the right answer or the best grades (though she usually did). She was the best because she tried so hard and had such a great attitude. There was never a hint of sarcasm or disrespect in her voice. She was wide-eyed and innocent, the product of her grandparents' careful rearing and now something was out of whack.

"What are you doing?" I asked.

"Hunh?" she responded.

"What...are you doing?" I repeated.

"Uhm...I dun-no," she answered in her quiet, sing-song voice.

"Sit down. We don't do that during class."

"O-kay...sor-ry."

We had different versions of that same conversation over and over for the next week or so. "Why are you talking while I'm teaching?" "Why are you turned around in your chair?" "Why didn't you do your homework?"

"I dun-no. I dun-no. I dun-no. Sor-ry."

I knew. They had all been doing whatever they wanted for so long they had forgotten how to behave in a proper classroom setting. I blamed it on an absentee teacher and a dominant Student X. He did whatever he wanted. Why shouldn't the other kids follow suit? Well, not on my watch. I was determined to re-establish order and a focus on learning. X didn't take kindly to this new direction. He constantly pushed to see what he could get away with. Though his STS worker was very good, she wasn't by his side every moment of the day, as I'd hoped. But she was often in the room and she removed him without hesitation before he became too disruptive. This allowed the rest of the class, including Janelle, to settle down and regain focus.

There was also a wonderful parent who volunteered her mornings. She had two sons in the school. One in fifth or sixth and the other in Awesome Grade Lead's class. Since she was accustomed to third-graders, the Principal asked her to help out in New Teacher's room, which didn't last long.

"Yeah, I got the impression she didn't want my help. She didn't really include me in her daily plan. Plus, one of her kids told me he was going to 'get my fat-ass fired.' I didn't need that crap. So the Principal switched me to this room."

From day one, I made it clear that I wanted and needed her help. She helped re-organize the class, sorting through the stacks of papers covering Regular Teacher's desk. She put together a job board for the kids, gave out assignments and paid them out of her own pocket with chips and lollipops. She made photocopies, watched the class when I stepped into the hallway to deal with issues and backed me up when the kids were out of hand—even X. Unfortunately, within two weeks, my amazing parent volunteer was snatched up by the Climate Team.

"I spend so much time here; I might as well get paid for it."

I understood. Most people can't afford to work for free. But this announcement followed pretty quickly on the heels of X's STS worker quitting.

"Yeah, I'm out," she said, literally heading for the door. "I'm going to Comcast. But good luck. I can tell you have what it takes to work with kids."

Then why was I so panicked?

A few days later, two new STS workers took over X's care. However, since they already had full case loads, managing him continued to be a challenge—one that distracted me from what was going on with Kevin and Kurt. Unlike before, they were both now defensive and argumentative, especially with the other boys in the class. Getting them to quiet down and sometimes even to sit down was a chore. Getting them to focus on work was even harder. Kurt, who had always been an enthusiastic student, now sometimes wouldn't even attempt his assignments. Even when everyone else was working.

"I'll do it for homework," he'd say, then sit watching his brother and the other boys in the class.

Something was wrong and I was missing it. Usually, the twins were the first to let me know what was going on. When one of the girls in the class was knocked down by a fourth grader, Kurt and Kevin told me what happened and insisted on walking me to the teacher's room to point the boy out. They weren't scared and they weren't sucking up. They did it because they felt it was the right thing to do.

This time, nothing. So, after school one day, I walked with them to where their father usually waited. After I explained the situation, he promised that I wouldn't have any more problems with them and I didn't. Then he dropped a bomb. Someone had been taking Kevin's lunch and, since he had severe allergies, he couldn't replace it with the school lunch.

"By the time I get here to pick them up, the boy is starving. What can we do about that?" he asked.

These kids were being bullied right under my nose. Obviously, it had been going on for a while, yet no one mentioned it to me. The next day, instead of just dropping the kids off at the lunchroom door, I walked in and took a seat next to Kevin and Kurt.

"So who are these kids? Point them out," I said, looking in the direction of some of the older students in the room—

"It's X," Kurt said.

"And Harry," Kevin chimed in quietly.

I turned to find X and Harry eyes wide and watching very closely. The thought of Kevin walking around hungry...being bullied by his own classmates...and I had missed it...I felt like my head was going to pop off. I waved them over.

"Have you been taking Kevin's lunch?"

"He's lying...!" X started to shout but Harry responded with a quiet, firm "Yesh."

"Listen to me," I heard myself saying, low and calm like my mother when she was really annoyed. "I better not ever hear that you have put your hands on Kevin, Kurt or their food again. Do you understand me?"

"Yes/Yesh."

"If you think I'm hard on you now...it's nothing in comparison to how hard on you I'll be if you do it again. Do you understand?"

"Yes/Yesh."

Knowing how honest Harry is, I gave him a job. "In fact, Harry, I'm making you responsible for letting me know if anything like this happens again. Got it?"

"Yesh," he nodded.

"Go." As they scurried away, I turned back to Kurt and Kevin, who were trying very hard not to smile.

While Kevin's lunch was safe, X still provoked him daily. When he wasn't verbally attacking Kevin, X was accusing him of saying or doing things that he hadn't said or done. One day, I caught X pushing other kids into Kevin in the hope of starting a fight. A foot taller than Kevin, Kurt had taken on the responsibility of protecting his smaller twin. So he often wound up scuffling with the other boys, which made him very unpopular. I ran interference as much as possible, but I also tried to help Kurt repair his friendships. I talked to him and them, and provided opportunities for him to partner up with different students. After a while, things settled down and both of them were back to participating more. Though their mother told me Kevin, in particular, had been angry because I "just left" without warning, he was back to shooting me his unexpectedly devilish grin.

Academically, the class seemed to be going backwards. I did my best to get on top of the actual teaching part. This time around, the Principal included me in grade group meetings, which were brief and focused mostly on visual compliance with District protocols.

"Put the day's goals on the board."

"Make sure the school principles are in plain view."

"Reinforce SLANT (Sit up, Listen, Ask & Answer questions, Nod your head, Track the speaker) by putting it on the board."

It's not that these things weren't helpful. It's that the emphasis seemed to be on impressing the District officials who occasionally walked the building vs. teaching. After a while, all that stuff was just taking up valuable board space we needed for work. (The smart board was still broken.) The one thing that did help was creating anchor charts. Awesome Grade Lead helped me think through content to distill it into quick concept reviews on poster-sized charts. I was pretty proud of them until Trouble A to Z and a couple of his buddies from New Teacher's room snuck in during lunch and ripped them down. I put them back up but other than getting the kids to copy them into their notebooks, I didn't have time to reinforce the concepts the way I should have. Mostly, I was just trying to maintain a minimum of order while teaching as much as I could.

As usual, I spent a lot of my afternoons posted up in the office calling parents, many of whom were shocked to discover that their son or daughter a) had homework they hadn't been doing and/or b) hadn't done well on the last language arts or math quiz. My evenings were spent planning lessons, printing out worksheets, marking papers, and updating my spreadsheet with grades and checkmarks for completed homework. Perhaps this would have been a breeze for an experienced teacher, but for this untrained sub, it was pretty challenging. I didn't have processes in place, so I had to make them up as I went along. Clearly, there were areas where I could have done better, reinforced more and introduced more enjoyment of learning. But spending so much time on discipline issues—with X in particular—devoured my time and energy.

In between all of this, I was still trying to put an end to the culture of bullying that had enveloped 110. I re-instituted lunch detention on an ongoing basis. Hitting, kicking or doing anything violent to another kid was an automatic detention. Not doing class work, another automatic detention. Missing lunch detention was an automatic two detentions. Sometimes, we did the old fashioned sit there in silence and be bored thing. But, often, we talked through problems or caught up on homework or class work that had been neglected.

We also gathered on the rug to discuss why they were so mean, calling each other "ugly," "fat" and "stupid." (Thankfully, most of them stopped calling each other "gay" after I explained that it wasn't an insult.) So few of them worked and played nicely together. Some of the kids wanted to talk. They explained how it made them feel when someone was mean to them. Others said nothing. Depending on his mood, X alternately mocked his classmates or cheered them for admitting things they'd done that weren't so nice.

"At least that's honest, right? Good job..." he'd say, leading a clap.

Harry usually giggled, wiggled and ignored whatever meaningful discussion we might be having. His only contribution being, "I hate this class."

I understood why. There was too much work, too many calls to parents, too much Miss Harris. He wanted to be back in New Teacher's class where he could do whatever he wanted...all day long. But she didn't want him and I was tired of taking the blame for it.

"You want to be in New Teacher's class?" I asked, one day.

"Yesh."

"Go ask her."

"Go ask her what? If I can be in her class?" he responded as though this were some kind of trick.

"Yeah," I said. "Maybe she'll let you come back." I knew she wouldn't, but I hoped.

He took off as the rest of us continued our discussion. We hadn't gotten very far when Harry slid back into the room and plopped down in his place on the rug.

"What'd she say?" I asked.

He shot me a slightly embarrassed smile. "She said 'no.'"

"Okay," I said, "moving on."

I didn't bring it up again after that day and neither did he. This was the turning point in our relationship. Harry became a lot easier to deal with. He listened more and argued less, which made it easier for me to figure out that he was struggling with reading, but he wasn't so bad in math. One day, as I was helping him with his homework, I decided to have an honest conversation.

"You know if you stop hanging with the hall-runners (meaning X) and focus, the work will be easier."

"What's a hall-runner?" he asked.

"The little kids who spend all their time running up and down the halls instead of in class learning," I answered, watching as the words sunk in. "Your choice, but I think you can do better."

I started calling him to the blackboard more and putting him out less, even when he was bouncing around the room. As long as he didn't bother the other kids, I didn't mind that he seemed to think better in motion, especially after he told me how hard it was for him to be still.

Overall, the physical fights diminished, but the name-calling, pushing and other pettiness continued. I was especially worried about the damage it was doing to some of the girls who were routinely called "ugly" or "beast" by the boys. I gave them all an assignment to write two poems: one with 10 lines starting with "I am not..." and another with 10 lines starting with "I am..." In addition to the expected ("I am not ugly." "I am not dumb.") the kids delivered some surprising statements.

Kurt wrote, "I am not Kevin." Perhaps because he was sick of fighting his brother's battles.

One of the more introverted and troubled girls in the room wrote, "I am a king..." which, of course, the boys jumped all over.

"You can't be a king...you're a girl!"

With encouragement, she opened up, saying she chose "king" because "No one is higher than a king. No one can tell a king what to do." I had to give her a high-five on that one, even though I often had to tell her to sit down.

Several of the boys wrote, "I am good at math," while the two best math students in the room (both girls) each wrote: "I am not good at math." (Apparently, the Imposter Syndrome starts early.) I made them both change it to "I am good at math," which sparked a quiet, ongoing competition between them.

X wrote only a few sentences. Things like, "I love my family. I protect my family. I do not start trouble. I do not fight."

"But you do start trouble...and fight," his mother responded when she saw his paper. "That's the problem."

It took Harry a couple of days to finish. He had been pulled out of class by the counselor and it was very difficult for him to stay focused once the rest of the class had moved on. But finish he did, ending with: "I am not a hall-runner...I am a good boy." While some of the kids were clearly just delusional, Harry's statement struck me as aspirational. Once he dropped the tough-guy act, he *was* a good boy: sweet, vulnerable, helpful, forgiving and slow to anger. He never left class without permission and never wanted to be sent out. He even did his homework a couple of times.

While things were getting better overall, X was getting worse. Though many of the teachers, climate staff and STS workers kept an eye on him, X had a knack for wreaking havoc during the "in-between" times. He stole a cell phone during recess and candy from New Teacher's room on his way home. He tripped kids in the stairwell and knocked another kid into the wall at lunch. And those were just the things I was aware of. There just wasn't enough manpower to watch this kid every second of every day.

One morning, as it occasionally happened, Harry became the focus of X's anger. Usually when they fought, X started it but as soon as he let up, they'd be back to laughing and joking. This particular morning began, once again, with the two boys nose-to-nose.

"Come on then if you ain't scared," taunted X, while Harry calmly waited for him to strike first.

After separating them, we headed up to class. Harry rushed ahead to hold the door, but X beat him to it. Since neither was assigned to this job, I asked them both to get back in line.

"But tie your shoes, Harry, before you fall."

As he knelt to do so, X stood over him, silently opening and closing his fists, as though he were contemplating punching Harry or pushing him down the stairs.

"X, move away from him," I called out, which alerted Harry who quickly slid away and stood up.

"F****t," spat Harry.

X didn't flinch, perhaps because he often used the word himself, sometimes even toward the girls. Instead, he moved toward Harry who braced for a fight.

"That's enough!" I yelled, taking the steps a few at a time. "Both of you, let's go."

Stepping between them, I directed all of the students to head into the class. X refused but Harry headed in with the rest of the kids.

The last to straggle in, X sat down, waited for everyone to settle, then began his counterassault. From the back of the room, he calmly and steadily berated Harry loud enough and long enough for everyone to hear.

"You're stupid...you're so dumb...you're the only kid in the class who can't read...in the whole grade...you're poor...you wear the same hoodie every day..."

Harry turned to look at X but said nothing in response.

"Turn around, Harry. Just ignore him." I stood in front of him, as though blocking his view somehow blocked the words that X flung spitefully into the air.

"You had those pants on yesterday...with that same hoodie...look at you... that's why the girls don't like you..."

He was crushing Harry's spirit and no matter what I said, he wouldn't stop. I called the STS room, but no one was there. Thankfully, I spotted the head STS worker in the hallway and waved her over. Soon as X heard her voice, he stopped berating Harry and sat quietly in his seat. After I explained everything that had happened, she called X over.

"So you were thinking about pushing someone down the stairs, huh? How would you like it if I told Harry to come out here and get a free swing at you while we all watched? You wouldn't like that, right?"

"No," he responded.

"Get your stuff," she commanded and he obeyed.

These two had some weird history. She had been his STS worker when he was in the first grade. She was the only adult in the school he seemed to respect and he listened to her when he wouldn't listen to anyone else.

X obediently grabbed his bookbag and followed her out, while Harry sat very still, looking down at his desk. He was humiliated. Though I tried to comfort and encourage him, I suspected that there might be repercussions. Sure enough, before I left for the day, one of X's STS workers stopped me in the hallway.

"Harry beat the *shit* out of X. Sent him home crying." Then, she smiled.

I still say it takes a special kind of person or an extreme level of fear or frustration to stand by and do nothing while two children hurt one another, even if the law is on your side.*

The next day, X picked a new game and a new target. When I collected the kids from art, the instructor said they'd all been pretty rowdy but X, as usual, was over-the-top. He had chased the girls around the room and destroyed jars of paint by mixing them together. Back in class, I went over how the students should behave when visiting another teacher's room. In response, they all proclaimed their innocence, while simultaneously throwing each other under the bus. Kurt was the only one quietly and politely raising his hand.

"Yes, Kurt?"

"When X was running around the room, he smacked me in the head."

Before I could respond, X jumped out of his seat screaming at the top of his lungs, "He's lying! He's lying! I hate you...fuck you...FUCK YOU!!"

---

*In 2014, two years after the Jerry Sandusky scandal, PA legislators added teachers, administrators and other school personnel to the definition of possible perpetrators of child abuse, effectively implementing a "no touch" policy for all. *Every* school employee is also now a "mandated reporter," and required to report any suspicion of child abuse. Statewide, claims of child abuse have skyrocketed. In 2017, there were 280 claims of child abuse against SDP employees. Eighteen were validated.[1]

The kids and I stared in shock as he stormed out, slamming the door behind him. Kurt shook his head and quietly said, "I am not lying."

I was exhausted. Nothing was working with X. I tried being tough and being kind. I tried giving him more responsibility and letting him work with a partner. Everything eventually deteriorated into a struggle with me or a fight with another student. Even with one of his STS workers sitting right next to him, he wouldn't do his work. His grandmother came to check on him several times. His mother texted every day. I never had good news for them. One day, he flipped out on me because I picked his bookbag up off the floor. One of the male STS workers had to intervene and physically restrain him. Later, it occurred to me we should have looked inside. X had a habit of collecting things that didn't belong to him.

Another day, I asked for the bottle of water he was "flipping" before art class. Aside from the fact that he wasn't supposed to have it, I was sure it would result in someone getting hurt or wet.

He threw it on the floor, "Pick it up, if you want it."

"You can pick it up and hand it to me or I can call the STS room and you can spend art class with them."

Though he took his time, holding the bottle out and demanding that I "come and get it," he finally walked over and placed it in my hand. Of course, we had wasted five minutes of the class's art time and my lunch, but stuff like that happened all day, every day.

Even when X tried, and sometimes I think he did, he just could not behave in a general classroom setting. Once, after being sent to his STS worker, he came back with the new counselor.

"We wanted to understand why X has been put out of the class," she said politely, nodding at X.

"Because he won't stop talking and he won't stay in his seat," I answered.

"Is that true?" she asked and he nodded that it was.

"That's understandable then," she said and they left.

Maybe he doesn't understand, I thought. I knew she didn't. She was new and X is absolutely charming...one-on-one. It's when there are other children in the mix that there's a problem.

Sometimes X would begin the day with a pronouncement. "I don't feel like doing work today. So I'm gonna leave now to keep from getting in trouble." And he was off to run the halls.

I'd report him to his STS workers, who had to track him down, then text or call his mother. Inevitably, he'd return...usually at the point when the lesson was going well and the other students were engaged and learning.

"Can I come back now? They said I had to come back. Can I? I'll be good. I promise."

Yet somehow, the learning process would be derailed within 15 minutes of his return. Why let him come back? Because the law is on his side. He has the right to be the room, the right to learn...and the right to stop others from learning. I don't think that's fair. Neither did the other students.

One day—after months of being bullied, bossed and harassed by X—the whole class stood up to him. We heard the usual knock on the door after one of X's daily timeouts. He had been gone for hours.

"Don't let him in," said Marshall.

Of course, I had to. It's the law. I opened the door and asked if he was ready to behave.

"Yes," he said as usual, but when I turned to let him pass, the entire rest of the class was standing right behind me blocking the entrance.

"We're playing a game," said Janelle.

"Don't ruin it," warned Harry.

Not one of the students moved until he agreed, "Alright, alright."

And he didn't ruin it because we only had five minutes left in the day. Just enough time to finish the game and go home. The next morning, it was back to business as usual. I lost count of how many times I stepped between X and another student, or called the Climate team, or sent him to his STS workers or called his STS workers to come sit with him in the room. He created an environment of chaos and anxiety for all, including me. Though I loved the kids and lived to see their eyes light up when they "got it" or when something was funny, soon I was bugging the Principal again, "When is Regular Teacher coming back?"

Once, she called right in front of me to show me what she was dealing with.

"Hi, how are you? I'm calling because we have the sub and we were wondering...oh okay. Alright. Thank you." She hung up.

"What did she say?" I asked.

"Keep the sub."

Everyone...*everyone* said Regular Teacher was gone for good and that I'd be there 'til the end of the year. Then, one day, the Principal stopped me in the hallway.

"Looks like she put her resignation in. I'm waiting for them to send over a copy now." She was smiling. I was smiling.

Shortly after that, the school Literacy Specialist approached me.

"Now that we know you'll be here permanently, I'm allowed to work with you. I was hoping to be able to get in earlier, but I can still help you set up reading stations and lesson plan with you for the rest of the year..."

I was thrilled. I had at least three kids, including Harry, who desperately needed help with reading. But since they were native speakers, there was no reading program like ESOL (English for Speakers of Other Languages) for them. This would be just the help they needed.

Awesome Grade Lead came up with a plan to align my class with hers for everything else so she could do the rest of the lesson plans for both of us. (New Teacher was gone again and we had no idea when she was coming back.) I was scared and excited at the same time. 110 was really my class now!

And then, it wasn't.

Raring to go, I left a message for the Principal asking if there was anything I needed to do or tell Kelly in anticipation of taking over the class permanently. She called me back over the weekend.

"Where'd you hear that?" she responded.

"Uh...from everybody..." including you, I wanted to say.

"Who's everybody? I want to know," she said. "That's why I don't like people gossiping before things are set. I'll let you know when it's set, okay?"

"Uh...okay. Thanks."

Monday, she swung by the room during lunch and blurted out in front of a few of the kids that Regular Teacher would be back next Monday. The news circulated quickly. Teachers and staff members told me they were sorry to see me go, but expected that I would be back soon. New Teacher texted to tell me she'd be out one more week and offered up her class. A couple of the Fab Senior Teachers tried to talk me into taking on the out-of-control second-grade class. I passed on all of it. It was time to get back to writing and touring the District to see what other schools had to offer.

This time, I wanted to make sure we all had closure. The next morning, I gathered the kids on the rug and broke the news. Some of them already knew but were too polite to say anything.

"…I want you all to know how happy I am that I had the chance to get to know you. You're some smart cookies and I'm going to miss you very much. I love you all."

"Even me?" asked X?

"Of course, you too, X. All of you," I answered, trying to sound as upbeat as possible so they wouldn't be upset. "Regular Teacher will be back on Monday! Isn't that exciting?"

"Yeah, but what about Tuesday?" Harry asked.

Another bright little girl chimed in. "So she's not, 'sick' anymore?" she said, making air quotes.

"I see her in the store sometimes," said another. "She doesn't look sick."

"Maybe someone else is sick and she's been taking care of them," I reasoned. "We don't know. The point is if you are all very good for the rest of the week, maybe we can have a party on Friday."

A cheer went up accompanied by the Floss, the Whip, backflips and other demonstrations of their dancing expertise. All that week, I gave away prizes for kindness, thoughtfulness and academic skill. Of course, Janelle won the first bear for solving a math problem and Jaloni won for being helpful. But even more notably, X won for helping me pull Trouble A to Z off of another boy in our class. Okay…at first he cheered them on…but once I said "help me," he did jump in along with Jaloni to pull the boys apart. While X was thrilled to get the teddy bear, Jaloni wanted to know why he didn't get one, too.

"So, how did X get that bear?" he casually asked.

He helped me just like you did, but you already have a bear and you don't need two."

"Yes I *do*," he laughed but he understood.

On my last day, the kids drew pictures, wrote letters and stories for me. We ate lunch and had lots of snacks while watching *Hidden Figures*. I drew comparisons between what was happening in the movie and the stories of segregation we discussed during black history month. Many of them had already taken note.

"They can't even use the same bathroom?"

"That's just stupid."

Marshall whispered something under his breath and Janelle took offense.

"He said the lady in the movie is smarter than Miss Harris." The room went silent in anticipation of my reply.

"The lady in the movie is waaaay smarter than Miss Harris," I replied and we all laughed.

X was on his best behavior, but even with one of his STS workers sitting right in the room, he could not sit quietly and watch the movie. Eventually, he returned to his desk to finish drawing a picture for me. Noon dismissal brought the party to an early close. While the rest of us cleaned and said our good-byes, Marshall gave out goodies from the candy-filled bear he won for sharing the last of the popcorn. All was well. My time with them was ending on a high note...until X jumped on Marshall, wrapped his hands around his throat and began choking him.

As I pulled X off of Marshall, tears sprang to his eyes. *"What is wrong with you?!"* he yelled at X.

Stunned and, for the first time I'd ever witnessed, angry, X's other STS worker ushered him out of the room. Once he was gone, the other kids, including Marshall, returned to cleaning, packing up and saying their good-byes like nothing had happened. They had become far too accustomed to X's erratic and violent nature. As for me, my heart was breaking. Is this what being an educator is about? Falling in love with a new group of kids every year; then saying, "Good-bye?" Teaching is just a tough gig—all the way 'round.

March 19, 2018

A text message from the Principal of P.S. #7 popped up at 8:19 am: "Hi, Miss Harris. Can you come in today?"

Regular Teacher hadn't shown up and there was no word about what happened or when she'd be there. I couldn't make it that day, but I was there bright and shiny the next morning.

With a pat on the back, a wink and various versions of "Told you so," everything went back to business as usual. I was happy. The kids were relieved. Then, in the middle of the math lesson on Thursday, the class phone rang. I didn't want to answer. For once, the entire class seemed to be on the verge of getting it: Length x Width = the Area. But I had to answer...

"Hi, Miss Harris. This is Regular Teacher. I'm coming back on Monday." She sounded upbeat and cheery.

Surprised, I stepped into the hallway so the students wouldn't overhear. "Are you...*freaking kidding me?*" I wanted to say. Instead, I settled for... "sure?"

She laughed. "Yes, I'm sure."

"It's just...the students thought you were coming last Monday and they were so...disappointed."

"Oh...no, I'll be there this Monday. I just wanted to talk with you about where they are in their text books. Would it be okay if I call you later?"

"Of course, I'll talk to you then," I responded. Right then, I dove back into the math lesson. Later, I caught up with the Principal.

"I don't know if she's going to show up this time either," she reasoned.

"I think she will. She wanted to know where the kids are in their text books."

"Hmm," she responded.

"I could come in on Monday. Help transition the class," I volunteered.

"Yes," said the Principal. "That way, if she doesn't show up, you'll already be here."

I was planning to bring in music the next day. You know, to celebrate my third last day. But that morning, I woke to a flooded house and for the first time ever called out. The following Monday, I discovered no one had told the kids where I was, even though I specifically asked them to. They'd had enough unreliability to last a lifetime. Instead, they were divided up and shuttled off to the three fourth-grade classrooms. They couldn't wait to tell me about their different experiences.

"It was boring. We didn't have anything to do."

"Nuh-unh, they were doing really hard work."

"I was scared. They were crazy in there. Nobody was listening to the teacher."

As I listened to their stories, I was trying to decide whether or not I should tell them Regular Teacher was coming back, but it was getting late and so far she hadn't shown up. Then, suddenly, in she strolled looking rested and ready. The whole cafeteria went silent, but then some of the girls ran to give her a hug, belatedly looking to see if that was okay with me.

Disappointed though I was, I welcomed Regular Teacher back and explained that I was there only to help transition the class.

"Alright," she said to the kids in a loud, firm voice, "let's go." The kids slowly lined up, as we continued to chat.

Suddenly, she turned back to them: "You're taking way too long." (She was right. They did that to me sometimes...most times really.) "Let's go!" she yelled.

They snapped to, got in line and walked upstairs quietly, stopping at each landing without being reminded.

"Huh," I thought. "They don't walk up that nicely for me."

Once in the room, I took a seat in the back and helped out where I could. When students came to me instead of her with questions, requests and complaints, I referred them back to Regular Teacher. They needed to make the switch and make it fast. No point pissing her off. So, I did my best to quietly keep them from talking to me and each other, but they were a little chatty.

"One, two..." Regular Teacher yelled out, snapping her fingers.

"Eyes on you. Tell me what you want me to do." They shot right back.

"Okay," I thought, "now she's just showing off." But I got it. Regular Teacher knew what she was doing. I marveled at how she broke down the math concepts into very simple, understandable components. Sometimes, I felt like I was speaking an alien language and, I suspect, the kids probably did, too.

During lunch, Regular Teacher and I laughed and talked like old friends. She wasn't the horrible human being I thought she was. Since she hadn't called me,

I tried to catch her up on everything she needed to know, like that there was another new student in the class and where the kids were in their text books.

"Half of them didn't have their math workbooks anymore. I made sure they all got one and we finished up volume one. They're ready to start volume two."

"I don't even use those things," she commented.

That explained a lot. Many of the teachers felt the math books were too challenging, including me. Nevertheless, they were tied straight to the PSSAs and the approved curriculum. How are the kids supposed to pass the test if she's not using the book? It's her class I reminded myself and I promised to send her a copy of the quarterly grades when I finished them. I also told her that one of the last things I had done was write up X.

"I covered everything he did over the last couple of weeks from stealing candy and a cell phone to choking, punching and berating other students, humping Janelle's desk while she was in it, cursing and fighting. There's a new part-time vice principal. He suspended X. That gives you a couple of days to ease back in."

I thought she'd be happy, but she sighed and her eyes went blank.

"He makes me not want to come to school," she said quietly.

While I admit to being guilty of judging this woman, in that moment, my heart went out. I'd felt the very same way many times. The difference was my assignments are temporary. All I had to do was hang in until the Regular Teacher returned or, if things really started to get bad, switch assignments. Unfortunately for her, she was the Regular Teacher.

I hung in through the afternoon, helping the kids with their work and checking out the new stools and beanbags that had been donated to Regular Teacher. When it was time to say good-bye, I didn't dawdle. I had my moment with the kids. It was her turn. I hugged her good-bye and wished her luck.

"Why did I come back?" she quietly complained. "I'm exhausted already. My back is hurting from standing...I don't think I can do this."

"Yes, you can. The year's almost over. You've got PSSAs in about a week or so. That'll take a couple days. Then, there's the holiday weekend. Then, it's June."

"Yeah," she said, nodding. "It's almost over."

"Look, if you need a day or two here or there, call me," I offered. "Not two or three weeks now..." which made us both laugh. I headed out waving a quick goodbye. It was for the best. The students were getting the experienced teacher they needed and I got to focus on my water-logged house.

Mid-May 2018

First came the text messages. Kurt and Kevin's mother letting me know that the bullying had started again. X had punched Kevin three times in one day. Once in his stomach. The very thought infuriated me.

"You go up to that school and demand that they do something. Your child has a right to be cared for and safe!" I shot back.

Then the Principal, asking if I could come in. I couldn't. I had other commitments. Plus, all the start and stop wasn't good for the kids or me. How many times did we have to say good-bye?

Next, a supervisor from Kelly called. "There's another sub in the spot who's willing to stay but they want you." Finally, I agreed to call the Principal to find out what was going on.

"She's gone. For good," the Principal informed me.

"What's wrong with the sub in the spot now?" I asked straight out.

"They're not working," she said.

"The kids don't like him?"

"No, I mean, whenever I stop by the class, they're sitting around talking or sitting on the rug...talking. He's not teaching."[†]

That wasn't good. "I'm out of town," I responded. "I won't even be back until next week."

"That's fine."

"And I won't be available for the last week of school."

"That's okay, too. There are only two days that last week. It'll be fine."

"What the heck?" I figured. It was only a couple of weeks.

[†] The substitute who "wasn't teaching," was transferred to the completely out-of-control, second-grade class no one else wanted to deal with, including me. Not only did he stick it out through the end of the year, he also had grades for the 110 kids.

I couldn't help but notice the new classroom arrangement. Some of the boys were sitting at a long table together, while three of the girls had their desks abutting the teacher's desk, with another row of girls behind them. Other desks were completely alone or in little clusters. There were lots of drawings on the wall and small plants on the window sill. Books and papers were all over the place. It looked like fun, sort of a Montessori vibe, but the thought of dealing with X in this unstructured setting gave me an immediate headache. I switched the desks back to the tried and true. The students didn't complain so much as express their frustration with having to change the desks around again.

The other new thing was that Kevin and Kurt had transferred back to New Teacher's room, though she still hadn't returned. And there were two new kids in the class who were completely aghast that I would even consider giving them homework. The other students broke it down.

"We get homework every day," said one.

"Fridays, holidays…" chimed in another.

"What?!" said one of the new kids.

"I'm not doin' it," replied the other.

"We'll see," I commented, shooting them both a smile.

In my previous visits to P.S. #7, I had learned so much. The first time I came face-to-face with the realities of a struggling neighborhood school: students running the halls, absentee teachers, a filthy, crumbing building, intermittent heat and limited resources. During my second extended visit, I came to truly understand the extent of the impact a child like X has on students who are otherwise happy and enthusiastic. The anxiety and chaos he introduced into the environment made ordinarily strong students agitated, unengaged, even fearful.

This last time out, I think I finally developed real empathy for students suffering with uncontrolled disorders. Yes, I acknowledged early on that these students weren't getting the attention and support they needed. That's obvious. What I hadn't comprehended, is how these students can become ostracized as the rest of the class begins to mature. Or, how they may become targets as kids who have previously been bullied grow taller and angrier. The whole thing is just painful to observe.

Before my last departure, Marshall was coming around. He was smiling and participating more and sneering less. He had become friends with Kevin and even started doing his homework consistently. He was super enthusiastic about math and spelling bees, and he went out of his way to avoid X as much as possible. I had even come to rely on him to referee our games of silent ball because he was always fair.

In a little less than two months, Marshall had changed. He was angry all the time, something his mother also pointed out. He wasn't taking direction well and he was quick to walk out of class, behavior I thought we'd left behind long ago. Now a couple of inches taller, Marshall reserved his greatest anger for X. He no longer avoided him; no longer let snide remarks slide by unanswered. If X said anything Marshall didn't like, he was up out of his seat and in X's face. They pushed, kicked and punched each other until I broke it up. One day, as I pulled him away from X, I could feel Marshall's heart thumping hard and fast.

"I'm not afraid of you!" he kept yelling at X who, cool as a cucumber, shot back, "Then do something... "

Marshall's mother blamed the school for a lot of the issues he was having and I didn't completely disagree. She was seriously working on transferring him to a private or charter school, either way his admittance was contingent upon a record with no discipline issues. I did my best to help...stopping things before they escalated; refusing to let him walk out of class; giving him lunch detention instead of writing him up. (There was a good chance nothing would happen if I did, but every once in a while, kids were suspended and that remained in their records.) P.S. #7 had failed Marshall. It allowed X to harass him and ruin his year, but I was determined Marshall wouldn't miss out if he had the chance to transfer to a better school.

It wasn't just Marshall who'd had enough of X. Most of the kids cringed at his behavior. They never cheered for him and never wanted him back in the room. Every student, except X and Harry, had spoken with their parents about transferring to another school at the end of the year. (A couple were gone by the time I returned.) Between X and the absentee teacher, parents were fed up. But the chances of all of them finding a spot in a better public school were slim. One of Philly's better charter schools once received 9,190 applications for ninety-six spots.[2] And transferring to any old charter school is certainly no guarantee that things will be better academically.

The kids were quick to tell me when X did something "bad." Suddenly, he couldn't get away with anything. One day, when I took the kids to the restroom, a few of the boys came out and told me that X had urinated all over the floor. I immediately flagged down the counselor who happened to be passing by.

"Why did you do that?" she asked him.

"Aw... they were gonna do it, too. It was a dare."

"You dared us but we didn't do it and you still did," Jaloni responded, disgusted. (The kids constantly complained about how dirty the bathrooms were. One day, I marched them around for 20 minutes looking for clean, dry, unlocked restrooms they could use. Those reserved for the adults weren't much better.)

"Do you do that at home?" the counselor asked.

"No," X said, like "of course not."

She took him along to her office so they could discuss the situation and I updated his folks when they texted. For the first time ever, they did not respond. The next day, I asked what they had said.

"They asked why I did it but I didn't get in trouble or anything."

"Why did you do it?"

"I don't know," he shrugged.

Even the kids in New Teacher's class, which had finally been taken over by a steady sub, were frustrated with X. Shortly after I returned, a few of her hardcore hall-runners (including Bang-Bang and Trouble A-Z) stopped by to see me during lunch. They wanted me to know that when 110 didn't have a teacher, they came to their room. And they hated it.

"They mess up and don't clean up," Bang-Bang complained.

They weren't just talking about paper on the floor and desks turned over, though that was part of it. X had slammed their door so hard he finally broke the glass panels.

"And it's still broke," said another kid. "He didn't even get in trouble. It's not fair."

There was absolutely no consequence for this incident and many, many others. Once again, I found myself crying on Awesome Grade Lead's shoulder, "I can't do it. I can't handle him."

"You can," she said. "You just don't see it," she encouraged.

"I put him out every day—every single day."

"Yeah, but each day you keep him longer and longer. That's progress."

I was embarrassed that this is what was passing for progress. But at least it gave me something concrete to work on. In that moment, I made it my goal to keep X in the room and productive for a full day. Unfortunately, he did nothing to help with my mission. He continued to fight, argue and disrupt. And I continued to send him to his STS worker. At this point, we couldn't even trust him to walk from my class to the STS room or Awesome Grade Lead's room across the hall. One day, as one of his STS workers and I stood in the hallway watching him cross, he took off running in the opposite direction. We both called to him pointlessly, as he hauled-ass around the corner and out of sight. His STS worker's face said it all. She'd had enough of chasing this little boy down. She called his folks to come deal with him.

His grandmother showed up, as she had a couple of times before. But this time, there was no discussion, no bargaining, no winning her over with his adorable smile and big eyes. She took him straight to an empty room and spanked him. Afterwards, she brought him back to me and warned him that if she got one more call from anyone, next time she would spank him in front of his entire class

"When you're not at home," his grandmother continued pointing to me, "this woman is your parent. So listen to her."

These words landed on my head like an elephant. His grandmother was according me both a great deal of respect and a huge responsibility.

I looked down at him, as he tried to shield himself behind me.

"If you were my child," I thought, "I'd be moving heaven and earth to get you out of this school and into one with specialized classes and teachers trained to deal with whatever is wrong with you." But since he was only my student, I decided maybe I could just be more patient and understanding.

X must have come to some similar realization, as well. From that day on, he never argued with me, or sucked his teeth or treated me with any kind of disrespect. He even showed up for lunch detention, which in the past had always been a fifty-fifty proposition. With each passing day, he seemed to grow more and more attached to me.

"Miss Harris," he'd say grabbing my arm, "you're my favorite teacher."

Occasionally, I'd have to ask if he would prefer to do his work or if I should call his grandmother. He always opted for the work, especially if I stood by his side or even better walked him through it. He understood the material just fine. He just couldn't stay focused by himself. By this point in the year, most of the students could plow through a two-sided worksheet in ten minutes. For X, this was a near impossibility.

Though I greatly appreciated the change in attitude toward me, there was very little change toward the other students. And for me, violence was always a deal breaker. If he did his homework but tripped a kid in the hallway, I sent him to an STS worker or Awesome Grade Lead's room. If he walked nicely in the line, but punched a girl in the stomach, I sent him out. If he participated in class, but called another student "stupid," he had to go. Regardless of what the other students were forced to tolerate, physical and verbal abuse should not be a part of the package.

In the last couple of weeks at P.S. #7, grades were in, PSSAs were done and everyone was coasting except the kids in 110. I was still teaching and giving homework because they had lost so much instruction time. None of the students who had started out in New Teacher's room had done well on the PSSAs which, given the circumstances, was to be expected. They hadn't even taken their final benchmarks (practice exams) which were supposed to help prep them. I know they completed the first one because one of the Fab Senior Teachers took time out of her schedule to help me administer it. A few of the students had shined on that first test, but there were wide gaps in what they'd learned in the meantime. And when they finally took the last benchmark, after the PSSAs were over, none of them did well.

The only thing I could think to do to help with next year's testing, was to give them as much experience with laptops as possible. To be honest, I didn't even know they had their own laptops until this last visit. I thought we were sharing. Nope. These laptops belonged specifically to 110 but the cart stayed in Awesome Grade Lead's room because the cart lock was broken and Regular

Teacher never locked the room door. I would have locked the door, but no one could find the spare key I turned in the last time I left. And Regular Teacher hadn't turned hers back in.

The laptops didn't go to waste. Awesome Grade Lead's class was twice as big and she didn't have enough to go around. So they used them. Once I realized they belonged to 110, I started sending kids for the cart every morning and returning it before the day ended. They finally had a chance to play word and math games on ABCya.com and work on internet research projects. They loved it.

During the last full week of school, we cleaned the room, watched movies and had extended recess and parties. Things were pretty laidback, until one morning when the sub for New Teacher's sub approached me.

"Are the children allowed to bring sharps to school?"

"What? You mean like to test blood glucose or something?" I responded.

"No, like a box cutter. The girl on the end," she pointed. "She has one."

I knew "Taliya," but not well. She had never been in my class and she was pretty quiet. Her father volunteered in the mornings for a while. He was absolutely disgusted with P.S. #7 and willing to tell anyone who'd listen that "the school is a disgrace, the Principal is a joke and the kids aren't learning a damn thing." And don't let him get started on New Teacher.

I walked over to Taliya and asked what was going on.

"Nothing."

"Taliya, do you have a box cutter?"

"He keeps messing with me and nobody does anything."

"Who's messing with you, Taliya?"

"X. He won't leave me alone."

I suspected that she was telling the truth, but I didn't have any proof, other than the guilty look on X's face as he watched from a safe distance.

"You should have told someone, Taliya."

"I did. I told my teacher but she didn't do anything."

Which teacher had she told? New Teacher? The sub? Or this new lady who showed up today? Yesterday, they didn't have a teacher at all. They were split up between four or five classes. (We had three of them in 110, including Kurt and Kevin who immediately upon hearing they were all going to different classes, marched down the hall and informed me they were coming to mine. God, I love those kids.)

"You cannot have that in school, Taliya. Please give it to me."

She shook her head, "No."

"Okay, get your stuff and come with me."

She calmly grabbed her little bookbag and followed. Once out of sight of the other students, she asked where we were going.

Where did she think? "To see the Principal."

All of a sudden, she fell out on the floor and started screaming and crying, "Noooo, I don't want my dad to give me a whippin'!"

"Taliya, I have to take you to the Principal's office. You won't give me the box cutter."

Lickety-split she pulled it out and handed it to me. It was way bigger than I'd imagined. Way. This thing could have sliced someone open.

"Please don't tell on me. Please..." She was absolutely panicked, but what could I do? You cannot bring weapons to school. You just can't.

I left Taliya sobbing in the stairwell and headed to the Principal's office, where she was ever-so-slowly wrapping up a meeting.

As time ticked on, I started to get antsy. The new sub had been left with all of the students in the lunch room and Taliya was having a breakdown in the stairwell. I needed to get back so I tried turning the weapon in to the Principal's assistant.

"No, unh-unh. I don't want that," she said walking away.

In this instance, who could blame her? After waiting a few more minutes, I started flicking it open and closed to reveal the huge razor blade inside.

"Okay, Miss Harris," the Principal responded. "You don't have to do all of that. Come on in here."

She asked the head of the climate team—you remember Boss Man—to join us, too. Handing over the weapon, I explained what happened. Neither of them knew anything about X bullying Taliya. Neither did I, but it didn't mean it wasn't happening. That kid got around.

Boss Man instructed me to "write it up," then released me to retrieve my class. By the time we made it back to the room, the kids were hyped up. Following up on a previous conversation we'd had, a few of the girls, including Janelle, told me they didn't "feel safe." One girl had called her parents who were ready to pull her out of school that day.

First, I locked the door from inside so the girls would feel more comfortable. Next, I explained that it was a box cutter, not a knife, as some had heard. Third, I assured them that I had taken the box cutter from Taliya and given it directly to the Principal and Boss Man, and they would be dealing directly with Taliya and her parents. Finally, I spoke to the parents who kept calling. Once I explained what happened, and that the box cutter had been removed from the girl's possession, they agreed to let their daughter stay for the end-of-year party we were planning.

While X was conspicuously quiet, the rest of the students were in overdrive. They all wanted to know if Taliya would be suspended.

"Probably," I hedged, just in case she wasn't.

Apparently, this wasn't the first time something like this had happened with Taliya, but they were all talking at once so I couldn't quite get it.

"Some kids got sick from these cookies," Jaloni finally offered up.

"Taliya," a bunch of them responded.

"Yeah, Taliya was one of them," he agreed.

Later during lunch, I ran into one of the Fab Senior Teachers and asked about the cookie incident.

"Oh yeah, we were on the news. Seventh graders were selling marijuana-laced cookies. (A lot had happened while I was gone.) We only found out because they overdid it and kids started getting sick. I've been at this school for over a decade and this is the worst I've ever seen it. Did they tell you about the girl who brought in the spoon and lighter?"

"Uhn-uh."

"She heated up the spoon and burned a boy on his neck. I heard the boy's mother was furious. I don't blame her. The girl wasn't suspended. It's ridiculous. This school is going straight downhill..." She muttered as she walked away, "And it smells like a bus station."

Awesome Grade Lead and I met up on the way to the yard.

"I heard there was a knife..."

"Box cutter, but it was huge and sharp."

"I bet nothing happens to her," she remarked.

"She hasn't gone back to class. I checked. I think they suspended her."

"It's just getting worse and worse. Did I tell you about 'my Student X?' He slammed the door on a second grader's hand. Severed the tip of her finger. She's wearing a cast now. *And,* he broke the door glass but I had it replaced. No suspension. His mother thinks it's all the school's fault. I couldn't do it anymore. He's in New Teacher's class now."

Despite all the turmoil, our last couple of days were fairly uneventful. We had our party on Thursday, so no one would miss it. Early in the day, I kicked X out for punching one of the girls. He was supposed to be cooling out in the STS room, but every single time I stepped out of class he was right there begging to come to the party.

"I'm sorry, Miss Harris. I'll be good. I promise. Please can I come to the party? Please...please..."

What could I do? He was nearly hysterical, especially after he heard me ordering pizza. I walked him back to 110 and checked to see if it was okay with the rest of the kids. X immediately and sincerely apologized to the girl he had punched.

"I'm sorry, 'Shauna.' Okay? It was my bad. I'm sorry."

Every last single one of them gave him the go-ahead. And I could be wrong, but I don't think it was out of fear. They truly didn't want him to miss out. Good thing too, because it was a great party. Several of the kids brought goodies, including Janelle and Jaloni. We had pizza, cupcakes, chips of all kinds, soda, juice and candy. We danced and played musical chairs and some frozen statue game.

Eventually, we settled into two groups: one playing Uno and the other playing Trouble. I partnered with one of the girls who was a little shy about playing by herself. (We may have won.) X brought his own brand of drama to the game. He tried to quit every five minutes, which would've been fine with the other kids, but I wouldn't let him. I wanted him to have the experience of playing nicely with the others. When it was time to switch games, he declared, "I only want to play if Miss Harris plays."

"I'm right here if you need me," I said. "You guys go ahead." I had to start cleaning up. Unfortunately, without me standing right next to him, X started banging on the game board and using foul language.

"Okay, let's go," I said, walking him over to Awesome Grade Lead's room. Within thirty or so, she stormed back into my room fuming. X followed contritely behind her.

"He choked two of my students. I need his grandmother's number. I'm calling her right now!"

I texted the number and they returned to her room. But later, she told me she was so upset, she couldn't remember where it was.

"I was searching and searching for a piece of paper. Then X said, 'Don't you remember? Miss Harris texted it to you.' You gotta love him," she said shaking her head.

Lucky for X, the day and the year were both almost over.

On my last day at P.S. #7, we finished cleaning up and cleaning out. We also reorganized the front closet, stacked the book shelves and cleaned out their desks. The kids were so helpful, even X as long as I gave him specific tasks. Once finished, he chased the girls (and some of the boys) around the classroom with a broom. He was playing, but the problem was they never knew when the playing might turn into something else. During one of X's sojourns out into the hallway, he learned that one of the Fab Senior Teachers was giving ice-pops to the kids who helped pack up her room. He came back to let me know that he was going with her. I stuck my head out the door and she gave me a wave to let me know it was okay, and he took off down the hall.

The rest of us spent the remainder of the day peacefully playing ball and going to another pizza party in New Teacher's room where only seven kids and the latest substitute had bothered to show up. At the end of the day, I was, once again, sad. The more I came to know these kids, the more I loved them. The more I loved them, the more I wanted better for them than a substitute teacher could ever provide.

Shouldn't we all want better for them?

Though a ton of my time at P.S. #7 had been focused on X and a few others who negatively impacted the class and impeded everyone's progress, there's so much more I'll remember. Like how the majority of the kids really wanted to learn and wrote me notes telling me so:

"I love the way you teach me but I hate it when the class talks when you are trying to teach...my favorite subject that you teach is math because there is a lot of fun stuff you can do."

"It's hard trying to learn when it is a lot of people talking in the classroom. I will try my best and I will work very hard."

"You're the best teacher ever and I love when you teach us and you are fun. All the things you teach us are things we didn't know before so thanks for the education."

"We all love you for making us smarter."

"Please don't leave because you helped me learn a lot and gave me homework."

"Please remember you are my favorite teacher."

"I will never forget what you have done for me."

"Thank you for teaching, Miss Harris."

I'll remember the thank-you texts and calls from parents and encouragement from experienced teachers and staff members. And how Harry went from "hating" me and hall-running to asking if he could stay with me instead of going to lunch or group counseling, even if it meant doing his homework. I'll remember writing up one of the new boys for taking a swing at me (yes, he missed; yes, he was suspended; yes, his mother and father and I had lots of conversations) but later naming him Student of the Month for his incredibly improved attitude and behavior. And how could I ever forget the whip smart girls and boys who always rose to the occasion, or the kids who started out doing no work and having little confidence, but who developed a stronger work ethic and more faith in their own ability. If I had the privilege of witnessing this type of growth in that whacked-out environment, imagine what these kids could achieve in a safe, supportive school setting focused on academic achievement and cultural enrichment?

———————

The fallout from the 2017-2018 school year was fairly extensive. The art teacher, who had spent a high percentage of her instruction time covering for absent grade teachers, was badly injured when she and another teacher tried to stop a fight. She went out on medical leave and never returned.

Both Regular Teacher and New Teacher were transferred to different schools. I heard through the grapevine that Regular Teacher was happier, though that was early in the year. New Teacher told me herself that she liked her new school.

"It's not perfect, but it's definitely better than P.S. #7...and I'm doing better now."

The Principal, who was in her first assignment, was removed from her position and transferred to another school as an Assistant Principal. I ran into her one day, during my travels and she shared that what she appreciated most about the new school is that they "worked as a team." Ironically, quite a few of the teachers at P.S. #7 blamed her lack of experience and refusal to include them in decision-making for the rapid decline of the school.

"She says she's open to suggestions, but she's really not. She doesn't listen," I heard several times from different teachers. Unwilling to "suffer through" another newbie principal or worse, quite a few of the Fab Senior Teachers made the difficult decision to leave P.S. #7 after many years at the school.

On the other side of the fence, I recall that the Principal seemed to feel that the teachers of P.S. #7 weren't taking enough responsibility for their students. One day, as I was catching her up on my first week back, I shared that four of my students (X, Harry, Marshall and a new kid) wouldn't come in from recess on my first day. I called the office twice to report them, but no one did anything and they stayed out in the yard playing for about two hours. (We could see them from the room window.)

"That's cutting class," she said, shocked. "They need to be suspended."

"If you want," I answered, "but it's handled. When they finally came in all happy and sweaty, I sent them to the office. Then, I called their parents and gave them all lunch detention. They haven't done it again."

She paused, then shook her head: "If I had ten more of you, things would have gone real different here."

A nice compliment, though I suspect it was less about me and more about the relationships she didn't have with the other members of her staff. In addition to whatever disciplinary problems the school had, there were huge communication and cooperation issues that contributed to its continued decline. Teachers and staff constantly complained about how the school was "going downhill," but the Principal felt the same. Once, as I was waiting to speak with her, she was informed that a second grader, who had walked out of class and out of the building, had been found. As we stood there shaking our heads, she blurted out, "This school is... a mess."

Before I thought to edit myself, I agreed: "It really is." Then I held my breath, hoping I hadn't overstepped.

"It really, really is," she responded. "And it just didn't get this way when I came." She pulled out the School Progress Report from the previous year— before she had arrived—and showed it to me. P.S. #7 had scored 0% for progress and an overall 9% out of a possible 100%, which clearly identified it as a school that required intervention.[3]

"Did you know," I asked? "Did they tell you this was a tough school and they wanted you to turn it around?"

"No," she said. "Nobody told me a thing."

As much of a mess as P.S. #7 was, it's neither an anomaly, nor considered to be one of the worst schools in the District. Following up the next school year, I discovered that in addition to the mass exodus of teachers, a significant portion of its student body had also transferred. Though my "source" liked the new administrators, she admitted that the school was no better and perhaps even a little worse because a lot of the older students had started hanging out in the hallways upstairs, as well as coming down to the first floor, where they set a bad example for the younger kids.

Also, the third-grade hall-runners were now fourth-grade hall-runners who, while trying to enter what they thought was an empty classroom in the basement, ran smack into the homeroom teacher. She claimed that as she tried to push past them, they "grabbed her private parts and used sexually explicit language." The students claimed she used racial epithets. Later, the teacher informed the new principal that she didn't feel safe continuing to teach at the school. The principal reportedly warned her that not showing up for work would be considered "abandoning her class." She quit anyway and is now employed at another District school.

Discussions about "fixing" P.S. #7 have also finally begun. The plan is to turn it into an "accelerated" school, a.k.a. "promise academy," a.k.a. "turnaround" school, etc.

"It's all the same," commented a current P.S. #7 teacher. "And they never stick with any one thing long enough for it to work. But they need something."

This teacher also informed me that during one school meeting, it was acknowledged that P.S. #7 has a very high percentage of students with emotional and behavioral problems. When the teachers asked if some of those students would be transferred to other schools...no answer was given.

Of everything I heard about and witnessed during the following year at P.S. #7, the thing that disappointed me most was discovering that X was still wreaking havoc on his classmates, which included Kurt, Kevin, Harry and Marshall. And just like the year before, the class had been abandoned by its regular teacher and left in the willing, but inexperienced hands of a very discouraged substitute teacher.

The reason why we have failed at school reform is because we're trying to do school reform cheap for poor kids..."[1]

—Julian Vasquez Heilig, Ph.D.
Dean and Professor
University of Kentucky College of Education

> Update on the District

*O*nce considered one of the worst public school systems in the United States, the SDP has made significant progress over the last fifteen plus years. It was immediately obvious to me as a returning substitute that many of Philly's administrators, teachers, parents and students are pushing for academic success. The SDP continues to make smart moves that are in line with current trends for improving education. Under Superintendent William Hite, the District has not only invested considerable funds in new classroom resources, it has won awards for environmental excellence—a bit perplexing considering the widespread issues with lead and asbestos. Nevertheless, Governor Wolf and the PA Dept. of Environmental Protection recognized GreenFutures, the SDP's sustainability program, for pursuing opportunities to reduce energy consumption, increase waste diversion, establish green spaces (five new schoolyards per year for schools that previously had nothing but cement to play on), etc.[2,3]

The SDP has also boldly embraced the idea that all children do not learn the same way by investing in the development of diverse school models through its School Redesign Initiative (SRI) and Innovation Network. The SRI empowers educators to redesign the approach to education in (mostly failing) neighborhood schools,[4] while the innovation schools offer a range of options that include project-based learning, real-world problem solving, community partnerships and self-paced and virtual curriculums.[5] Some of these schools have students who are achieving test scores equal to or better than the state average, while others are "non-academically selective" and emphasize hands-on mentoring and training vs. a traditional curriculum and standardized test taking. For some students, these new schools represent a second chance for success.

The Early Literacy Initiative is, perhaps, the most impressive of the SDP's newer projects. It includes the revamping and re-supplying of all K-2 classrooms to better facilitate reading instruction[6] and education in general. This effort dovetails with the Read by 4th program, which is supported by school officials, parents, neighborhood reading captains and over 100 corporate partners. The goal is to ensure all students are reading on grade level by the start of fourth grade, which has been identified as the critical turning point "when instruction shifts from learning to read to reading to learn." Something nearly 2/3rds of Philadelphia students entering fourth grade for the 2016-2017 school year were unable to do. Administered by the Free Library, Read by 4th promotes quality reading opportunities and support inside and outside of school. The program establishes neighborhood reading captains and encourages quality classroom instruction and consistent attendance—a component the SDP pushes hard with weekly acknowledgement and prizes for perfect and near-perfect attendance.[7]

Some of my most disappointing encounters have been with students in fifth, sixth and seventh grade who played, yelled, lied, fought and feigned disinterest—anything to hide the fact that they couldn't read. Pushing younger children to master this incredibly important life skill while they are still enthusiastic, cooperative and minimally self-conscious is not only brilliant, it could lead the way in rebuilding Philly's entire public school system from the bottom up. It already seems to be working. On 2017-2018 standardized tests, all grades from third to seventh made progress on the PSSA reading exam, but third graders who have been the primary beneficiaries of this new program achieved the largest gains.[8] Like me, you may be wondering what happens to the students who have moved on from early elementary, but still need help? I don't know. Perhaps, as in the past, they just get left behind.

The SDP also works to promote excitement and enthusiasm about education with free back-to-school events and high-school selection tradeshows that feature entertainment, giveaways and guidance. Accurate information about most public and charter schools in Philadelphia is available on the School District's website (https://www.philasd.org/performance/programsservices/school-progress-reports/available-spr-reports/). Unlike in the past, when the SDP seemed to operate under a "hide-in-plain-sight" philosophy, parents are now encouraged to review and understand School Progress Reports. In a struggling district where both parents and students are desperate to get into

"one of the good ones," this type of information is invaluable. As you may recall, Philadelphia schools are ranked by tiers:
- Model (75-100%)
- Reinforce (50-74%)
- Watch (25-49%)
- Intervene (0-24%)[9]

I'm sure it comes as no surprise that there are more public and charter schools in the bottom two tiers than in the top two. Philly has always had a small group of "private" public and charter schools to which most students never gain access. The difference today is that the pool of higher performing schools seems to be growing. According to the SDP's 2017-2018 SPR Fact Sheet:
- Overall school performance has increased three years in a row
- There are almost twice as many higher performing schools (from 36 to 68 in the Model and Reinforce tiers)
- There are nearly 50% fewer schools in the lowest tier—Intervene (from 88 to 45)
- 53% of schools have improved achievement
- 69% have improved climate[10]

What the 2017-2018 SPR Fact Sheet does not tell us is exactly how many of Philly's schools are still in the bottom half of the performance tiers. So let's do the math. If there are 316[*11] schools and 68 are in the top two performance tiers (Model and Reinforce) and 45 are in the very bottom tier (Intervene) then there are (316 – [68 + 45] =) 203 schools in the Watch tier, "needs intensive support to improve."[10] If we add the two bottom tiers together (203 in Watch + 45 in Intervene), there are 248 (or 79%) of Philly's public and charter schools that are still struggling or outright failing.

Is this really the progress the SDP would have us believe it is?

Comparing 2017-2018 stats with those from just two years earlier, tells a different story:

School Year	2015-2016[12]	2017-2018[10,11]
Total Schools	318*	↓316*
Model & Reinforce	78	↓68
% of schools in top half of performance tiers	25%	↓22%
# in Watch tier	131	↑203
# in Intervene tier	109	↓45
# and % of schools in bottom half of performance tiers	240 or 76%	↑248 or 79%

318* schools were rated in the 2015-2016 school year. 78 were in the top two performance tiers, 131 were in the Watch tier and 109 were categorized as Intervene.[12] In just two years, 64 schools have moved from the very bottom tier to the next one up, Watch. This is significant progress by anyone's standards and likely the result of very hard work on the part of all involved. Yet, the next tier up is described as "needs intensive support to improve," hardly something to celebrate. There are also now more total schools in the bottom half of the performance tiers. Granted, schools are dynamic organisms that fluctuate with changes in leadership, funding, faculty, etc., but this indicates that some schools are achieving less now than in the time period directly after the implementation of more rigorous standards. Some may argue that there's not a huge difference between 76% and 79%. In this case, it adds up to eight more underachieving schools. If we're looking for substantial progress; if our goal is for all children to attend schools capable of giving them a competitive education; then, this just isn't good enough.

---

* According to the SDP Dashboard and Open Data Philly spreadsheet, a few schools lacked sufficient data and therefore were excluded from overall totals. Specifically, the 2017-2018 SPR Overview indicated 339 schools though only 316 had sufficient data for year-to-year comparison, while the 2015-2016 school year, Raw Data spread sheet indicated 324 total schools with six excluded due to insufficient data.[10, 11,12]

Most of the schools I visited this time around were like P.S. #7, struggling neighborhood schools in the bottom half of the performance tiers. But I also had the opportunity to visit a couple of Philly's best, along with a few in the solidly improving category. My last long-term assignment was at one of these "improving" schools in the far Northeast of the City. A one-day assignment with twenty-two kindergarteners turned into over three months working with one of the most ethnically diverse classes I've ever had the good fortune to teach. For the most part, they all got along and when they didn't, it had nothing to do with race, ethnicity or culture. Once again, I found myself covering for a teacher who was on medical leave. The difference was that everyone knew there was a serious medical issue and the teacher was in touch with the administration. From the start, they told me they didn't know how long the assignment would run, but they suspected at least two months. Everyone made me feel welcomed and supported. They promised to help me and they did.

The Classroom Assistant and I worked as a team. The wonderful Grade Partner created the lesson plans and printed out homework for both classes. Every single day. She also helped dig out books and other materials and answered a million questions. The Computer Teacher made sure I was outfitted with a laptop and login and showed me how to use the SMART Board during my first full week. (In the five months total I spent at P.S. #7, no one ever lent me a laptop or fixed the broken SMART Board, which impeded instruction. All of the math lessons had corresponding videos to which we did not have access for the whole year.)

The Principal stopped in frequently to check on me and backed me up when I ran into a craz...er...*challenging* parent and an unreasonable member of the engineer's team who, despite the fact that we were in the middle of a Hand, Foot & Mouth Disease outbreak, didn't feel extra sanitizing measures were warranted. And the School Based Teacher Lead went above and beyond. She is the only member of any school administrative team anywhere who actually sat in the room while I taught and gave me feedback. She also hung charts, made folders and helped me do report cards. Not only did this woman encourage me, she also patiently coached me on the particularly demanding schedule and curriculum for the kindergarteners. I will never be able to adequately express how much I appreciated the support and kindness of the whole team.

Thinking back to all those years ago when I was subbing at P.S. #15, I was pretty certain we were providing little more than babysitting service for the kindergarteners. This assignment confirmed my suspicions. These kids at this school were being educated. Two of the kindergarten classes had participated in a University of Pennsylvania pilot program. After it was over, the school adopted the curriculum for all four of its kindergarten classes. The students began the day with ABC and counting worksheets, while I took roll and directed them to hang up jackets and put completed homework in their cubbies. Then they had an hour and a half of English Language Arts, with lots of phonics, story time (fiction and non-fiction), drawing and writing (words and short sentences related to the latest book). After lunch and recess, they had an hour and a half of math. Then, they had 45 minutes of computers or another enrichment class, 15-20 minutes of independent reading practice, 40 minutes of "constructed" play (computers, learning games and guided reading) and then either social studies or science to finish off the day. They also took home books to read with their parents and caregivers.

The curriculum is tough but some of these kids were up to it, actually reading and writing and doing the required higher-order thinking...in kindergarten. Of course, others were struggling. A couple started crying in the middle of one math test. One truly lovely little boy looked at me with his big, blue eyes and shrugged as if to say, "Yeah, I got nothin' for ya." But for the most part, they were all trying and they were all learning.

At one point, I informed the Teacher Lead that a few kids were acting out and disrupting class. She responded that the class was due for testing so we'd soon see what was going on academically. Within a week, we knew which students needed help and exactly what kind. Most of them turned out to be the students who were acting out.

"We always start from the point of academics. Does this child need additional instruction? If that doesn't help, then we start to explore other areas," the Counselor explained.

We did have to explore other areas for some. In the three months I worked at this school, the team was responsible in part or in whole for children receiving extra reading and math support, ESOL tutoring, psychological observation and speech therapy, as well as dental services and eyeglasses. Soon after, one child began taking medication that calmed him down enough so that he could do his class work. Three others were assigned to a Therapeutic Support Staff (TSS) worker.

Children were not left to flounder and neither were teachers. There were plans and procedures in place to support both. The Teacher Lead even made arrangements for my class to be covered so I could attend grade group meetings where we actually discussed teaching methods. Not big picture, high-concept stuff, but nitty-gritty "to get across this concept, I say x, y and z, then I do this..." Might seem like a small thing, but when you're struggling to reach some of the kids, this is what you need. Yes, I could follow the video presentations, read ahead in the teacher's guide and explain 'til the cows come home. But teaching is more than that. It's explaining in a way that allows children to discover the connections. The ability to do that, I think, comes from a combination of innate talent and experience. And nobody gets there alone.

Every single day I wondered why this school was so much better than P.S. #7. Was it because they had a plan and P.S. #7 did not? Or did they both have the same District-prescribed plan, but this team was better at implementing? Demographically, the two schools are similar. Both have about the same number of students. They have similar levels of low-income students, around 65%. But where they differ greatly is in the number of students with disabilities. The school in the Northeast had roughly 12%, while P.S. #7 has a reported percentage of about 21%[13,14] and an unofficial estimate somewhere north of 25%.

Don't get me wrong. The school in the Northeast wasn't perfect. There were disruptive students (and a couple of condescending teachers) but acting out and screaming down the halls wasn't the norm. The one time I witnessed a student having a meltdown, he was confined to the hallway and surrounded by adults, including the Principal. The one time a student in my class had a meltdown (because I let someone else play with the blocks) he cried for over an hour, still didn't get to play with the blocks and I told his mother. In fact, I started giving her a daily report. She talked to him at home and we made sure he received the extra academic support he needed at school. It took a long while but, finally, he was able to show us what a lovely boy he is. And when I went back to visit, he pulled out some of his worksheets to show me that he could now write his letters.

There was an overall sense of community in this place that did not exist at P.S. #7. There was no anxiety that at any moment something crazy might happen. There were canned-goods drives, door-decorating contests, plays, sports and music lessons. Kids actually held doors for me and said "good morning" at the start of the day. Not all of them all of the time, but enough to contribute to the general vibe of wellbeing that permeated the hallways. Again, I grew attached to the kids. Again, I was sad to leave. I'll always treasure the drawings and gifts they gave me, as well as the time I got to spend with them. But unlike when I left P.S. #7, I didn't worry about whether or not these students would be okay. I knew they were in good hands and a good environment. I didn't need an SPR to tell me this school was doing okay, but it did confirm it. Their overall score was 54% landing them...just barely...in the Reinforce tier.[15] My expectation is that this number will continue to rise, as long as they are able to maintain a setting that is conducive to teaching, learning and growing.

So now...are *Philly's* schools any better?

When it comes to the overall number of students with emotional and/or behavioral challenges who are allowed to disrupt the educational process, I'd have to say, "No." In that particular area, Philly's schools are probably worse. (We'll take a more in-depth look at this in the next chapter.) Academically, I'd say, "Mostly." Even in the most underachieving schools, there is now a greater emphasis on academic rigor, more access to resources and more teachers and administrators with "by-any-means-necessary" attitudes. (One principal actually wrote her personal cell number on the blackboard in case I needed help during the day. In a school system where some administrators have been known to hide in their offices, she demonstrated incredible commitment.)

If a child is fortunate enough (or their family is connected enough) to get into one of the new, recently improved and/or just plain superior public or charter schools in the city, their educational experience is definitely better. But if a child is stuck in a bottom-tier school, there's a good chance her educational environment is not hugely different than it would have been 15 plus years ago. In many cases, it may be worse. P.S. #7 was definitely worse this time around. And though I haven't detailed my experiences, the environments in several of the schools I re-visited, including P.S. #13, had also declined. At P.S. #13, the behavior seemed to vary by class. Some seemed to be completely under control, while others weren't. The students I subbed with had a reputation for ignoring the work given to them and terrorizing subs, as well as their regular teacher. That assessment came not just from my one-day return visit, but from a regular staff member and students.

"Can you believe this is supposed to be a magnet school?" one of the more diligent and well-behaved kids asked me. "They act like this every day."

"Even when the regular teacher is here?"

"Even when she's here," another answered, which explained why she wasn't.

Despite District improvements and what seems to be a methodical, yet slow-as-molasses plan to turn the SDP around a few schools at a time, the majority of Philly's public and charter schools continue to underachieve. On an institutional level, the SDP still faces huge budget shortfalls and staffing deficiencies. And according to a radio interview with Superintendent Hite, a significant portion of the teaching community still believes "all students are not capable of succeeding."

It's my personal belief that even if all educators had the right attitude and right resources, turnaround would still be nearly impossible. Why? Because of two huge, hopelessly intertwined obstacles: inclusion and funding. Though education financing is a hot-button topic, very few people outside of educators are talking about how nearly impossible it is to teach or learn in a continuously disrupted, undisciplined and unsafe environment. Poor standardized test results reflect this reality. But instead of fixing the disrupted environments, there has been a statewide—and perhaps countrywide—de-emphasis on the importance of well-formulated, culturally fair standardized tests, which are our only means of determining whether or not an individual school is doing its job. Perhaps, it's time to take a closer look at where we went wrong.

> Author's Note #2

Before continuing, please allow me to take this opportunity to say that I have worked with students who have autism, Down syndrome, hearing disabilities, speech impediments, ADHD and other special needs. And they were simply a joy to teach. In this next section, I am specifically addressing the challenges associated with uncontrolled emotional and behavioral disorders and learning disabilities that cause students to act out and disrupt the educational process. This is not a judgment of these children. Truly, it is heartbreaking to watch them attempt to navigate the educational environment without the proper assistance. My goal is neither to condemn these students to an inferior education, nor to make them the scapegoat for all of the problems of the public education system. However, I am convinced that forced full inclusion is a huge stumbling block for Philadelphia and other school districts that are under pressure to improve both the experience and academic outcomes for all students.

> The Burden of Inclusion

*W*hen I first began this journey, I knew very little about students with special needs and I had never heard of inclusion. To be honest, I thought I was just dealing with very poorly behaved kids...and sometimes I was. However, I came to understand that a significant portion of these children were struggling under the burden of disabilities and, in the process, hampering their own educational progress, as well as the progress of their classmates. New and veteran teachers shared my concerns and explained that inclusion—a federally mandated push to educate children with special needs in the general classroom setting—had resulted in constant disruption and frequent violence in public school classrooms throughout Philadelphia and around the U.S.

A little background

Inclusion began to take shape in the 1950s and 60s when parents of children with disabilities petitioned courts and elected representatives for access to public schools. By 1975, the Education for All Handicapped Children Act (EAHCA) was implemented and it declared:

> "...all children, regardless of disability, have the right to a free, appropriate education in the least restrictive environment..."[1]

This law freed children with special needs from the limited options of home care and institutionalization, and precipitated the establishment of "special" education classes in public schools.[1] Unfortunately, special education was considered by many to be an inferior program in which children with disabilities were isolated and babysat until graduation day.

Madeleine Will, Assistant Secretary for the Office of Special Education and Rehabilitative Services and the parent of a child with Down syndrome, hoped to eliminate the gap between "general" education and special ed., while at the same time providing disabled students with greater social benefit. In 1986, she proposed that "greater efforts be made to educate mildly and moderately disabled students in the mainstream of regular education." Soon after, support also began to grow for educating students with more severe disabilities in the general classroom setting as well.[1]

In 1990, the EAHCA was reissued and renamed the Individuals with Disabilities Education Act, better known as "IDEA."[1] Though a few words have been changed here and there over the years, generally it states:

> "...**to the maximum extent appropriate**, children with disabilities, including children in public or private institutions or other care facilities, are [to be] educated with children who are nondisabled, and [that] special classes, separate schooling, or other removal of children with disabilities from the regular educational environment occurs **only if the nature or the severity of the disability is such that education in regular classes with the use of supplementary aids and services cannot be achieved satisfactorily."**
>
> —IDEA Sec. 300.114[2]

What some people took away from this passage is that pretty much all special needs students should be "included" in general classrooms, even if they have disruptive disabilities and disorders, such as Oppositional Defiant Disorder, Obsessive Compulsive Disorder, Attention Deficit/Hyperactivity Disorder, etc.[3] Suddenly, cash-strapped school districts all over the U.S. were abandoning expensive special education programs that have smaller class sizes and higher-paid, specialized instructors. They began to shift as many students with disabilities as possible into general education, despite the fact that studies had indicated inclusion is not the best choice for all students with disabilities.

Before we go further, let's take a look at three terms that are often used interchangeably:

- **Mainstreaming** refers to "the selective placement of special education students in one or more [general] education classes,"[4] during the school day, while the special ed. classroom remains their primary home. In this model, a child is expected to demonstrate an ability to keep up with the work assigned by the general classroom teacher.

- **Inclusion** commits first "to educate each child, to the maximum extent appropriate" in the school and classroom he or she would normally attend. It requires only that the child benefit [socially, emotionally or academically] from being in that class"[4] vs. a special ed. environment. Support services are brought to the child in the general education environment.
- **Full inclusion** places all students, "regardless of handicapping condition or severity," in a general ed. classroom full time. All support services are brought to the child in that setting.[4]

In 1980, a full decade before IDEA made inclusion the law of the land, researchers analyzed 50 different studies comparing separate special education with inclusion. The conclusion was that special ed. was better for children with emotional, behavioral and learning disabilities.

> "**Special [education] classes were found to be** significantly inferior to regular class placement for students with below average IQs and **significantly superior to regular classes for behaviorally disordered, emotionally disturbed and learning-disabled children.**"
>
> —C. Carlberg, Ph.D & K. Kavale, Ph.D
> *The Efficacy of Special vs. Regular Class Placement*
> *for Exceptional Children: A Meta-Analysis*[5]

Many advocacy groups, including the Council for Children with Behavioral Disorders and the Learning Disabilities Association, opposed full inclusion and said so.[6] Justine Maloney, former Legislative Chairman of the Learning Disabilities Association wrote: "For some students with learning disabilities, total inclusion is a disastrous reality."[7]

Teachers and administrators also warned that inclusion would have a catastrophic effect on the educational process. They turned to the American Federation of Teachers (AFT) to help put an end to the devastating effects that it was having on their classrooms. In response, Albert Shanker, who was then president of the AFT, went on record stating that school administrators were "rushing to bring all students into the regular classrooms, regardless of their ability, in an effort to save money."

Robert Chase, former president of the National Education Association, also commented at the time saying, "There's no question that the inclusion movement is being abused in some places."[8]

Guess what? The studies, the experts, the teachers and administrators... they were right. While it cannot be denied that some special needs students do fine or even thrive in general education classrooms, others are unable to cope and keep pace with the academic and emotional demands. In response, they act out, behave violently, ignore teachers and disrupt the daily learning process. Subsequently, the classroom environment has devolved, requiring many public school teachers to serve as therapists, disciplinarians and, sometimes, even medical personnel; all in addition to performing the job they were hired to do—*teach*.

While schools did receive *some* additional funding to help children with disabilities be successful in the general ed. setting, it wasn't and still isn't enough. Experts have debated the costs of inclusion vs. special ed. for decades. The only true consensus seems to be that implementing inclusion effectively costs a lot more than abandoning children with disabilities in the general ed. environment without the full range of necessary support services.[8,9]

Tawanna Jones, SDP Psychologist and former special ed. teacher, describes Philadelphia as a "high-needs city without enough supports," such as psychologists, staff trained in dealing with special needs students, etc. "And that makes it nearly impossible to attend to the needs of all disabled students."

A true believer in inclusion, Dr. Jones commented, "If you put the same kind of people in the same space, your results are going to plateau at some point because everyone is sort of thinking alike. That's what seems to happen when you pile a bunch of students who have significant learning or behavioral needs into one space. They never get used to the rigor or the standard of a general education class. So they're always behind."

When asked if placing students who are not ready for or comfortable with the general ed. setting into one of these classrooms could translate into disruption, Dr. Jones responded, "Absolutely. It translates into disruption or a withdrawal so much so that [students are] not really learning or participating or gaining anything from the space."

That's why Dr. Jones does not support "full" or "forced" inclusion.

"How did you make the decision?" she asked, explaining the types of questions that need to be considered. "That this was going to be okay for that student? Who's doing the remediation? Who's making sure the student gets the accommodations? Least restrictive environment means the child is getting what they need, not that the school decides we're going to do inclusion and that's what [all students with disabilities] need."

Dr. Jones has a lot of experience in this area. She helped develop and implement a model that integrates ongoing, individualized planning and support for each special needs student. In addition, general education classrooms are staffed with both content and behavior-modification specialists:

"In a really well-running school, you would have one of both types of teachers in the classroom [general ed. and special ed.] at least for the core subjects, as well as people who float between other areas to provide the support students may need. And that's expensive. The District doesn't have that kind of money."

School police, city police, climate staff and STS workers

What Philadelphia does have to handle the daily challenge of safety and the discipline of out-of-control students (with or without special needs) is school police, city police, climate staffs and Student Therapeutic Services workers, also known as STS, TSS, One-on-Ones and Wraparounds. Again, I'll use P.S. #7 as an example. It had one school police officer who ran from crisis to crisis all day. She took the job seriously and the students took her seriously, but she couldn't be everywhere at once and she also couldn't stop teachers and climate staff members from being injured by violent students.

Other school police I encountered in my travels ranged from no-nonsense and always on-guard to literally being afraid of the students. There were also officers who were quick to call the real police or to encourage others to do so, which directly conflicts with the District's shift away from suspensions, expulsions and referrals into the criminal justice system. Shortly after Superintendent Hite arrived, he began to dismantle Philadelphia's Zero Tolerance policies. Likely because studies across the state and around the country have shown that under these regulations, students of color have been punished more severely and for less serious offenses than white students. Zero Tolerance policies have also resulted in a very high percentage of minority students, especially those with special needs, being expelled and referred as criminals.[10]

Over the last few years, the School District in combination with Philadelphia's Police Department and other City agencies have created a compassionate, trauma-informed Student Diversion Program. The goal of this program is to provide second chances to first-time offenders. Instead of being disciplined in court for minor offenses, eligible students are given off-site counseling and direction to help them cope better and avoid future entanglements with the law. Under the direction of former Deputy Police Commissioner, Kevin Bethel, Philadelphia police officers became the first point of contact for this program, which diverted 1800 students from involvement with the court system in its first four years.[11,12]

"Climate" is a relatively new term used in the District. It refers, generally, to safety, engagement and orderliness. According to a District job posting, the official duties of a climate staff member are to "provide assistance to staff during lunch and recreation periods, assist in monitoring student behavior in and around the school building and assist security and instructional personnel in monitoring and directing students' activities."[13] What the posting doesn't say is "be prepared to be hit, kicked and/or disrespected on any given weekday."

Some climate teams are very effective, ensuring that students clear hallways between classes, checking on visiting subs (thank you) and, generally, maintaining order. But I've also come across climate teams members who were hostile, indifferent (to students and teachers) overwhelmed and/or burned-out. The team at P.S. #7, as a whole, usually seemed to be hanging on by its fingernails. It had a great deal of turnover, especially after one of its core (and hardest working) team members was injured in a confrontation with a student. Once the team was shored up with more males, it seemed to function better... but again, there were only a few of them and over 500 students. They couldn't be everywhere at once.

STS workers are a special breed. Back in 2002, when I first encountered them, I was skeptical about the value they brought to the classroom. They sat in the room with their assigned student all day, looking bored. If the student acted out, the STS would spring into action, often removing the child until he or she calmed down. To me, it seemed like an incredibly inefficient use of time and money, until the day a quiet unassuming young man was absent and I was left to deal with his surprisingly combative student all on my own.

Today, there seems to be an even greater need for STS workers and many split their hours between two, three and more students. As a substitute teacher, I often viewed them as lifesavers. Other times, not so much. Like all professionals, STS workers vary in ability, temperament and style. Some were unobtrusive in their interactions, patient with their students and helpful with other children in the room who were acting out. Others were constantly on their cell phones or laptops, and sometimes even trying to strike up conversations with me while I was trying to teach. In other words, they were doing everything except paying attention to the students they were supposed to be supporting. Then, there were those who caused even more of a ruckus than the kids they were supposed to be managing by yelling across the room for a student to behave or dramatically snatching them up and out the door when they didn't listen.

The absolute worst STS workers were the ones who literally brought everything to a standstill, including lessons, as they embarrassed, belittled or otherwise intimidated a student into compliance. Granted, some students seemed only to respond to this type of an approach; however, I'm pretty certain it's not the right example to set for a child who is prone to bullying. Once the STS worker has moved on to the next student in the next room, it's back to business as usual for a child who's now embarrassed, angry and waiting for an opportunity to lash out.

To be fair, I've also come across STS workers who have established strong, almost parental relationships with their charges. (I have no doubt that the STS program helped Harry.) Others are known to have a calm demeanor and considerable patience. But even for them—after the fiftieth time they have told a child to sit down and be quiet or to stop hitting, kicking or choking another kid—that patience begins to wear thin. Still, at the outset, everyone hopes this extra, one-on-one guidance will help. Unfortunately, sometimes, students will languish on the waiting list for months before an STS worker becomes available. In the meantime, and sometimes even after an STS worker has been assigned, it's the teacher in the room who bears the responsibility for that child's behavior.

The challenge for teachers

Back when I started subbing in 2001, I was stunned by the number of miserable, frustrated and burned-out teachers I encountered. Rarely did anyone speak of loving or even liking their profession. A great deal of that discontent came from being forced to deal with the unchecked emotional and behavioral disorders of their students.

Said Dr. Jones, on this aspect of teaching, "There's a lack of understanding. Training just isn't sufficient for what teachers need to know...I've been having this conversation with [established] developmental teachers, as well as people who come into the District right now. I say the same thing. It's like the company line: This is the job."

This time around though, I have been impressed with the quality and attitude of many of the teachers I met, especially those working in the inner-city. For the most part, they seem to be committed, prepared, enthusiastic, good humored, deeply immersed in their profession and impatient with those who do not follow suit. The worst possible condemnation of a teacher, administrator or school is:

"Those kids are not learning."

From what I've observed, senior teachers are overburdened. They're expected to adeptly handle discipline and disruption issues in their own classes and support newer teachers and substitutes, all while meeting the now, more aggressive academic goals of the District. (Lots of pressure). New teachers are often struggling to reconcile their idealized version of teaching with the daily realities of the profession. (They're in shock.) Other teachers are dealing with serious personal issues that—combined with the challenge of managing students with disruptive disorders—are just too much. (They're overwhelmed.) The end result? An extraordinarily high rate of teacher absenteeism. [14] In the 2017-2018 school year, only 62% of teachers were present for at least 95% of their classes.[15]

Though I sympathize on a human level, working three long-term assignments in one school (and three others in different schools) allowed me the opportunity to experience firsthand how high, repetitive absence rates destabilize the learning process for everyone involved. Other teachers, administrators and substitutes scramble to cover for the M.I.A. In one single day at P.S. #7, there were 17 faculty and staff absences. While that may have been a record, it wasn't highly unusual. Teacher absences often resulted in classes being split up and farmed out to other teachers who probably already had more than the approved number of students.

Other times, entire classes had extended recess or spent hours sitting in the auditorium doing nothing. On more than one occasion, students were left sitting in the lunchroom with no one to pick them up at the start of the day because "the office" was still trying to figure out who was going to cover what. And it was understood throughout the building by students and staff alike that both of the seventh-grade teachers were gone, just like in 2002 when all of the sixth grade teachers at P.S. #7 stopped showing up all together. (No wonder the seventh graders were able to establish a thriving marijuana-cookie business.)

Four of the eight regular teachers on the hall where I worked were out for weeks at a stretch. New or inexperienced subs often picked up these assignments; but then, quickly moved on citing a "lack of support from the main office." When there were no subs available, the regular teachers were forced to give up their free periods (meant to be spent preparing materials for their own students) to cover. Or, art, dance, computer and other enrichment classes were cancelled for all students while those teachers covered for the absent teachers. This was an everyday thing at P.S. #7. So it should be no surprise that the school had a serious discipline problem. At any point during the day, you could find children running up and down the halls—crying, fighting and arguing with adults. While I tried to help as much as possible, I admit that sometimes I kept the door closed and the students in my room calm, safe and as focused as possible on work instead of on the kids who were literally screaming in the corridor.

I have spoken at length with many, many teachers about classroom management and "taming" an unruly class. One of the best answers I received came from Awesome Grade Lead at P.S. #7:

"The only way to avoid having a crazy class is for teachers to show up every day and get their classes well in hand from the first day of school forward. If they have to spend the entire first week marching up and down halls so the students learn how to line up properly, that's what you do."

The teachers who were known to have well run rooms were rarely absent. Sick or not, tired or not, frustrated or not, they showed up—despite the number of challenging students they had or the personal issues they were dealing with at home. Obviously, like everyone else, teachers have a right to personal problems. But should those who are struggling to perform be shielded by union regulations or administrators who allow them to be in and out of school for extended periods of time? Should principals have absolutely no idea what's going on with their teachers, or when they're coming back? Or, be afraid to ask because they may be accused of harassing someone on an "approved" leave? Should principals be held accountable if they have been too nice, too busy or too lazy to document the problems they're having with one of their own? Because, according to Dr. Jones, "that's how you put an end to that type of irresponsible behavior." You document it.

Teachers who are struggling or in trouble deserve to get the help they need. They should be released from the responsibility of a classroom quickly and not allowed to return until they are truly ready. No in and out because teaching is not an ordinary 9 to 5. Teachers hold the futures of their students in their hands. And far too often that future is dropped into the hands of subs. Not to demean substitute teachers, as the SDP has learned, it's extraordinarily difficult to operate its schools without them. But we all know that a parade of subs or even a long-term uncertified sub is not optimal.

Let's be honest, inclusion is one of the main reasons why our schools are the way they are. If student management issues were not so completely out-of-control in so many schools, more teachers would show up to work. In the *2017 Educator Quality of Work Life Survey*, 61 percent of the nearly 5000 educators surveyed found work to be "always" or "often" stressful. That's twice the rate of other professions. Twenty-seven percent said they have been threatened, bullied or harassed. At this point, it should be no surprise that 50 percent of those who claimed to have been threatened said it was a student who was doing the harassing or bullying.[16] At the end of every year in Philadelphia, 27 percent of teachers leave their schools and, often, the District.[17] How can schools be expected to thrive with over a quarter of their full-time employees leaving at the end of every year?

Removing disruptive students

It's a well known fact that suspension, expulsion or any type of permanent removal of a disabled student from a general ed. classroom is nearly impossible in the SDP. Even in 2004, when the Individuals with Disabilities Education Act was again revised, supposedly giving more authority to school districts to determine if a disruptive disabled student should remain in the general classroom setting, there was only one major difference. Legislators added "committing serious bodily injury" to bringing in "guns, bombs or drugs" as a reason for removal.[18] The new version of IDEA left teachers and students in the same vulnerable position.

On my last day of subbing back in 2002, I was placed in a first-grade class where the teacher had been pushed backwards over a chair by one of her students. This particular child had been a consistent problem but nothing could be done until the teacher was injured. So with a couple of months left to go in the school year, the teacher went out on medical leave, the "troubled" student was finally removed from the class (and hopefully given the counseling and support he needed) and the rest of the students were condemned to a parade of substitutes of which I was the last. The new version of IDEA did nothing to make the situation any better. This type of scenario was playing itself out again and again.

> "In communities across the United States, educators, mental health practitioners, parents, and students have come face to face with the fact that even young elementary schoolchildren can become a threat to society and themselves."[19]
>
> —S. Duckworth, S. Smith-Rex, S. Okey, et al, 2004
> *Wraparound Services for Young Schoolchildren*
> *with Emotional and Behavioral Disorders*

Wouldn't it make more sense to remove these students from the environment *before* someone is hurt? Better yet, why make the general education classroom the default setting in the first place? IDEA did not _demand_ full inclusion of all students with disabilities. The law says "...to the maximum extent appropriate." How is allowing disruptive and sometimes dangerous students to remain in general classroom environments appropriate? Unfortunately, the SDP, along with the U.S. education system in general, has aggressively adopted inclusion. When graduation rates of children with disabilities began to rise, supporters of inclusion attributed this success to the fact that those children were participating in general education classes with their peers. What they did not acknowledge is that the children who benefitted most from inclusion were those with visual impairments, traumatic brain injuries and hearing impairments, who had graduation rates of 75 percent, 70 percent and 69 percent, respectively. However, along with children who were intellectually disabled, children with emotional and behavioral disorders—the very same students that study after study said would learn and perform better in separate special ed. classes—had the highest dropout rates at nearly 60 percent.[20]

So why, as time progressed, did the SDP continue to push more students with disabilities into general education classes at such high rates? Three words: Class. Action. Suit. In 2002, the school year I first began subbing, the U.S. Dept. of Education reported that Pennsylvania was the "7th lowest state" for including students with disabilities in "regular" education classes. By 2005, the state of PA and the Public Interest Law Center of Philadelphia—which represented the plaintiffs—settled with the agreement that PA would increase the number of students with disabilities in general education classrooms throughout the state.[21] (Similar actions were taking place across the U.S.) By 2014, nearly 66% of U.S. children between three and five who had special needs were placed in general education programs for part of the day, while 63% of special needs students between six and twenty-one spent 80% or more of their day in general ed. classes.[22] Across the U.S., almost 95% of special needs students between the ages of six and twenty-one spent some portion of their day in the general ed. environment.[23] This is their federal right. Whether or not they are disruptive, dangerous or hampering their own or someone else's educational progress.

All kids are special

Perhaps parents of children who have been bullied, harassed and distracted from their education by students with special needs should consider suing their school districts and states, as well as the federal government. With few exceptions, the inclusion discussion exclusively revolves around what's best for students with special needs. Which classroom environment is best for them? Which method of teaching is most appropriate for them? Not that these aren't important considerations. They definitely are, but what about the other children? Are the other children's rights secondary to those of children with disabilities? Is what's best for them merely an afterthought? From what I've witnessed, seems like the answer is "yes."

In the haste to accommodate children with special needs and to ensure they are not unfairly disadvantaged, or sometimes just to save money, we have deprived the greater number of public school students across America of the education they need. We have turned their classrooms into places where the primary focus is discipline and behavior management, and where there are no real consequences for disruptive behavior. In many instances, a dominant special needs student can supplant the teacher as the central authority in the classroom and become the "blueprint" from which the other kids model their behavior. I've seen it far too many times.

During this most recent outing as a sub, I had the opportunity to re-visit P.S. #11 where the sixth and seventh graders were as big as (or bigger than) me. In each class, there were a few particularly challenging students who argued, challenged, refused to do work, walked in and out of class at will, etc. They brutally cursed each other, "You monkey-looking whore." They harassed their classmates, "You actin' like you some goody-goody...trying to do work." And frustrated teachers complained about the lack of consequences for out-of-bounds behavior—another thing I heard over and over, this time and before.

Not surprisingly, I also encountered an older and bigger "Student X" type. She played around, instigated trouble and generally ignored me and the assignments at hand. I asked her to leave; she wouldn't. I called for backup. Someone came and escorted her out. (That's when I found out she didn't belong in the class in the first place. Since I had no class lists, how was I supposed to know?) Didn't matter anyway, she came right back.

I wouldn't have minded her being in the class. When you're a sub you have to be flexible, figure out which tactic is going to get the best result from and for the students. Nothing worked with this kid. I tried appealing to her sense of pride: "Be a leader. Set the tone. If you get to work, so will the others." I tried being firm. I called for backup a couple more times and tried to flag down a female school police officer who, seeing me in distress, rushed in the opposite direction. The same woman who came the first time eventually returned and escorted this child out again. Again, she was back within five minutes and when the class ended, she told me point blank, "I'll see you after lunch."

When she returned, I tried to lay down some rules: "If you want to stay in here, you have to do your work."

"Okay," she said, sliding past me. But instead of working, she locked her arms around another girl who was clearly uncomfortable.

"This is a hug," she said as I approached. "We're hugging."

"Can you hug after class?" I asked and she let go.

A short while later, she was arguing with the same girl. Before I could intervene again, she had grabbed this girl by the back of her head and slammed her face down on a desk...hard. Then she followed as the crying girl ran out of the room to "persuade" her not to tell.

I called the office again, "I need help now."

This time, one of the men from the climate team showed up, but the girl who had been attacked refused to go to the office to make a report.

"They haven't been able to do anything about it before. Why is this time any different?"

"She's gotta go," I said and the sympathetic and unafraid "Climate Guy" made her leave. Even though he was supposed to be somewhere else, he remained in the class to make sure she didn't come back.

Once she was gone, the rest of the kids settled down, stopped playing and got to work.

"You're one of the few subs who..."

"Cares?" a student cut in.

"...actually tries to do work with the kids," he said to me. "Stay out of grown folks' conversation," he said to the student.

Lowering his voice, Climate Guy confided that just the day before, the same student I was struggling with had stolen another sub's cell phone and sent out embarrassing text messages to her husband and friends. The substitute had to call the police...the real police...to get it back. (The police also made an appearance the day I was there but no one told me why.)

"She's dangerous," he continued. "She does what she wants when she wants. And we can't do anything about it because she's special needs."

When he finally left, I closed the door. I had kept it open all day 1.) because it's usually safer if people can see you from the hallway and 2.) because it was stiflingly hot in the room and the door tended to jam. It's not cool to get locked out of or inside your class. I decided to risk it though because I didn't want that girl coming back. Everything was going fine. The kids were quiet and working. I was helping out where needed. Then we heard a knock at the door.

"Look first. It might be her," one of the boys warned.

As the others mumbled their agreement, the knob jiggled. Luckily, the door had jammed and didn't budge. By the time I lifted the shade, whoever had been there was gone. I heard a sigh of relief that could've just as easily come from me as one of the students in the room.

> School _Is_ the Trauma

*C*ountless students throughout the District are being educated in a state of anxiety and, for some, real fear on a daily basis. Kids fighting and running up and down the hallways; STS workers and climate staff physically removing students who often don't want to go; classmates who berate, bully and stalk; and teachers who are ignored, threatened and occasionally injured. Conditions like these are frightening to children. The kids in my class at P.S. #7 wanted to learn and have fun. They didn't want the stress of dealing with a troubled classmate. I know because they told me:

"Can you put X in another class?"

"I don't want him in here."

"Can he go back with New Teacher?"

They wanted X out but I certainly didn't have the authority to make it happen. The person they expected to teach and protect them was powerless. All I could do was try to put an end to whatever inappropriate thing he or any other student was doing, as quickly as possible.

I'm not claiming that all of the other kids in the class were angels, but most were manageable in the environment though some would have benefitted from more specialized instruction. I felt bad for these kids. They were stuck with a classmate who terrorized them. That year, the year before and probably the next one coming. (And if not him, someone else.) What kind of impact does learning in this type of environment day-in and day-out have on the developing mind of a child? Tonya D. Armstrong, Ph.D., M.T.S., a Licensed Child/Family Psychologist and Owner of the Armstrong Center for Hope in Durham, NC answered my question.

"Children who are exposed to such troubled students in the classroom are at risk for a number of psychological challenges, including higher levels of anxiety (from the real or perceived threat of a bully), disrupted academic achievement and, in some instances, suicidal behavior. From a psychosocial perspective, children [in disrupted environments] additionally suffer from the loss of social support, the absence of modeling and practice of pro-social behaviors, such as cooperation and healthy competition. They're also at increased risk for negative peer influence and may adopt and utilize bullying behaviors themselves."

There it was. Confirmation that the "blueprinting" I had been witnessing was real. Children are easily influenced but they are not stupid. Some of them will begin acting out if they see that this type of behavior gets the attention they want and need. Others will align themselves with the bully to avoid being bullied. Either way, this mimicry multiplies the threat and the disruption other students must endure and throws the classroom further into chaos.

The trauma/inclusion connection

One of the hot topics right now is early childhood trauma and how it affects current behavior and long-term health risk. Dr. Vincent Felitti, Chief of Kaiser Permanente's Department of Preventive Medicine and (from the CDC) epidemiologist Dr. David Williamson and Dr. Robert Anda, MD, MS designed and implemented the Adverse Childhood Experiences (ACE) study. This was a huge study that surveyed over 17,000 predominantly white, middle-class, middle-aged people with jobs and good health insurance. The participants were physically examined and asked to complete confidential surveys that included 10 questions related to different categories of childhood abuse, neglect and household challenges.[1,2] Below are examples of the types of questions asked:

1. "Before your 18th birthday, did a parent or other adult in the household often or very often... swear at you, insult you, put you down or humiliate you? Or, act in a way that made you afraid that you might be physically hurt?"

   Yes No

2. "Before your 18th birthday, was a biological parent ever lost to you through divorce, abandonment or other reason?" (This question seems to have been modified over time to include "abandonment or other reason.")

   Yes No

For each "yes" answer, participants were assigned one ACE. The results revealed that 2/3rds of the 17,000 participants had experienced at least one ACE.

And of that group, 87% had experienced more than one ACE, which means they experienced more than one form of childhood trauma. The more ACEs or "yes" answers, the greater the long-term risk for a wide variety of medical, social and emotional problems, such as lung cancer, heart disease, diabetes, some autoimmune disorders, alcoholism, depression, suicide, chronic absenteeism, being violent or the victim of violence, etc.[1,3] You can take the quiz yourself at https://acestoohigh.com/got-your-ace-score/.[*]

There has also been a lot of discussion about the link between the ACEs and ADHD-related behavior, which—once again—seems to be rampant in the SDP. Whether childhood trauma actually causes ADHD is still being debated; however, one thing physicians seem to agree on is that children who have experienced trauma often exhibit symptoms (inattention, hyperactivity and impulsiveness) that mimic ADHD but require a different type of treatment.[5]

In light of the ACE evidence, Philadelphia and other school districts throughout the U.S. have started to place more emphasis on "trauma-informed" teaching practices. This is a new approach designed to more compassionately and effectively manage children suffering from the effects of traumatic home circumstances.[6] I doubt that anyone would object to dealing with traumatized children in a more compassionate, sensitive and informed manner. I certainly don't. However, from what I've observed, **for a significant portion of children, the trauma they are experiencing is being introduced into their lives through the public school environment.** It's the result of being trapped in classrooms with students who are emotionally erratic, behaviorally challenged and sometimes violent—year after year after year. It's constantly hearing other children screaming or watching them fight during lunch or recess or class. It's sitting silently while classmates have meltdowns and STS workers and climate staff swoop in to remove them until the "episode" has passed. It's being hit, cursed and kicked. It's never knowing when they may become the target of another child's aggression or obsession, no matter how hard they try to fly under the radar.

Where is the compassion and sensitivity for these children?

---

[*] Though the ACEs are strong predictors for future development of chronic disease and emotional and social disorders, psychologists have pointed out that some people are just more resilient and may overcome difficulties more easily. Also, having at least one positive relationship with an adult (a grandparent, a teacher, a coach, a caretaker, etc.) can lessen the effects of the trauma a child experiences.[4]

There are those who will say that I am speculating; that I don't have the appropriate background to address this situation or that I don't know anything about the home lives of the P.S. #7 kids. I know I met or spoke with all of the parents and caregivers of the 110 students multiple times and gained a fair sense of what they were dealing with at home: One family had become displaced. They weren't on the street, but they also hadn't landed on their feet yet: trauma. Another family had been caught in the middle of a violent shooting, which resulted in an extended absence for the student: trauma. Another mother seemed to neglect her child, who was desperate for attention: trauma. One student in the class didn't seem to consistently have one person who was responsible for his wellbeing: trauma. And a couple of students had lost their fathers to illness or incarceration: trauma. It just so happens that five of these six kids were also the most challenging to manage. Their behavior ranged from jumpiness and excessive talkativeness to unprovoked crying and wandering around the class to outright hostility and violence.

The rest of the kids appeared to come from fairly stable homes where they were dealing with ordinary challenges. I spoke to moms, dads, grandparents, aunts and uncles. One thing they all expressed was a genuine concern for their children and a desire for them to do well in school. Quite honestly, most of them were angry and frustrated about the "crazy" environment in which their child was being educated. So was I. I can't tell you how many times I had to explain what happened at school that day. Why there was a bruise or scratch on someone's son or daughter. At the start of the 2017-2018 school year, I encountered students at P.S. #7 who were bright, thoughtful, helpful, enthusiastic about learning and who always had their homework done and their hands up. Each time I returned to the school, that enthusiasm had dried up a little more. I saw noticeable differences in their behavior that ranged from distraction and lethargy to agitation, anger, fear and physical volatility. In speaking with their parents, nothing seemed to have changed at home, but their school environment had continued to deteriorate with an in-and-out teacher, a classmate who bullied and harassed them and no consistent structure.

I fully acknowledge that I am not a medical doctor, psychologist or a research scientist. I am, however, a concerned citizen who has the right to care. And I can't help but wonder how much more insight we might gain if the ACE study were adapted or extended to include the environment where children spend the majority of their time—at school.

The ACEs Adapted for the School Setting[3]

1. Before your 18th birthday, did a ~~parent or other adult in the household~~ **student in your class** often or very often...swear at you, insult you, put you down, or humiliate you? **Or,** act in a way that made you afraid that you might be physically hurt?

Yes   No

2. Before your 18th birthday, was a ~~biological parent~~ **teacher** ever lost to you through ~~divorce~~, illness, abandonment, or other reason?

Yes   No

3. Before your 18th birthday, did a ~~parent or other adult in the household~~ **student in your class** often or very often...push, grab, slap, or throw something at you? **Or,** ever hit you so hard that you had marks or were injured?

Yes   No

4. Before your 18th birthday, was a ~~household member~~ **student in your class** depressed or mentally ill... **Or,** did a ~~household~~ **class** member attempt suicide?

Yes   No

A "yes" answer to any of these questions could indicate a negative impact on a child's current stress level and their future health. I expect most of the students in that P.S. #7 class would answer yes to all of these questions. I only adapted four questions because four "yes" answers is considered a very high score; one that indicates an extremely high risk for developing physical and/or social dysfunction, as well as odds of having a learning behavior problem 32 times higher than kids who have no ACEs.[1]

What are we condemning these children to? And what impact will that have on society as a whole?

Trauma-informed teaching practices may be helpful for children who come to the school environment already suffering from the effects of adverse experiences. But if trauma is being introduced in the school environment, wouldn't it make more sense to stop it before it starts? Placing emotionally and behaviorally challenged students in a specialized environment where they can get the extra help they need will not only benefit them, it will benefit the other students, as well.

What is the District doing about this?

Though the School District has done a fair amount to address the level of general violence in Philadelphia schools, it appears to have sat idly by while the negative effects of inclusion multiplied. Finally, in 2017, the SDP took steps to open a modern, 600-seat, $54-million school dedicated exclusively to the needs of students with disabilities. But after prolonged and vocal protests from parents, politicians and inclusion advocates who accused the SDP of building "a segregated school," the proposal was scaled back to $10M and 100 seats integrated into existing general education schools. The main goal of the initial proposal was to build a school so that special needs students in or headed to private placement with Wordsworth—a contractor that lost its license when the death of a student in its care was ruled a homicide—could be accommodated closer to home. In addition to bringing the Wordsworth students back under District supervision, the new school would also have been able to enroll additional students in need of more intensive services.[7]

One hundred seats may support many of the former Wordsworth students, but what about the students on waiting lists, or those who have yet to be diagnosed? According to District counselors and teachers and from what I've seen, Philly's school system is overburdened by the number of students who need support that cannot be obtained in a general ed. setting. We should be finding ways to create more specialized seats, not fewer. According to Eugene Frasier, M.Ed. in counseling and psychology and 17-year veteran of the SDP, some children have more intensive needs.

"I worked in several social services programs. One of them being Carson Valley, which is a program that works with students who have been separated from their parents because of problems in their homes."

In addition to behavioral and emotional problems that are the result of coming from an environment where they were abused or neglected, Mr. Frasier stated that some of the students also had "undiagnosed cognitive issues that required evaluation, observation and ongoing treatment."

Originally founded in 1907 as a school for indigent white female students, Carson Valley is a private institution that began to accept students regardless of race or gender in 1965.[8] Funded through the Department of Human Services, it currently supports students ranging from elementary through high school.

"We provided them with the services they needed so they would be able to go to school while [receiving help]," explained Mr. Frasier.

Though treatment is based on individual needs, the students have access to a comprehensive suite of services from medication and individual or family therapy to supervision of social interactions. The goal for all students is to be able to return to their families, communities and the public school system.

"Many of them came to Carson Valley in that program, got the help they needed, got the therapy, got into [the] social environment, did very well and then returned to their families. It's like a kid in a public school [who's] in special education—it's a service, not a sentence."

While the majority of the students in the Carson Valley program were victims of their home circumstances, Mr. Frasier acknowledged that some of the students were the source of the problems in their homes and also sometimes in their regular school environments.

"Many times family members are in denial that a child really has a problem... That means [teachers have] to talk to those parents intimately and find out what the needs of their son or daughter are. Get them to share if they have any medical or psychological problems... Nobody wants to admit that their child has a problem. They will deny [it] and say, 'He doesn't act like this at home.'"

Continuing, Mr. Frasier pointed out how crucial it is for teachers to establish a partnership with parents on day one in elementary school.

"So [they] can find out everything about this child; so [they'll] be able to really make the right interventions... However, in order for that to happen, parents have to share with [teachers] when that child starts school that he does have some problems. 'He will not sit down. I have to tell him to do things repeatedly...'"

According to Mr. Frasier, establishing this type of partnership between parents and teacher will ultimately show the child that somebody really cares about him.

"I can't stress enough how important this is."

Though many of the students in the Carson Valley program were able to successfully return to their families and their schools, a few continued to live and go to classes on campus until graduation, which afforded them the advantage of a low teacher-student ratio.

Said Mr. Frasier, "They were more prepared than some of the students that went back to the public schools because they got an intensive education intervention."

While he's very proud of the work at this full-service program, Mr. Frasier also feels that the regular public schools could be the right setting for children with complex emotional and behavioral needs, if the classroom has the right kind of supports.

"So if I'm teaching and I have 25 students but at least five of those students have problems following directions, staying on task, comprehending what's going on in an educational setting and I have a classroom assistant, I can delegate to that assistant to work with that child. If I don't have that kind of support in class, then, as the teacher, I've got to spend my time constantly redirecting other students that just do not have the ability to stay on task, to focus [and] follow directions. This also impedes their ability to get what's going on in reading, math and whatever is being taught."

"What about the other students?" I asked. "Does that behavior, being unable to focus and stay on task, disturb the other students and impede their ability to learn?"

"Yes," he said. "They do disturb the other students. And the teacher has to try to keep those students focused and stop them from buying into the distraction. But some students are influenced. Peer pressure is very powerful in the classroom."

As we parted, Mr. Frasier shared one final thought.

"There has always been a lot of talk about creating full-service schools that have a clinical component. These schools would offer all the services—medical, dental, psychological and therapeutic—that students and their families need. Then [parents] wouldn't have to take the child out of school to take him somewhere else to get the service. That's the idea," he said, "but it's still not being done."[†]

What is painfully obvious to anyone who spends a portion of time in the average SDP classroom is that whatever we are doing isn't working. There are solutions out there. We've discussed quite a few in this book alone. But solutions cost money. Lots of it. Interestingly, I've been told—point blank—on many occasions that there's no more money for Philly's public schools.

"There just isn't."

It's as if people view Philadelphia as this huge, money-guzzling monster that wastefully squanders its allotment check then greedily returns to beg for more.

"Where's this money coming from?"

That's another question I get when I bring up the funding shortage and scarcity of resources in Philadelphia schools. And up until recently, my response was always the same: "Where do we get the money for everything else? For wars and weapons...and a wall?"

The answer is we get it from the middle-class tax base, which literally pays for everything in America. Whether we agree with it or not. However, while researching this book, I learned that most of the SDP's money issues have been the result of the state of Pennsylvania's nearly criminal underfunding of the School District of Philadelphia. There *is* money. Let's take a look at why Philly isn't getting its fair share.

---

† In 2016, Philadelphia Mayor Jim Kenney shepherded a new soda tax through City Council. The revenue from that tax is dedicated to free head start/pre-school programs, park clean-up and the support and development of community schools, where students have access to counseling and other social services. According to a 2018 Research for Action study, the formula for community schools isn't quite right yet, but they're still working on it.[9]

> Show Me the Money

*E*ducation financing is complicated. So bear with me while I try to break it down into simpler terms. Money for U.S. public schools primarily comes from three sources: the federal government, the home state and local taxes. We all know that wealthier townships/districts within states can afford to direct more local tax dollars toward educating their students. What you may not know is that poorer schools have been victimized at every funding level starting at the top. Back in 2006, *the Funding Gaps Report* from the Education Trust offered a series of articles on public school financing that really opened my eyes to this travesty. Here's what you need to know:

> "Wealthier, higher-spending states receive a disproportionate share of Title I (federal) funds, thereby exacerbating the profound differences in education spending from state to state. Title I makes rich states richer and leaves poor states behind."[1]
>
> —Goodwin Liu, former Assistant Professor of Law at U.C. Berkeley Co-director of Chief Justice Warren Institute on Race, Ethnicity & Diversity, "How the Federal Government Makes Rich States Richer"

The Report also examined the unfair manner in which many states distributed funds to their own school districts. Some States turned a blind eye to the higher costs of educating poorer students and the smaller contributions less wealthy districts received in local taxes. Across the U.S., poorer districts were receiving between $800 and over $1,000 less *per student* in combined state and local revenue.

> "In 26 of the 49 states studied, the highest poverty school districts receive fewer resources than the lowest poverty districts... Four states–Illinois, New Hampshire, New York, and *Pennsylvania*–shortchange their highest poverty districts by more than $1000 per student per year."[2]
>
> —Ross Weiner and Eli Pristoop, Education Trust, "How States Shortchange the Districts That Need the Most Help"

Unfortunately, this bias also existed within school districts, as well. Administrators routinely directed more money toward teacher salaries and other resources in more affluent neighborhoods instead of to the schools that needed it most.

> "...almost universally, school districts themselves magnify those initial inequities by directing more non-targeted money to schools and students with less need."[3]
>
> —Marguerite Roza, former Research Assistant Professor in the Center on Reinventing Public Education at Washington University, "How Districts Shortchange Low-income and Minority Students"

By 2015, the Education Trust's *Funding Gaps Report* showed that many states were still providing more in combined state and local funds to more affluent districts, while the poorest districts were getting even less, about $1200 per student less. When viewed based on race, the situation was even worse. Many school districts across the U.S. with high percentages of children of color were being shortchanged by an average of $2000 per student.[4]

That same year, respected Data Scientist and Visual Analytics Consultant, David Mosenkis, testified on behalf of POWER* in front of PA's Basic Education Funding Commission. Using charts, graphs and hard figures, he made it painfully clear that in Pennsylvania, it is race—not poverty—that is a more reliable predictor for which school districts receive less money. Many poor, predominantly white school districts were still getting their fair share

---

*POWER is an interfaith organization committed to building communities of opportunity that work for all. They represent over 50 congregations throughout Southeastern and Central Pennsylvania.[5]

of funding, while districts with higher percentages of children of color, like Philadelphia, were being short-changed by over $1900 per student.[6] $1900 x Philly's 130,000 plus[†] students added up to $247 million less than what the SDP should have received for a district its size.[7] (Visit tiny.cc/pafairfunding for a brief video overview.)

In response to Mr. Mosenkis's testimony, the bi-partisan PA Funding Commission hammered out the first-ever **fair funding formula**. This new method determined exactly how much each district should receive based on various factors, including number of students, poverty level, local taxing capacity, number of English language learners and population density.[8] The Commission then submitted its new formula to the General Assembly, which instead of making educational funding fair once and for all, chose to double down on injustice and write a 30-year-old "hold harmless" policy into law[6].

The 2016 PA General Assembly, Act 35, House Bill 1552 states, "The hold harmless provision in basic education funding ensures no school district will receive less basic education funding than it received in the previous year."[9]

The problem is that in the above amendment, "the previous year" refers to 2015—the year before the fair funding formula was created.

"The way the law is written, no district can ever get less than they got [in 2015] even though that means a lot of districts are getting more than twice their fair share according to the formula."

—David Mosenkis, POWER

PA politicians made one concession: Any *extra* money that might be set aside for education in the future would be distributed fairly, through the new formula.[6] Some considered this progress. It wasn't. In 2016, Mr. Mosenkis completed a study in which he compared the amount districts were actually getting with what they *should* be getting according to the fair funding formula. (Philadelphia should have been receiving an additional $300 million per year.[10]) The results clearly demonstrated that despite small budget increases distributed through the formula, whiter schools were still receiving way more money.

---

† This total excludes students in charter, alternative, out-of-district special education schools, etc.

"People are under the illusion that it's getting better," said Mosenkis, "but in the 2018-2019 school year, 91% of education money was distributed in the old, unfair way and 9% went through the fair funding formula."

That's 5.5 *billion* dollars[8] distributed in a way that leaves school districts with high numbers of children of color under-resourced, overcrowded and ill-supported. And according to Mosenkis, it's getting worse:

"In 2016, predominantly white districts received around $1900 more per student. Now it's up to $2300 more per student and it'll be $2400 by 2020."

We actually have a solution that politicians have chosen to ignore. *Why?*

"There are a lot of districts [in PA] that are not wealthy," Mr. Mosenkis shared, providing more insight. "They may be lower middle class or working class districts that are rural, overwhelmingly white...but they're struggling, too. They're not struggling as bad as Philadelphia, Reading and Chester, but they're struggling. They're not getting enough funding. They're getting more than their fair share of an insufficient pot of money. But they don't know they're getting more than their fair share. They just know they don't have enough resources... and they don't know that these urban districts are struggling even worse than they are. So to ask those districts, 'Hey, how 'bout if we cut your funding next year so that urban districts can have more...why would they be interested in that? And why would their representative in the legislature support something like that?"

He paused, then continued, "Another side is that working class white districts don't tax themselves nearly as heavily as urban districts do. They've been able to not kill themselves on property taxes because they are getting more than their fair share [of education funding] from the state...the fair funding formula takes that into account."

Anyone who's paying attention knows the only real way to make PA education funding equitable is to start from scratch and apply the fair funding formula across the board. This may sound like a fight that can't be won, but there is already growing support for it. In March of 2019, State Representative, Chris Rabb, D-Phila., introduced House Bill 961, which calls for "...100 percent of state funds for public schools to be distributed through the fair funding formula..."[11] The bill is co-sponsored by a group of 63 democrats *and* republicans.[10] And in

June of 2019, more than 1000 protesters representing over 60 individual groups marched on the state capitol to demand an end to racial bias in funding.

In the meantime, since elected PA State Representatives allow this injustice to continue, several PA school districts, state organizations and individual parents—represented by The Education Law Center of Philadelphia and The Public Interest Law Center—have joined forces to sue the state for biased and inequitable education funding. This is the first time a suit against PA's discriminatory funding practices hasn't been blocked by the State Supreme Court.[12] PA is not the first in the union to be sued and it probably won't be the last. About half of America's 50 states have been court-ordered to make their funding practices fair for all schools within their jurisdiction.[13]

Just in case you were wondering, there are other states where the whitest school districts still receive more money in combined state and local funding. According to the 2018 *Funding Gaps Report*, those states are: Alabama, Colorado, Florida, Idaho, Illinois, Iowa, Kansas, Montana, Nebraska, New York, North Dakota, Texas, Virginia and Wyoming. A big shout-out to the states that seem to be doing their best to provide equitable funding to all school districts and all children: Ohio, Louisiana, New Jersey, Minnesota, Massachusetts and Arkansas.[‡14] If they can do it, any state can—and should—do it.

Is Philly really *that* broke?

Let's take a look at a few reasons why school funding has been such an ordeal for Philadelphia:

1. **High poverty.** Philadelphia is the poorest big city in America. One in every four people live in poverty; half of them with an average income of less than $10,000 for a family of three. (One adult and two kids.)[15]
2. **Historically low/unfair real estate taxes.** In comparison to neighboring counties, Philadelphia County taxes are quite low. Within the City, the value of similar properties varies widely. Even after reform in 2018, an independent auditor labeled Philly's method of tax assessment "flawed," with "residential home values [and subsequent tax payments] off by an average of 20%." You guessed it. Owners of lower-priced houses

---

‡ Vermont, Alaska, Hawaii and Nevada were excluded from analysis by The Education Trust for various reasons.[14]

are paying too much, while owners of higher-priced properties are paying too little.[16]

3. **Tax-exempt buildings and land.** Philly is an old, historic city. The *Declaration of Independence* was signed here. There are tons of monuments, museums, churches and other non-profit organizations. In fact, Philly has one of the highest percentages of land owned by nonprofits in the country. And these nonprofits pay either low or no real estate taxes.[17]

4. **10-year tax abatements.** To stimulate real-estate improvement and development, Philly launched a Tax Abatement Program in 2000. Residents and developers were given a pass on real estate taxes for 10 years. That means no or very low real estate taxes on renovated and new construction properties for a full decade after renovation and/ or purchase.[18]

5. **Historically corrupt Parking Authority.** The state of PA took control of Philly's Parking Authority in 2001, around the same time it took over the School District of Philadelphia. Between 2012 and 2017, the Parking Authority cheated the SDP out of over $77 million through "wasteful spending and uncollected fees." During this same time, the Parking Authority also came under scrutiny for workplace harassment, payouts,[19] patronage (hooking up buddies with jobs)[20] and excessively high ticketing in poor communities of color where people are least likely to challenge fines.[21]

6. **Inadequate funding contributions from the state of PA that are not only discriminatory, but which helped dig the financial hole from which Philadelphia has yet to escape.**

This confluence of economic and political issues, along with some past "mismanagement" of funds within the SDP itself, has nearly bankrupted Philadelphia and its schools, again and again.

So, where *should* the money come from?

Let's say we all agree. Poor and/or minority kids deserve the same, first-rate public education that rich and/or white kids receive. Here's where we get the money.

#1 The Great State of Pennsylvania: We're all clear on this one, right? PA needs to increase the overall education funding budget and distribute all of the money through the fair funding formula. *Period.*

#2 Philly's 10-year Tax Abatement Program: It's time to say bye-bye to big real-estate tax breaks for the wealthy. Supporters of Philly's Tax Abatement Program claim that construction costs are expensive and completed buildings do not generate the higher rents of places like New York and San Francisco. A tax break encourages developers to do business in Philly. According to the *Building Industry Association Abatement Summary,* as these tax breaks expire and people are required to pay what they owe, Philadelphia will be able to collect more money. They projected that by 2020, expired abatements would add up to over $100M per year in new taxes and over $160M per year by 2026 and every year thereafter, as long as the tax abatement program remained the same.[18] And with 55% of that money earmarked for the SDP, that means between $55M and $88M a year for Philly's schools. Here's the problem: *It's not fair and it's not enough.*

There's no denying that the abatements have had a profound impact on the revitalization of some (not all) areas of the city, but continuing the program would just be unfair. The people who benefitted most (wealthy developers and homebuyers) could, if required, scrape together the money to pay their taxes. In the meantime, middle and working class Philadelphians pay their taxes. Also the City and School District have been gypped out of millions in revenue for 20 years. During that time, public schools have fallen more deeply into disrepair and further behind. While $55 million is nothing to sneeze at, it's a mere drop in the bucket for a District in need of more than $4 *billion* in remediation and repairs that do not include upgrades like air conditioning and laptop computers.

The issues are critical and ongoing. In October of 2019, *6 ABC Action News* reported that over a thousand students from two different Philadelphia schools were displaced because of dangerous asbestos conditions. Two weeks later, both student bodies were relocated to temporary housing where classes were able to resume. After more than a year of focused, intensive efforts, mess-ups and re-starts, the SDP is still only at the beginning of fixing this District-wide problem. What's that expression about "the tip of the iceberg?" *That's* where we are, folks.

So kudos to Philadelphia Mayor Jim Kenney and City Council members who commissioned an independent analysis to help determine the economic impact of limiting or eliminating the tax abatement program all together. Ten different scenarios were studied, including options for phasing out the abatement over time and capping the tax break for selected areas. Weighing short-term revenue gain against long-term construction revenue and job loss, the study determined:[22]

A. The Abatement Program allowed Philadelphia to remain competitive with other Northeastern cities during the recession.
B. Though the recession is over, all options for changing or stopping the program would result in less construction revenue and fewer construction jobs in the future.
C. The two options with the least impact on future construction revenue and jobs were:
   1. Continuing to offer the abatement, but with diminishing percentages (10% less for each year, e.g., 90% in year 2, 80% in year 3 and so on) which, reportedly, would eventually cut the abatement by about 50%.[23]
   2. Completely eliminating the School District's portion of the abatement (55% of every tax dollar), which would generate the most immediate funds (between $58-68M per year[22]) now... not ten or fifteen years down the line after we've failed another generation of children.

Unfortunately, in December of 2019, City Council voted to move ahead with option A, which will require more time to generate desperately needed funds. The new program also won't apply to commercial real-restate endeavors, which I suspect account for a high amount of lost tax revenue.[23] I also suspect that this part of the program was left intact to lure businesses that will generate jobs...for people who either live in the suburbs or who have relocated to Philadelphia from other cities. While I am disappointed (and a bit indignant) about this outcome, I still give this current iteration of City Council points for beginning to curtail a program that has relentlessly siphoned money from Philly and its public schools for the last 20 years. I also give them points for including a reassessment clause that kicks in every three years. Perhaps next time, they will be braver.

#3 Charter Schools: Though the SDP is not participating in the fair funding lawsuit against the state of PA, Superintendent Hite appears to be fighting back from within the system. In his 2015-2019 *Five-Year Financial Plan*, Hite revealed that charter schools across PA were receiving $350 million dollars annually for services that support special ed. students; however, collectively charter schools "only spent $156 million on those students."[24,25]

If you're like me, you're probably wondering if this is legal and what happened to all of that extra money? It's simple. In an interview with *The Philadelphia Notebook*, the Education Law Center of Philadelphia revealed research showing that not only do charter schools enroll fewer students with disabilities; they also tend to enroll students who have less expensive disabilities to support (illegal). The schools are then free to do whatever they want with the leftover money (legal). Though the spokesperson for the Education Law Center acknowledged that all charter schools do not discriminate based on disability, he did label it a *"city-wide pattern."*[26]

Superintendent Hite tactfully requested that the state change its funding formula to more accurately address the expenses of District-run public schools across PA, which educate the vast majority of special needs students (including those with the most expensive disabilities).[25] Correcting the special needs payment formula could add "an extra $100 million dollars" to the annual budget of Philadelphia's District-run schools alone.[24,25]

#4 Philly's Beverage Tax: In 2017, Mayor Kenney and City Council implemented a special tax on drinks that contain added sugar—1.5 cents per ounce. Granted it's steep, almost 50 cents on a thirty-two ounce Snapple, but the majority of the real complaints seem to come from a few politicians, beverage manufacturers, distributors and retailers. In 2019, lobbyists for the American Beverage Association unleashed a torrent of commercials claiming that since Philadelphia (for the first time in a long time) had a budget surplus (around $300M, which is not a lot for a city of its size) the soda tax should be eliminated.[27]

The reason the beverage tax was instituted in the first place was to fund park clean-up, community schools and pre-school programs,[27] which experts have identified as the single most important component of a successful start to an education. It should be a requirement for all of Philadelphia's children, not a luxury for a chosen few. By 2023, the beverage tax is expected to provide revenue of about $75 million per year.[28] That money will fund 20 community schools with built-in social services and over five-thousand additional pre-school seats.[29] I could be wrong but I think the residents of Philly get it: pay a little more for soda and get a better education for children in the neighborhood, including their own.

#5 The Philadelphia Parking Authority: City Council members have been lobbying the state of PA to relinquish control of Philly's Parking Authority. While the agency has made progress under new leadership and contributions to the SDP have increased, there still seem to be too many ties to the past (when the Parking Authority was steadily gypping Philly out of money) and too many mistakes. With the proliferation of Uber, Lyft and other ridesharing companies, the agency will need very careful oversight to avoid repeats of the 2018 failure to collect nearly $250,000 in owed taxes. Luckily, Uber discovered the error and fessed up.[30] It's time for authority over The Authority to return to the City that has a vested interest in making it an efficient and transparent organization.

Real-world impact

It's obvious that a lack of funding affects everything from the cleanliness, safety and maintenance of school buildings to a lack of resources, such as textbooks, technology and quality teachers. But when it comes to inclusion, reading about a bunch of statistics, trends and policies can distract us from the fact that we're talking about real children who grow up to be real adults facing the truly unfortunate consequences of being poorly educated. At a recent community meeting, members of my church and surrounding neighbors watched a presentation about turning our newly vacant convent into housing for homeless college students. About halfway through, a young woman shared her story, which once again brought me back to the lasting impact of an insufficient education.

Though now a stable and successful professional with a master's degree, Marissa Meyers from Northeast Philadelphia found herself among the rapidly growing numbers of college students who experience housing insecurity.

"Here I am looking like I come from privilege," she said, "but I didn't. I grew up in the foster system."

Thanks to student loans, Marissa was able to get the funds she needed to pay college tuition, but there wasn't enough to cover housing, especially after she paid for "the never-ending cycle of remedial classes" she was forced to take. Though she never slept on the street, Marissa did a lot of "couch surfing," crashing with different friends or college staff members every night, never knowing where she'd be staying long-term.

A product of the SDP, Marissa ties her desperate financial situation directly to being academically unprepared for college.

"Remedial classes counted for absolutely nothing and they cost the same as regular college-level courses. They say public school is free. It's free until you get to college and have to pay a lot of money to learn what they didn't teach you for free in public school."

Like Marissa, some kids are fortunate enough or resilient enough to rise above the circumstances of a poor education. Others aren't so lucky. For many, inclusion has become a reliable component in a system of oppression that creates and maintains Philadelphia's cycle of poverty. Let's take a look at how the inclusion effect plays out over and over again:

THE INCLUSION EFFECT

1. Students with uncontrolled, disruptive disabilities go without the support needed to help them be successful in a general classroom setting—leaving them to distract and detract from the education process *every day.*

2. Inappropriate, upsetting and sometimes violent behavior becomes a "normal" part of the classroom setting, depriving *all* students of a first-rate academic and social education *year after year.*

3. A high percentage of students either drop out (30% in Philly)[31] or graduate with academic and/or social deficiencies that leave them unprepared for college and the workforce.

4. Some former students end up in the criminal justice system, while many others find themselves stuck in low-paying jobs with a lack of upward mobility or forced to take remedial college courses to gain basic knowledge and skills.

5. The next generation of students—often the children of the above children—attend the same underfunded, underperforming schools where continuous disruption all but guarantees an insufficient education and a place in Philadelphia's underclass.

©Clayvon C. Harris

Inclusion has had a devastating effect on both the School District and the communities of Philadelphia. Yet this is not just an inner-city problem. Let's take a look at how our neighbors in the suburbs are handling some of these same issues.

> A Nationwide Concern

*B*ack in 2001, when I first started subbing, people claimed that school environments like the ones I describe in this book were confined to urban schools. They blamed "the deep poverty of the inner-city" or "the parents." This time around, I heard similar claims. While I do not discount the important roles either of these two factors play, I do believe they have become catch-all excuses for inaction. The truth is that administrators in the suburbs and on the outskirts of Philadelphia are less inclined to allow students with emotional and behavioral challenges to diminish the orderliness of their institutions. Some ensure that students get the help they need quickly. Others are more willing to suspend, transfer or block admission.

One of my recent assignments was in the lower Northeast at a predominantly white, special-admit school with a fairly decent reputation. As usual, there were a couple of kids in each class who were out-of-control: harassing and fighting with other students and disrupting the work at hand. When I called for assistance, members (plural) of the climate team showed up quickly to remove them from class. To one of these kids, a woman said, "You? Oh, keep it up. *Please...*" and she clasped her hands as if in prayer. "We're building a file on you and you will be outta here by the end of the year." At some schools, this is a strategy for dealing with difficult-to-manage students. Build a case and get them out. They have the manpower and determination to protect their school environment from volatile students and they do.

Later, I shared this experience with my friend "Tessa," who is white and lives in Bucks County, a predominantly white suburban area. In turn, she shared a deeply personal story about her son, "Mason," who has special needs that began to manifest when he was in preschool.

"He was disruptive and destructive," said Tessa. "He didn't hit kids but he would hit teachers. He would climb on tables. He would throw things. He would find your weakness and exploit it."

Over the next two years, she fought for an official diagnosis that would get her son the support he needed.

"I could not find a single [agency] that would provide services I could pay for. It didn't exist. It's all paid by Medicaid and I'm not eligible for Medicaid. But Mason *had* to have Medicaid."

Tessa also couldn't find a preschool that was able to handle her son's disability. She and her husband enrolled Mason in a Southampton preschool with a good reputation.

"It was pretty clear he wasn't going to make it. They'd be calling us twenty minutes after we dropped him off. "

During this period, Tessa worked continuously to secure services for Mason through Bucks Intermediate Unit (BIU). But it took so long to get someone to come observe him that she and her husband were politely invited to enroll their son in a different school. They transferred him to a pre-school that guaranteed they could handle his special needs.

"But they could not. Mason's teacher would scream at him and get very frustrated, which made him act out even more," said Tessa.

Within six months, the new school was begging the people at BIU for an evaluation. This time, they came and determined that Mason qualified for services.

"But one teacher. Specializing in autism. One time a week. Didn't help," remarked Tessa.

Once again, she and her husband were asked to remove Mason. Surprisingly, his previous preschool allowed him to return.

"They knew what they were getting into," said Tessa. "But I think they had forgotten."

The staff helped as much as possible, supporting Tessa's appeal for more comprehensive services. Finally, BIU did a full behavior assessment and gave Mason the services he needed.

"But it was too late," she said. "It's a great school and they tried their damnedest...but apparently screaming 'motherfucker' 200 times at the top of your lungs is the breaking point."

Again, they were asked to remove Mason from school and he spent the remainder of the year at home, awaiting the start of kindergarten. Tessa's husband took a leave of absence to watch and work with their son.

"[My husband] told his job, 'You can fire me, but I have to be home with my kid. I won't be back until we get this worked out. And I don't know how long that's going to be.'"

To Tessa, it was clear Mason needed medication, but he was too young. The only psychiatric practice in their area refused to see him before he turned five. Even then, only one of their doctors was willing to treat a child that young. He confirmed what Tessa suspected all along: "ADHD and high intelligence. A really bad mix," she said.

In college, Tessa had majored in pharmaceutical business with a concentration in chemistry. Because she had a general understanding of how medications work, she had already begun to do some research.

"I went in requesting Ritalin, but the doctor recommended and prescribed Adderall. When I say it fixed him..." she said, pausing. "He is a completely different child on Adderall. The medication allows him to focus and sit still."

By this point, Centennial School District had identified Mason as a student in need of extra behavioral support, "above and beyond what can be provided in a typical classroom."

"You have the right to an education," Tessa commented. "And you have the right to be as close to your regular classroom as possible. For Mason, his typical classroom would be at Davis, which is a mile from our house. They can provide a one-on-one aide. They can also provide a different curriculum. They can modify that curriculum in any way for any student in any class. But if [a student] needs to be reminded six different times to do whatever, they can't accommodate that in a regular classroom. And Mason needed more than that— way, way more than that."

Fortunately, Centennial had a plan in place. There are three general elementary schools and each one supports a specific disability. With this format, the three schools are able to accommodate all of the disabled students in the District.

According to Tessa, "McDonald focuses on occupational therapy for children with physical disorders. Davis focuses on support for autism. And Willow Dale focuses on emotional support for kids who are troubled, violent and/or socially behind. My son is behaviorally behind but intellectually ahead; he's high IQ, very low EQ [emotional quotient]. So he was sent to Willow Dale, which is a 45-minute bus ride away."

Willow Dale offers small classrooms that have ten or less students, a teacher and an aide who are both trained to support students with emotional and behavioral challenges.

"They also have a small room with white painted walls, no windows, nothing on the wall," commented Tessa. "A child can go in there and they can scream and curse and kick, whatever they want to do, safely away from everybody else."

The main goal for students in this program is to transition 100 percent into the general classroom setting. But to start, Tessa had to fight so that Mason could spend at least 20 percent of his time in the general education class, even though he had a one-on-one aide.

"Typically, [the students] don't get a one-on-one in addition to being in this class because that's a lot. Mason was identified to have a one-on-one *and* be in the class. He was considered the worst of the worst coming in. But that was all pre-Adderall."

The medication worked so well for Mason that starting on day one, he was allowed to remain in the general education classroom full time.

"He's actually excelling in school. Maybe three or four times over the last six months, he's been pulled into the emotional support class, which I say is pretty darn good for him."

In fact, in just one month after he started school, Mason was approved to return to his neighborhood school, Davis, which has tests scores above the state average and is generally considered a better school.[1] But instead of switching him back immediately, Tessa decided that he would finish the year at Willow Dale.

"His regular ed. teacher is amazing and really connected with him. And the emotional support services are in the same building. He still has access to that teacher as well, who works with him on things that he doesn't inherently know or that he has a harder time learning."

At the start, every day for fifteen minutes or so, Mason would go to her and she would teach him about feelings and about the different zones. Like, 'I'm in the green zone, so I'm happy. I'm in the yellow zone, which means I'm frustrated; or I'm in the red zone which means I'm angry. And any zone is okay, but for school we need you to be in the green zone...' Or, 'When you hurt someone, you have to say you're sorry...' Now, when the baby falls down, Mason is the first to run over and see if he's okay. "

Tessa is quick to acknowledge how much progress her son has made and how highly she thinks of Willow Dale.

"The teachers, the principal...everyone is very involved with the whole emotional support aspect of the school. When Mason had a problem on the school bus, the *principal* drove to meet the bus to straighten it out."

Tessa believes that early intervention in a supportive school setting along with the appropriate medication were the keys to Mason's success. She also feels that her son can now be just as successful at Davis. And, since her other son will be starting there in the fall, she'd like both of them to be at the same school.

"I won't be able to be as involved as I want if I'm splitting my time between schools."

So back he goes to Davis...*with* the continued support of his one-on-one aide. Reflecting back on all the family has gone through, Tessa admits that it was very hard.

"During the most challenging times, my husband and I had this running joke—ADHD and high intelligence. Is he going to use his powers for good or for evil? Elon Musk or Charles Manson? We were joking but we knew Mason had great potential, but the behaviors were getting in his way. So we had to get him the help he needed in order to become a productive and compassionate member of society. Instead of someone who is just constantly in survival mode."[*]

Not too far away in another suburb of Philadelphia is Montgomery County's North Penn School District. Median home values range from $280K to $318K and the average household income is about $106K.[2] In 2016, full inclusion was implemented in the school district. In 2018, the School Board began to reconsider how they could make full inclusion work better for all students.

Said Jenna Ott, School Board Director for North Penn, "There are areas where inclusion is really working for the entire population. Children with disabilities, as well as the rest of the students who are having the opportunity

---

[*] Mason is now doing so well at his new school that he's being evaluated for the gifted program and his one-on-one aide is being phased out.

to interact and develop those compassion skills that a lot of kids are lacking these days."

According to Ms. Ott, inclusion is working best for North Penn at the middle and high-school levels because older students in the district were not educated under the new, full-inclusion model.

"They were getting more of the one-on-one [support] they needed, so I think they were more prepared, more ready to be a part of full inclusion as older students."

But North Penn still has "more work to do" at the elementary level.

"Going to full inclusion, we're not able to meet all the needs of the younger students. That's an area where there needs to be a little more one-on-one, a little more support. Some of these kids might need an hour or two a day where they are not in a classroom because they need that time to focus themselves and to regulate their emotions."

While acknowledging that there are some younger students who are thriving in the full-inclusion environment, Ms. Ott is another person who cautions against a one-size-fits-all education model because no two children are the same. In order to gain greater insight into how full inclusion was working for North Penn, she and another board member visited schools and talked to the people who are in the trenches every day—the teachers.

"We heard [about] kids putting teachers in chokeholds when they're upset. That's something we've heard multiple times. We've also heard and seen the effects of a child that actually pulled the shelves off the wall..."

All at the elementary level.

Another issue Ms. Ott is concerned about is the response to that behavior. Rather than removing the child who is having difficulty and providing that child with a "safe space to calm down and to work through those emotions," the response has been to remove all of the other students. That's because teachers do not have the right to remove a child who doesn't wish to be removed. So, instead of learning, the other kids are ushered into the hallway to wait and later, go home upset.

"To a certain degree," Ms. Ott continued, "I think we're normalizing that behavior for all these other kids. So not only then do we have to have the support in place to address that particular child, but we have to address the impact [that child] is having on the other children who are witnessing [the behavior], having their day interrupted and falling behind."

Two years into full inclusion, North Penn also began to face a teacher shortage which, according to a 2019 Economic Policy Institute press release, "... is large and growing for our nation's schools." (When certification, training and experience are taken into account, the deficit is particularly severe in areas of high poverty, like Philadelphia.[3])

"Some [teachers] have been injured by children on the job, others are frustrated by policies that don't allow them to give a child a hug to help them work through the issues they're having," said Ott. "We're losing good teachers because they're retiring early or they're walking away for other careers. We're asking too much of them."

In July of 2018, the North Penn School District Board of Directors unanimously voted to hire one of the leading behavioral threat assessment consultants to train school personnel in the identification, assessment and management of students who may have emotional issues. The proposed plan would also increase the availability of mental health resources for students who need them. Training and implementation of the new program was scheduled to begin on August 1 of 2018 and continue into 2019.[4]

When asked why North Penn chose to go full inclusion in the first place, Ms. Ott responded: "To be fair, I don't know because I wasn't on the Board at the time, so I wasn't involved with the decision. I would speculate that it was a combination of money and, really, just trying to make sure we were doing the best for the students."

These two stories made me question whether or not there is a link between the surge of students with emotional and behavioral disorders being integrated into America's general ed. classrooms and the increase in school shootings throughout the country. Often, after one of these horrifying episodes, we hear that other students could tell something was "off." Or, that the shooter had a "history of mental illness." Rarely, if ever, do we hear anything about what was being done or had been done to help the student navigate his or her challenges beforehand. Were they attending sessions with counselors or psychologists?

Were they enrolled in a class that provided emotional and behavioral support? Why have we been missing the signs?

According to everytown.org, a gun safety advocacy group backed by Michael Bloomberg, there have been about 500 school-related shootings throughout the U.S. (grade schools, high schools and colleges) since the 2012 tragedy that took place at Sandy Hook Elementary School. These shootings have occurred in every type of community all across the U.S.[5] CNN.com has also been tracking school shootings. When you look closely at these numbers, a couple of things jump out. While there are more school-related shootings in communities of color, black communities in particular, the incidents normally take place after regular school hours. In predominantly white communities, the shootings usually take place while classes are in session and more people—students, staff and teachers—are hurt or killed.[6] In both scenarios, people are dying and it's tragic. The inclusion trend has flooded a staggering number of volatile students into inner-city classrooms. Perhaps this same trend has funneled volatile, white, suburban students into the general ed. setting where their emotional and mental health issues are being overlooked.

A recent report on discipline issues from the ACLU revealed that American schools are dangerously understaffed when it comes to counselors and psychologists. Despite the fact that students (low-income students in particular) are *21 times* more likely to visit school-based mental health professionals,[7] 14 million students are in schools that have no counselor, nurse, psychologist or social worker." Sadly, what they do have in abundance is school police officers which, according to studies, have not contributed to a safer environment or reduced mass shootings in any way.[8]

Sometimes specialized programming *is* the answer.

After I finished subbing the first time around, I volunteered once a week for two years at Northern Home for Children's After-School Partial Program where I helped kids with their homework. My most startling moment came while working with one of my favorite students. Though we normally got along great, one day, he had a meltdown I couldn't handle. Luckily, there were others nearby who were trained to deal with his emotional challenges. As I watched Kevin, the Program Director, calm this child, it occurred to me that he (along with the other kids in the program) was one of those students I routinely kicked out of my classes for disrupting the environment and preventing the rest of the students from learning. Shamefully, I had written those kids off. This program showed me that given the right structure—personal attention, trained counselors and instructors, high ratio of adults to children, academic rigor—there can be hope.

Providing emotionally and behaviorally disordered children with additional support will help them reach their full potential. Isn't that what we want for them? *And* if special education was not doing that…if it was not working the way it was supposed to…if it was not providing a safe and productive environment… perhaps the solution should have been to *fix* it, instead of breaking general education, too.

Now that we know the truth…that education funding is inequitable and, in many instances, corrupt; that decrepit, old school buildings like those in Philadelphia expose students and staff to toxic substances with lasting physiological and neurological effects; and that when it comes to inclusion, we are allowing political correctness to override common sense…our next step is to acknowledge that Philadelphia does not stand alone. These issues affect millions of children across the U.S. and it's time to do something about it. Parents and caregivers, listen to what your children are saying about school…*and demand better.* Educators, tell the truth…*don't help hide the problems.* Elected officials, *it's time to get to work.* Though well intentioned, the inclusion mandate in the Individuals with Disabilities Education Act (IDEA) has been misinterpreted and abused. It often does more harm to the general population of students than it does good for the students it is meant to serve. *Fix it.* For real, this time. For the sake of all students (with and without special needs) who are being cheated out of a first-rate education.

> *Afterword*

*I*n May of 2019, the School District of Philadelphia announced a Comprehensive School Planning Review to, among other things, examine projected changes in population and communities and optimize building use and capital investment. This initiative is meant to help make good on Superintendent William Hite's goal of ensuring that "all children have a great school close to where they live."[1] While this project is said to be one of the most ambitious education reform programs in Philly's long history, it's important to remain clear-eyed: Having a great school in a neighborhood is not the same as all students in that neighborhood being able to attend that school.

In November of the same year, Superintendent Hite (with support from Board of Education President Joyce Wilkerson, Councilwoman and long-time education advocate Helen Gym, Councilwoman Cindy Bass and State Senator Vincent Hughes) outlined a new environmental safety improvement plan. Among other things, it includes the hiring of outside consultants to help assess, implement and manage the cleanup of asbestos, lead and other toxic substances in Philly's schools. The plan had an aggressive timeline of having all asbestos-related remediation completed by the start of classes in 2020.[2]

The Philadelphia Federation of Teachers initiated a lawsuit against the District in January of 2020, asking for more capable management of the situation, more collaboration and greater transparency. By February of 2020, ten different schools had been closed because of severe asbestos issues; only a few had reopened.[3] *Then came coronavirus.* Hite and his team responded swiftly to the developing crisis, requesting and receiving $11M to provide every public school student in the City with laptops to finish the school year from home.[4] In one fell swoop, the entire District was dragged into the 21st century, while also freeing many teachers and students from ongoing lead and asbestos exposure, under-resourced classrooms and distracting and sometimes violent student behavior.

During this same period, the SDP came under fire for results from the 2019 National Assessment of Educational Progress (NAEP). Philly students performed poorly: Only 17% of fourth and eighth graders scored proficient or better in reading on the NAEP. 18% of fourth graders and 16% of eighth graders scored proficient or better on the math portion of the test.[5] Overall, that's fewer than 20% of students "passing" the test, similar to results from previous years.

In December of 2020, Philadelphia's School Board introduced the aspirational "Guides and Guardrails" plan to combat Philly's low student achievement. The plan listed "questions, visions and conditions," such as:

- "Every school will be a safe, welcoming and healthy place where our students, staff and community want to be and learn each day."
- "Every student will have a well-rounded education with co-curricular opportunities."
- "Every parent and guardian will be welcomed and encouraged to be partners in their child's school community."[6]

And no practical, actionable explanation for how they were going to get there.

By August of 2021, Philadelphia's students returned to in-person learning. Experienced and thoughtful administrators, educators, public health experts and other consultants put together a plan to keep students and teachers safe while coronavirus rages on. But children, younger ones in particular, act on instinct. And their human instincts tell them to hug, hit, kiss, argue and otherwise invade the personal space of other kids and teachers. Then there are students who have specific disabilities that make it very difficult for them to exercise self-control under the best of circumstances. For this complex plan to keep everyone safe and healthy, *everyone will have to follow the rules pretty perfectly.* And no one is perfect.

At the federal level, President Joe Biden signed into law the $1.9 trillion American Rescue Plan Act of 2021. It includes $122 billion in support for states and schools to help address the effects of the pandemic on U.S. students, as well as $3 billion specifically earmarked for "special needs."[7] It is projected that the SDP has $1.1 billion coming its way through September 2024. According to its website, the administration has put forth a plan for allocating funds[8]:

- $350M to Support Educational Recovery and Accelerate Learning (summer programs, after-school programs, career immersion opportunities, etc.)

- $325M to Improvements for Safety, Health and Modernization of Philly's schools (asbestos and lead paint removal, etc.)
- $150M for Support of Social and Emotional Needs of Students (increased social services, counselors, discretionary funds for schools, etc.)
- The last "focus area," More Supports in Schools to Help All Learners and Educators Succeed, includes special education resources: "50 psychologists, 10 occupational therapists, 20 speech therapists in the short-term **to accelerate student evaluations and pursue long-term system wide redesign.**"[8]

Unfortunately, this last focus area is the only one that does not have a financial commitment associated with it. And in the SDP's more comprehensive "Lump Sum 5-Year Fiscal Plan," the bullet point addressing "long-term system wide redesign" is missing all together.[9] Is this is an oversight? Was system-wide redesign of special education an afterthought or an update to the website that came after the initial plan was presented? Are they still evaluating the necessary funding commitment?

Clearly, the District's environmental hazards, overcrowding, under-resourcing, etc., need to be eliminated. But we must also put a stop to the daily disruption of the education process by students who are struggling under the weight of unmanaged emotional and behavioral disabilities. Disabilities, which according to studies, would be better addressed in smaller classroom settings staffed with teachers and aides who are specifically trained to support them. Making this a priority is critical to the success of these students, as well as the success of their current classmates, teachers and the SDP overall. The restructuring, reimagining and refunding of Philly's public school system is an opportunity that may not come again. *So, we have to get it right. This time.*

Note: In September 2021, School District of Philadelphia Superintendent William Hite announced that he would not be renewing his contract, which ends in August of 2022.

> *Acknowledgements*

*W*hen it comes to the City's schools, native Philadelphians and newcomers alike have stepped up. In addition to individual volunteers, nearly every local company, foundation, organization and club sponsors some type of program, service, grant or party that supports Philly's schools. Much of this sustained awareness and commitment is the result of unrelenting coverage of all school-related matters by *The Philadelphia Public School Notebook* and *The Philadelphia Inquirer/Daily News*, local ABC, CBS and NBC news affiliates, as well as WHYY, WURD, WDAS, *The Philadelphia Tribune* and many other media outlets in Philly and across the country. For the last 20 years, they have alerted us to the fact that one of the most basic rights of U.S. citizenship—access to a free, quality education that enables the pursuit of happiness—was vanishing from Philadelphia's landscape. I shudder to think where the School District would be without these watchful journalists. They deserve the grateful thanks of an entire city. They definitely have mine.

On a personal note, I'd like to thank: Sr. Marianna R. Fieo, SSJ and Roy McKinney, Jr. for their professional guidance and honest feedback; Nancy Hills for reading and checking and re-checking every single PSSA and Keystone score in the book; my beloved aunt, the late Edith V. Roberts and my "godfather," Paul Styer, for passing along education news I may have missed; Pastor Joseph Okonski, Ted Travis and Larry Notis for allowing me to print and photocopy to my heart's content; Constance D. Lindsay, DMA, D.Min for her thoughtful comments; Robyn Tucker and Diana Mitchell for their insight into suburban services for children with special needs; Sr. Joan Alminde, SSJ, Karen Savin Benjamin, Doreene Hamilton, Ann Marie Miller, Najah Haqiqah, Marilynne Diggs-Thompson and the late Michael Ajakwe, Jr. for their encouragement over the years; Joel Catindig for his initial thoughts on the cover design; Monica Hagen for that last critical proof; Liz Shope for her calming presence and beautiful designs; Sid Holmes who first said the word "book;" and all of the candid, forthright and concerned educators, counselors, parents and students who spoke with me on and off the record. *May God bless you all.*

> *End Notes*

Introduction

1.   Lori Shorr, Executive Advisor & Chief Education Officer to Mayor Michael Nutter, "The Philadelphia Great Schools Compact," School Reform Commission Meeting Presentation, November 16, 2011.

2.   Eva Travers, "Philadelphia School Reform: Historical Roots and Reflections on the 2002-2003 Under State Takeover," *Perspectives on Urban Education Journal*, 2, no 2, Fall (2003), accessed March 3, 2017, http://www.urbanedjournal.org/archive/volume-2-issue-2-fall-2003/philadelphia-school-reform-historical-roots-and-reflections-2002-

3.   "About Us, Charter Schools," School District of Philadelphia website, accessed March 4, 2017, link no longer available. Data on file, Angelwalk LLC.

4.   Brian Gill et al. *State Takeover, School Restructuring, Private Management, and Student Achievement in Philadelphia.* © Copyright 2007 RAND Corporation, accessed August 3, 2017, http://www.rand.org/content/dam/rand/pubs/monographs/2007/RAND_MG533.pdf

5.   Cremata, Davis, Raymond et al. *National Charter School Study 2013, Center for Research on Education Outcomes (CREDO)* Stanford University, Stanford, CA.

6.   Press release: "Online Charter School Students Falling Behind Their Peers," Mathematica Policy Research & Center on Reinventing Public Education (CRPE) & Center for Research on Education Outcomes (CREDO) Stanford University, (2015) accessed January 31, 2019, https://www.crpe.org/search/site/Online%20Charter%20School%20Students%20Falling%20Behind%20Their%20Peers

7.   Arianna Prothero, "Is There a Growing Political Backlash to For-Profit Charter Schools?" *Education Week* website, Charters & Choice Blog, September 17, 2018, accessed February 9. 2019, https://mobile.edweek.org/c.jsp?cid=25920011&item=http%3A%2F%2Fapi.edweek.org%2Fv1%2Fblog%2F129%2Findex.html%3Fuuid%3D77462

8.   *High School & the Future of Work—A Guide for State Policymakers*, XQ Institute, Fall 2018, Issue 1.

9.   *The Condition of College and Career Readiness, 2017*, ACT Internet Site, accessed September 10, 2019, https://www.act.org/content/act/en/research/condition-of-college-and-career-readiness-2017.html.

10. Laura Jimenez et al. *Remedial Education: The Cost of Catching Up*, Center for American Progress, September 28, 2016, accessed September 10, 2019, https://www.americanprogress.org/issues/education-k-12reports/2016/09/28/144000/remedial-education/

11. Robert G Lynch and Patrick Oakford, *The Economic Benefits of Closing Educational Achievement Gaps: Promoting Growth and Strengthening the Nation by Improving the Educational Outcomes of*

Children of Color, Center for American Progress, November 2014, accessed September 10, 2019, https://cdn.americanprogress.org/wp-content/uploads/2014/11/WinningEconomyReport2.pdf.

12. *The Economic Impact of the Achievement Gap in America's Schools,* McKinsey & Company, Social Sector Office, National Dropout Prevention Center website, April 2009, accessed September 10, 2019, https://dropoutprevention.org/wp-content/uploads/2015/07/ACHIEVEMENT_GAP_REPORT_20090512.pdf

13. *The Condition of Education 2019,* National Center for Education Statistics, Reading Performance, p.1, accessed February 2, 2019, https://nces.ed.gov/programs/coe/pdf/coe_cnb.pdf.

14. Eric A. Hanushek et al. "Economic Gains from Educational Reform by US States," *Journal of Human Capital,* 11, no. 4, 447-486, doi: 10.1086/694454.

PART 1: Inside the SDP (2001-2002)

1. "Race/Grade Report," School District of Philadelphia, December 5, 2000.

2. Connie Langland, Susan Snyder, et al. "Report Card on the Schools," *The Philadelphia Inquirer,* March 3, 2002: 10-12.

3. "PSSA Results, Academic Year 2000-2001," State of Pennsylvania Department of Education, accessed March 24, 2017, link no longer available. Data on file, Angelwalk LLC.

4. *Mental Health: A Report of the Surgeon General.* Rockville, MD: U.S. Department of Health and Human Services, Substance Abuse and Mental Health Services Administration, Center for Mental Health Services, National Institutes of Health, National Institute of Mental Health, 1999.

5. Seth Gershenson et al. *The Long-Run Impacts of Same-Race Teachers,* Working Paper 25254, National Bureau of Economic Research, doi:10.3386/w25254.

6. Jill Rosen, "Black students who have one black teacher are more likely to go to college," November 12, 2018, accessed October 20, 2019. https://hub.jhu.edu/2018/11/12/black-students-black-teachers-college-gap/.

PART 2: Update on the Schools

Between Then & Now

1. Vince Lattanzio, "Nearly 4,000 Philadelphia Teachers, School Staff Losing Jobs," NBC 10 Philadelphia, June 7, 2013, accessed January 29, 2017, https://www.nbcphiladelphia.com/news/local/Layoff-Notices-Looming-Over-Philadelphia-School-District-210577111.html

2. Greg Windle, "In Philadelphia, school police outnumber counselors," *The Philadelphia Public School Notebook* website, March 16, 2017, accessed March 18, 2017, http://thenotebook.org/articles/2017/03/16/school-police-outnumber-counselors.

3. "Persistently Dangerous Schools," Pennsylvania Commission on Crime and Delinquency website, Office of Safe Schools Advocate, School Safety, Persistently Dangerous Schools, accessed March 15, 2020, https://www.pccd.pa.gov/ossa/school-safety/Pages/Persistently_Dangerous_Schools.aspx

4. Mike DeNardo, "Superintendent of Philly schools receives performance report card," CBS Philly 3 website, December 22, 2016, accessed January 20. 2019, http://philadelphia.cbslocal.com/2016/12/22/superintendent-of-philly-public-schools-receives-performance-report-card

5. Kristen A. Graham, "Philly teachers OK new contract; now, how to pay for it?" *The Philadelphia Inquirer* website, June 19, 2017, accessed January 21, 2019, http://www.philly.com/philly/education/philly-teachers-ok-new-labor-contract-now-how-to-pay-for-it-20170620.html

6. *Action Plan Update 2018, Progress + Priorities,* ©2018 School District of Philadelphia.

7. "2017-2018 Dashboard, City-wide, Performance Overview," School District of Philadelphia website, accessed March 19, 2019. https://dashboards.philasd.org/extensions/philadelphia/index.html#/

8. "2017-2018 Dashboard, City-wide, Student Achievement," School District of Philadelphia website, accessed March 19, 2019. https://dashboards.philasd.org/extensions/philadelphia/index.html#/keystone.

9. *Facility Condition Assessment* report, Parsons Environment & Infrastructure Group, Inc., School District of Philadelphia website, January 2017, p. 8, accessed March, 20, 2019, https://www.philasd.org/capitalprograms/wp-content/uploads/sites/18/2017/06/2015-FCA-Final-Report-1.pdf

10. John Kopp, "These are the 12 most rundown schools buildings in the School District of Philadelphia," *Philly Voice* website, January 27, 2017, accessed July 28, 2017, http://www.phillyvoice.com/these-are-the-12-most-rundown-school-buildings-in-the-school-district-of-philadelphia/

11. Barbara Laker et al. "Toxic City. Sick Schools. Danger: Learn at your own risk" *The Philadelphia Inquirer* website, May 3, 2018, accessed July 16, 2018, http://www.philly.com/philly/news/lead-paint-poison-children-asbestos-mold-schools-philadelphia-toxic-city.html

12. Press Release: "Governor Wolf, Philadelphia officials announce 15.6 million to improve conditions at public school," Governor's Office of Communications, School District of Philadelphia website, July 5, 2018, accessed July 19, 2018 https://www.philasd.org/communications/2018/07/05/governor-wolf-philadelphia-officials-announce-15-6-million-to-improve-conditions-at-public-schools/

13. "Building Improvement Update," The School District of Philadelphia website, December 6, 2018, accessed March 20, 2018, https://www.philasd.org/facilities/wp-content/uploads/sites/71/2018/12/Winter-Building-Improvement-Update-12.6.18.pdf.

14. Wendy Ruderman et al. "Philadelphia school kids get added protection from lead perils," *The Philadelphia Inquirer* website, December 13, 2018, accessed March 20, 2019, https://www.philly.com/news/philadelphia/lead-paint-philadelphia-schools-protections-toxic-city-20181213.html

15. Oliver Milman and Jessica Glenza, "At least 33 U.S. cities used water-testing 'cheats' over lead concerns," *The Guardian* website, June 2, 2016, accessed January 20, 2019, https://www.theguardian.com/environment/2016/jun/02/lead-water-testing-cheats-chicago-boston-philadelphia

16. "Lead Toxicity: What Are Possible Health Effects from Lead Exposure?" Centers for Disease Control website, Agency for Toxic Substances & Disease Registry, Environmental Health and Medicine Education, June 12, 2017, accessed March 20, 2019, https://www.atsdr.cdc.gov/csem/csem.asp?csem=34&po=10

17. Xu G et al. "Twenty-year trends in diagnosed attention-deficit hyperactivity disorder among US children and adolescents, 1997-2016," *JAMA* Netw Open, doi:10.1001/jamanetworkopen.2018.1471.

18. "State-based Prevalence Data of Parent Reported ADHD Diagnosis by a Health Care Provider," Centers for Disease Control website, accessed March 21 2019, https://www.cdc.gov/ncbddd/adhd/prevalence.html

19. Greg Windle, "School lead testing bill moves out of Council committee unanimously," *The Philadelphia Public School Notebook* website, December 3, 2018, accessed December 5, 2018, https://thenotebook.org/articles/2018/12/03/school-lead-testing-bill-moves-out-of-council-committee-unanimously/

20. Marilyn V. Howarth, MD, FACOEM, Director, Community Engagement Core, Center of Excellence in Environmental Toxicology, Perelman School of Medicine, University of Pennsylvania, "Prepared Remarks," December 3, 2018.

21. Wendy Ruderman et al. "Toxic City. Sick Schools. Hidden Peril." *The Philadelphia Inquirer* website, May 10, 2018, accessed July 16, 2018, https://www.inquirer.com/news/inq/asbestos-testing-mesothelioma-cancer-philadelphia-schools-toxic-city-20180510.html

22. "Dashboard Facts, Total Number of Schools 2017-2018," School District of Philadelphia website, accessed July 30, 2018, https://dashboards.philasd.org/extensions/philadelphia/index.html#/

23. Press release: "Governor Wolf: Restore Pennsylvania Would Help Remediate Contaminants in Pennsylvania Schools," PA Dept. of Education website, March 21, 2019, accessed March 22, 2019, https://www.governor.pa.gov/wp-content/uploads/2019/02/20190204-Restore-PA.pdf

24. Kristen Graham, "Price tag for fixing all urgent Philly school building problems? $170M, union, lawmakers say," *The Philadelphia Inquirer* website, March 29, 2019, accessed September 26, 2019, https://www.inquirer.com/education/philadelphia-school-district-lead-asbestos-building-safety-million-fix-20190329.html

A Word on Standardized Testing

1. "PSSA Results, Academic Years 2000-2001," State of Pennsylvania Education Website, accessed March 24, 2017, link no longer available. Document/s on file, Angelwalk LLC.

2. Diane Ravitch, *Reign of Error–The Hoax of the Privatization Movement and the Danger to American Public Schools.* New York, NY, Vintage Books, A Division of Random House LLC, 2014.

3. Meredith Broussard, "Why Poor Schools Can't Win at Standardized Testing," *The Atlantic* website, education archive, July 15, 2014, accessed June 23, 2017 https://www.theatlantic.com/education/archive/2014/07/why-poor-schools-cant-win-at-standardized-testing/374287/

4. "School Progress Report – Parent and Family Guide," School District of Philadelphia website, Office of Evaluation, Research and Accountability, March 31, 2017, accessed August 18, 2018, https://www.philasd.org/performance/wp-content/uploads/sites/85/2017/07/SPR-Parent-Guide_English_Final.pdf

5. "About the Standards, Myths vs. Facts," Common Core website, accessed March 27, 2017 http://www.corestandards.org/about-the-standards/myths-vs-facts/

6. William R. Hite, Jr., Ed.D, Superintendent, "Letter to School District of Philadelphia Community," August 6, 2015.

7. Shannon Puckett, Director, *Defies Measurement*, March 26, 2015, accessed August 17, 2017, www.defiesmeasurement.com or www.youtube.com

Update P.S. #1

1. James R. Sadler, "No School Left Uncorrupted: How Cheating, High-Stakes Testing, and Declining Budgets Affected Student Achievement in Philadelphia,"01 April 2013. *CUREJ*, 163 (2013), University of Pennsylvania, https://repository.upenn.edu/curej/163/

2. "SY 2007-08 Persistently Dangerous Schools," Pennsylvania Department of Education website, accessed May 4, 2017, link no longer available. Document/s on file, Angelwalk LLC.

3. "SY 2008-09 Persistently Dangerous Schools," Pennsylvania Department of Education website, accessed May 4, 2017, link no longer available. Document/s on file, Angelwalk LLC.

4. "Philadelphia School District Accepts $730,676 Multi-Year Grant to Improve School Climate from the Philadelphia Foundation's Fund for Children," Philadelphia Foundation website, accessed March 22, 2017, https://www.philafound.org/press-releases/philadelphia-school-district-accepts-730676-multi-year-grant-to-improve-school-climate-from-the-philadelphia-foundations-fund-for-children/

5. Aaron Moselle, "3 Northwest Philly principals honored with Lindback award," NBC 10 Philadelphia website, April 16, 2015, accessed August 22, 2017, https://www.nbcphiladelphia.com/news/local/philly-principals-honored-lindback-award/66228/

6.   PSSA Results, Academic Years 2001-2002 through 2011-2012, State of Pennsylvania Education Website, accessed March 24, 2017, link no longer available. Document/s on file, Angelwalk LLC.

7.   "Keystone Exam Results, Academic Years 2012-2013 through 2017-2018," State of Pennsylvania Education website, accessed January 25, 2019, link no longer available. Document/s on file, Angelwalk LLC.

8.   "Safe Schools LEA Report, District Level Report, Philadelphia 2015-2016," PA Dept of Education website, accessed January 9, 2017, link no longer available. Document/s on file, Angelwalk LLC.

9.   "Safe Schools LEA Report, District Level Report, Philadelphia 2011-2012," PA Dept of Education website, accessed January 9, 2017, link no longer available. Document/s on file, Angelwalk LLC.

10. "Safe Schools Statewide Report, 2015-2016," PA Dept of Education website, accessed March 24, 2017, link no longer available. Document/s on file, Angelwalk LLC.

11. "Safe Schools School Report, 2015-2016," PA Dept of Education website, accessed May 5, 2017, link no longer available. Document/s on file, Angelwalk LLC.

Update P.S. X:

1.   "PSSA Results, [P.S. Y] Academic Years 2008-2009 through 2010-2011," State of Pennsylvania Education website, accessed July 22, 2017, link no longer available. Document/s on file, Angelwalk LLC.

2.   James R. Sadler, "No School Left Uncorrupted: How Cheating, High-Stakes Testing, and Declining Budgets Affected Student Achievement in Philadelphia," *CUREJ*, 163 (2013), University of Pennsylvania, https://repository.upenn.edu/curej/163/

3.   Benjamin Herold for *NewsWorks*, "Philly district suspends school rating system, seeks fix," November 1, 2012, *The Philadelphia Public School Notebook* website, accessed April 10, 2017, http://thenotebook.org/articles/2012/11/01/philly-district-suspends-school-rating-system-seeks-fix

4.   "PSSA Results, Academic Years 2001-2002 through 2011-2012," State of Pennsylvania Education website, accessed March 24, 2017, link no longer available. Document/s on file, Angelwalk LLC.

Update St. Athanasius School

1.   "St. Athanasius," GreatPhillySchools.org, accessed March 25, 2017, https://greatphillyschools.org/schools/st-athanasius-school

2.   "Mission Statement," Philadelphia School Partnership website, accessed March 15, 2020, https://philaschoolpartnership.org/

3.   "TerraNova Tests Scores," data on file, St. Athanasius School, September, 2019. Tabulated by CTB/McGraw-Hill Companies, Inc.

4. Coleman Poses, "An Analysis of How Philadelphia School Partnership Has Implemented Its Mission," Alliance for Philadelphia Public Schools website, August 25, 2015, accessed June 30, 2017, https://appsphilly.net/an-analysis-of-how-the-philadelphia-school-partnership-has-implemented-its-mission-2/

5. "School Progress Reports, All Schools Batch Report," School District of Philadelphia website, District Performance Office, accessed April 10, 2017, https://www.philasd.org/performance/programsservices/school-progress-reports/available-spr-reports/

6. Press Release: "Governor Wolf Announces PSSA Testing Reduction to Benefit Students, Teachers, and Parents," PA Governor's Office, August 14, 2017, accessed November 14, 2017, https://www.governor.pa.gov/governor-wolf-announces-pssa-testing-reduction-benefit-students-teachers-parents/

Update P.S. #2

1. Kristin A. Graham and Dylan Purcell, "City School's Fast-rising Test Scores Questioned," May 1, 2011, *The Philadelphia Inquirer* Archives.

2. Kristin A. Graham and Dylan Purcell, "Tighter Scrutiny, Lower PA Test Scores," July 29, 2012, *The Philadelphia Inquirer* Archives.

3. "PSSA Results, Academic Years 2001-2002 through 2017-2018," State of Pennsylvania Education website, accessed January 25, 2019, link no longer available. Document/s on file, Angelwalk LLC.

4. Susan Snyder et al. "Underreporting Hides Violence," March 28, 2011, *The Philadelphia Inquirer* Archives.

5. Mike DeNardo, "Parents' Protest Disrupts SRC Meeting On School Closures" CBS Philly Eyewitness News, February 22, 2013, accessed June 23, 2017, http://philadelphia.cbslocal.com/2013/02/22/parents-protest-disrupts-school-reform-commission-meeting-on-school-closures/

6. Kevin McCorry, "4 Elementaries Added to Philly District Schools Slated for Intervention." Whyy.org, March 4, 2016, accessed June 23, 2017, https://whyy.org/articles/4-elementaries-added-to-philly-district-schools-slated-for-intervention/

7. Press Release: "District Announces New Turnaround Schools Model," School District of Philadelphia, March 10, 2016.

Update P.S. #3

1. "Mission & History," Mastery Charter School Website, accessed September 17, 2019, https://www.masterycharter.org/about/mission-history/

2. "PSSA Results, Academic Years 2001-2002 through 2017-2018," State of Pennsylvania Education website, accessed January 25, 2019, link no longer available. Document/s on file, Angelwalk LLC.

3. Dale Mezzacappa, "Mastery Chief Speaks Out about Oprah," *Philadelphia Public School Notebook* website, Sept 21, 2010, accessed June 23, 2017, http://thenotebook.org/ articles/2010/09/21/mastery-chief-speaks-about-oprah

4. Barack Obama, "The Importance of Education Reform," Obama addresses National Urban League, YouTube website, accessed June 3, 2017, https://www.youtube.com/ watch?v=ZCHMyFU6aEU

5. John Thompson, "The 70% Solution," Alexander Russo's This Week in Education website, November 16, 2009, accessed June 3, 2017, http://scholasticadministrator.typepad.com/ thisweekineducation/2009/11/thompson-the-70-solution.html#.WTIOrWgrJPY

6. "Programs, School Improvement Grants: Examples of Successful Efforts," U.S. Department of Education website, Mastery Schools, Philadelphia, PA, August 26, 2009, accessed June 3, 2017, https://www2.ed.gov/programs/sif/examples.html

7. Jenny Seng, "Mastery Shoemaker–Sweating the small stuff," *The Philadelphia Public School Notebook* website, December 1, 2009, accessed July 12, 2017, http://thenotebook.org/ latest0/2009/12/01/mastery-shoemaker-sweating-the-small-stuff.

8. Kristen A. Graham and Kelly Heinzerling, "Philly principal hit with a brick at dismissal," June 1, 2017, *The Philadelphia Inquirer* Archives.

9. "Keystone Exam Results, Academic Year 2015," State of Pennsylvania Education website, new link accessed March 18, 2020 https://www.education.pa.gov/DataAndReporting/ Assessments/Pages/Keystone-Exams-Results.aspx

10. "Demographics & Data," StartClass website, Graphiq Knowledge Graph database, Graphiq Research Sites, Public-schools.startclass.com, accessed July 10, 2017, link no longer available. Document/s on file, Angelwalk LLC.

11. "School Progress Report Parent and Family Guide," School District of Philadelphia website, accessed March 18, 2019, https://cdn.philasd.org/offices/performance/SPR_Files/Parent_ Guide/SPR_Parent_Guide_English.pdf

12. "School Progress Reports, 2015-2016 High School Batch All Schools," School District of Philadelphia website, District Performance Office, accessed April 10, 2017, https://www. philasd.org/performance/programsservices/school-progress-reports/available-spr-reports/

13. Kristen A. Graham, "Top, most improved Phila. schools named," January 31, 2017, *The Philadelphia Inquirer* Archives.

14. Avi Wolfman-Arent, "Has Mastery lost its mojo? The quest to fix Philly's biggest charter network," WHYY website, November 14, 2016, accessed March 16, 2019, https://whyy.org/ articles/has-mastery-lost-its-mojo-the-quest-to-fix-phillys-biggest-charter-network/

15. "College Signing Day," Mastery Charter Schools, June 24, 2013, accessed July 17, 2017, YouTube website, https://www.youtube.com/watch?v=mC5ak6jBnAo

16. Casey Fabris, "Mastery students celebrate 'College Signing Day.'" June 4, 2014, *The Philadelphia Inquirer* Archives.

Update P.S. #4

1. Celeste Lavin, "School-specific data related to closing decisions obtained," March 14, 2011, *The Philadelphia Public School Notebook* website, accessed June 3, 2017, http://thenotebook.org/articles/2011/03/14/school-specific-data-related-to-closing-decisions-obtained.
2. "PSSA Results, Academic Years 2001-2002 through 2013-2014," State of Pennsylvania Education website, accessed March 24, 2017, link no longer available. Document/s on file, Angelwalk LLC.

Update P.S. #5

1. Susan Snyder, "27 Phila. schools labeled dangerous by state officials," August 23, 2003, *The Philadelphia Inquirer* Archives.
2. "Public Hearing on the Proposed Closure of Middle School," presentation, February 23, 2009.
3. PSSA Results, Academic Years 2001-2002 through 2009-2010, State of Pennsylvania Education website, accessed March 24, 2017, link no longer available. Document/s on file, Angelwalk LLC.

Update P.S. #6

1. "PSSA Results, Academic Years 2001-2002 through 2017-2018," State of Pennsylvania Education website, accessed January 25, 2019, link no longer available. Document/s on file, Angelwalk LLC.
2. "School Progress Report, 2015-2016," School District of Philadelphia website, accessed July 27, 2017.
3. "School Progress Report, 2017-2018," School District of Philadelphia website, accessed June 27, 2019.

Update P.S. #7

1. "School District of Philadelphia, Facilities Master Plan: Summary of Recommendations," CBS Local website, February 2013_final, accessed March 20, 2020, https://philadelphia.cbslocal.com/wp-content/uploads/sites/15116066/2013/02/fmp-revised-recommendations-feb2013_final.pdf
2. James R. Sadler, "No School Left Uncorrupted: How Cheating, High-Stakes Testing, and Declining Budgets Affected Student Achievement in Philadelphia," *CUREJ*, 163 (2013), University of Pennsylvania, https://repository.upenn.edu/curej/163/
3. "PSSA Results, Academic Years 2001-2002 through 2017-2018," State of Pennsylvania Education website, accessed January 25, 2019, link no longer available. Document/s on file, Angelwalk LLC.

Update P.S. #8

1.   "PSSA Results, Academic Years 2001-2002 through 2017-2018," State of Pennsylvania
     Education website, accessed January 25, 2019, link no longer available. Document/s on file,
     Angelwalk LLC.

2.   Bill Hangley, Jr., "Waiting for the Renaissance," *The Philadelphia Public School Notebook* website,
     February 1, 2010, accessed June 24, 2017, http://thenotebook.org/articles/2010/02/01/
     waiting-for-the-renaissance

3.   Dale Mezzacappa, "What went wrong with Promise Academies?" *The Philadelphia Public
     School Notebook* website, April 1, 2015, accessed March 22, 2020. https://thenotebook.org/
     articles/2015/04/01/what-went-wrong-with-promise-academies/

4.   Kati Stratos et al. "Philadelphia's Renaissance Schools Initiative After Four Years," The
     University of Pennsylvania Graduate School of Education's Online *Urban Education Journal*.
     12, no. 1 (2015): 1-7, http://www.urbanedjournal.org/archive/volume-12-issue-1-
     spring-2015/philadelphia%E2%80%99s-renaissance-schools-initiative-after-four-years

5.   Dale Mezzacappa, "After schools are chosen, District discloses some Promise Academy
     details," *The Philadelphia Public School Notebook* website, April 7, 2010, accessed August 2, 2017,
     http://thenotebook.org/articles/2010/04/07/after-schools-are-chosen-district-discloses-some-promise-
     academy-details

6.   Benjamin Herold, "Promise Academy teaching staffs include many who are new,
     inexperienced," *The Philadelphia Public School Notebook* website, December 21, 2010, accessed
     July 28, 2017. http://thenotebook.org/articles/2010/12/21/
     promise-academy-teaching-staffs-include-many-who-are-new-inexperienced

7.   Martha Woodall et al. "Ackerman could be entitled to $1.5M in severance," July 23, 2011, *The
     Philadelphia Inquirer* Website, accessed March 28, 2020, https://www.inquirer.com/philly/
     news/homepage/20110723_Ackerman_could_be_entitled_to__1_5_million_severance.
     html#loaded

8.   Brian Gill et al. *State Takeover, School Restructuring, Private Management, and Student Achievement
     in Philadelphia*, © Copyright 2007 RAND Corporation, accessed August 3, 2017, http://www.
     rand.org/content/dam/rand/pubs/monographs/2007/RAND_MG533.pdf

9.   Press release, "District Announces New Turnaround Schools Model," School District of
     Philadelphia, March 10, 2016.

10. "School Progress Report, 2015-2016," School District of Philadelphia website, accessed
     August 2, 2017.

11. John Kopp, "These are the 12 most rundown schools buildings in the School District of
     Philadelphia," *Philly Voice* website, January 27, 2017, accessed July 28, 2020, http://www.
     phillyvoice.com/these-are-the-12-most-rundown-school-buildings-in-the-school-
     district-of-philadelphia/

12. "Acceleration Network," School District of Philadelphia website, accessed February 7, 2020,
     https://apps1.philasd.org/onlinedirectory/view-network.jsp?ulcs=3570

Update P.S. #9

1. "PSSA Results, Academic Years 2001-2002 through 2017-2018," State of Pennsylvania Education website, accessed January 25, 2019, link no longer available. Document/s on file, Angelwalk LLC.

2. "School Progress Report, 2015-2016," School District of Philadelphia website, accessed July 26, 2017.

3. Kevin McCorry for *NewsWorks*, "Philly SRC votes to phase out two middle schools," February 19, 2016, accessed June 26, 2017, *The Philadelphia Public School Notebook* website, https://thenotebook.org/articles/2016/02/18/src-votes-to-phase-out-two-middle-schools/

4. Bob Brooks, "Mom says bullying led to 10-year-old son's death in Germantown," 6ABC News website, May 13, 2017, accessed July 24, 2017, http://6abc.com/news/mom-says-bullying-led-to-10-year-old-sons-death/1986682/

5. Alicia Victoria Lozano, "Philadelphia School District Reeling From 3 Student Suicides," NBC Philadelphia website, May 25, 2017, accessed July 24, 2017, http://www.nbcphiladelphia.com/news/local/3-Philadelphia-Area-Students-Die-By-Suicide--424398114.html

6. "Three recent deaths among Philadelphia students," Fox 29 Philadelphia website, May 24 2017, accessed March 22, 2020, https://www.fox29.com/news/three-recent-deaths among-philadelphia-students

7. "High School Youth Risk Behavior Survey," Philadelphia, PA 2015 and United States 2015 Results, Centers for Disease Control website, Accessed July 24, 2017, https://nccd.cdc.gov/youthonline/App/Results.aspx?TT=G&OUT=0&SID=HS&QID=QQ&LID=PH&YID=2015&LID2=XX&YID2=2015&COL=&ROW1=&ROW2=&HT=QQ&LCT=&FS=S1&FR=R1&FG=G1&FSL=&FRL=&FGL=&PV=&C1=PH2015&C2=XX2015&QP=G&DP=1&VA=CI&CS=N&SYID=&EYID=&SC=DEFAULT&SO=ASC&pf=1&TST=True

Update P.S. #10

1. Evan Leach, "Arts Link: Building Competencies in Mathematics and Science through an Arts Integration Model," Final Report for the U.S. Department of Education, Executive Summary, pp. 2-3, Philadelphia Arts in Education Partnership website, accessed August 9, 2017, http://www.paep.net/images/images/Arts_Link_Final_Report_TAP.pdf

2. "Dashboards: Enrollment, Student Demographics, Students by Race/Ethnicity, Gender and Age," School District of Philadelphia website, accessed March 22, 2020.

3. "School Progress Report, 2015-2016," School District of Philadelphia website, accessed August 9, 2017.

4. "PSSA Results, Academic Years 2001-2002 through 2017-2018," State of Pennsylvania Education website, accessed January 25, 2019, link no longer available. Document/s on file, Angelwalk LLC.

5. Kristin A. Graham, "Top, most improved Phila., schools named," Philly.com, January 31, 2017, *The Philadelphia Inquirer* Text Only Archive.

6. Barbara Laker et al. "Toxic City. Sick Schools. Danger: Learn at your own risk," *The Philadelphia Inquirer/Daily News* website, May 3, 2018, accessed July 16, 2018, http://www.philly.com/philly/news/lead-paint-poison-children-asbestos-mold-schools-philadelphia-toxic-city.html

Update P.S. #11

1. "Test Security Violation Reports," School District of Philadelphia, Posted to Dropbox, October 23, 2012, accessed August 17, 2017, link no longer available. Document/s on file, Angelwalk LLC.

2. Benjamin Herold for WHYY/NewsWorks, "New cheating concerns at Philly school met with 'baffling' response," October 23, 2012, *The Philadelphia Public School Notebook* website, accessed August16,2017,https://thenotebook.org/articles/2012/10/23/new-cheating-concerns-at-philly-school-met-with-baffling-response/

3. Daniel Denvir for *Philadelphia City Paper*, "How Pennsylvania schools erased a cheating scandal," July 18, 2013, *My City Paper NYC* website, accessed June 30, 2017, https://mycitypaper.com/cover/how-pennsylshyvania-schools-erased-a-cheating-scandal/

4. Jackie Zubrzycki, "Philadelphia District's Response to Cheating Questioned," October 29, 2012, *Education Week* website, accessed July 28, 2017, http://blogs.edweek.org/edweek/District_Dossier/2012/10/philadelphia_districts_respons.html?qs=nationwide+cheating

5. James R. Sadler, "No School Left Uncorrupted: How Cheating, High-Stakes Testing, and Declining Budgets Affected Student Achievement in Philadelphia," 01 April2013. *CUREJ*, 163 (2013), University of Pennsylvania, https://repository.upenn.edu/curej/163/

6. Paul Socolar, "Investigative journalism can shake up a school system," June 5, 2014, *The Philadelphia Public School Notebook* website, accessed August 18, 2017 http://thenotebook.org/latest0/2014/06/05/investigative-journalism-can-shake-up-a-school-system

7. Dale Mezzacappa and Paul Socolar, "So far, 23 educators have been disciplined by the state for cheating," December 8, 2015, *The Philadelphia Public School Notebook* website, accessed July 28, 2017, http://thenotebook.org/latest0/2015/12/08/so-far-23-educators-have-been-disciplined-by-the-state-for-test-cheating

8. Kristin A. Graham, "Some districts and charters cleared of cheating on '09 state tests," January 13, 2012, *The Philadelphia Inquirer* Archives.

9. "School Progress Reports 2015-2016," School District of Philadelphia website, accessed August 21, 2017.

10. Laura Benshoff for *NewsWorks*, "Hundreds of Philly students opted out of standardized tests this year," June 5, 2015, *The Philadelphia Public School Notebook* website, accessed August 15, 2017, http://thenotebook.org/articles/2015/06/05/hundreds-of-philly-students-opted-out-of-standardized-tests-this-year

11. Kathy Boccella, "As protests rise over high-stakes tests, more students likely to opt out," February 28, 2016, *The Philadelphia Inquirer* website, accessed August 15, 2017, http://www.

philly.com/philly/education/20160228_As_protests_rise_over_high-stakes_tests__more_students_likely_to_opt_out.html

12. *Defies Measurement*, directed by Shannon Puckett, March 26, 2015, accessed August 17, 2017, www.defiesmeasurement.com or www.youtube.com, film

13. Kathy Matheson, "Testy over testing: More students snub standardized exams," February 23, 2015, *The Morning Call* website, http://www.mcall.com/news/nationworld/pennsylvania/mc-pa-students-snub-standardized-tests-20150222-story.html

14. "PSSA Results, Academic Years 2001-2002 through 2017-2018," State of Pennsylvania Education website, accessed January 25, 2019, link no longer available. Document/s on file, Angelwalk LLC.

Update P.S. #12

1. "Race/Grade Report," School District of Philadelphia, December 5, 2000.

2. "Persistently Dangerous Schools: 2009-2010," PA Dept of Education website, accessed August 23, 2017, link no longer available. Document/s on file, Angelwalk LLC.

3. "Persistently Dangerous Schools: 2010-2011," Pennsylvania Commission on Crime and Delinquency, PA Office of The Safe Schools Advocate, accessed March 26, 2020, https://www.pccd.pa.gov/ossa/school-safety/Pages/Persistently_Dangerous_Schools.aspx

4. "Persistently Dangerous Schools: 2015-2016," (5-year summary) Pennsylvania Commission on Crime and Delinquency website, PA Office of The Safe Schools Advocate, accessed March 26, 2020, https://www.pccd.pa.gov/ossa/school-safety/Pages/Persistently_Dangerous_Schools.aspx

5. "School Progress Reports 2015-2016, All High Schools," School District of Philadelphia website, accessed July 23, 2020.

6. "PSSA Results, Academic Years 2001-2002 through 2011-2012," State of Pennsylvania Education website, accessed March 24, 2017, link no longer available. Document/s on file, Angelwalk LLC.

7. "Keystone Exam Results, Academic Years 2012-2013 through 2017-2018," State of Pennsylvania Education website, accessed January 25, 2019, link no longer available. Document/s on file, Angelwalk LLC.

8. Aaron Moselle for *NewsWorks*, "3 Northwest Philly principals honored with Lindback award," April 15, 2015, accessed August 22, 2017, WHYY website, https://whyy.org/articles/3-northwest-philly-principals-honored-with-lindback-award/

9. "Philadelphia School Partnership big donation," 6 ABC website, videos, October 10, 2016, accessed July 23, 2020. https://6abc.com/society/philadelphia-school-partnership-big-donation/1548646/

Update P.S. #13

1. Susan Snyder, "Growing opportunities for city's gifted students," March 10, 2005, *The Philadelphia Inquirer* Historical Archives.
2. "Blue Ribbon Honor Crowns 'A Cinderella Year'," *No Child Left Behind Achiever*, November 2008, Vol. 7. No. 7, Department of Education website, Archived Information.
3. "PSSA Results, Academic Years 2001-2002 through 2017-2018," State of Pennsylvania Education website, accessed January 25, 2019, link no longer available. Document/s on file, Angelwalk LLC.
4. James R. Sadler, "No School Left Uncorrupted: How Cheating, High-Stakes Testing, and Declining Budgets Affected Student Achievement in Philadelphia," *CUREJ*, 163 (2013), University of Pennsylvania, https://repository.upenn.edu/curej/163/
5. "School Progress Reports 2015-2016," School District of Philadelphia website, District Performance Office, accessed September 9, 2017, https://www.philasd.org/performance/programsservices/school-progress-reports/available-spr-reports/
6. "School Progress Reports 2016-2017," School District of Philadelphia website, District Performance Office, accessed August 18, 2017.

Update P.S. #14

1. Kristin A. Graham, "New art-oriented high school in Phila. praised," January 12, 2010, *The Philadelphia Inquirer* Archives.
2. Benjamin Herold, "Setting an example," September 21, 2011, *The Philadelphia Public School Notebook* website, accessed July 12, 2011, http://thenotebook.org/articles/2011/09/21/setting-an-example
3. "PSSA Results, Academic Years 2001-2002 through 2006-2007," State of Pennsylvania Education website, accessed March 24, 2017, link no longer available. Document/s on file, Angelwalk LLC.
4. Kristin A. Graham, "At one school, no optimism things will get better," June 8, 2014, *The Philadelphia Inquirer, The Philadelphia Inquirer & Daily News* Text Archive
5. "Keystone Exam Results, Academic Years 2012-2013 through 2017-2018," State of Pennsylvania Education website, accessed January 25, 2019, link no longer available. Document/s on file, Angelwalk LLC.
6. "School Progress Reports 2015-2016, All High Schools," School District of Philadelphia Website, accessed August 21, 2017.
7. "Best High Schools, Rankings 2017," *U.S. News and World Report* website, accessed August 21, 2017.

Update P.S. #15

1. Chris Palmer, "School in Frankford on lockdown after man is shot nearby," June 10, 2016, *The Philadelphia Inquirer* Archives.
2. Martha Woodall, "A new day, a big test, Mastery's most ambitious mission: Turning three low-performing elementary schools into charters." September 2, 2010, *The Philadelphia Inquirer* Archives.
3. Benjamin Herold, "Philly charter group doesn't shy away from restarts," February 24, 2011, *Hechinger Report* website, originally published on PoliticsDaily.com, accessed August 22, 2017, http://hechingerreport.org/philly-charter-group-doesnt-shy-away-from-tough-restart-school-reform/
4. "PSSA Results, Academic Years 2001-2002 through 2017-2018," State of Pennsylvania Education website, accessed January 25, 2019, link no longer available. Document/s on file, Angelwalk LLC.
5. "School Progress Reports 2015-2016," School District of Philadelphia website, accessed August 28, 2017.
6. "School Progress Reports 2017-2018," School District of Philadelphia website, accessed September 24, 2019.

PART 3: Back Inside the SDP...*15 years later*

Back in the Saddle

1. Dale Mezzacappa, "District Gives up on Source4Teachers," *The Philadelphia Public School Notebook* website, May 6, 2016, accessed March 22, 2017, http://thenotebook.org/articles/2016/05/06/district-gives-up-on-source4teachers-poised-to-hire-new-firm

Public School #7, Back...and Back Again

1. Claudia Irizarry-Aponte, "As child abuse allegations in Philly schools rise, 'teacher jail' thrives and reputations are at stake," Philly.com/*The Philadelphia Inquirer* website, July 23, 2018, accessed July 24, 2018, http://www.philly.com/philly/news/child-protective-services-law-amendment-teacher-jail-philadelphia-school-district-abuse-20180721.html
2. Walter Perez, "9,190 Apply for 96 Spots in Philadelphia School Lottery," 6ABC website, February 21, 2017, accessed April 11, 2017, http://6abc.com/education/9190-apply-for-96-spots-in-philadelphia-school-lottery/1766103/
3. "School Progress Report, 2016-2017," School District of Philadelphia, accessed July 27, 2017.

Update on the District

1. *Defies Measurement*, a film by Shannon Puckett, March 26, 2015, accessed August 17, 2017, www.defiesmeasurement.com or www.youtube.com, film

2. Press Release: "Wolf Administration Honors 23 Organizations and Individuals with Environmental Excellence Awards," Commonwealth of PA website, Dept. of Environmental Protection, Harrisburg, April 18, 2018, accessed March 28, 2019, http://www.ahs.dep.pa.gov/ NewsRoomPublic/articleviewer.aspx?id=21443&typeid=1

3. Press Release: "School District's GreenFutures Sustainability Program Earns Statewide Recognition," School District of Philadelphia website, April 23, 2019, accessed March 28, 2019, https://www.philasd.org/blog/2018/04/23/ school-districts-greenfutures-sustainability-program-earns-statewide-recognition/

4. "School Redesign," School District of Philadelphia website, accessed March 29, 2020, https:// www.philasd.org/sdptest/greatschools/schoolredesign/

5. "New School Models," School District of Philadelphia website, accessed March 28, 2019. https://www.philasd.org/newschoolmodels/our-schools/

6. Avi Wolfman-Arent, "Philly flaunts early literacy approach for national audience," WHYY. org, July 24, 2018, accessed March 26, 2019, https://whyy.org/articles/ philly-flaunts-early-literacy-approach-for-national-audience/

7. "About Us," Readby4th website, accessed March 26, 2019, http://readby4th.org/

8. Action Plan Update 2018, Progress + Priorities, ©2018 School District of Philadelphia.

9. School Progress Report Parent and Family Guide, School District of Philadelphia website, updated March 31, 2017, accessed March 24, 2019, https://cdn.philasd.org/offices/ performance/SPR_Files/Parent_Guide/SPR_Parent_Guide_English.pdf

10. "2017-2018 SPR Highlights/Fact Sheet," School District of Philadelphia website, accessed March 19, 2019, link no longer available. Document/s on file, Angelwalk LLC.

11. "Dashboard, City-wide, SPR Overview," School District of Philadelphia website, accessed March 19, 2019.

12. "2015-2016 School Progress Report 20170203, Raw Data for SPR, Open Data Initiative," School District of Philadelphia website, accessed April 11, 2017, link no longer available. Document/s on file, Angelwalk LLC.

13. "School Demographics, [Unnamed Northeast Phila. School] 2017-2018," Great Philly Schools website, accessed May 1, 2019.

14. "School Demographics, [P.S. #7] 2017-2018" Great Philly Schools website, accessed May 1, 2019.

15. "School Progress Report, [Unnamed Northeast Phila. School] 2017-2018," School District of Philadelphia website, accessed March 24, 2019.

The Burden of Inclusion

1. "Inclusion: The Pros and Cons, Historical Background," *Issues ...about Change* 4, no 3 (1995), Southwest Educational Development Laboratory legacy website (SEDL merged with American Institutes for Research in January 2015), accessed April 30, 2019, http://www.sedl. org/change/issues/issues43.html

2. "IDEA Regulations, Part B, Sub-part B, Sec. 300.114 LRE requirements," U.S. Department of Education website, accessed May 14, 2018, https://sites.ed.gov/idea/regs/b/b/300.114

3. "A Parent's Guide to Special Ed/Special Needs: Disabilities covered under the Individuals with Disabilities act (IDEA)," The Council for Disability Rights website, accessed October 4, 2019, http://www.disabilityrights.org/appendix.htm

4. Katie Schultz Stout, "Special Education Inclusion, Definitions," Wisconsin Education Association Council (WEAC) website, accessed October 12, 2019, https://weac.org/articles/specialedinc/

5. Conrad Carlberg and Kenneth Kavale, "The Efficacy of Special vs. Regular Class Placement for Exceptional Children: A Meta-analysis," *The Journal of Special Education* (1980): 295-305.

6. Douglas Fuchs and Lynn S. Fuchs, "Sometimes Separate Is Better," *Educational Leadership*, Vol 52, No 4, p. 26, December 1994/January 1995.

7. Justine Maloney, "A Call for Placement Options," *Educational Leadership*, Vol 52, No 4, p. 25, December 1994/January 1995.

8. Sara Sklaroff, "A.F.T. Urges Halt to 'Full Inclusion' Movement," *Education Week*, 1993, accessed 8/14/06, https://www.edweek.org/ew/articles/1994/01/12/16speced.h13.html

9. Philip Murphy, "The Biggest Barriers to Inclusive Education," Think Inclusive website [blog], September 14, 2015, accessed November 16, 2019, https://www.thinkinclusive.us/barriers-to-inclusive-education/

10. Harold Jordan, *Beyond Zero Tolerance: Discipline and Policing in Pennsylvania Public Schools*, A Publication of the American Civil Liberties Union of Pennsylvania, February 2015.

11. Kevin Bethel, "Expanding the Philadelphia Police School Diversion Program," Stoneleigh Foundation website, accessed February 10, 2019, https://stoneleighfoundation.org/project/expanding-the-philadelphia-police-school-diversion-program/

12. Dale Mezzacappa, "With police diversion, arrests plummet," *The Philadelphia Public School Notebook* website, December 9, 2018, accessed February 10, 2019, https://thenotebook.org/articles/2018/12/09/with-police-diversion-student-arrests-plummet/

13. "Climate Staff Job Posting: #4600152384, SY 2018-19," School District of Philadelphia Job Board, March 23, 2018.

14. Dale Mezzacappa, "District gives up on Source4Teachers," May 6, 2016, *The Philadelphia Public School Notebook* website, http://thenotebook.org/articles/2016/05/06/district-gives-up-on-source4teachers-poised-to-hire-new-firm

15. "Teacher Absence Rate SY 2017-2018, District Score Card," *School District* of Philadelphia website, accessed October 4, 2019, https://www.philasd.org/performance/programsservices/school-progress-reports/district-scorecard/#note

16. *The 2017 Educator Quality of Work Life Survey*, American Federation of Teachers and the Badass Teachers Association, Copyright © American Federation of Teachers, AFL-CIO (AFT 2017), accessed August 31, 2019, https://www.aft.org/sites/default/files/2017_eqwl_survey_web.pdf

17. Matthew P. Steinberg et al. *Teacher Mobility in the School District of Philadelphia, 2009-10 through 2015-16.*" (2018) Philadelphia: The Philadelphia Education Research Consortium.

18. Christine A. Samuels, "Reauthorized IDEA Could Shift Power to School Districts," *Education Week* website, November 30, 2004, accessed September 14, 2006, http://www.edweek.org/ew/articles/2004/12/01/14idea.h24.html?print=1

19. Susanna Duckworth et al. "Wraparound Services for Young Schoolchildren with Emotional and Behavioral Disorders," (2001), p. 110, *Educating Exceptional Children*, Fifteenth Edition, 03/04, McGraw-Hill/Dushkin, Guilford, Connecticut.

20. "High School Graduation Among Students with Disabilities, Graduation and Dropout Rates by Disability," *23rd Annual Report to Congress on Special Education*, section I/p.2; Archived Information, U.S. Department of Education, 2002.

21. Disabilities Rights, "Pennsylvania Agrees to Changes in Special Education to Increase Inclusion of Students with Disabilities in Regular Education Classes," Public Interest Law Center of Philadelphia website, accessed January 15, 2007, link no longer available. Document/s on file, Angelwalk LLC.

22. *38th Annual Report to Congress on the Implementation of the Individuals with Disabilities Education Act*, US Dept of Education website, 2016, pp. 29-30, accessed April 15, 2017, https://ed.gov/about/reports/annual/osep/2016/parts-b-c/38th-arc-for-idea.pdf

23. *38th Annual Report to Congress on the Implementation of the Individuals with Disabilities Education Act*, US Dept of Education website, 2016, pp. 47-48, accessed April 15, 2017, https://ed.gov/about/reports/annual/osep/2016/parts-b-c/38th-arc-for-idea.pdf

School *Is* the Trauma

1. Jane Ellen Stevens, "The Adverse Childhood Experiences Study—the largest, most important public health study you never heard of—began in an obesity clinic," AcesTooHigh.com, October 3, 2012, accessed July 26, 2018, https://acestoohigh.com/2012/10/03/the-adverse-childhood-experiences-study-the-largest-most-important-public-health-study-you-never-heard-of-began-in-an-obesity-clinic/

2. "About the CDC-Kaiser ACE Study," Centers for Disease Control website, Violence Prevention, accessed July 26, 2018, https://www.cdc.gov/violenceprevention/acestudy/about.html

3. Robert F. Anda and Vincent J. Felitti, *Adverse Childhood Experiences and their Relationship to Adult Well-being and Disease: Turning gold into lead*, ACE National Webinar, August 27, 2012, The National Council for Behavioral Health website, accessed May 30, 2017, https://www.thenationalcouncil.org/wp-content/uploads/2012/11/Natl-Council-Webinar-8-2012.pdf

4. Laura Starecheski, "Take the ACE Quiz—And Learn What it Does and Doesn't Mean," National Public Radio website, March 2, 2015, accessed May 30, 2017, https://www.npr.org/sections/health-shots/2015/03/02/387007941/take-the-ace-quiz-and-learn-what-it-does-and-doesnt-mean

5. Rebecca Ruiz, "How childhood trauma could be mistaken for ADHD," AcesTooHigh.com, July 7, 2014, accessed July 26, 2018, https://acestoohigh.com/2014/07/07/how-childhood-trauma-could-be-mistaken-for-adhd/

6. Dale Mezzacappa, "Schools focus on being more 'trauma aware,'" *The Philadelphia Public School Notebook* website, April 18, 2017, accessed August 15, 2018, https://thenotebook.org/articles/2017/04/18/notes-from-the-news-april-114/

7. Kristin A. Graham, "New, $10M special-ed school for Philly kids, draws fire," *The Philadelphia Inquirer* website, updated July 5, 2017, accessed August 27, 2017, http://www.philly.com/philly/education/new-10m-special-ed-school-for-philly-kids-draws-fire-20170705.html

8. "Carson Valley School Records, Urban Archives, Historical Note," Temple University Libraries, accessed April 9, 2019, https://library.temple.edu/scrc/carson-valley-school-flourtown

9. Mark Duffy and Alyn McCarty, *The Philadelphia Community Schools Initiative*: Year 1 Report, ©2018 Research for Action, accessed May 3, 2019, https://www.researchforaction.org/publications/the-philadelphia-community-schools-initiative-year-1-evaluation/

Show Me the Money

1. Goodwin Liu, "How the Federal Government Makes Rich States Richer," *Funding Gaps 2006* ©The Education Trust, Washington, D.C., http://edtrust.org/resource/the-funding-gap-2

2. Ross Wiener and Eli Pristoop, "How States Shortchange the Districts that Need the Most Help," *Funding Gaps 2006*, ©The Education Trust, Washington, D.C., http://edtrust.org/resource/the-funding-gap-2

3. Marguerite Roza, "How Districts Shortchange Low-income and Minority Students," *Funding Gaps 2006*, ©The Education Trust, Washington, D.C., http://edtrust.org/resource/the-funding-gap-2

4. Natasha Ushomirsky and David Williams, "Too Many States Still Spend Less on Educating Students Who Need the Most," *Funding Gaps 2015*, ©The Education Trust, Washington, D.C., https://edtrust.org/wpcontent/uploads/2014/09/FundingGaps2015_TheEducationTrust1.pdf

5. "About POWER," POWER Interfaith website, accessed April 23, 2019, https://powerinterfaith.org/

6. David Mosenkis, *Systemic Racial Bias in Latest Pennsylvania School Funding*, POWER Interfaith website, July 2016, accessed April 23, 2019, https://powerinterfaith.org/wp-content/uploads/2016/08/PA-Racial-School-Funding-Bias-July-2016-1-1.pdf

7. "Enrollment Projections Report, Actuals, Philadelphia City District, 2015-2016," p 923, PA Dept. of Education website, Division of Data Quality, December 30, 2016, accessed January 21, 2019, link no longer available. Document/s on file, Angelwalk LLC.

8. Joe Markosek, "PA's Fair Funding Formula Explained," Primer, House Appropriations Committee (D), PA House Democrats website, January 10, 2018, accessed June 18, 2019, http://www.pahouse.com/Files/Documents/Appropriations/series/3013/BEFC_BP_011018.pdf

9. "2016 Act 35, HB 1552," Pennsylvania General Assembly website, accessed April 23, 2019, https://www.legis.state.pa.us/cfdocs/legis/li/uconsCheck.cfm?yr=2016&sessInd=0&act=35

10. *Pennsylvania Education Funding Inequity* video, 100% Fair Funding Campaign, POWER website, accessed December 22, 2019, tiny.cc/pafairfunding

11. Press Release: "Rabb calls for end to educational apartheid. Introduces legislation to ensure full and fair funding for public schools," May 17, 2019, PA House Democrats website, Philadelphia County, accessed June 19, 2019, http://www.pahouse.com/Rabb/InTheNews/NewsRelease/?id=107382

12. Dale Mezzacapa, "Court allows historic school funding case to proceed," *The Philadelphia Public School Notebook* website, May 7, 2018, accessed May 15, 2018, http://thenotebook.org/articles/2018/05/07/court-allows-historic-school-funding-case-to-proceed/

13. Dale Mezzacappa, "Democratic legislatures say fixing school funding is a moral imperative," *The Philadelphia Public School Notebook* website, January 24, 2019, accessed January 26, 2019, https://thenotebook.org/articles/2019/01/24/democratic-legislators-say-fixing-school-funding-is-a-moral-imperative/

14. Ivy Morgan and Ary Amerikaner, "An Analysis of School Funding Equity Across the U.S. and Within Each State," *Funding Gaps 2018*, ©The Education Trust, Washington, D.C., accessed July 13, 2018, https://1k9gl1yevnfp2lpq1dhrqe17-wpengine.netdna-ssl.com/wp-content/uploads/2014/09/FundingGapReport_2018_FINAL.pdf

15. *Philadelphia 2018, The State of the City, A Report from The Pew Charitable Trusts*, April 2018, © 2018 The Pew Charitable Trusts, accessed May 25, 2019, https://www.pewtrusts.org/en/research-and-analysis/reports/2018/04/philadelphia-2018-the-state-of-the-city

16. Laura McCrystal, "Philly property assessments are flawed, audit finds," January 3, 2019, *The Philadelphia Inquirer* website, accessed January 24, 2019, https://www.inquirer.com/news/assessment-audit-opa-city-council-philadelphia-property-taxes-20190103.html

17. Daphne A. Kenyon and Adam H. Langley, "The Property Tax Exemption for Nonprofits and Revenue Implications for Cities," p. 4 (2011), Tax Policy Center website, https://www.taxpolicycenter.org/publications/property-tax-exemption-nonprofits-and-revenue-implications-cities/full

18. "Philadelphia's 10-Year Property Tax Abatement," Building Industry Association, March 2017, accessed July 30, 2018, http://phillytaxabatement.com/pdf/BIA_Abatement_Summary_Final.pdf

19. Greg Windle, "Audit: Mismanagement and corruption at the Parking Authority cheats district out of nearly $80 million," December 7, 2017, *The Philadelphia Public School Notebook* website, accessed June 25, 2019, https://thenotebook.org/articles/2017/12/07/mismanagement-and-corruption-at-parking-authority-cheats-district-out-of-nearly-80-million/

20. Jolley Bruce Christman, "Pay Up PPA!: Philadelphians deserve a public forum to discuss the parking authority," February 22, 2019, *The Philadelphia Public School Notebook* website, accessed June 25, 2019, https://thenotebook.org/articles/2019/02/22/pay-up-ppa-philadelphians-deserve-a-public-forum-to-discuss-the-parking-authority/

21. Charles D. Ellison, "Reality Check: How does the parking Authority Spend its Revenue?" *The Philadelphia Citizen* website, October 30, 2017, accessed June 25, 2019, https://thephiladelphiacitizen.org/reality-check-how-does-the-parking-authority-spend-its-revenue/

22. *City of Philadelphia, Economic Impact Analysis of Proposed 10 Year Tax Abatement Adjustments,* ©2018 Jones Lang LaSalle Americas, Inc., NY., City of Philadelphia website, accessed August 17, 2018, https://www.phila.gov/media/20180524153805/City-of-Philadelphia-2018-Abatement.pdf

23. "Equitable or not enough? Philly Council just changed the 10-year tax abatement," Jake Blumgart, December 12, 2019, WHYY website, accessed March 3, 2020. https://whyy.org/articles/its-unanimous-philly-council-passes-tax-abatement-bill-reducing-a-controversial-tax-break/

24. *School District of Philadelphia, Five-Year Financial Plan,* 2015-2019, December 2014, SCRIBD website, accessed April 1, 2017, https://www.scribd.com/document/250499600/SDP-Five-year-Financial-Plan-2015-2019

25. Pennsylvania Association of School Business Officials (PASBO) et al. "Special Education Legislation Press Conference Call/Web Forum," May 13, 2014.

26. "Franklin Town accused of discriminating against special needs student," Greg Windle, July 19, 2018, *The Philadelphia Public School Notebook* website, accessed July 24, 2018. http://thenotebook.org/articles/2018/07/19/franklin-towne-accused-of-discriminating-against-special-needs-student/

27. "A Timeline of Philadelphia's soda tax," Laura McCrystal, April 29, 2019, *The Philadelphia Inquirer* website, accessed May 3, 2019, https://www.philly.com/news/timeline-philadelphias-soda-tax-20190429.html

28. James F. Kenney, "Mayor's Operating Budget in Brief for Fiscal Year 2020," March 2019, City of Philadelphia website, accessed May 11, 2019, https://www.phila.gov/media/20190306124654/FY20-Budget-in-Brief_All_Proposed.pdf

29. Claudia Vargas and Laura McCrystal, "Mayor Kenney to request $5 billion spending plan with big investments in Philadelphia schools, public safety," March 7, 2019, *The Philadelphia Inquirer* website, accessed May 11, 2019, https://www.philly.com/politics/philadelphia/jim-kenney-philadelphia-budget-no-tax-increase-education-public-safety-20190307.html

30. Alison Burdo, "PPA has $15.8M for city schools, but Uber miscalculation raises funding doubts," May 23, 2018, *Philadelphia Business Journal* website, accessed June 25, 2019, https://www.bizjournals.com/philadelphia/news/2018/05/23/ppa-fy18-school-funding-uber-tnc-taxes.html

31. "Tackling the Dropout Rate," Philadelphia Education Fund site, accessed May 14, 2019, http://www.philaedfund.org/node/1483

A Nationwide Concern

1. "Davis Elementary School," Great Schools website, accessed April 1, 2019, https://www.greatschools.org/pennsylvania/southampton/436-Davis-Elementary-School/

2. "North Penn School District Demographics and Statistics," Point2Homes website, accessed September 2, 2019, https://www.point2homes.com/US/Neighborhood/PA/Montgomery-County/North-Penn-School-District-Demographics.html

3. Emma Garcia and Elaine Weiss, *The teacher shortage is real, large and growing, and worse than we thought, The first report in "The Perfect Storm in the Teacher Labor Market" series,* March 26, 2019, Economic Policy Institute website, https://www.epi.org/files/pdf/163651.pdf

4. Dan Sokil, "North Penn School Board OKs contract for behavioral threat assessment," *Montgomery News* website, July 30, 2018, accessed February 13, 2019, http://www.montgomerynews.com/northpennlife/news/north-penn-school-board-oks-contract-for-behavioral-threat-assessment/article_515eef75-8b53-567a-bcaf-3a95dc24af20.html

5. "Gunfire on School Grounds in the United States," ©2019 Every Town for Gun Safety Support Fund, Every Town Research website, accessed October 28, 2019, https://everytownresearch.org/gunfire-in-school/#ns

6. Christina Walker et al. "10 years. 180 school shootings. 356 victims." CNN.com/Interactive, © 2019 Cable News Network, Turner Broadcasting System, Inc, accessed October 27, 2019, https://www.cnn.com/interactive/2019/07/us/ten-years-of-school-shootings-trnd/

7. Linda Juszczak et al. "Use of Health and Mental Health Services by Adolescents Across Multiple Delivery Sites," *Journal of Adolescent Health*, 32, no. 6 (2003:108-118).

8. Amir Whitaker et al. *Cops and No Counselors: How the Lack of School Mental Health Staff Is Harming Students,* a report on discipline from the ACLU, March 4, 2019, ACLU website, pp. 4-5, accessed May 21, 2019, https://www.aclu.org/sites/default/files/field_document/030419-acluschooldisciplinereport.pdf

Afterword

1. Press Release: "District Announces Comprehensive School Planning Review to Better Plan for, Design Neighborhood Schools Citywide, Multi-year initiative to analyze changing communities throughout city and solicit input about how to serve shifting school populations." May 28, 2019. School District of Philadelphia. Accessed12.31.19. https://www.philasd.org/blog/2019/05/28/district-announces-comprehensive-school-planning-review-to-better-plan-for-design-neighborhood-schools-citywide/

2. Press release: "District Outlines New Environmental Safety Improvement Plan," November 19, 2019, School District of Philadelphia website, accessed March 8, 2020, https://www.philasd.org/communications/2019/11/19/district-outlines-new-environmental-safetyimprovement-plan/

3. Michaela Winberg, "Philly school asbestos problem: What's closed, what's open and what's being done," February 19, 2020, Billy Penn website, accessed March 5, 2020, https://billypenn.com/2020/02/19/philly-school-asbestos-problem-whats-closed-whats-open-and-whatsbeing-done/

4.   Press release: "School District Will Use $11 Million to Help Bridge the Digital Divide Among Students," March 26, 2020, School District of Philadelphia website, accessed March 29, 2020, https://www.philasd.org/communications/2020/03/26/school-district-will-use-11-million-to-help-bridge-the-digital-divide-among-students/

5.   The Nation's Report Card, How did U.S. Students perform on the latest assessment, Philadelphia 2019, National Center for Education Statistics (NCES), within the U.S. Department of Education and the Institute of Education Sciences (IES), Accessed 9.12.21. https://www.nationsreportcard.gov/

6.   "Board of Education Goals & Guardrails Presentation," December 10, 2020. School District of Philadelphia website. Accessed 9.12.21. https://philasd.novusagenda.com/agendapublic/CoverSheet.aspx?ItemID=3563&MeetingID=163

7.   U.S. Department of Education Fact Sheet: "American Rescue Plan Act of 2021 Elementary and Secondary School Emergency Relief Fund," Office of Elementary & Secondary Education Website. Accessed 9.12.21. https://oese.ed.gov/files/2021/03/FINAL_ARP-ESSER-FACT-SHEET.pdf

8.   "American Rescue Plan Funding: Helping our Students Heal, Recover and Emerge Stronger from the COVID-19 Pandemic," June 2, 2021 update. School District of Philadelphia Website. Accessed 9.12.21. https://www.philasd.org/arp/

9.   "Moving Forward: Returning & Learning with Care, Lump Sum Presentation (FY21-22) Five-Year Plan (FY22-26)," March 25, 2021. School District of Philadelphia Website. Accessed 9.12.21. https://www.philasd.org/budget/wp-content/uploads/sites/96/2021/03/FY21-22-Lump-Sum-and-Five-Year-Plan-Presentation.pdf

Please note:

All referenced documents and other supporting materials
on file at Angelwalk LLC.

> *About the Author*

Photo credit: Michael A. Roberts

Writer and advocate for fair and equal education, Clayvon C. Harris earned an MFA in Cinema-Television/Screenwriting from the University of Southern California's School of Cinematic Arts. She also holds a BA in English literature from Swarthmore College where students are taught they have the ability to change the world. Harris lives and writes in the Philadelphia area where she specializes in messaging strategy, digital content creation and script development. She is also a member of the Writers Guild of America. Her first book is the award-winning collection of essays *Year of Trial, Year of Grace—A Catholic's Search for Faith.*

CPSIA information can be obtained
at www.ICGtesting.com
Printed in the USA
BVHW040819100122
625105BV00007B/67

9 780988 179721